# THE ARAB OEDIPUS

## FOUR PLAYS

# THE ARAB OEDIPUS

Four Plays from Egypt and Syria

Edited with an Introduction
by
Marvin Carlson

Martin E. Segal Theatre Center Publications
New York

LIBRARY OF CONGRESS CATALOGING-IN PUBLICATION DATA
The Arab Oedipus: four plays from Egypt and Syria / edited with an introduction by Marvin Carlson.
p. cm.
ISBN 0-9666152-8-X (alk. paper)
1. Arabic drama-20th century. 2. Oedipus (Greek mythology)-Drama. I. Carlson, Marvin A., 1935- II. Hakim, Tawfiq (1898-1987). Malik Udib. English. III. Ba Kathir, 'Ali Ahmad (1915-1959). Ma'sat Udib. English. IV. Kumidiya Udib. English. V. Ikhlasi, Walid, 1936-. Udib. English.

PJ7665.A725                  2005
892.7'2609351-dc22       2005054122

Copy-editing by Amy E. Hughes

# TABLE OF CONTENTS

### Editor's Introduction
The Arab Oedipus

Aristotle, whose comments on tragedy have dominated Western writing and thinking on the subject of tragedy, considered Sophocles' *Oedipus* to be the most perfect example of the form. Despite this commendation, or perhaps because it set so formidable a benchmark for subsequent dramatists, the story of Oedipus, while inspiring dramatic imitations throughout the Western tradition, has been less attractive to major dramatists and inspired fewer canonical works in that tradition than the stories of Electra and Orestes, Phaedra, or even Amphitryon. The dramatic fortunes of the Oedipus story have been quite different in the Arab world, where some of the most important dramatists of the past and present have found this myth useful for their purposes.

Despite a strong interest among medieval Arabic scholars in the classic Greek writings in philosophy and science, in Plato, Aristotle, Ptolemy and others, comparatively little attention was paid to the Greek literary forms in general and the drama in particular. After the Arab renaissance (*al-Nahdah*) of the late nineteenth century, strongly influenced by Western sources, finally succeeded in establishing a European-style dramatic tradition in the Arab world, scholars devoted much speculation as to why Arab culture had previously proven so resistant to this major Western form, particularly in view of the extensive knowledge of Greek thought. A number of the prevalent theories are summarized in the opening section of Tawfiq al-Hakim's introduction to his own version of Oedipus, a major theoretical statement on Arab tragedy in general and his aesthetic in particular, which is included in this volume.

It is of course impossible to say which of the many possibilities mentioned by al-Hakim and others or which combination of them explains the late development of Western-style dramatic literature in the Arab world, but classical tragedy in particular clearly would have presented some serious problems to traditional Islam. Al-Hakim argues that as an Easterner he still retains a certain religious orientation now lost in the Western theatre that in fact ties him more closely to the religious-based Greek tragedy. This may be true so far as the cosmic echoes of the drama are concerned, but the Greek humanistic stress on individualism and the search for one's individual destiny so common in Greek tragedy has little in common with the traditional Islamic concept of fate and submission to the will of God, a problem even more serious than the obvious difference between a polytheistic and a monotheistic religion. This problem would seem to be particularly pronounced in the case of Oedipus, where this theme is more clearly and directly articulated than in almost any other extant Greek tragedy.

Nevertheless, as al-Hakim explains, certain features of Oedipus fitted so well with central occupations of his own that he was able to change the focus of the drama to stress that aspect and turn it away from its individualistc orientation. This is a pattern we will see in each of the works in this volume, and is of course true of reworkings of classic material throughout dramatic history. New adaptations, and even new translations of a work from another era, will inevitably, to a greater and lesser extent and with varying degrss of conscious manipulation on the part of the dramatist, reflect the changed concerns and assumptions of their new cultural context. Al-Hakim notes but does not expand upon this phenomenon when he observes that the classic story of Phaedra in the hands of Racine contained a certain measure of its original religious concern, but now filtered through the Jansenist religious orientation of its seventeenth-century adaptor.

Apparently the first exposure of the Arab world to the Sophoclean legend came in 1905, when the modern Arabic drama was still in its infancy, in the form of a translation into Arabic of Voltaire's neoclassic version of the drama by Najib al-Hadad (1867-1899) entitled *Udib, aw al-sir al-ha'il* (*Oedipus, or the Great Secret*). To a modern English-speaking reader this choice might seem strange, but an understanding of the origins of the modern Arab drama during the Arab renaissance of the late nineteenth century goes far toward explaining this choice. The first major center of experimentation with the new Western style of theatre took place in Syria, and particularly in Beirut (present-day Lebanon being at that time a part of Syria), a European-oriented city whose intellectual and literary community was largely French oriented and indeed French speaking.

European-oriented Arabic drama traces its birth to the year 1848 when the Lebanese businessman Marun an-Naqqash staged in his home in Beirut a play of his own, *al-Bakhil*, inspired by Molière's *The Miser*. Interestingly, *The Miser* was also among the first adaptations of the first European-oriented theatre established in Egypt, by Yacub Sanua in 1871. Adaptations from the French and new plays based on French models dominated the repertoire of Sauna's theatre, which in 1872 presented the first tragedy in Arabic, al-Misri's *Layla*, based on Voltaire's 1743 tragedy *Mérope*. This French orientation was reinforced by the arrival in Cairo in 1878 of a troupe of Syrian actors headed by Salim al-Naqqash, a nephew of the Beirut theatre pioneer. Adib Ishaq and others provided this company with translations from all the great dramatists of the French neoclassic tradition: Molière, Racine, Corneille, and Voltaire up until the Urabi revolt of 1882 closed all theatres in Egypt.

During the 1890s, with the theatres reopened, French influence remained strong, with the adaptations of Muhammad Uthman Jalal (1829-94) in particular gaining growing popularity for the work of Molière. It was not until this period that the first Arabic versions of major English tragedies appeared. The prolific Najib al-Hadad, translator of the Voltaire *Oedipus*, created an Arabic *Romeo and Juliet* in 1890. The first Arabic *Hamlet* was by Tanyus Abduh in 1901.

Al-Hadad's *Oedipus* has not survived, but we do possess a note relating to it which provides some fascinating details about its staging. This note remarks that although the text contains both prose and poetry, the poetry, consisting of songs and chants, was in fact added by acting companies and was not composed by the author. This information is valuable not only because it shows that al-Hadad's undertaking was not a purely literary exercise; its remark on the addition of songs is equally interesting. A modern reader might assume that these were added in an attempt to replicate the choric odes of the original Greek, but such a project would have surely been the concern of al-Hadad himself, a leading literary scholar, and not the emendation of actors seeking a popular success. Clearly this material was added in fact to make the rather alien literary drama more accessible to a public familiar with staged song and dance but not yet with the spoken theatre. This practice is often seen in late nineteenth- and early twentieh-century Arabic adaptations of Western dramas as well as in original works.

A more direct translation of Sophocles' own work, although almost certainly through the medium of some modern language, probably French, was created in 1913 by another prominent writer, Farah Antun (1874-1922). This version, which has also not been preserved, was created specifically for the company headed by Georges Abyad (1880-1959), then the leading theatrical group in Cairo. It was presented before the Khedive at the Cairo Opera, built for European-style performance half a century earlier and still at this time the leading venue in the city for dramatic performance, and remained in the repertoire of this company and subsequently in that of the National Theatre into the early 1940s.

The first scholarly translation of *Oedipus* into Arabic was the work of one of Egypt's leading men of letters in the early twentieth century, Taha Husayn (1889-1973). Husayn studied in France under André Gide and championed a Western-oriented educational system in Egypt that would further its ties with European literature and culture. His translation of *Oedipus* appeared in 1939, in a volume which also included *Ajax*, *Electra*, and *Antigone*.

In addition to his translations and critical writings, Husayn is today remembered among theatre historians for being one of the first and most enthusiastic supporters of Tawfiq al-Hakim, who emerged during the 1930s as the first major modern Egyptian dramatist. The appearance of his play *The People of the Cave* (*Ahl al Kahf*) and his novel *The Soul's Return* (*Awdat ar Ruh*), both in 1933, immediately established him as the leading Arabic writer of his generation. Among the many articles heralding al-Hakim's arrival, the most famous was that on *The People of the Cave* written by Husayn for the newspaper *Ar-Risala*. In this essay, Husayn hailed the work as "epoch-making," important "not in modern Arabic literature alone, but in the whole of Arabic literature." "I have not hesitation in stating," he continued, "that it is the first work in Arabic literature which may be properly called drama," and, perhaps the highest possible praise from Husayn, he felt the work "raised the status of Arabic literature, making it possible to stand comparison with modern and ancient European traditions."[1] Although their relationship was not always smooth, Husayn remained an important champion and supporter of the man hence-generally acknowledged as Egypt's leading dramatist.

---

1. Cited in M. M. Badawi, *Modern Arabic Drama in Egypt* (Cambridge: Cambridge University Press, 1987), 27.

Al-Hakim was the first Egyptian dramatist to undertake a serious reworking of Sophocles' *Oedipus*, which he is thought to have begun in the early 1940s. It was published in 1949. Given Husayn's interest in and support of al-Hakim and his program of encouraging Egyptian use of European materials, not to mention his own translations of the *Oedipus* of both Gide and Sophocles, it seems quite possible that Husayn was one of the influences that led al-Hakim to consider creating his own version of this major legend. Al-Hakim's extensive preface to the work, published ten years later, does not make any such suggestion, however, and there are many other possible sources of inspiration for his undertaking.

Like Husayn, al-Hakim spent some of his formative years (1925-28) in Paris, where he devoured French culture and literature, reading on the average 100 pages a day and frequenting museums, concerts, and theatre. Not surprisingly, his introduction to *Oedipus* is primarily indebted to French thinkers and artists: Hugo and Brunetière, Corneille and Racine, Gide and Bouhélier. He even reports on a performance of *Oedipus* he attended at the Comédie Française, with Albert Lambert, the leading tragedian of the period, in the title role. In this interpretation, Lambert was following the footsteps of Jean Mounet-Sully, whose creation of this role in 1881 had restored the Sophoclean classic to the major European stage where it remained the signature role of this actor for the rest of his career. Long before going to Paris, however, al-Hakim mentions in his autobiographical work *The Prison of Life* (*Sijn al-Umr*) that while still a schoolboy he went often to see his favorite actor, Georges Abyad, performing *Oedipus* and *Othello* at the Cairo Opera and that he was able to recite "whole pages" of these works to his schoolmates.[2]

Al-Hakim himself insists that his attraction to *Oedipus* was less a result of any specific literary or theatrical experience, however, than of a recognition of the fact that it could be used to revisit a type of conflict which al-Hakim felt could be the basis for modern tragic insight and which he had first fully engaged in his breakthrough work, *The People of the Cave*. This, as the dramatist explains in his Introduction, is not so much the traditional struggle between man

---

2. Tawfiq Al-Hakim, *The Prison of Life*, trans. Pierre Cachia (Cairo: American University Press, 1992), 140.

and fate as that between the forces al-Hakim designates as "fact" and "truth." In the earlier play al-Hakim's doomed lovers Mishilinia and Prisca were torn between the "fact" of their love and the "truth" that Mishilinia has returned from an enchanted three-hundred-year sleep and that Prisca is actually only a remote descendent of his original love. Al-Hakim specifically identifies Oedipus and Jocasta as "none other than Mishilinia and Prisca," who like them must confront the conflict between the fact of their love and the hidden truth of their actual relationship to each other. Not surprisingly, then, one of the most striking innovations al-Hakim makes in the traditional story is the first scene of the third act. Instead of moving rapidly as in the original from the exposure of the dark secret to the suicide of Jocasta and the blinding of Oedipus, al-Hakim introduces here a lengthy discussion between Oedipus and Jocasta precisely upon the conflicting demands of what the dramatist has identified as the fact and the truth of their relationship.

"My whole concern was to prevent any trace of reasoning from appearing in the dialogue so that it would not overwhelm a scene or weaken the action," al-Hakim notes in the concluding section of his Introduction. "I strove to conceal the thought within the action and to fold the idea into the scene." For most of the play this is the case, but in much of the third act al-Hakim allows discussion to dominate, as Bernard Shaw suggested should in fact be the practice of the new drama of ideas.

Although al-Hakim claims to have restored something of its original religious foundations to the tragedy, in fact it has a distinctly secular feeling, and not only because he has placed a philosophic rather than a religious debate at the intellectual center of his play. Related to this, and equally important, is that the gods, and their principle manifestation in Oedipus, the workings of destiny or fate, have almost entirely disappeared in al-Hakim's version. This can be most clearly seen in al-Hakim's radical revision of Tiresias. This is not the divine seer of Greek tragedy, but a very contemporary political manipulator, interested in power and control over the royal house of Thebes. In fact much of the background of Oedipus is a fabrication by Tiresias, who spread the tale of the sphinx and the riddle whereas Oedipus in fact killed only a predatory lion.

There is thus no question that al-Hakim's *Oedipus* is much more directly involved with Theban political intrigue than that of Sophocles, and the critic Sami Munir has gone so far as to consider the play in part a specific political allegory, referring to the major events of February, 1942, shortly before al-Hakim began work on it. At that time British troops surrounded the royal palace in Cairo and forced King Farouk, whom they suspected of Axis sympathies, to appoint Mustafa el-Nahhas, leader of the Wafd party, prime minister.  Although the Wafd party was opposed both to the totalitarian monarchy and British influence in Egypt, their popular support and strong opposition to the Axis seemed to offer Britain the best opportunity to secure and stabilize this important area.

Munir argues that Tiresias' manipulation of Oedipus in al-Hakim's play is a conscious echo of the British manipulation of the Wafd party, the rightful leaders of the nation, bringing him to power by lies and the show of force.  In both cases, Oedipus' and el-Nahhas', the power gained through such means, although originally legitimate, becomes corrupted and tragically lost.[3]

Critics have disagreed about the degree of direct political reference in al-Hakim's *Oedipus*, but there is no question that the *Tragedy of Oedipus* (*Ma'saat Udib*) by Ali Ahmad Bakathir (1910-1964) was directly inspired by current political events, namely the defeat of the Arab armies in Palestine in 1948.  "At that time," Bakathir wrote, "I felt despair regarding the future of the Arab nation and shame, disgrace and ignominy.  Our dignity had been trampled underfoot.  I remained in the grip of this deep, heavy pain a long time, not knowing how to relieve it."[4]  Not surprisingly, Bakathir, who had emerged in the mid-1940s as an important new Egyptian dramatist, one of the first to appear in the wake of al-Hakim's success, found his release in the creation of a play, his own version of *Oedipus*.

Bakathir's background and intellectual orientation was very different from al-Hakim's.  Al-Hakim was Egyptian by birth and training, exposed to the European classics from his earliest schooldays, and further internationalized, like many of his generation, by several years as a young intellectual in Paris.

---

3. Sami Munir, *The Egyptian Theatre after World War II* (Cairo, 1979).
4. Quoted in Nehad Selaiha, "Manifold Oedipus," *Al-Ahram* 563 (6-12 December, 2001), 3.

Bakathir was born of Arab parents in Indonesia, and before coming to Cairo in 1934 (at roughly the same age when al-Hakim departed for Paris) had a traditional Islamic education, which included no exposure at all to European culture or languages. In Cairo, however, Bakathir became fascinated by English literature and especially the work of Shakespeare. While a student at Cairo University he experimented with a translation of *Romeo and Juliet* in Arabic verse and graduated with a degree in English.

Throughout his career, however, Bakathir remained a strong supporter of Islam and of Arabic nationalism and his first play, *Ikhnaton and Nefertiti* (1940), sought to claim classical Egypt as a part of the Arab heritage. Bakathir's first major drama was the 1947 *Secret of Caliph al-Hakem (Sirr al-Hakem bi Amr Illah)*, which deals with a despotic tenth-century ruler of Egypt who is lead into apostasy by his Machiavellian councilor Hamza, until a religious conversion restores him to Islam and an acceptance of his deserved punishment.

Although Bakathir credits the 1948 war as the catalytic agent for his *Oedipus*, there are sufficient similarities to the characters, the political dynamics, and the religious orientation of *The Secret of Caliph al-Hakim* to suggest that these were already established central concerns of the dramatist. In addition to the particular crisis of the war, the late 1940s saw an intensification of the Islamic movement in Egypt, one product of which, Sayed Qutb's book *Social Justice in Islam (Al-Adala al-ijtima'iyya fil-Islam)*, was highly influential on Bakathir and his generation and might almost serve as a guide to the politics of Bakathir's Oedipus. In the face of a rising tide of Marxism and materialism, Qutb called for an integrated, coherent, Islamic theory of social justice, and Bakathir's play demonstrates an Oedipus who begins as a kind of proto-Marxist, an atheist who preaches social justice and confiscates the goods of the temple to distribute to the people but who is ultimately led by Tiresias to an understanding that his social aims can in fact only be attained by faith in God and total submission to His will.

These influences result in an *Oedipus* which provides an interesting counterpart to that of al-Hakim. Both plays have a strong political dimension, depicting a powerful and well-meaning leader who is led into evildoing by manipulative counsellors. One of the most striking and significant differences in the two dramas is in the depiction of Tiresias, radically changed in both from the seer of classic Greece. In al-Hakim he is a purely amoral political intriguer, while in Bakathir he is a devout Muslim who speaks in language redolent of the Qur'an and whose advice at last leads to Oedipus' enlightenment. The role Tiresias plays in al-Hakim is essentially played in Bakathir by Lucasius, the high priest, a wily, calculating politician intent on preserving the riches of his temple. Even more fully than in al-Hakim Oedipus' background, from the first prophecy of his danger to Laius through his killing of the sphinx and assumption of the throne of Thebes is revealed not as the workings of fate or the gods, but as the result of conscious manipulation and outright deception on the part of the evil Lucasius.

After the simultaneous appearance of these versions of *Oedipus* by leading Egyptian dramatists almost thirty years passed and then, rather surprisingly, another two versions appeared, within two years of each other. The first of these, which does not appear in this anthology and which has received less critical attention, was *The Return of the Absent* (*Awdat al Gha'ib*), published in 1977, one of the first plays by Fawzi Fahmi, a professor of theatre and later president of the Academy of Arts in Cairo. The second, presenting a much more radical departure from the dramatic tradition, was a scathing political satire by Ali Salim boldly entitled *The Comedy of Oedipus* (*Kumidiya Udib*) with the subtitle *You Who Killed the Beast* (*Inta Elli Qatalt al-Wahsh*). It was presented, with great success, in 1979 at the now defunct El-Hakim theatre and has remained a popular favorite, although a much more subdued version was demanded by the government shortly after its opening.

When Salim first appeared on the literary scene in the mid 1960s he immediately established himself as an imaginative satirist, taking as his targets Egyptian bureaucracy, the jargon of scientists and literary critics, the new social class of post-revolutionary Egypt, and despotism of all sorts. Not surprisingly, every one of his first five plays had some difficulty with the censor, and his *Oedipus* was the first to reach the stage uncut, somewhat surprisingly, since it is as cutting in its social and political satire as anything Salim had yet written. Perhaps it was the use of a foreign classic that mollified the censors, and the setting of the play in a vague period described by its author as "a long time, a very long time ago." Even so, Salim made little attempt to hide the fact that his real concern was contemporary Egypt. Despite the claimed time, the characters and situations are clearly current or very recent, and unlike his predecessors, Salim transports his action from the Greek to the Egyptian Thebes. It has been suggested that this change was inspired at least in part by the 1960 book *Oedipus and Akhnaton*, by Immanuel Velikovsky, which advanced the theory that the life of the visionary pharaoh was the original inspiration for the Greek myth.[5] The leading contemporary Egyptian critic Nehad Selaiha has recently discovered another drama basedon Velikovsky, written in 2002 by Alexandrian dramatist Mahdi Bunduq.

Selaiha has suggested that "maybe any Egyptian play based on the Oedipus legend is perforce political," citing al-Hakim's speculation in the preface to his own version that the Greek concept of tragedy is inherently antithetical to the Islamic view of the relationship between human beings and God. "A Muslim Oedipus," suggests Selaiha, "can only grapple with earthly issues and fight sordid politicians and mean-spirited foes."[6] Certainly, despite their very different tonalities and character depiction, this is a quality that unites the adaptations of these three major modern Egyptian dramatists.

Whatever the judgment of the censor, it was immediately apparent to Salim's audiences that his version, like the previous ones of Bakathir and perhaps al-Hakim as well, was in significant measure a specific political metaphor, referring in this case to the recent history of Egypt and especially to Nassar, who in 1956 gained heroic stature in the eyes of his people by confronting, almost alone, the beast of Israel, France, and England, but who then allowed his moral authority to be eroded by the cult of personality, the suppression of truth and the political indoctrination of the mass media, while he turned his attention to technical matters, the improvement of the infrastructure. The defeat of 1967 showed that the beast was by no means destroyed and that the misdirected attentions of both leader and people had left them helpless to deal with it. The conclusion of Salim's play calls for a new orientation, a rejection of reliance on heroic saviors, and for the people to take their

---

5. Immanuel Velikovsky, *Oedipus and Akhnaton* (New York: Doubleday, 1960).
6. Selaiha, "Akhenaton a la Greque," *Al-Ahram* 754 (4-10 August 2005), 16; "Manifold Oedipus," 4.

destiny into their own hands.

Salim's Oedipus/Nassar, like the previous Egyptian Oedipuses, is more victim than villain, although all bear a certain responsibility for allowing themselves to become tools of repressive and manipulative forces that they are too preoccupied or idealistic to confront until it is too late to avert a catastrophe.  The play is a far more radical departure from the traditional story than its Egyptian predecessors, and not only in its changed locality and tonality. Oedipus does not kill his father or marry his mother.  Jocasta does not commit suicide nor does Oedipus blind himself.  The result is to shift the dilemma of Oedipus entirely from the personal to the political plane, to the distintegration of public life under the rule of the corrupt politicians, priests, and academics who surround the ruler and the appearance of a new or perhaps the same monster at the gates, for which Thebes is now woefully unprepared.

The only major part of the myth retained is Oedipus' encounter with the sphinx, which becomes central to Salim's version because it is the defining, quite likely incorrect but now mythologized, version of events upon which Oedipus' cult of personality is based.  All hesitations, all questions of his authority are answered by the mindless chant of the play's subtitle "You're the one who killed the beast."  All the major characters are present, but much changed, in this new context.  Jocasta is a sexually frustrated woman who has gotten rid of her previous unsatisfactory mates but is thwarted in her attempts to similarly dispose of Oedipus because of his godlike reputation.  Creon is a rather dense but well-meaning general who is eventually killed by the sphinx when he attempts to emulate Oedipus' previous victory.  Tiresias serves as the raisonneur of the play, opening and closing it and providing the moral, that the people cannot rely on heroes to solve their problems.  The evil High Priest of Bakathir's version here becomes the pompous but equally unprincipled Rector of the University of Thebes, who attempts to fabricate evidence for the divine origin of the hero.  Other corrupt functionaries, Onah, the President of the Chamber of Commerce, and Awalih, the Chief of Police, round out the rogues' gallery of advisors who surround the unfortunate Oedipus and use his reputation to keep the people in awe and subjugation. The play is full of innovative touches, one of the most interesting of which is the sequence of short scenes in the second act presenting amusing vignettes of the results of workings of the Oedipus personality cult, somewhat reminiscent of the brief illustrative episodes in the middle of an Aristophanic comedy. In his stage directions, Salim suggests that they might be presented in the style of the traditional puppet theatre, the type of theatre for which Salim's first work was created.

Although these Egyptian reworkings of the Oedipus story are those best known in the Arab theatre, the fourth version presented in this collection, a very different sort of approach, comes from the only other Arab nation whose contributions to the modern drama rival, historically, quantitatively, and qualitatively, those of Egypt. That is Syria, where the modern European-oriented drama was first established in the Arab world in the late nineteenth century.

After its preliminary leadership in the development of such theatre, Syria in the early twentieth century produced very little theatre of significance. The establishment of a National Theatre in 1960 and the inspiration of Egyptian dramatists like al-Hakim of the 1940s and 1950s influenced the development of an important new generation of Syrian dramatists. Among this generation, two dramatists were particularly noted for their interest in political drama and for their attempts to utilize both Western and local dramatic theatrical techniques: Sadala Wannus (1941-1997), who at his death was hailed as one of the greatest Arab dramatists, and Walid Ikhlasi (b. 1935). Although Ikhlasi, like Wannus, experimented widely with Syrian and Arab dramatic modes, his enormous output offers examples of almost unparalleled thematic and dramatic diversity. He was the first Syrian dramatist to employ the methods of the European theatre of the absurd, in the mid-1960s, and other plays have inspired comparison with dramatists as diverse as Brecht and Shaw. His dramas include tragedies, comedies, and allegories, and his subject matter ranges from Greek, Biblical, and Qur'anic legends to the most contemporary concerns.

Something of this range is suggested by Ikhlasi's 1978 *Oedipus*, created at the same time as the Egyptian versions of Fahmi and Salim but working in a completely different mode. Although all of the Egyptian versions have distinct contemporary echoes and that of Salim in particular claims an antique setting for what is obviously a contemporary culture, Ikhlasi frankly transposes his *Oedipus* into the most contemporary of contemporary settings, a modern computer laboratory. Like Salim, but in an even more extreme manner, Ikhlasi uses the traditional story largely as a point of departure.  Now even the names are gone, although the protagonist Suffian is clearly modeled on Oedipus and his colleague the computer scientist Dr. al-Bahi serves something of the expository functions of a Tiresias.  Here, as in Salim, the focus is upon a single part of the traditional story, in Salim the encounter with the Sphinx, and in Ikhlasi the original prophesy, which is generated, in appropriate late twentieth-century fashion, by a super-computer.

Ikhlasi's computer prophesy interestingly involves not the generation of Suffian's parents (the murder of his father, incest with his mother) but of his children (the murder of his son, incest with his daughter).  Thus his daughter/lover, Sulaf, is the closest parallel to the traditional Jocasta, but after the fateful revelation, very late in the play, she disappears from the action and attention focuses entirely on Suffian's suffering.  Sulaf's presumed father, Muder, thus parallels Oedipus' presumed mother Merope, and it is Muder who, like the shepherds in the original myth, reveals the truth of Sulaf's relationship to her lover.  Rather surprisingly in this contemporary retelling, Ikhlasi restores the classic Chorus, omitted by all the Egyptian adaptors, and uses it to provide short poetic meditations on the fateful story, especially at the opening and close of scenes.

In certain respects Ikhlasi's version, while obviously the furthest removed from the Greek original, in spirit marks a kind of return to it.  It is almost entirely devoid of the distinct political orientation of all of the Egyptian versions, returning to a highly personal study of an individual who imagines that he is control of his universe and finds that he is in fact the plaything of forces beyond his control and comprehension.  Ikhlasi does not position the computer as the dark force that shapes his protagonist's fate.  Its role is closer to that of the traditional oracle, which can look deeper into that mystery than the most intelligent human but ultimately has as little power over it.  Although Suffian himself has much less trust in the computer than his colleague (an echo of Oedipus' attempt to deny the authority of the oracle), clearly the use of the computer is made to emphasize that even in a world dominated by scientific achievements and rational thought, the primal forces that destroyed that early champion of rationalism, Sophocles' Oedipus, have lost nothing of their power.

Marvin Carlson

# KING
# OEDIPUS

by Tawfiq Al-Hakim

Translated by W. M. Hutchins

## Introduction to *King Oedipus*

*In the name of God, the Compassionate, the Merciful.*

Dramatic literature is a door which was not opened in the Arabic language until the modern age. Arabic literature has hesitated to accept this genre which was foreign to it. For some time it left it outside its walls. It heard about it from spectators without thinking of turning to it or wading into it.

There first appeared about a century ago in some of the Arab lands like Syria, Lebanon, and Egypt a type of theatre in which the serious was mixed with the comic, and acting with singing. Some Western stories were translated for it either literally or freely. They were presented either in their original garb or in the appropriate for the East. Sometimes they were in literary language and at other times in a language form more readily understood by the common people.

At that time, the theatre drew from French and English literature. We saw Molière's *L'Avare* presented in verse. We saw Shakespeare's *Romeo and Juliet* presented as a musical.

The originator of the Arab theatre in the East was, as is well known, Marun an-Naqqash. He was followed by his disciples, al-Qardahi and Abu Khalil al-Qabbani, among others. Then its banner was carried by ash-Shaykh Salama Hijazi followed in turn by the 'Ukasha family who inherited his stories and his songs. They followed his track, but the Egyptian revolution and the outpouring of national spirit impelled them to turn to Egyptianizing their stories. The writer of these lines began his theatrical life at that time. He wrote some plays for that troupe in the manner in which work was carried out in those days.

All this was happening without any one of those who wrote for the theatre desiring to call his work literature. Arabic literature gave no thought to considering this form of writing to be literature of any kind. Shawqi afterwards submitted some of his stories to the

Reprinted from *Plays, Prefaces and Postscripts of Tawfiq al-Hakim*, translated by William M. Hutchins. Copyright © 1981 by W. M. Hutchins. Reprinted with permission of Lynne Rienner Publishers, Inc.

theatre.  They were a success with the audience, but he as well did not think of printing them before they were acted.  He did not think they would have an illustrious existence at a distance from the lights of the theatre.  In his opinion, only the ode he submitted to the daily papers or to a publisher within a collection of poetry was ready for a victorious entry into the castle of literature with the heads of the literati bowing before them.  The barrier, then, between the world of the theatre and the world of literature was a perplexing matter requiring explanation.

This writer traveled to Europe at that time where a puzzling secret was revealed to him.  It was not difficult to come upon the key to the reason . . . the theatre world and the literary world in Europe are intertwined.  There is no separation or barrier between them. The cause for that is obvious.  Drama is a branch of literature studied in the institutes and universities as literature before being submitted to the stage.  Europe inherited this literature from the Greeks.  It examined and studied it.  It built and wove on its foundation. Drama was part of its national artistic tradition and grew and developed with the passing centuries, whether performed or not.  It had a separate existence.  It was similar to the sciences of logic, mathematics, and philosophy with their inheritance from the Greeks.  For that reason, the writer found it necessary to begin at the beginning and return to the source when he desired to study dramatic literature.

He thought the affair would be simple and the way easy.  He would begin wherever he wished.  He would devote his attention to this modern dramatic literature which would not require effort to study nor be difficult to understand.  He was told if he were serious, he should go back to the Greeks.  He returned to Aeschylus, Sophocles, Euripides, and Aristophanes.  Here he realized why Arabic literature pays attention to the ode and does not recognize the play even if it is poetry. The ode is a form inherited from the distant past, just as dramatic poetry is inherited by Western literature from the past.

Nothing is stronger than inheritance.  If immortality has a hand, it is this inheritance by which beings are transferred from one age to another.  The characteristics of individuals, the peculiarities of peoples, and the distinguishing marks of nations are nothing but an inheritance of attributes and characteristics which are handed down from generation to generation. What is said to be deep-rooted in a people is nothing but its qualities inherited from remote times. The characteristic originality of things and creatures is in that continual retention of inherited excellences from one who becomes adult to the next, link after link. This can be said of a people, a man, or a horse. It can likewise be said of art, science, or literature. The deep-rooted part of literature is its character preserved and handed down from the past.

America desired to find a shortcut for the art of music. It originated that variety of Black music called jazz. But it failed to persuade the cultured world to venerate that music with no venerable origin or revered lineage. Had America's language not been English, its literature would also have had this fate. But American literature could be a literature only because it rested on its recognized inheritance from English literature. The truth of the matter is that it is only a recent bough of the many-branched tree of Saxon literature.

Arabic literature, then, is like other deep-rooted literatures. It does not lightly accept change to its substance or character without research, examination, caution, and circumspection. When in the last century it took this cautious attitude towards the theatre, it was not to be censured or blamed for that. For the way the theatre was introduced in the Arab East it had no foundation which could justify it in the eyes of that deep-rooted literature.

If only a literary figure had risen among us during the last century or two to cry out questioningly: "O Arabic literature, from ancient times there have been between you and Greek thought close ties and bonds. You have reflected on it and taken the sciences and philosophy from it. You have, however, turned your face away from the poetry it has. How far will this rupture go? When will a truce be concluded between you and Greek poetry? Consider it a bit. Allow it to be translated and researched. Perhaps you will find in it something to reinforce your inheritance and to augment your bequest to future generations."

This voice was not raised during the past centuries. Therefore, the rupture continued to exist between Arabic literature and Greek literature. The persistence of this rupture has made it difficult for the theatre to stand on a solid foundation and to find a place among us within the colonnades of literature, thought, and culture.

There must be a truce then between the two literatures, if we wish to have established within the deep-rooted history of Arabic literature this dramatic genre, whether in poetry or prose, in a valuable and lasting way. But how is the truce to come about? We must first of all learn the reasons for the estrangement so that we can work successfully afterwards and take the measures necessary for a covenant.

Before anything else we must ask ourselves whose responsibility it was that Greek poetry was not translated into Arabic. This question leads us to study the way the Greek legacy was translated and the causes and reasons for that.

It is known that following Alexander's conquests the Greek spirit penetrated Asia. Syria, and the area of Mesopotamia, between the Tigris and Euphrates rivers, were among the most important regions which were subject to the influence of Greek civilization. There, in the cells of the Syrian ascetics throughout those areas, for a period of centuries an extensive movement of translation was energetically carried out for scientific and philosophical works from Greek to Syriac. It was from those Syriac translations that the Arabs later drew inspiration and made translations.

If this account is correct, the Arabs can say that they translated what they found. Poetry was not something those monks cared about . . . but what happened was that many Arabs afterward learned Greek and were able to translate from it directly.

Among the works translated into Arabic was the book of poetry or *Poetics* of Aristotle, containing his definitions of tragedy and comedy and their characteristics as parts of dramatic poetry. Ibn Rushd came and showed us with his famous commentary on the *Poetics* that the Arabs did not intentionally close their minds to knowledge of the art of poetry among the Greeks. How was it then that curiosity did not impel them thereafter to translate some of the representative tragedies or comedies into Arabic?

It is understandable that they would refrain from translating lyric poetry like that of Pindar or Anacreon, for in pre-Islamic or 'Abbasid Arabic poetry there are comparable works of that type. But why did they — since they were, as we know, eager to learn — fail to translate the tragedies of the Greek poets?

For us to answer that we must know first what tragedy is. How did it arise in Greece? There is no longer any doubt today that tragedy originated from the worship of Bacchus, the wine god known to the Greeks under the name of Dionysius. Every spring, religious celebrations were held for this god. There was boisterous drunkenness with an outpouring of gaiety. People danced and sang at these times around a statue of the wine god. They were decked out in goat skins and leaves.

This dancing and singing was at first improvised. After that, with the passing of time, the performance was refined. The people prepared them according to patterns with set elements. That singing was soon mixed with a type of praise for the deeds of that god in the form of a narrative recital of praise for his triumphs, his adventures, and his amazing journeys. Then the matter of the troupe of dancers developed till they began to vary their costumes and portray different characters — not just goats and animals. The narrative also developed and began to take on different ideas unrelated to the life of the god whose festivals they were celebrating. This led reactionary and conservative elders to make a row about the innovations. They said "There is nothing about Bacchus in this." This phrase later became proverbial in the Greek language.

But from this innovation which aroused criticism and anger came the dramatic art. It was not long before a man appeared, called Thespis, whose reflection led him to compose what the chorus would have to recite and the words of a dialogue for one actor to hold with the chorus. He gave this actor different masks and costumes. He was able in that way to take on a number of characters by himself.

In this fashion, the matter passed from the stage of narrative recital to that of dialogue and action. Drama was born and tragedy came into existence. After Thespis there came a poet named Phrynichos who took this art another step. It was said that he was the first to introduce women characters into the performance. He divided the chorus into two sections. One of them could address the actor in a tone of approval of his actions. Meanwhile the other addressed him in a tone of displeasure and criticism. It was as though the chorus with its two parts were the people in society, including those who support the deeds they see and those who oppose them. History also mentions to us that two of the poet's contemporaries, Choirlos and Pratinas, each played a part in improving this form of art. All of these prepared the way for the appearance of the great masters of tragedy: Aeschylus, Sophocles, and Euripides.

That is a quick look at the genesis of dramatic poetry in Greece. From it we see that worship of Bacchus was the mother of tragedy. This art then poured out to us like wine . . . from the jug of religion. In this way, the great poets of tragedy proceded to weave their immortal works from their religious legend, from mythology. They imbued them with a spirit of the struggle between man and divine powers.  Do you suppose it was this religious character which discouraged the Arabs from embracing this art?

This is the opinion of a group of scholars. They assert that Islam stood in the way of the acceptance of this pagan art. I do not share his opinion.  Islam has never been an obstacle for an art form.  It permitted the translation of many works produced by heathens. There was *Kalia and Dimna* which Ibn al-Muqaffa translated from Pahlavi.   There was Ferdowski's *Shahnameh* which al-Bundari translated from the Persian.  It is about their pagan age.  Similarly, Islam did not prevent the circulation of the wine poetry of Abu Nuwas, the carving of statues for the palaces of the caliphs, or the expert portraiture of Persian miniatures.   Likewise, it did not prevent the translation of many Greek works which mentioned pagan customs.  No, it was not the pagan quality as such which turned the Arabs away from dramatic poetry.  What did hold them back then?  Do you suppose it was the difficulty of understanding a story in poetry which revolves entirely around legends which could only be understood after a long explanation spoiling the pleasure of the person trying to understand them and ending the enjoyment of someone desiring to sample them?  Perhaps there is some truth to this explanation, for I was astonished by the comment of the ciritc Francisque Sarcey counselling the spectators when *Oedipus Tyrannus* was presented on the stage of the Comédie-Française in 1881 A.D.  I consider it, of the Greek tragedies, the one least immersed in religious mythology, the clearest and purest of them, and one closest to the soul's naked humanity.

The critic said: "I advise the audience — in particular the ladies among them — to open a book or dictionary of Greek mythology and to read in it before seeing the play performed, a summary of the Oedipus legend.  This will spare them the boredom of losing the thread and wandering through the obscurities of the first act."[1]

To whom was this advice directed?  To the public of a nation whose culture was based on the Greek legacy . . . a public most of whom had been to school where they were taught—and there is no doubt about what they were taught—Greek literature with its tragedies and comedies.  If a public like that, in the modern age, still needed a summary or dictionary to follow the tragedy of Oedipus, what are we to think of the Arab reader in the 'Abbasid or Fatimid eras?

But, despite the validity of this explanation, I do not believe that it, either, would have prevented translation of some examples of this art.  For Plato's *Republic* was translated into Arabic, and I have no doubt it contains ideas concerning that ideal city which would be difficult for the Islamic mentality to digest.  Yet that did not prevent its translation.  Indeed it was precisely this difficulty that moved al-Farabi to take Plato's *Republic,* wrap it in a gown of his thoughts, and pour it into the mold of his philosophic and Islamic mentality.

Something similar could have happened for Greek tragedy.  It would have been possible for a tragedy like *Oedipus* to have been translated and then afterwards taken up by a poet or prose author.  He would have removed from it the hard-to-understand mythological references and stripped it of the obscure pagan beliefs.  He would have presented it, clear and unambiguous in its bare human structure.  Or, he might have thrown over it a diaphanous gown of Islamic belief or Arab thought.

Why did that not take place?  Because there was another reason, no doubt, which turned the Arabs away from adopting Greek theatre.  Perhaps the reason was that the Greek tragedies were not considered at that time to be literature meant to be read.  At that time, they may have been something that would not be independently read the way Plato's *Republic* was.  They were written not to be read but to be performed.  The author knew that his work would be presented to the people in performance on a stage.  He would therefore leave his texts and his dialogue free of explanations, observations, or information necessary to grasp the story's atmosphere.  He could rely on the spectator's perceiving it visually, realized and portrayed, when it was produced.  In truth, the Greek

1. Francisque Sarcey, *Quarante ans de théâtre* (Paris: Bibliothèque des Annales, 1900-1902), III, 312.

theatre reached a precison and complexity in its machines and instruments that excites astonishment. It had machines that moved and rotated as well as theatrical tricks and devices sufficient to allow those people to produce *Prometheus Bound* by the poet Aeschylus which contains sea nymphs which appear out of the clouds and the sea. Prometheus comes in on the back of that fabulous animal with the head of an eagle and the body of a stallion.

Perhaps this is what made the Arab translator stop perplexed before tragedy. He would cast his eyes over the silent texts trying to see them in his mind throbbing and moving with their characters, atmosphere, locations, and times. But that mind would not comply with his wishes. For he had never seen this art acted in his land. The chorus among the Greeks created acting. It was the actor Thespis who created the play. The play did not create the theatre. The theatre was the creator of the play. So long as the Arab translator was certain that he had before him a work not made to be read, for what purpose would he translate it then?

Perhaps this is the reason that Greek dramatic poetry was not translated into Arabic. The activity of translation of Greek works was designed to be useful. It was not merely for the love of discovery or just from curiosity. In this case, the benefit from the ideas and thoughts of the tragedies was lost, because they could not be grasped or attained solely by reading. In order to make them clear, there had to be a means for presenting them. That was not something that was available or known. The question, however, which must then be posed is why there was not acting in Arab culture. Why wasn't it known?

The Arabs too had their pagan age. Among their poets of that age were those said to have traveled to "Caesar's land," like Imru al-Qays. There is no doubt he saw the Roman theatres looming tall. They inherited this art from the Greeks. Could not the sight of the theatre have inspired the pagan Arab with the idea of importing, transmitting, or adapting it?

Where would he have taken it? Here is the problem. The homeland to which the pagan Arab poet would have transmitted this art, had he wanted to, was nothing other than a desert vast as the sea. Through it hastened camels like ships, roaming from island to island. These were scattered oases which would gush with water one day and be green with plants. On the morrow the water supply would dwindle away and the green growth would wither.  It was a homeland moving on the backs of caravans, running here and there in pursuit of a drop from the clouds.  It was a homeland continuously rocked atop camels in a rhythmic, harmonic way enouraging the riders to sing.  From this, Arabic poetry was born.  It orginated with the camel chant, as the person holding the reins of the first camel raised his voice to chant to the beat of that faint, hidden music coming from the camels' hoof beats on the sand.

Everything, then, in the moving homeland separated it from the theatre.  The first thing the theatre requires is stability.  The Arabs lacked a settled feeling.  That is, in my opinion, the true reason for their neglect of dramatic poetry which requires a theatre.  The theatre of Bacchus, the ruins of which have been uncovered by archeological work in modern times, was a solid building with a massive foundation.  It was an establishment belonging to the state. Anyone who becomes acquainted, from the ruins or from drawings, with that enormous structure and its capacity for thousands of spectators will judge at once that this is something which must have been the product of a settled community and of a concentrated and united social life.  A researcher would have the right to object that the Arabs under the Umayyad and 'Abasid dynasties and thereafter experienced that sedentary community and united and concentrated society.  Why did the Arabs in those eras refrain from erecting a theatre when they were capable of it?  We see that they surveyed different cultures and adopted from their architecture elements they used to establish a stunning architecture bearing their new stamp.

There is a simple answer to that.  The Arabs under the Umayyad dynasty and later continued to consider the Bedouin and desert poetry the finest example to be imitated.  They looked to pre-Islamic poetry as the most perfect model to be followed.  They sensed their lack of architecture, but they never felt a shortcoming in poetry. When they wished to borrow and sample from others, they went in every direction and looked at every art—except the art of poetry. They believed that they had reached the ultimate in it long before. Thus we find ourselves turning round a complex group of reasons each of which could have discouraged the Arabs from becoming interested in drama.

However, was it necessary for Arab literature to produce tragedies?  Is tragedy a genre necessary for the development of

Arabic literature to complete its personality?

Anyone who reads the famous preface to *Cromwell* by Victor Hugo finds a partial answer. He divides the history of mankind into three ages. The primitive age in his opinion is the age of lyric poetry. Of it he says that in the primitive age man chants as though breathing. He is in the age of chilvalrous youth, of breaking into song, etc. Then comes the antique age, the age of the epic. The tribe has developed and become a nation. The societal urge has replaced the urge to travel. Nations have been formed and become important. One of them rubs against another. They clash and engage in battle. Here poetry arises to narrate the events that have taken place, to tell the story of what happened to the peoples and what befell the empires. Finally comes the modern age which is the age of drama. In his opinion, it is the complete poetry, because it includes within it all the varietes. It contains some of the lyric and some of the epic.

Let us listen to him summarize his thought: "Human society progresses and matures while singing of its dreams. Afterwards it begins to narrate its deeds. Then it finally undertakes to portray its thoughts."[2]

Hugo invites us to test his doctrine on each literature individually. He assures us that we will find that each bears out this division. According to him, the lyric poets always precede the epic poets, and the epic poets precede the dramatic poets.

Do you suppose this doctrine can be applied to Arabic literature? In my opinion it can be, if we disregard the genres and confine our investigation to the objectives. There is no doubt that Arabic poetry did sing of dreams, describe wars, and portray ideas. It did not change its method, leave its genre, or deviate from its principles. On its way, it followed the same order that Hugo set forth. In the 'Abbasid era alone we find al-Buhturi [d. 897 A.D.] is before al-Mutanabbi [d. 965 A.D.] and al-Mutanabbi before Abu al-'Ala' [d. 1057 A.D.]. Had these poets been planted in the Greek soil, al-Buhuti, the Arab cymbal player, would have been Pindar. Al-Mutanabbi who makes our ears resound across the generations with the ring of swords would have been Homer. Abu al-'Ala' who

---

2. Victor Hugo, *Oeuvres complètes: Cromwell* (n.p.: Editions Rencontre, 1967), 26.

portrayed for us thought about man and his destiny and the heavenly hosts would have been Aeschylus. The development, then, in terms of content was completed. But the development with respect to form was hindered by those circumstances which attended the growth of the Arab state. The circumstances, which as we have seen did not limit the Arabs' mentality or restrain their artistic nature, were able in any case, against their will, to keep them away from this one of the literary arts at that stage of their history.

There is then no inherent animosity between the Arabic language and dramatic literature. It is a question rather of a temporary estrangement, resulting from a lack of the instrument. The matter for the Arabs here is like that when they knew no riding animals other than the camel. Had circumstances conspired to deny them the horse, they would have continued to the present day without knowing how to ride it. But no sooner had the horse entered the desert than the Arabs became horsemen. They mastered the arts of rearing it and of describing it. What is there to say today anywhere in the world about the original horse before the Arabian? If a splendid description of the traits of the horse is sought, where is it but in Arabic poetry?

The whole question then is one of instrument. It is as though the Arabs in the age of camels were saying: "Give us the horse; we will ride it." They might similarly have said: "Give us the theatre and we will write for it."

There is no doubt that the world has changed today. Theatre in the broad sense of the word has become one of the necessitites of contemporary life. It is not restricted to any one class. It is the daily nourishment for the minds of the people. Its richness varies according to their cultural level. In the final analysis it is the instrument of art which spreads through the Eastern and Western lands of the earth. By "theatre" I mean here every art which sets out to portray things, persons, and thoughts on a stage, screen, page or over the air in such manner that they appear alive, conversing and debating, displaying their secrets and thoughts before a viewer, hearer, or reader.

There is no longer any way to ignore this worldwide style of presenting ideas in a living way in dramatic form. Wherever we go today in the Arab world we find high, lofty, ornamented buildings, the most luxurious in our cities. These are the theatres!

Thus we have the theatre, that is, the instrument. For our Arab way of life, it has become one of the necessities like bread and water. Every day the field of operation for this instrument called acting has expanded until it has become—with the spread of broadcasting—daily nourishment entering every home. All of this ought to have reached the ears of the deep-rooted Arabic literature and prompted it to pay attention to this art and lay foundations for it within its own procedures and categories. It is my guess that Arabic literature yearns to do that, for it is not a dead literature nor ossified.

But how can this be done? It cannot be expected to open a door into its noble frame and set within it an art with no foundations. For it is not a frivolous or spurious literature. These are the people who have preserved the lineages of human beings and horses. We must not give them cause for distress over their long-established literature at this late date. We must then create the missing link of the lineage and return to it so that it can firmly bond Arabic literature with dramatic art. This link can only be Greek literature.

For all these reasons, there must be a truce between the two long-established literatures. Here we approach the great question: how can this reconciliation be achieved? Is it sufficient to be, with care and concern, devoted to Greek dramatic literature, transmitting all of it to our Arabic language? This matter is obviously necessary, and most of that has been accomplished. Indeed, *Oedipus the King* by Sophocles was presented for all to see on the Arab stage more than a third of a century ago.

But the mere transmission of Greek dramatic literature to the Arabic language does not achieve for us the establishment of a dramatic literature in Arabic. Similarly, the mere transmission of Greek philosophy did not create an Arab or Islamic philosophy. Translation is only a tool which must carry us to a further goal.

The goal is to ladle water from the spring, then to swallow it, digest it and assimilate it, so that we can bring it forth to the people once again dyed with the color of our thought and imprinted with the stamp of our beliefs. This was the way the Arab philosophers proceded when they took the works of Plato and Aristotle. We must proceed in that same way with Greek tragedy. We must dedicate ourselves to its study with patience and endurance and then look at it afterwards with Arab eyes.

Before us, an analogous course was followed in the history of

French literature. Its tragedians returned to the ancient Greek works, to the works of Aeschylus, Sophocles, and Euripides. They ladled from them and transmitted them without changing the subject, characters, or action. Yet they bestowed on those works all of their French spirit.

That is the way to the truce, indeed the marriage between the two spirits and the two literatures. There must occur a marriage between Greek literautre and Arabic literature comparable with respect to tragedy to the marriages that took place between Greek philosophy and Arab thought and between French literature and Greek literature. If that is completed in any fashion, whether in poetry or in prose, I have no doubt that Arabic literature will recognize this new-old form without regard to the age in which that marriage took place. For time is of no significance in the long history of literature, so long as the links for it are strongly connected, logically fastened, with a progression that makes sense.

It has always been my opinion that modern Arabic literature is nothing but a continuation of the innovative movement which al-Jahiz undertook in the third century of Islam. This is so despite an occasional relapse as well as reliance on tradition during intervening periods over this long time. It is so despite what has been said of its blind imitation of Western literature in the recent past. This [Western] influence, which some of the superficial Orientalists have noticed, does not go beyond the form, appearance, and dress. It is a natural matter in the history of the literatures of all nations. The outer cloak is a property owned in common by the prevalent culture in any age. The difference is in the substances, the character, the sensitivity. Arabic literature never lost its spirit, thought, or sensitivity over the years, whether it stood still or advanced, frozen or developed.

Thus I was moved to study the dramatic literature of Greece. I did not look at it as a French or European scholar but as an Arab scholar, an Easterner. The two viewpoints are very different. This became clear to me later. Despite the European clothing I wore to the Comédie-Française to see *Oedipus* by Sophocles with [Raphael] Albert Lambert and despite that French spirit [of the production] derived from the tragedies of Corneille and Racine, something in the depths of my soul brought me close to the spirit of tragedy as the

Greeks felt it.

What is the Greek spirit of tragedy? It is that tragedy springs from a religious feeling. The entire substance of tragedy is that it is a struggle, manifest or hidden, between man and the divine forces dominating existence. It is the struggle of man with something greater than man and above man. The foundation of true tragedy in my opinion is man's sense that he is not alone in existence. This is what I mean by the expression "religious feeling." No matter what the play's form, style, or the effect it produces in the soul, it is not permissible in my opinion to describe it as tragedy so long as it does not rest on that religious feeling. This divine element in the spirit of tragedy has not retained its heat and radiance over the course of the centuries. Since the age of Latin, you find poets who precisely imitate the Greek tragedies in all their external aspects and yet preserve little of the substance. When the Renaissance came, they went further down this road. Poets no longer distinguished between tragedy and atrocity. Whenever they piled on terror and heaped up horror, they thought they were making a tragedy resembling the Greek tragedies. In the seventeenth century we are confronted by tragedy which has become a struggle between a man and his soul. With Corneille it is based on incidents of history. Let us listen to the schoar Brunetière as he says approvingly: "But is not history the spectacle of the struggle between one will and another? . . . It is natural therefore that history should beome an inspiration for theatre which . . . rests totally on the belief in the sovereignty of the will."[3]

With Racine, tragedy became a struggle between one emotion and another. Love with the jealousy, envy, malice, and hatred which accompany it became the domain in which his feeling and thought moved. Both of them, in addition to that, wrapped their tragedies in the French spirit. The poet Corneille "Frenchified" history to some extent. Napoleon, in a later time, preferred him to all other poets. He used to say of him: "This man discovered the meaning of politics. Had he had practical experience, he would have been a statesman . . . A decree of the state has taken the place with the modern poets

3. Ferdinand Bruetière, *Les epoques du théâtre français (1636-1850)* (Paris: Calmann Lévy, 1892), 65.

of a decree of fate among the ancients. Corneille is the only one of the French poets to have sensed this truth."[4]

Napoleon's admiration for this attitude of Corneille's is apparent in his frequent praise for it and in his expression of regret that Corneille did not live in his era. Otherwise, as he said, "I would have made him a prince. Indeed, I would have appointed him prime minister." Napoleon found nothing to do for this Corneille except to search for his descendants. Of them he found only two women. He ordered that they be provided with pensions of three hundred francs a year.[5]

At precisely this time, it seems it was not easy for the people to experience the Greek tragedies in their true form nor even for the elite among them to penetrate to their spirit. Napoleon desired to see Sophocles' *Oedipus* performed on stage. He encountered stiff opposition from France's leading actor at that time, the great [François-Joseph] Talma. Napoleon explained his point of view as follows:

> I do not desire with this request to rectify our contem-
> porary theatrical situation. I did not wish to introduce
> any innovation into it. I wished rather to witness the
> effect the antique art might produce on our modern
> notions and circumstances. I am convinced that that
> undertaking would bring the soul pleasure. I would
> like to know what impression the sight of the Greek style
> troupe and chorus would have on our tastes.[6]

That was with respect to Corneille. Racine did not go beyond portrayal of the psychological condition of his epoch, presenting it on the stage in that framework to which he gave the name "tragedy."

With the passing years then that religious feeling which made the first tragedies a conflict between man and what is greater than man has been dispersed and has evaporated in the winds of time. Perhaps this was a harbinger of the scientific renaissance of that century.

---

4. cf. L.-Henry Lecomte, *Napoléon et le monde dramatique* (Paris: H. Daragon, 1912), 401.
5. Ibid.
6. Ibid., 421-22.

Whatever the reason may have been, the poets and people had changed in their belief. They had come to believe that there is nothing but man in this existence—his state, his government, his leaders and his authority.

Once this religious feeling is extinguished, in my opinion, there is no hope of producing tragedy. Perhaps this is the reason for the death of tragedy in our present age. There is not a single poet in the world today who can write a single tragedy of lasting value, comparable to the tragedies which came before. The reason for that is that no thinker in the Western world today truly believes in the existence of a god other than himself.

The last of the ages for tragedy, properly understood, was the seventeenth century. In spite of what we mentioned about Corneille and Racine, they at least had a remnant of the religious feeling which provided their works an ember from the heavenly heat. Racine's relationship with the Jansenist religious sect and the explanations critics expounded for some of his tragedies, especially *Phèdre*, according to the light of the teachings of that sect, are matters the history of literature has explained in detail.

I think there is no need to speak of the tragedies of Voltaire! This sarcastic doubter had in his heart belief only for his intellect. He looked at Shakespeare more than back to the Greeks. Voltaire is the person who prepared the way for the modern artistic mentality and a first model for the Western thinker and the European author of the present day.

In this atmosphere of the present century from the sky of which that religious feeling in its former sense has disappeared, I was reading and watching tragedy. I perceived its true substance with a hidden sensitivity. What was the secret?

It is not a strange secret at all. All there is to the matter is that I am an Easterner, an Arab. I still retain some part of my original religious sense. I have not traversed those previously mentioned stages that the European mentality has. My position before Greek tragedy is that of an Arab thinker of the third century of Islam.

With this feeling I returned to Egypt. Not much time had passed before I wrote the play *The Sleepers of Ephesus* [*The People of the Cave*]. That was in the year 1928. The 'Ukasha troupe had finally gone out of existence. So I had in mind no vision of a special theatre or of a particular actor. I found no one to confide my work to but paper.

When the writer lacks a theatre and his thoughts take control of him, he sets up his theatre at once between the covers of a book. My aim in composing *The Sleepers of Ephesus* was to introduce the element of tragedy in an Arab and Islamic subject. This was tragedy in its ancient Greek meaning which I have retained: the conflict between man and the unseen forces beyond man. I desired my source to be not the legends of Greece but the Qur'an. My aim was not simply to take a story from the Holy Book and put it in the dramatic mold. The goal was rather to look at our Islamic legends with the eye of Greek tragedy. It was to effect this intermarriage between the two mentalities and literatures. I did not wish to provide that work with an introduction when it was published to avoid directing the reader's thought and pointing him to someone else's opinion. What concerned me was to see the effect of the work on the souls of its readers removed from any guidance or suggestion. No matter what interpretations that book received, what was firmly established in the minds of the literary people of that day was that there was something which had been composed on some foundation. The literary figures without exception considered this work a form of Arabic literature, whether acted or not.

In this way, the goal I referred to at the opening of this introduction was realized. It was for Arabic literature to accept this dramatic literature without reference to the theatre. It is an amazing result. For Shawqi, as I have said, had plays which were known first to the theatre before they were known to literature as a book to be read. Moreover, it is easy for a scholar to notice that Shawqi in his plays has absolutely no connection to the Greeks. He proceeds in them in the manner of the French tragedians. He too wove the subjects for his plays from history and love as in *The Death of Cleopatra* and *Layla's Majnun*. There is no question that the conflict between one emotion and another or between one will and another is the easiest type of conflict to present to an audience.

For that reason, the difficulty of presenting plays centered on a conflict between one idea and another on a stage other than that of the mind is evident. Yet this mental theatre is necessary, so long as there are subjects which must be presented which are based on bare thought and immaterial characters. The struggle between man and the unseen forces which are greater than man, like time, reality space, etc., cannot be given a bodily form appropriate for the material theatre, unless we have recourse to the pagan method of personification.  Aeschylus, for example, did this when he made power and the sea actual characters who speak.  This is an affair I think the Islamic, Arab mentality would not swallow.  It has purified "Allah" of any personification and compelled the mind to accept the concept as it appears solely in thought, bare and unblemished by any coarse outer cover.

Aeschylus, moreover, himself, despite his personification of the hidden forces, was tucked by critics into the group of authors who are better read in a chair than presented on stage.  That question has also been raised in relation to Shakespeare, although it is an obstinate exaggeration in my opinion.  I have read of a study by a critic called Boulanger about what he terms, "theatre in an armchair."  In it, he expressed his astonishment that Shakespeare's plays have more the spirit of the book in them than of the theatre. Remy de Gourmont was also of this strange opinion.  He said, "There is none of Shakespeare's plays which has not disappointed me on the stage."[7]

Confronted by these views, the critic Thibaudet undertook to divide dramatists into two groups: one group which takes human life in itself as the subject of its action and endeavor and a second which makes of that life an intellectual melody.  One group portrays the movement of human beings in life.  The other portrays the thought of human beings in life. In his opinion, the first group can be easily presented in the material theatre.  He includes Shakespeare among them despite the intellectual melodies in some of his plays. Of the Greeks he includes Sophocles and Euripides.  In the second group he puts Aeschylus.[8]

Our conclusion based on all this is that it is the play's subject which determines the type of theatre.  If the play is based on the motion of human beings, its place is the material theatre.  If it is based on the motion of thought, its place is the mental theatre.

Here a question appears: is it not possible to present to the audience in the material theatre some Greek tragedy covered with a veil of the Arab mentality in which there appears the conflict

---

7. cf. Albert Thibaudet, "Les Spectacles dans un Fauteuil," *Reflexions sur la littérature* (Paris: Fallimard, 1938), I, 83.
8. Ibid., 86.

between man and the sublime, unseen forces, without so baring the thought in it that it falls into the mental type of plays? To answer the question, I devoted no small amount of time to studying Sophocles. I ended up selecting *Oedipus* as the subject for my experiment.

Why did I choose *Oedipus* in particular? For a reason that may appear strange. It is that I considered it a long time and saw in it something that never occurred to the mind of Sophocles. I saw in it a struggle not between man and fate, the way the Greeks and those following them to the present day have thought of it. I saw in it rather the same hidden conflict that arose in [my] play, *The Sleepers of Ephesus.*

This struggle was not just between man and time as its readers were wont to think. There was rather another concealed war that few have paid attention to, a war between fact and truth. There is the fact of a man like Mishilinia who returned from the cave to find Prisca. He loved her and she loved him. Everything was ready for them to lead a life of ease and happiness. Only one obstacle stood between them and this beautiful fact. That was the truth. The truth of this man Mishilinia which became clear to Prisca was that he was the fiancé of her great-aunt. The two lovers strove to forget this truth which rose to destroy their fact. But they were unable with their tangible fact to repel this mysterious, intangible thing called truth.

Oedipus and Jocasta, themselves, are none other than Mishilinia and Prisca. They too loved each other, but when they learn the truth of their relationship to each other it destroys what they had in common. Man's strongest adversary is always a ghost. It is a ghost given the name "truth." This was my motive for choosing *Oedipus* in particular. I had my view and idea of it, but there remained the execution. In what manner should I treat this tragedy?

At this point I succumbed to anxiety for a time. I knew the pains which had tormented those poets and authors who had dealt with it before me over the course of the centuries. When I recollected Seneca's shortcoming in *Oedipus,* Corneille's failure in *Oedipus,* and Voltaire's puniness compared to Sophocles in *Oedipus,* I was afflicted by vertigo. Then if I left those poetic geniuses and turned to those of the contemporary rebels who have treated Oedipus and to the failure and defeat to which they have exposed themselves, I was overcome by anguish. I remained for a time despairing and indolent, postponing the execution of this work. At last I began to take heart. I said: Let me work. It is better for me to err than to be anxious and paralysed. Let me take those who have failed as my model. Let me fail like them, for they in any case did their duty. They still deserve praise, because they courageously advanced and made mistakes. I can benefit from that and avoid their errors. I can turn my face in another direction where perhaps there is another type of error. So be it. The mistakes of artists and authors are sometimes beneficial and preferable to what is correct.

I knew that among the living poets who had treated Oedipus were the English language poet Yeats and the German poet [Hugo von] Hofmannsthal. The two did not add anything to Sophocles' tragedy.

Then I knew of three contemporary French prose writers who each adapted *Oedipus* from Sophocles. The first of them was Saint-Georges de Bouhélier. The second was Jean Cocteau and the third André Gide. De Bouhélier cut up the story of Oedipus. He divided it into numerous scenes, following the practice of Shakespeare in his plays. No sooner was it performed on the stage than the critic Lucien Dubech said of it:

> While in Sophocles Oedipus is preoccupied with the action he is directing and living through without time for him to ponder his destiny, de Bouhélier leaves him alone for long periods. He confides his doubts, regret, and the wakefulness of his conscience like Hamlet or Lady Macbeth . . . .
> It is futile for us to remind de Bouhélier that nothing surpasses [in Sophocles' immortal tragedy] that great dramatic force which issues from that massing of action and the accumulation of events, in that strong unity and narrow focus. . . .[9]

I truly have benefitted from this error, for it had occurred to me as well to put the story of Oedipus in numerous scenes as I did in *Shahrazad* and *The Wisdom of Solomon*. God protected me from the evil of this action, for I saw the experiment fail at the hand of de Bouhélier. Jean Cocteau also composed an *Oedipus* with numerous scenes which he named *La Machine Infernale*. He presented it on the

---

9. Lucien Dubech, *Le Théâtre 1918-1923* (Paris: Librairie Plon, 1925).

stage, but I have never seen it acted nor read the critics on it.  I perceived from reading it printed in a book, however, that Cocteau was superficially influenced by the Greek theory about *Oedipus*.  But he too was artistically influenced by Shakespeare.  He had the spirit of the father of Oedipus appear on the walls like the spirit of Hamlet's father.  It is amazing that there should be so much influence on *Oedipus* from Shakespeare instead of from Sophocles who is indisputably the peak of the tradition of the art of tragedy.

After that comes André Gide with his story *Oedipus*.  In it he moved towards Sophocles, but he made us feel a loftiness in Oedipus that does not originate from man's link to what is greater than man so much as from man's link to himself.

André Gide was able to derive from his faith in man the substances of a humility taking the place in the soul of that submission to the sublime, hidden forces.  He summarizes for us with truth and sincerity the whole European credo today: there is nothing in existence but man; there is no value in existence but man's.  André Gide is not the only one responsible for this belief.  It had existed for about a century before him, since Blanche saw in Aeschylus' character Prometheus, "Man forming himself by himself."  Indeed, Edouard Schuré saw in *Oedipus* what André Gide did.  Schuré, in his book *L'Evolution divine du Sphinx au Christ*, published in 1912, said the following:

> Oedipus is not an initiate, or even an aspirant; he is the
> strong, proud man who plunges into life with all the energy
> of his unbounded desires, and dashes himself against
> obstacles like a bull against his adversaries.  The will for
> pleasure and power ruled in him.  By a sure instinct he
> guesses the riddle that the Sphinx-Nature asks of all
> humanity on the threshold of life, and gives the
> answer as "Man."[10]

This is the gist of Schuré's idea.  This is what Gide as well saw in *Oedipus*.  I believe he summarized in it the current European mentality. We can trace that mentality back to the days of Voltaire. He was the one who began to level the fortress of belief in hearts with the varieties of sarcasm with which he pelted the Supreme

---

10. Edouard Schuré, *From Sphinx to Christ*, trans. Eva Martin (Philadelphia: David McKay Company, n.d.), 217.

Being.  He was, however, indulgent on occasion.  He allowed the concept of God to live on without frankly rejecting it.  It was Renan in the nineteenth century who began to raise doubts for people about what he called the antique ideas about God.  He said, "People are living on whiffs of perfume which emanate from an empty container."

Afterwards, Nietzsche devastated intellects and souls with his views which frankly denied the existence of any unseen world or of any divine sovereignty.  He declared it certain that nothing above man existed!  The will for power in him is his excellence and his paradise.    He announced: "The super man has today taken the place of God. God has died."[11]  Under the influence of that, religious belief was shaken.  No one believed any longer in anything besides man.    That is Europe's belief today which Gide summarized excellently in the story of Oedipus.  It has resulted in man's victory, even in his tribulation, over the manifest and hidden forces.  Thus contemporary European thought sees nothing but man, alone in this existence.  It is something that my intellect can apprehend as it follows the developments of the human intellect, but my religious, Eastern heart does not believe it.  I too have seen in the story of Oedipus a challenge of man to God or the unseen forces.  I have made this challenge stand out, but I have also emphasized at the same time the consequences of this presumption.  For I have never felt that man is alone in this existence.

This feeling is the basis of all my work.  Anyone who reads at one time the thirty books I have published may sense this feeling pervading all of them just as Gide's idea of man alone in existence pervades his works.  The dedicated reader or specialist critic may see this idea or feeling in cloaks, recesses, and tendencies which have escaped me.

Our modern Arabic literature does not yet know the reader or critic who pursues an idea or tendency through the works of an author.  Literary criticism here is still at the stage of newspaper criticism, which reviews the book divorced from the author's body of works.  There is no doubt that this stage will be followed by a higher level, that of constructive criticism in which the critic

---

11. cf. Friedrich Nietzsche, *Thus Spoke Zarathurstra* (Los Angeles: Gateway Editions, Inc., 1957), 342-43.

concentrates on the totality of a particular author's works in order to extract an idea from them and formulate a doctrine.

My feeling is that the Easterner always lives in two worlds in the way I mentioned in *Bird of the East*. That is the last fortress left for us to shelter from Western thought which lives in a single one, the world of man alone. This feeling of mine is nothing other than an extension of the feeling of Islamic philosophy.

The substance of the renewal which Islamic philosophy brought and which influenced Europe in the thirteenth century A.D. was not that it transmitted the works of Plato and Aristotle nor that it alone wrote commentaries and explanations for them. It was that it had also studied the thought of the School of Alexandria, Neoplatonism, and the thought colored by the religious spirit of the first period of Christianity. It had then taken all of that and combined it, although it was difficult to combine. It combined the logic of Aristotle with the religious spirit, not the way it was received from the School of Alexandria but stamped with an Islamic character. Thus Europe learned what it called Arab or Islamic philosophy, that is, the amazing doctrine which rests on two pillars one would not have thought would stand side by side: the intellect and religious dogma.

It is not strange then if someone like me preserves some trace of that philosophy and finds it pacing through his blood in spite of himself. Our contact with European civilization is responsible for providing us with imported styles and modern clothing, but it is not capable of plucking out the spirit or erasing the character.

I always move in two worlds and base my thought on two pillars. I think that man is not alone in this existence. I believe in man's human nature. I think his greatness is that he is a human being, a human being with his weakness and defects, his limitations and errors. But he is a human being inspired from on high.

This is the nature of the difference between me and André Gide or those preceding him who deified man. They put him in a single world to be master of himself and of existence, ruling by his command with no master over him other than his will and intellect.

Gide was sincere in his admiration for man. He put Oedipus in a framework of veneration for man's pride. He went to the limit of belief in this boasting and of praise for this arrogance. It is a noble framework which shook my soul and delighted my mind. There is no way for me to deny that.

The splendor with which André Gide has surrounded his story, however, does not prevent me from rejecting his method of proceeding. It is a purely intellectual splendor which delights those like myself who love abstract thought. Those with a taste for works of the theatre of the mind will have no objection to it. Had I done an *Oedipus* ten years ago, I too would have stripped it of everything except the opinions I wished to pour into it. I acted in the manner in 1939 with the play *Praxa: The Problem of Ruling*, which I adapted from Aristophanes and then in my play *Pygmalion*.

But today, I wish to pay attention to the elements of plays with respect to their being something presented to an audience. I have asked myself with respect to André Gide's story why he did not preserve the theatrical splendor of the tragedy of Oedipus. He seems to have deliberately removed everything in it of dramatic value, sometimes without cause. Consider this inquiry that Oedipus carries out to discover the truth. As a former investigative prosecutor, I think he shows great skill in its direction and in his debate with the witnesses. Spectators over the centuries have thought it a breathtaking theatrical experience with great impact on the soul. Why did Gide abbreviate it this way? Why did he contract and disguise it as though it were irrelevant? He took his idea and rose with it to the intellect without support from the situations which inspire it.

It would be an error then to call Gide's story a tragedy. He had no intention of presenting tragedy to us in its artistic beauty and emotional splendor. What can we call this work of his then?

I rather think it is an intellectual commentary on *Oedipus* by Sophocles or a mental tragedy from which all the theatrical elements of tragedy have been removed.

For that reason, I was most desirous to preserve all the dramatic power and the theatrical situations of the tragedy Oedipus. My whole concern was to prevent any trace of reasoning from appearing in the dialogue so that it would not overwhelm a scene or weaken the action. I strove to conceal the thought within the action and to fold the idea into the scene. I have encountered difficulties, however, which I believe I have not surmounted. I remembered Sarcey's advice to the audience at the Comédie Française to turn to a dictionary of Greek mythology before the performance. I would have to summarize, then, what happened to Oedipus before the beginning of the play. I had to strip the story of some of the superstitious beliefs that the Arab or Islamic mentality would scorn. I had to violate the principle of unity of time and place which Greek tragedy observes. I was compelled to violate this principle. I would have wished to retain it, but I thought the family atmosphere in the life of Oedipus was something which ought not to be neglected. For it is the pivot around which revolves the idea for the sake of which I chose this tragedy in particular. The family atmosphere in *Oedipus* cannot be set outside the house. It is true that the events in Greek tragedy always occur in a public square or out of doors. This was a result of the spirit of ancient Greek life. Otto Müller says:

> The action of plays was moved from inside homes to the
> outside. In Greece, all important events and great
> matters transpired only in a public place. The social
> relationships between people did not arise in houses
> but in the markets and on the roads. The Greek poets
> were forced to observe these traditions of Greek life
> when they wrote their dramatic works.

I thought, however, despite that, of the possibility of retaining this principle in this story if a theatrical director were to insist upon it. I have provided him with a stratagem whereby he can show the house and the square at the same time without the need to change scenes or violate the principle of unity of time and place.

In conclusion, I do not know what I have made of this tragedy. Have I been right to proceed with this or wrong? Will Arabic literature accept it in this form?

I have tried. This is all I have been able to do.

Tawfiq Al-Hakim

# KING OEDIPUS

A Play in Three Acts
by Tawfiq Al-Hakim
1949

## CHARACTERS

ANTIGONE

JOCASTA

OEDIPUS

A VOICE from the crowd of Thebans

HIGH PRIEST of Thebes

TIRESIAS

CREON

A HERDSMAN from Thebes

A THEBAN who returns with the herdsman

AN OLD MAN from Corinth

A SERVANT from Thebes

CHORUS OF THEBANS

ANTIGONE'S YOUNGER SISTER AND TWO YOUNGER BROTHERS

PEOPLE OF THEBES

TIRESIAS' SERVANT BOY

**Act One**

*KING OEDIPUS is leaning against one of the columns of the hall of his palace. He is motionless, like a statue, and looks long and thoughtfully at the city beyond the spacious balcony. QUEEN JOCASTA appears surrounded by her four young children. She is gesturing to them to slow down and walk quietly. Meanwhile ANTIGONE, the eldest, whispers to her mother.*

ANTIGONE (*whispering while looking at OEDIPUS*): Mother! Why is he looking at the city this way?

JOCASTA: You go to him, Antigone. Cheer him up, for he always listens to you.

ANTIGONE (*approaching him gently*): Father! What are you thinking about, alone like this?

OEDIPUS (*turning towards her*): Is it you, Antigone? (*He sees the QUEEN and the other children.*) And you, Jocasta? . . . All of you here around me. What brings you here?

JOCASTA: This worry oppressing you, Oedipus . . . Don't tell us it's the plague which has settled on the city. For you have no way to repel it. You have done what you could. You hastened to seek out Tiresias so he could advise you of any inspiration he had gathered from his knowledge of the human sciences and secrets of the unknown. Why then do you remain downcast like this for so long?

OEDIPUS: The ordeal of Thebes . . . This city which entrusted its destiny to me . . .

JOCASTA: No, Oedipus! It is not simply the city's ordeal . . . I know you as I know myself. There's another reason . . . There's a disturbance in your soul. I see its traces in your eyes.

OEDIPUS:  A disturbance the cause of which I don't know . . .  It's as though some powerful evil were lying in wait for me.

JOCASTA:  Don't say that!  It's nothing but the people's pains reflecting their specter on your pure soul.  We are your family, Oedipus.  It is our duty now to cheer you up.  Here we go, children!  Come round your father and disperse these dark clouds from his head and heart.

ANTIGONE:  Father!  Let me ask you something you mustn't refuse. Tell us the story of that beast you killed long ago.

OEDIPUS:  I suspect, Jocasta, that you're the one who inspires your children to ask me that always.  They have heard that story from me many times.

JOCASTA:  Why does that trouble you, Oedipus?  In any case, it is a page from your life that is right for our children to know thoroughly.  Every father is a hero in his children's eyes.  So why not you, when you are a true hero in the eyes of all of Thebes.  Despite that, rest assured that your children are the ones who yearn to hear that from you all the time.  Look at their eager eyes and bated breath.

ANTIGONE:  Yes, Father.  Tell us how you defeated the beast.

OEDIPUS:  Do you really want that, Antigone?  Haven't you tired of it yet? . . . and your sister and brothers?

ANTIGONE (*shaking her head with the others in the negative*):  We shall never tire of it.

OEDIPUS (*taking a seat with his children around him*):  Then listen . . . That was twenty years ago . . .

JOCASTA (*sitting down near him*):  Seventeen years ago, so far as I recall . . .

OEDIPUS:  Yes, you're right.  That day as I approached the walls of

Thebes, it happened that . . .

ANTIGONE:  From the beginning, Father!  Tell it to us from the
    beginning.

OEDIPUS:  That has no relationship to the incident with the beast.
    Nevertheless, let it be the way you wish . . .  You know that I
    grew up, like you, in a royal palace.  Like you, I found love
    and affection in the care of a generous father – King Polybus
    – and an affectionate mother – Queen Merope.  They raised
    and educated me like a prince until I became a strong, sturdy,
    intelligent youth.  I was proficient in horsemanship and was
    wild about knowledge. Yes, Antigone, I had the glow your
    eyes have.  I loved to investigate the realities of things.  Then
    one evening, I learned from an old man in the palace whose
    tongue was loosened by wine that I was not the son of the
    king and queen.  They had never had a child.  I was, rather, a
    foundling they had adopted.  From that hour, I never had a
    moment's rest and never ceased thinking about the truth of
    my origin.  I departed from that land.  I wandered aimless in
    search of my reality until my travels brought me to the walls
    of Thebes.

ANTIGONE:  And here you met the beast.

OEDIPUS:  Yes, Daughter.  It was a terrifying beast . . . a lion.

JOCASTA:  With a woman's face!

ANTIGONE:  And the wings of an eagle.  You always forget, Father,
    to tell us about its wings.

OEDIPUS:  Yes! . . . yes.  It had wings like an eagle.  It advanced
    against me from the forest.

ANTIGONE:  Walking or flying?

OEDIPUS:  Walking like a bird . . .  It opened its mouth . . .

ANTIGONE: And posed you the riddle.

OEDIPUS: Yes, before eating me, it cast me a riddle . . . that riddle
it is said it used to pose to any of the Thebans it met . . .

JOCASTA: And none of them was able to solve it! Then it would
assault them and kill them immediately. Thus it devastated a
great number of people in the city. Indeed, Oedipus, the
people of Thebes continued for a time to avoid remaining on
outside the walls till sunset for fear of meeting the beast.
They called it "Father of Terror." It frightened people for a
long time. My husband, King Laius, had died shortly before
and left me in the prime of life to live in this cold palace. I was
trembling with fright from the rumors spread in the city
about Father Terror and his victims. My brother Creon was
at that time the regent. He was not able to repel the disaster.
The people rioted asking protection from that danger. Then
he did not hesitate to announce his wish that the city's throne
be bestowed on the person who rescued it from the beast.

OEDIPUS: Not just the throne, Jocasta. There was another reward
even more precious . . . the hand of the widowed queen. I
knew none of all this when I met the beast. If I had known
that lovely prize awaiting, I wonder what I would have done
. . . Perhaps my heart would have been in turmoil, my hand
would have trembled, and I would not have been victorious.

ANTIGONE: How did the beast die?

JOCASTA: When your father solved the riddle which no one else
could, Father Terror was enraged and threw himself into the
sea. At that time I was here in my palace listening to what
people had to say about that riddle the beast posed its
victims. I didn't know what it was, for no one before your
father had returned alive to us to tell us about it. I won't
conceal from you, Oedipus, now that at that time I too was
posing myself a question, rather, a riddle: who do you
suppose the victor will be? Will I love him? For a
long time I cried out from the depths of my soul in the still of

the night: who will be the winner? . . . not over the beast . . .
but of my heart . . . my heart which had not yet known love
— despite my early marriage to the good king Laius.  But
when I saw you, Oedipus, and loved you, I perceived that
my riddle had also been solved.

ANTIGONE: How did Father Terror present his riddle to you,
Father?

OEDIPUS:  He said to me when he had ruffled his wing feathers:
"You who approach, what have you come to do here?"  I told
him, "I have come to search out my reality."  He said, "I have
a question for you.  If you are unable to answer it, I will
devour you.  What animal walks in the morning on four feet,
at noon on two, and in the evening on three?"

ANTIGONE:  Don't you answer, Father.  Let me solve the riddle
today in your place.  You answered it in this way: "Beast, you
have frightened the city, but you will not conquer me.  That
animal you ask me about is man!  When young he crawls on
all fours.  When adult he walks upright on his two feet.  In old
age, he hobbles on his feet and stick."

OEDIPUS:  The answer, as you see, is obvious, Antigone.  I am
amazed that so many people failed to get it.  Perhaps we may
contain many answers to our questions without knowing or
seeing . . .

JOCASTA:  Perhaps the beast wanted to make fun of man who does
not see himself.  But you, Oedipus, saw and answered.  In this
way, you disheartened the beast, silenced him, and threw him
into the sea.  You entered Thebes.  You found it ready to
welcome you, to seat you on its throne, and to bestow on you
the hand of its queen.  Thus you came to me and lived with
me.  You fathered these fine, handsome offspring and gave us
this happiness.

OEDIPUS:  Yes, this happiness which pervaded me and made me
forget my reason for setting out and the object of my search.

JOCASTA:  Your reality?  Of what importance to us is this reality?
. . . so long as we're happy!  I've told you often not to think
that I would prefer you to be a descendent of kings.  I and our
children are proud that you are instead from the elite of
heroes.  For this reason, I like you to narrate your heroism to
our young ones and to give them your lesson on every
occasion.  Indeed, I shan't deny that I too always love to hear
this story from you.  It reminds me of those moments when
my heart was awaiting you, anxiously, trembling, not
knowing whether you would win its key or whether it
should throw itself into a sea of oblivion.  Oedipus!
My husband!  It seems I – and you too – were destined to have
complete and unsullied happiness.  I had a child by Laius.
But no doubt god desired happiness for us and inspired him
to repudiate this child, since he would have become an ill
omen for him.  He handed him over after his birth to
someone to kill him on the mountain  Thus there is no
phantom to rise between us and spoil your happiness . . .
Oedipus!  What's troubling you?  The dark cold has
returned to settle on your face.

OEDIPUS:  My anxiety is for the people in their ordeal.  I trembled
when you mentioned the word "happiness" . . . I sensed
something.  This word frightens me now . . . Listen!  What is
this sound?

(*JOCASTA and THE CHILDREN turn to the balcony.*)

ANTIGONE: They are coming down from the hills, crowding the
streets, carrying branches . . .

JOCASTA:  Yes, Oedipus! . . .  It's the people of Thebes, coming to
you, no doubt, bearing branches in supplication.

(*OEDIPUS silently looks from the balcony, surrounded by his family.*)

THEBANS (*outside shouting*):  Oh King Oedipus! . . .  King Oedipus!

VOICE (*from the crowd outside*):  Oh you who are king, sitting on the throne of Thebes! You see the throngs of your people, men and women, young and old, rushing to throw themselves at your portal's threshold, raising in their hands the branches of supplication which quiver over their weakened bodies.

Misfortune has stormed through the city as you can see with your eyes. Death afflicts the herds in the pastures and strikes children at random in their cradles. The plague is harvesting spirits throughout your realm and spreading destruction. It mocks our bloodied hearts and our flowing tears . . . Oedipus! You who rescued this city from Father Terror, rescue it today from this plague. The people who proclaimed you a hero and seated you on the throne of this nation – so you would protect it from tribulations – now demands that you act to aid it and rise to its succor.

OEDIPUS: My wretched people! I am not oblivious to your pains nor unaware. I am deeply hurt by your plight. I have not forgotten that you raised me to this throne to protect you and that you expect action from me to save you. So let me have time to think, to plan, and to act.

VOICE (*from outside*): Oh King, seek an oracle from God. Here is the High Priest entering your palace. Listen to him.

PRIEST: Oedipus! I have come to say one thing to you and then depart. Your people are falling around you like leaves from the tree. If no leaf has yet fallen from your branch, this should, we think, not prevent your concern for the state of others. But concern alone is not enough. The matter, as you see, cannot be helped by solving riddles or by finding the answers for enigmas. Nothing will deliver us save a return to God.

OEDIPUS: And do I prevent you from returning to God?

PRIEST: You don't prevent us . . . You can't, but you are always investigating what you ought not and always asking questions which you should not pose . . . Heavenly revelation is for you a subject for scrutiny and exploration.

OEDIPUS:  If only I were able to free myself from my nature . . .

PRIEST:  There is no need of that for you or for us.  We have sought another to go to the temple at Delphi to ask God's guidance in what is right for us to do to lift this wrath from us.

OEDIPUS:  Who is this man you have dispatched?

PRIEST:  He is Creon!

JOCASTA:  My brother?

PRIEST:  He is, as we all know, a man who does not debate reality nor dispute actuality.  He will not say to the priests in the temple at Delphi: furnish me tangible evidence that this oracle truly came down to you from God and did not originate in your minds.

OEDIPUS:  I am happy that Creon has your confidence, but I have not yet understood what you came to ask of me . . .

PRIEST:  Creon will no doubt return soon.  If he brings a command from the temple, are you ready, Oedipus, to carry out his command to save the city?

OEDIPUS:  Now I understand . . . (*after a moment's thought*)  I can answer you, High Priest . . .  I shall not hesitate to carry out whatever can help save the city.

PRIEST:  I am going then, to return to you with Creon and the heavenly oracle he brings.

(*The HIGH PRIEST leaves.  OEDIPUS and his family remain, silent.*)

JOCASTA (*after a moment*):  Mercy on us, Oh Heaven.  I'm . . . afraid.

OEDIPUS:  Don't be afraid . . .  I'm not afraid.  Nothing would truly frighten me unless I saw danger threatening you and our children . . .  As for the prattle of these priests . . .

JOCASTA:  Don't say that, Oedipus!  Don't say that in front of our children.  You should know that I owe my happiness to God.

OEDIPUS:  Are you sure of that?

JOCASTA:  Put aside these ill-omened questions . . .  You are no longer sure of anything since you learned you were a foundling.  It was a shock to you.  You grew up with loving parents.  You never doubted that they were your parents.  When the veil was suddenly lifted for you to reveal as counterfeit what you thought reality, your confidence in things was destroyed.

OEDIPUS (*turning to the balcony*):  Hush . . .  What's this commotion?

THEBANS (*outside shouting*):  Oh King Oedipus! . . .  King Oedipus!

VOICE (*outside among the people*):  This is Tiresias who has come.  Seek his advice.  He may give you a message from the heavens.

(*The blind TIRESIAS enters.  A BOY leads him.*)

TIRESIAS:  You sent for me, Oedipus?

OEDIPUS:  Yes!

(*JOCASTA leads the children out.*)

OEDIPUS (*on seeing the chamber empty*):  Now we are alone.

TIRESIAS:  I know without needing divine revelation your reason for summoning me.  I can read your soul.  The people demand that you save them.  It is not only a cure for the plague which arouses your concern . . . it is the danger rising round you . . .  The priests don't like your way of thinking.  They are disturbed by your mentality.  They are comfortable with a person like Creon.  The situation in Thebes today is one which could alarm a king.  It is propitious for a revolt.  For every trial which shakes the masses shakes at the very same time the props of the throne.

OEDIPUS: Do you think Creon can overcome the plague the way I overcame the beast?

TIRESIAS: Who knows? Creon went to seek an oracle. He will soon return with the command vouchsafed him.

OEDIPUS: And you, Tiresias . . . whom the people believe acquainted with the human sciences and privy to heaven's secrets . . . Have you no remedy to bring an end to this ordeal which afflicts the people?

TIRESIAS: I have grown old . . . It is proper for me to watch what happens from a distance. Proceed on your way alone, Oedipus.

OEDIPUS: You wish to rid yourself of me now that you see danger advancing on me and know the circumstances which will endanger my sovereignty.

TIRESIAS: Oedipus, you have will, a strong hand, and a clear eye. What do you want from an old man like me who is feeble and blind?

OEDIPUS: I perceive what is behind your words . . . I know you, Tiresias! A person like you does not withdraw his hand from what is around him without a reason.

TIRESIAS: I am withdrawing my hand this time in order to see what will happen.

OEDIPUS: To see me fall the way you saw me rise?

TIRESIAS: It is a great enjoyment for me to see what will happen when I leave matters to the hand of fate.

OEDIPUS: You will not have a chance to enjoy this, Tiresias. I know how to spoil your plan for you.  You think you have the reins of my throne in your hand, but your veil is in mine.  I will tear it away in front of the people and disclose your true countenance whenever I wish.

TIRESIAS:  Not so fast, Oedipus.  Don't let anger make you lose course.

OEDIPUS:  Be confident that I shall not allow you to trifle with me.  Indeed, I am quite capable of having the people trifle with you.

TIRESIAS:  What can you tell the people?

OEDIPUS:  Everything, Tiresias . . . everything!  I don't fear the truth.  Indeed, I am looking forward to the day when I can free myself of that great lie I have been living for seventeen years.

TIRESIAS:  Don't be insane!

OEDIPUS:  I may go insane any moment, open the gates of this palace, and go out to the people shouting: listen, Citizens of Thebes!  Hear the story of a blind man who wished to mock you and of a well-intentioned man with no ulterior motive who joined him in the farce . . .  I am not a hero, I never met a beast with the body of a lion, wings of an eagle, and a woman's face which posed riddles.  It is your naïve imagination which liked this picture and made popular this image.  What I actually met was an ordinary lion which was preying on people who tarried outside your walls.  I was able to kill it with my cudgel, throw its body into the sea, and rid you of it.  But Tiresias, this brilliant blind man, inspired you – for his own purposes, not for God's sake – to appoint that hero your king.  Yes!  He's the one who desired that and planned it.  He is the one who taught me the solution for that puzzle about the animal that crawls on its hands and feet . . .

TIRESIAS:  Hush!  Hush . . . lower your voice!

OEDIPUS:  He is the one who in former times inspired Laius to kill his son in the cradle by leading his father to believe that it was heaven which revealed to him that the child would kill his father if he grew up.  For Tiresias, this dangerous blind man, resolved with a will of iron to deprive the throne of Thebes of its legitimate heir.  He wished the throne to go to a foreigner.  What he wished for has come to pass.

TIRESIAS:  I told you to lower your voice, Oedipus.

OEDIPUS:  Yes . . .  This is Tiresias . . . who has had you believe that he can read the unknown mysteries and hear heavenly voices, while he hears nothing in reality but the voice of his will and peruses nothing but the lines of his scheme and plan.  He wished – and was proud of it – to change the course of events, to change the established system of inheritance, and to challenge the will of heaven which had produced a son and heir for Laius.  He did that in order to put on the throne with his mortal hand a person who was the offspring of his head and the product of his thought.

TIRESIAS:  Calm yourself, Oedipus . . .  The soul's storms extinguish the intellect's lamp.

OEDIPUS:  You know now what I can do to you?

TIRESIAS:  And to yourself?

OEDIPUS:  I have no fear of the truth for myself . . . even if it casts me off the throne.  You know that sovereignty is not my goal.  I was in Corinth, my cradle where I grew up in the arms of the excellent Polybus and the compassionate Merope.  Their sole aim was to convince the people that I was their son and to put me on their throne.  But I fled from that kingship to search for the truth of my origin.  I fled from Corinth, because I could not bear to live a lie. I came here . . . only to live a greater lie.

TIRESIAS:  Perhaps the lie is the natural atmosphere for your life . . .

OEDIPUS:  And your life too, Tiresias.

TIRESIAS:  And my life too . . . and the life of every human being. Don't forget you're the hero of this city.  For Thebes needs a hero.  It believed in the story of Father Terror!  Beware of depriving the people of their myth.

OEDIPUS:  Nothing forces me to keep silent except my fear of depriving my wife and children of their belief in my heroism . . . And nothing causes me such pain as being forced into this lengthy lie with them.  I force myself not to shout to them when they are reciting before me the story of Father Terror: don't believe this nonsense!  The truth, my children, is . . .

TIRESIAS:  Beware, Oedipus! . . . Beware!  My great fear is that your reckless fingers will trifle with the veil of Truth and that your trembling fingertips will come too close to her face and eyes . . . You fled from Corinth, roaming in pursuit of her, but she escaped from you.  You came to Thebes announcing you lacked origin or lineage in order to display her to the people. She drew away from you.  Leave Truth alone, Oedipus . . . Don't challenge her!

OEDIPUS:  Why do you challenge heaven, Tiresias?   Do you suppose you are of a stronger fiber, are more resolute and sharper-eyed than I?

TIRESIAS:  I am not sharper-eyed than you, Oedipus . . . I see nothing.  And I see no god in existence save our volition.  I willed and to that extent was divine . . . I truly compelled Thebes to accept the king I wished for it.  I got what I wished for.  As you see . . .

OEDIPUS (*in a sarcastic tone*):  Lower your voice, Tiresias!

TIRESIAS:  Don't make fun of me . . . and don't presume—if your determination to execute your threat is real—that I am incapable of confronting the people.  Open your gates, if you wish.  Go to your people and raise your voice with whatever you wish.  Then you will know what Tiresias has to say!

OEDIPUS:  What will you say?

TIRESIAS:  I will shout at the top of my voice: People!  I have not imposed my will on you for any glory I cover but for an idea I believe in: that you have a will . . .  It was not because of hatred between me and Laius or antagonism between me and Creon . . . rather I wished to turn the page on the hereditary monarchy of this ancient family, to make you the ones who choose your king from a wide spectrum, without regard to descent and lineage, with nothing to recommend him except his service to you and with no title for him other than his heroism for you.  Thus there exists in your land only your will.  That's all that should exist.

OEDIPUS:  And what of your will, you brilliant blind man!  You know the people find no pleasure in having a will.  The day they have it in hand, they hasten to give it to a hero their legends have contrived or to a god enveloped in the clouds of their dreams.  It seems to be too much for them to bear. They are not strong enough to preserve it and wish to be free of it to cast aside its burden.  But you are a man blinded by delusion.  You don't truly strive for public glory.  You want, however, to be the fountainhead of events, the source of upheavals, the motive force changing and replacing human destinies and natural elements.  I see in you this cloaked presumption.  I read in your soul this hidden conceit!

TIRESIAS:  I have a right to boast a little, Oedipus . . .  You don't deny that I have succeeded.  That you are on the throne is nothing other than a manifestation of my will.

OEDIPUS:  I am tired of hearing that from you.  I summoned you to hear your opinion of this ordeal, not the hymn of your glory.  I am not clear about your position with me . . .  Are you with me?  Have you turned against me?  I don't see the grounds on which you have founded your will.

TIRESIAS:  You will learn that at the appropriate time, Oedipus.

OEDIPUS:  When?

TIRESIAS:  When Creon arrives with that oracle from the temple at Delphi.  I am well advised to learn something of the will of heaven before proceeding to form my will.

OEDIPUS:  Am I able to rely on your support, Tiresias?

TIRESIAS:  It would be stupid, Oedipus, to fear anything from me.

OEDIPUS:  Let's await then what Creon will bring . . .

TIRESIAS:  Let me go now . . . until it is time for action.  At this hour I will say to you only: confront your destiny, Oedipus!  Don't be afraid . . . I am with you!

OEDIPUS:  Are you confident, Tiresias?

TIRESIAS:  Where is the boy who leads me?

OEDIPUS (*as though addressing himself*):  My destiny? . . . What is my destiny?

TIRESIAS:  Where's the boy?

(*OEDIPUS goes to the door and opens it.  The BOY enters.  He leads TIRESIAS out.  OEDIPUS remains alone, leaning his head against a pillar, downcast.  It is not long before JOCASTA enters by herself.*)

JOCASTA (*searching the chamber with her eyes*):  The prophet Tiresias has departed?

OEDIPUS (*turning to her*):  Yes!

JOCASTA:  Perhaps he has told you how to drive away this affliction and end this ordeal . . .

OEDIPUS (*speaking to himself*):  I must not rely on anything but this hand of mine . . . This hand which knows how to deal harshly with anyone who threatens evil to you or me . . . whether a beast, a person . . . or a god!

JOCASTA:  Don't scorn God, Oedipus!  You owe our happiness to Him . . .  It's not possible He would wish you harm.  He is the one who led you from Corinth to this place where you found me and where we have lived in contentment producing these dutiful children.

OEDIPUS:  I no longer see anything in the fog surrounding me.  I know only that a disaster threatens me . . .  From what direction?  I don't know!  From what hand?  I don't know!  I am like a lion in the forest which senses a snare set near it but doesn't know where it is or who set it.  I am fumbling and groping like a blind man.  I see nothing and no one!  I merely smell the scent of danger near me . . .

JOCASTA:  Your love for us, my beloved husband, is what is making you imagine this.  The plague will not approach our house!  It will not touch anyone of our young children!  It is rather another infection which I think you are doubtless giving me . . . that anxiety disturbing your peace of mind.  I, too, Oedipus, am filled by that alarming foreboding.  I almost feel as if there were something coarse strangling me . . . here around my neck.  I can hardly breathe.  I sense a dark melancholy in which my soul sinks like a corpse into the darkness of the tomb.

OEDIPUS:  Hush!  Don't mention death, Jocasta.

JOCASTA:  Do you see how my depression distresses you just as your anxiety and concern distress me?  It would be good, Oedipus, for us to banish these ghosts from us.  It is no doubt the atmosphere of this city, heavy with suffering, which has spread these dark, gloomy clouds through our souls . . .

OEDIPUS:  Perhaps . . .

JOCASTA: Whatever the cause is, it's our duty to be resolute and to pretend to be joyful for the sake of our children.

OEDIPUS: Yes! . . . Where's Antigone?

JOCASTA: This girl, Oedipus, believes in you more than you do yourself. I left her just now telling the other children that you will no doubt vanquish the plague the same way you did Father Terror, because God did not put you on this throne in vain . . .

OEDIPUS (*in almost a whisper*): My dear daughter!

JOCASTA: She believes that her destiny is bound to yours . . . For a long time she has told me that she hopes for nothing for her future except to live in the temple of your heroism and to see the world as you see it . . . to have your eyes, to see life's riddles, puzzles, and secrets with them.

OEDIPUS (*as though speaking to himself*): I hope to have her eyes to see for me the soul's tranquility, the heart's truthfulness, and existence's purity . . .

JOCASTA (*listening*): Listen, Oedipus! . . . What is this din?

THEBANS (*outside shouting*): Creon has come! . . . Creon's come!

OEDIPUS (*looking towards the balcony*): Yes! He's come . . . What do you suppose your brother has brought?

JOCASTA (*looking towards the balcony*): He must have brought good news, for he has fastened a garland of flowers to his forehead.

OEDIPUS (*at the balcony*): Here's the High Priest with him. They are making their way through the crowds of people and waving a greeting to them.

JOCASTA: They are nearing the palace gate. I shall go to allow you to devote yourselves to the city's welfare.

OEDIPUS:  I have a burning desire to know what he has brought.

JOCASTA:  I hope you will learn from him now something that will comfort your soul and spread peace through it.  (*She departs.*)

OEDIPUS (*in a whisper*):  Yes! . . .  I will learn now.

(*The HIGH PRIEST enters with CREON.*)

PRIEST:  Here is Creon who has returned from the Delphi temple with a mighty oracle.  I would like him to reveal it to you in private, Oedipus, if you will permit him to speak.

OEDIPUS:  I am listening to him.  Let him reveal to us everything he brings.

CREON:  Oedipus, here's what I've learned . . .  The oracle has revealed to us the secret of this anger which heaven has sent down on our land.

OEDIPUS:  What is this secret?  Quickly?

CREON:  There is an abomination in this land which must cease.  Otherwise, we are destined to perish.

OEDIPUS:  What abomination?

CREON:  A sin befouls Thebes which must be erased.

OEDIPUS:  Explain!

CREON:  Blood from our land has been shed and that must necessarily be washed away with blood.

OEDIPUS:  Whose blood! . . .  Who did it?

CREON:  Laius!  Before you came to us, we had a king named Laius.

OEDIPUS:  I know!  I know! . . .  I know his name, but I never saw him.

CREON:  This king was killed.

OEDIPUS:  Killed?

CREON:  The order of God is unambiguous.  Justice must be done and revenge taken on the killer.

OEDIPUS:  If this is all you've brought, then it's true . . .  but this crime, so far as I can see, happened long ago.

CREON:  It's been about seventeen years.

OEDIPUS:  Will it be easy after this length of time for us to follow its tracks and lift the veil from the killer's face?

CREON:  The God said: "Search and you shall find!"

OEDIPUS:  I love nothing better than searching . . . my whole life is nothing but a search.  So long as God — as you say — is the one ordering me now to search and investigate you will find me thoroughly obedient.  Do you hear me, High Priest?

PRIEST:  I have heard . . .  I hope you will pursue to the end your search for the killer.

OEDIPUS:  Here I begin the search, at once . . .  Tell me, Creon. Where was Laius killed?  Was it in his palace?  Or in the city? Or outside it?

CREON:  Laius had left Thebes on pilgrimage to the temple at Delphi to consult the oracle, as he said, on the matter of his son whom he had delivered up to death long before, on the command of heaven.

OEDIPUS (as though speaking to himself):  On the command of heaven . . . yes . . .  That poor king! . . .  And then?

CREON: There isn't anything more . . . He did not return to us after that day he set forth.

OEDIPUS: Was there no witness who saw or heard anything of what happened to him?

CREON: All the witnesses were taken by death . . . except for one. He was able to escape with his skin . . . We learned only one thing from him.

OEDIPUS: What was it?

CREON: He related that a gang of thieves waylaid King Laius and killed him and his attendants.

OEDIPUS: Would thieves dare attack a king this way?

CREON: This is the account he gave us.

OEDIPUS: I don't think people like that would attack the king unless someone here had incited them to it, spurred them on, and paid them a price for that.

CREON: This is what occurred to us too at that time.

OEDIPUS: In spite of that, you did nothing to search for the killers or to disclose the hand which directed the crime?

CREON: At the time, we were preoccupied. Our attention was seized by a more alarming disaster which took us by surprise and left us sleepless.

OEDIPUS: What catastrophe is greater than the murder of your reigning king?

CREON: Father Terror had appeared at the time killing people with his riddles outside the walls of Thebes!

OEDIPUS: Yes! . . . Yes, how stupid you all are. My eye sees everything clearly now.  I can almost see the person who planned all that . . . and know the hand which moved and the will which incited . . .

PRIEST:  What are you saying, Oedipus?  Repeat once more what your lips uttered.

OEDIPUS:  What my lips uttered is no concern of yours.  You are awaiting my action and seek justice . . .  The killer of Laius must be presented to you, even if that is not entirely to my liking . . .  Truly! . . .  You are right!  It had not occurred to me that the pillars of my throne are plunged in a king's blood.  I wouldn't have thought that the person who wanted that would go so far as crime.  I will not hesitate!  Yes!  Do you hear?  I shall not hesitate to hand over the killer . . . not just to save Thebes but to save my conscience.  High Priest! . . .  Go and announce to the people that I will promptly carry out the command Creon brought.  I will give them the killer.

PRIEST:  Do you know, Oedipus, who the killer is?

OEDIPUS:  It is not difficult for me to know now.  Go at once and leave the matter to me . . .  Amazing! . . .  Why are you frozen to the earth like statues?

PRIEST:  Are you confident that you will take vengeance on the killer of Laius?

OEDIPUS:  Do you doubt that, Priest?  Whatever the standing of this man among you, I will deliver him to you to receive the recompense for what his hand committed.  This is my promise that I will never go back on, no matter what it costs me to be faithful to it.  For everything dear to me is reduced to insignificance by this hideous crime.  Who can trust — after today — a man who dared kill a king!  I will tear the veil from his face and present him to justice, even if that is a curse for me and leads to my destruction.

PRIEST:  Your knowledge of the criminal, Oedipus, has relieved us of a heavy burden.

OEDIPUS: What burden?

PRIEST: The burden of disclosing his name to you.

OEDIPUS: Did you too know who he was?

PRIEST: We knew . . . Creon brought his name with the oracle from the temple at Delphi.

OEDIPUS: And weren't you astonished when you learned who he was?

PRIEST: Totally astonished, Oedipus . . . for he's the last person one would have suspected.

OEDIPUS (*as though speaking to himself*): Yes! . . . That man of exalted standing, high status, venerated by everyone.

PRIEST: He truly is that . . . We are sad he is the one who committed an offense like this.

OEDIPUS: My sorrow is no less than yours . . . but justice is superior to any rank. The victim's blood must be washed away with the killer's. This is what heaven has commanded you, Creon, and I will obey the command.

PRIEST: We did not suppose you would obey heaven's command with such alacrity . . . Forgive us our previous suspicion of you. You are more magnanimous than we imagined . . . But may we ask you what has kept you silent all this time about the killer?

OEDIPUS: I knew nothing of this crime until today.

PRIEST (*looking at CREON*): What are you saying, Oedipus?

OEDIPUS: Why are you exchanging these glances?

PRIEST:  We are amazed that you could have been ignorant of it . . .

OEDIPUS:  Why are you amazed?

PRIEST:  Because you have the closest link to the crime's secret.

OEDIPUS:  If you mean Jocasta, you can rest assured that she knows nothing of the affair.  If you mean my link to the killer or the instigator of the murder, then I am astonished that you never suspected him all the time he has maintained a position of trust among you and been sought for his counsel.

PRIEST:  Would you have wanted us to suspect the lofty soul without proof? . . . to accuse this high rank without a command from God or an oracle from heaven?

OEDIPUS:  Now that you know the oracle from heaven and the veil has been removed from the killer's face, here is my decision. He deserves punishment for the offense.  He wished to change with his hand the fates and destinies.  He let nothing stand in the way of his will . . . not even conscience . . . Go to him and don't shrink back.  Hurl the accusation plainly in his face, without fear of his sanctity or awe of his majesty.

PRIEST (*looking at CREON*):  Will you truly permit us to do that, Oedipus?

OEDIPUS:  Once again you're exchanging these looks . . . What do you think me, Priest?  Do you think I'm not strong enough to execute this command? . . . And you, Creon?  Haven't you found me able before today to meet difficulties and with the daring to confront adversity?

CREON:  No one will deny you your courage, Oedipus.  You have confronted a danger that no one else among the people of Thebes could have.  The victory was yours alone.  But . . . not everyone is like you.  You bear for us an adversity which is too great for us and ask us to accuse that lofty rank . . .

PRIEST:  Truly . . . if it were possible for you to spare us this painful
      scene, you would do us a favor we would never forget.

OEDIPUS:  You want me to take charge of the affair myself?

PRIEST:  Yes!

CREON:  This is no doubt the best way.  The oracle of Delphi has
      reached you, Oedipus, and you know the killer's name has
      become known.  Quick vengeance is the price desired to save
      Thebes.  All that remains for you is to carry out this
      vengeance speedily, without clamor or commotion.
      Afterwards, it will be our  responsibility to announce the
      affair to the people.

OEDIPUS:  I will do this for you.  It won't cost me much hardship
      . . . But what distresses me . . .

CREON:  Your family?

OEDIPUS:  My family?  Of what relevance is my family here? . . .
      Yes . . . You're right . . . In truth, I think Jocasta believes
      strongly in this man.  In that respect, she resembles all the
      people in this land . . .  The echo will resound far and wide
      and have a great impact the day the killer's name is
      announced . . .  But what I ask you is to remember . . .

CREON:  What? . . . The effects of that, relative to the throne?

OEDIPUS:  I am not thinking now of that throne, for that hand has
      soiled it with blood . . . Certainly not . . . Rather I want you
      to remember that the sinner may deny the accusation and
      charge those who advance it with falsehood, slander,
      fabrication, and falsification.  He may call it a conspiracy
      trumped up to destroy him for personal reasons . . . It is best
      if you remain here.  I shall summon him so that you can tell
      him what the oracle revealed about him . . . After that I will
      take care of the rest . . .

PRIEST:  Who is it you will summon?

OEDIPUS:  The killer of Laius . . .  He's not far from this place . . .
     Wait!  I will send for him.

PRIEST (*looking at CREON*):  Oedipus!

OEDIPUS:  Strange!  Why do you keep exchanging these looks?

PRIEST:  You know he's not far from us now . . .

OEDIPUS:  Perhaps . . .  He promised to come on your arrival . . . as
     though he knew what awaited him.  He awakened doubt in
     me about what Creon would bring.  But I won't wait for him
     any longer . . .  He must be sought for. (*He moves.*)

PRIEST (*stopping him*):  Where are you going, Oedipus?  The killer of
     Laius is not far from us.

CREON:  He is not far from this palace.

PRIEST:  He is, as you know, in this palace now . . . only a step away.

OEDIPUS:  In this palace now? . . .  What do you mean?

PRIEST:  You know, Oedipus, what we mean and whom we mean.

OEDIPUS:  The killer of Laius is in this palace?

PRIEST:  And in this chamber . . . as you no doubt know.

OEDIPUS:  Explain!

PRIEST:  Woe! . . .  Haven't you known all the time what we mean?
     Who besides yourself were you accusing then, Oedipus?

OEDIPUS:  Besides me? . . .  What's this I hear from you?

PRIEST:  Strange! . . .  Didn't you know that you, Oedipus, are Laius' killer?

OEDIPUS:  I . . . the killer of Laius?  Have you gone mad, Priest?

PRIEST:  I am not mad . . .  It is the oracle Creon brought from the temple at Delphi.

OEDIPUS:  The oracle said I am the killer?

PRIEST:  Speak, Creon!

CREON:  Yes! . . .  That's the truth! . . .  I will relate it as I heard it without adding a word.  This is the revelation from heaven . . .  "Oedipus is the killer of Laius."

OEDIPUS (*racked by laughter*):  I the killer?  Is this credible?

PRIEST:  We are truly greatly distressed . . . but . . .

OEDIPUS:  When was your king, whom I never saw, killed? . . .  When did I do that and where?

PRIEST:  We don't know . . .  We can't answer these questions.  We can tell you only what the oracle revealed to us.

OEDIPUS:  Whose oracle? . . .  Creon's oracle or an oracle from you religious men?

PRIEST:  What are you saying, Oedipus?

OEDIPUS:  Here's a trick which has been uncovered! . . . a riddle disclosed in the land of puzzles and riddles! . . .  How stupid you are!  Not one of you can even devise an adequate trap.

PRIEST:  Don't overdo this kind of talk, Oedipus!

OEDIPUS:  Hush!  I see the affair now as plain as day.  The veil has truly been lifted . . . not from the face of a killer and a crime but from the face of conspiracy and of conspirators.  You must not think, Creon, and you, High Priest, that I am so dull-witted that I will fall into a trap like this which would not catch even small birds. I am not so weak as to be incapable of punishing you and all those who support you, openly or clandestinely, with every type of punishment.

PRIEST: Not so fast, Oedipus!

OEDIPUS: I have not yet shown you I am fit to be called a hero. My victory over a beast will not compare with that fortitude with which I shall conquer the traitors.

CREON: Who are these traitors?

OEDIPUS: You are at their head, Creon! . . . You who covet my throne. These priests have misled you, but I shall make you all the laughingstock of the people.

CREON: That's enough, Oedipus! I refuse to let you call me a traitor. Remember I am your wife's brother . . . I would never harm you nor would I harm Jocasta for the sake of ambition . . . Sovereignty was in my hand before you came to us. I released it to you for the sake of the people's welfare and in obedience to the counsel of the holy and inspired.

OEDIPUS: And today you attack me pleading the people's salvation again as well as obedience to the counsel of those men of religion who love you.

PRIEST: Don't speak blindly, Oedipus! The men of religion know that God's hand raises and lowers people to royal thrones. It is not for human hands to do. We would not have come to you on this grave matter had we not known that our God cursed this land. He inspired us to root out its causes and dispel His anger from us. You yourself promised to aid us and execute God's command. We who have brought it to you are racked by pain and distress. You ought to have received heaven's will submissively. You ought not hurl your thunder and lightning at us, in an attempt to hide the voice of truth which has come down from on high.

OEDIPUS:  The voice of truth!  What is the voice of truth?  Is it what you hear and I don't?  Don't I have two ears on my head like you?

PRIEST:  The voice of truth, Oedipus, is not heard by the ear or the head . . . but by the heart!

OEDIPUS:  Yes! . . .  With words like these, Priest, you wish to make me feel I am far removed from your heaven . . . that I am subject to its curse and the object of its anger . . .  It afflicted this land with the plague merely because I am dwelling here . . .  Why am I cursed by God?  Is it because I do not accept what you attribute to Him until after an inquiry which satisfies my intellect?  If you said that, if you dared, you would find no objection from me.  But you say something that corresponds to your obvious scheme. You say I am cursed by heaven, because I killed Laius . . .  That the blood which soiled Thebes and brought the plague can only be washed away by the killer's blood . . .  What a conspiracy! What a conspiracy it is!

PRIEST:  Anger, no doubt, has blinded you, Oedipus!  We have passed on to you what the oracle revealed.  Make your plans accordingly.

OEDIPUS:  The matter does not require lengthy planning.

PRIEST:  You have all the time you wish . . .  We have nothing left to do but depart.

OEDIPUS:  Depart? . . .  Do you think a person who says what you have said today can depart in peace?

PRIEST:  What do you mean, Oedipus?

OEDIPUS:  Priest!  You don't know the Oedipus yet whom you dared term a murderer.  You claimed he had defiled the earth

of Thebes with blood.  You will not depart in peace, Priest
. . . nor you, Creon!

CREON:  Oedipus!

PRIEST:  We won't depart in peace?

OEDIPUS:  You have only two roads by which you can depart.
Choose between death and banishment!

PRIEST and CREON (*shouting*):  Death or banishment!

OEDIPUS:  There is no punishment for a traitor who conspires
against the sovereign except death, but I grant you the choice,
out of compassion for you . . .  Discretion would dictate I be
firm and pluck you from life by the roots like rank, stinking
weeds which disperse around them anarchy and corruption.
I have given my verdict on you: banishment or death . . .
Banishment or death!

## Act Two

*The square in front of the palace . . . A CHORUS of the people is*
*assembled. OEDIPUS, the PRIEST, and CREON stand before them as*
*though appearing before a court.*

OEDIPUS:  People of Thebes!  You have before you now a crime
against my person and throne committed by these two
conspirators.  I have pronounced a sentence on them which I
think just . . .  But I will not carry out my verdict until I
mount an investigation of their offense in your presence.  I
would not like to be blinded to truth by anger.  I shall now
disclose the face of truth to you so you can see the criminals
barefaced.

CHORUS:  Who would have thought, Oedipus, that Creon and the
High Priest would conspire against you?

OEDIPUS:  You in your simplicity, Citizens, do not see what is
fabricated in the dark . . . but I will tear aside the curtain for
you at this moment so you can see in the light those sinful
hands which wished to defile your throne with sin and
blood.

CHORUS:  Woe to anyone who would harm a single one of your
hairs, King.  We shall never forget that you are the hero who
saved us from Father Terror . . .  Strike down your enemies,
Oedipus, without mercy . . .  We are with you.

PRIEST:  How skillful you are, Oedipus, in rallying the people
against us . . . and in presenting us as criminal, when our
only crime is that we told you the command revealed by
heaven to free Thebes of this plague.

OEDIPUS:  Do you persist, treacherous priest, in terming this
conspiracy an oracle from heaven?

PRIEST:  Don't get angry, Oedipus!  You are the one who just said that you don't want anger to blind you to the truth.  Hold firm to prudence, seek the aid of patience and proceed with the inquiry you promised.  Do it quickly to keep the people from thinking about the misery they are suffering.

OEDIPUS (*to the CHORUS*):  People, do you actually think I am trying to distract you with this inquiry from the torment you suffer?

CHORUS:  Proceed, Oedipus, with what you have begun.  Strip back the curtain for us.  We are eager to see what is behind these affairs.

OEDIPUS:  Do you see, sinful priest, how your arrow has missed its target? . . .  This is the will of the people.

PRIEST:  How naïve they truly are, these people!  Yes, these people who are nourished by imagination not by realities!  They have forgotten the plague annihilating them.  They have forgotten that you have found no remedy to save them.  They have forgotten heaven's oracle which they were awaiting.  They remember only their desire to see the phantoms you claim to reveal.

OEDIPUS:  Don't scorn the people, Priest!  You are appearing before their court.  They are the ones who will find you guilty and support my punishment for you when they see your crime laid bare after I have stripped you of your secret.

PRIEST:  Do it, Oedipus, and quickly . . .  You are still the hero who fascinates people by disclosing secrets and solving riddles.  But the people will learn that I conceal no secret and harbor no riddle.  I merely sought in good faith to ask God's aid in dispelling this plague from our land.  I have informed you of the oracle . . .  That is my entire offense against you.

OEDIPUS:  Not at all, Priest!  You know your crime just as Creon knows his . . . and those who support you covertly . . . I shall not undertake its presentation to the people.  Rather, I leave you that honor, so it won't be said I reported it incorrectly or distorted it intentionally . . . You tell your story, Priest . . . or let your accomplice speak.

(*QUEEN JOCASTA comes out of the palace.*)

CHORUS (*turning*):  Queen Jocasta!

JOCASTA:  May I attend this trial?  The accusation you advance against these two men is grave, Oedipus.

CREON:  Do you believe, Jocasta, that your brother Creon would covet your husband's throne?

OEDIPUS:  It is not I, Jocasta, who will try your brother but the people.  I am only a man who has undertaken the investigation into the crime.  You will see now with your own eyes, just as the people around you will see, what the inquiry discloses.

CREON:  We have already been sentenced to death or banishment!

OEDIPUS:  I will never be satisfied with less than this penalty for those who conspire against the throne . . .  This conspiracy, had it been concluded, would have had among its consequences my death or banishment.

JOCASTA:  The evidence will have to be damning, Oedipus, before you carry out this harsh sentence on them.

OEDIPUS:  Here is the inquiry, conducted in public before you, Jocasta, and before all the people.  In it I will go to the pits and delve the depths to extract for you at the end of the affair the manifest and unambiguous truth.

CHORUS:  Proceed with your work, Oedipus . . .  You are the person best able to remove the cover from the secret of things.

OEDIPUS:  I would like the hearing to take place with Tiresias
        present.  I know his standing with you.  I sent for him
        before coming out to you.

CHORUS:  You did well, Oedipus.  The presence of this blessed
        elder among us at this hour will certainly increase our peace
        of mind.

JOCASTA:  No one so wishes for peace of mind as I do . . . for I of
        all people know Creon best.  He is my brother with whom I
        grew up.  His upright characters, his even temper, and his
        clear conscience all combine to make my soul amazed by his
        deed . . .  I have not yet learned how he conspired against
        the throne.  All I've heard is that he is accused of this crime.
        But I don't know how he came to that.

OEDIPUS:  You will learn now . . . not from my mouth, but from
        his!

(TIRESIAS appears led by his servant boy.)

CHORUS:  Here's Tiresias who's arrived.

OEDIPUS:  Make way for him!

TIRESIAS:  I know why you are gathered here . . .  Beware of
        asking my opinion, Oedipus, or of requesting me to speak!

OEDIPUS:  I shan't do it.  I merely wanted you to be present at this
        trial, because a person like you should not be forgotten in
        great undertakings.  Listen to what will be said now and
        grasp the import of these statements.

TIRESIAS:  I am listening, Oedipus.

OEDIPUS:  Now, People, hear how these men conspired.  I
        promised to let the accused state the case for the sake of

justice. I will not go back on this promise. Go ahead, High Priest . . . You speak first.

PRIEST: What shall I say? . . . You have put us into this shameful situation, Oedipus. You have affixed to us the stigma of accusation. You have presented us to the people's eyes as sinning traitors before we have learned what our offense was. . . I have nothing to say except what you and the people know . . . Your outcry against that plague which has been decimating you, People of Thebes, was raised. We saw no means to repel the plague from us except to seek an oracle from heaven . . . We thought a man from the royal house, known for prudence of opinion, forthrightness, and proper conduct, should go to the temple at Delphi . . . That man was Creon, as you know. Do you see anything the matter with this action, anything untoward about it?

CHORUS: Certainly not!

PRIEST: Creon went to the temple at Delphi. Then he returned with the oracle from God concerning this plague and its cause. I did not wish to reveal it except to the king in private. We wished to confine the matter to the narrowest limits and hoped to avoid upsetting you.

CHORUS: What was the oracle Creon brought?

PRIEST: It's up to Creon to reveal it to you, if he wishes . . .

CHORUS: Speak, Creon!

CREON: It's an alarming matter! I am not entitled to announce it to you without permission from Oedipus.

OEDIPUS: I give you permission to say everything here.

CREON: Here is what I brought . . . transmitting to you the exact text: "Heaven is angry, because the earth of Thebes has been defiled by impurity . . . Its king, Laius, was killed. No revenge has yet been taken on his murderer. The anger against Thebes will not be lifted unless that blood is washed away."

CHORUS: Our King Laius was killed?

OEDIPUS: This is not the amazing part, People . . . Ask him who the killer was . . .

CHORUS: Who was the killer? . . . Who was he?

CREON: You can be sure that it pains me deeply to utter his name. When I learned for the first time, I was struck by a terror I haven't the power to describe. Oedipus has been blinded by desire and fear. He has forgotten our relationship and my place with him and in his family. He has similarly forgotten my earlier days which I spent in his support . . . and my character which would reject what he has accused me of . . . and my nature which would shy away from what he suspects I did.

CHORUS: Who killed Laius, Creon? Who's the killer?

CREON: Don't force my mouth to mention this dear name! Ask the king standing before you to tell you.

OEDIPUS: No, you speak his name yourself, Creon.

CHORUS: Tell us the killer's name, Creon.

CREON: It is . . . Oedipus.

CHORUS: This Oedipus? . . . Oedipus our king? . . . He is the killer of Laius?

JOCASTA: What do I hear from you, Creon?

CREON: This is the way the oracle came from heaven, Jocasta.

CHORUS:  Oedipus is the killer? . . .  The killer is Oedipus?

OEDIPUS:  Do you see, People of Thebes, how the conspiracy was
hatched?  Can you imagine I killed Laius when I had never
seen him?  Don't you remember that when I came to your
land your throne was vacant and his resting place
unknown?  But they wish me to be the killer so that I would
deserve in consequence death or banishment.  For they are
distressed by my rule and dislike, for a reason best known to
themselves, that I should remain your king.

CREON:  Would I ask heaven to pour its curse on me even if I had
in my soul a vile objective like this?  I swear . . .  I swear I
added nothing to what I heard and learned by heart from
the oracle of the Delphi temple.

JOCASTA:  May I give my opinion about the disagreement which
has arisen between you?  I don't think either of you is a liar
or covetous.  I have no doubt that Creon heard what he
reported to you, Oedipus, with pure soul and clear
conscience . . .  But heaven's oracle is too elevated in status
for human beings to comprehend it, all the time.  People
rarely are able to understand the divine oracle properly . . .
God's will has goals which man's mind is not able to grasp.
Thus no person has complete sovereignty over the unknown
or the ability to prophesy.  I have at hand the example of
Laius.  A prophesy informed him that he would die at his
son's hand — his son from his loins and my belly . . .  I
believe Tiresias who is present remembers the story of that
prophecy.

TIRESIAS:  I remember that, O Queen.

OEDIPUS (*with concealed sarcasm*):  Indeed . . . he had better
remember that!

JOCASTA:  What happened after that? . . .  That son perished in
the cradle, for his father handed him over three days after
his birth to a shepherd who carried him off with his feet

bound to be destroyed on a desolate mountain. Laius met his death, as you know, outside this land. A gang of thieves, as I was informed at that time, attacked him. They killed him in a distant place at a spot where three roads meet. Thus the father died by a hand not his son's! What became of the prophecy then? The oracle, as you see, is not always borne out in all circumstances. Heaven does not whisper its words to every ear. It guards its secrets better than you suspect . . . Its language is not understood by every person . . . It prefers to reveal its intentions through actions not words. Speech is our human language . . . God's language is the deed . . . Beware of taking what Creon brought for a proof! It is only something he heard. It should have no effect. No decision should spring from it.

OEDIPUS: I hope, Jocasta, that my ear has misheard.

JOCASTA: Why? . . . What's this anxiety on your face?

OEDIPUS: It's nothing . . . It's merely the situation no doubt . . . with the strange talk and amazing accusations stirred up, which has landed me in confusion.

JOCASTA: Be more explicit, Oedipus. Disclose what is troubling you. Do you think I said anything injurious to you, unintentionally? Many pointless words slip at times, like rabble, into the parade of ideas.

OEDIPUS: I imagined I heard you say that Laius was killed at a place where three roads meet.

JOCASTA: That's true . . . That's what I said.

OEDIPUS: You said that? . . . You said that?

JOCASTA: What's come over you, Oedipus? . . . Yes. That's what I eventually learned then.

OEDIPUS: Where were those roads? . . . in what land?

JOCASTA:  In a land called Phocis . . . where the road branches into two courses.  One of them leads to Daulia, the other to Delphi.

OEDIPUS:  At what time did that take place?

JOCASTA:  Everyone knows that happened shortly before you ascended the throne.

OEDIPUS:  Oh Heaven!  Is it possible that is true?

JOCASTA:  What, Oedipus?  What's bothering you and causing this turmoil in your soul?

OEDIPUS:  Don't ask me anything . . .  Tell me what Laius looked like?  How old was he?

JOCASTA:  He was tall and slender with curly, grey hair . . .  His face resembled yours a bit.

OEDIPUS:  Do you suppose heaven's curse has truly struck me?

JOCASTA:  What are you saying, my husband? . . .  You frighten me.

OEDIPUS:  Do you suppose there's some truth in the oracle? . . . Tell me something else too . . . so that not a shadow of doubt remains in my soul.

JOCASTA:  You scare me!  I will tell you everything that came to my knowledge.

OEDIPUS:  What was King Laius' retinue like? . . .  How many guards did he have?

JOCASTA:  No more than five men guarded him on his trip . . . and a scout in advance.  There was only a single carriage in which the king rode.

OEDIPUS:  Enough, Jocasta! . . .  My eye sees everything clearly
and plainly now . . . but . . . who told you all that?

JOCASTA:  A servant . . .  He was the only one who returned alive
from that trip.

OEDIPUS:  Is he still in service here?

JOCASTA:  To the contrary!  He asked me to release him from the
palace service when he saw you had taken his master's place
and ascended his king's throne . . .  So far as I know he went
to the fields to work as a herdsman, far away from this city.

OEDIPUS:  Can we have him brought at once?

JOCASTA:  We can . . . but what do you want from that?

OEDIPUS:  Oh, my dear wife!  I fear I have divulged more than is
fitting . . .  I must see that man first.

JOCASTA:  You will see him . . . but have I not the right, Oedipus,
to know what is spreading this anxiety and turmoil through
your soul?

OEDIPUS:  You will know . . .  Send for that herdsman!

(*Some of the assembled people run off.*)

JOCASTA:  What do you wish to learn from him, Oedipus?

OEDIPUS:  This herdsman is my only hope . . .  I would like to
hear words from him contradicting what you said.

JOCASTA:  Contradictory in what respect?

OEDIPUS:  You said that the killer was a gang of thieves . . . and
that he is the one who told you that.  I must hear his
testimony to clear up that important matter.  Was the killer
truly a group or was he a single individual?  On this

testimony rests the verdict and hangs the destiny . . .

JOCASTA:  Whose destiny? . . .  Whose destiny, Oedipus?

OEDIPUS:  Mine! . . .  There's something I have concealed from
you, Jocasta.  Just as you concealed from me the information
of the circumstances surrounding the death of King Laius.

JOCASTA:  I haven't concealed anything from you . . .  It did not
occur to me to mention those details until there was some
call for it or some motive for us to go over them.  They are
not a pleasant topic for me to discuss with you when there is
no need.

OEDIPUS:  I too have not intentionally hidden anything . . .  It is
just a passing incident to which I attached no importance at
the time and paid little attention, because I did not know
who it was I met.

JOCASTA:  Whom did you meet, Oedipus?

OEDIPUS:  A man in a carriage . . . guarded by about five men
who blocked my way in the land of Phocis at the crossroads
between Daulia and Delphi.  A dispute broke out between
us over the right to pass first.  The dispute developed into a
quarrel, and the fervor and passion of youth drove me to
violence.  I raised my cudgel in the men's faces, and we
began to fight.  I vanquished them in the battle, but it seems
that a blow of my cudgel missed and struck the head of the
person in the chariot.  I set off afterwards on my way until I
neared the walls of Thebes and met the beast.  And you
know what happened to me then . . .  If that man in the
carriage was your King Laius, then I'm the one who struck
and killed him.

JOCASTA:  My god! . . . my god!

OEDIPUS:  But I was alone and you all said that Laius was killed
by a band of thieves . . .  This matter must be cleared up

before I pronounce sentence on myself.

CHORUS (*turning*):  Here's the herdsman.  They've brought him.

(*Some of the people who left to search for the HERDSMAN enter.  They are leading a feeble, old man.*)

THEBAN (*with the HERDSMAN*):  We hadn't gone far when we met him on his way here.  He had heard, so he said, news of the ordeal.  He was coming to pray with the people of Thebes and to entreat heaven to lift this plague from our land.

CHORUS:  What a decrepit old man he is!

OEDIPUS:  Come near me, Man, and answer the questions I ask you  . . .  Were you in the service of King Laius?

HERDSMAN:  Yes! . . .  I was born in his household and grew up in it.

OEDIPUS:  What was your employment with him?

HERDSMAN:  Herding his livestock.

OEDIPUS:  Do you remember how Laius was killed?

HERDSMAN:  That happened a long time ago . . . and my memory has grown weak and my mind feeble . . .

OEDIPUS: Recall!  Recall! . . .  Who killed Laius?

HERDSMAN:  He was killed . . . so far as I remember . . . by a strong-bodied youth.

OEDIPUS:  How?

HERDSMAN:  He jostled against the king's chariot at a crossroads between Delphi and Daulia.  A quarrel broke out between him and the guards in the retinue.  He conquered and killed them.  One of his blows struck the king's head.  It was a fatal blow and he died.  I fled from the battle with my skin.  No one else escaped.

OEDIPUS:  Was it a group which attacked the king?

HERDSMAN:  Certainly not, your Majesty!  It was a single man.

OEDIPUS:  Everything has become clear to me and to you all.  The veil has been removed from the killer's face . . .  You were right, Creon.  The oracle you brought from the temple at Delphi was right.  I ask your forgiveness and that of the High Priest.  I have erred in my suspicion of you and by falsely accusing you . . .  The killer of Laius is before you . . .  People!  I shall not attempt to defend him.  Judge him as you see fit.  Provide him the punishment he deserves.

JOCASTA:  Oedipus! . . .  Oedipus!  Don't exaggerate this way . . .  accusing yourself.  You didn't intend to kill him . . .  You didn't know the identity of the man you killed.

OEDIPUS:  Don't defend me, Jocasta, for you are part of me.  It is not right for us to undertake a defense of ourselves for the sins we have committed.

JOCASTA:  If you refuse me and yourself this right, here is Tiresias to speak on your behalf.

TIRESIAS:  If you need me, Oedipus, I am not far from you.

OEDIPUS:  Certainly not! . . .  Rather, stay in your place, Tiresias.  Don't interfere.  My case is clear.  I committed a crime and forgot it.  But heaven did not forget it . . .  Now it wants the price and demands the penalty.  Whatever doubts the intellect may have about the truth of the relationship between that crime and this plague, honor does not doubt the reality of the duty cast on my shoulders.  My duty now is to remove myself from the throne of a man who died by my hand.

JOCASTA:  He died by your hand against your will . . . I don't
think heaven demands of you this oppressive price for it.

OEDIPUS (*as though addressing himself*):  Heaven is never unjust, for
it is a set of scales which has no defect, tilt, deviation, or
passion . . .  When we perceive it to be unjust that is simply
because of our inability to see what consciences conceal and
our forgetfulness for our past account . . .  It adds to the
manifest sin the weight of the concealed one.  I have lied to
the people!  I have deceived the people . . .

TIRESIAS (*shouting and interrupting*):  Enough!  Enough!

(*At this moment a feeble OLD MAN with a stooped back appears.*)

OLD MAN (*shouting*):  O People!

CHORUS (*turning*): Who is this old man coming in from the fields?

OLD MAN:  Direct me to the palace of Oedipus!

CHORUS:  This is the palace before you! . . .  Who are you,
Stranger?  What do you want?

OLD MAN:  I am a messenger from Corinth.  I have brought a
message to Oedipus.

OEDIPUS:  Here I am, Man!  Approach!  What is your news?

OLD MAN:  Happy news! . . .  Although it contains something that
may stir your sorrow.

OEDIPUS:  Speak, Messenger!  Tell us what news you bring.

OLD MAN:  The people of Corinth greet you and ask you to be
their King.

CHORUS: King? Over the people of Corinth?

JOCASTA: Oh how heaven severs and binds! . . . Do you see how unjust you are to yourself, Oedipus? You wished to vacate the throne of Thebes and here's another throne coming to you from heaven!

OEDIPUS (*to the messenger*): What has become of your King Polybus?

OLD MAN: He has died and been entrusted to the earth.

OEDIPUS: Polybus has died? . . . How? Did he die of an illness or in some incident?

OLD MAN: Of the illness of old age!

OEDIPUS: I shall never forget that he was like a compassionate father . . . What has become of Queen Merope?

OLD MAN: Age weakened her . . . and she is on her way to rejoin her husband.

OEDIPUS: She loved me too, as though she were my mother . . . What good generous people they were . . . I remember their distress when I informed them of my discovery of the real nature of the tie binding me to them . . . that I was nothing more than a foundling they adopted . . . They exerted every effort to pluck this truth from my head. But I refused to accept their affection when it was like accepting alms . . . I hope they forgot me after I fled from Corinth and that in the course of time they found other things to think of . . .

OLD MAN: To the contrary! They did not forget you. They sent after you, at that time, someone to search for you. But you had disappeared. Polybus died mentioning your name and charging me to renew the search for you and to propose to you to be king after him.

OEDIPUS:   How did you know where I am?

OLD MAN:  It finally occurred to me to search for you in your
        birthplace.  So I traveled on foot to Thebes.  When I drew
        near its walls I learned that you are its king today.

OEDIPUS:  Who said Thebes is my birthplace?

OLD MAN:  I know that, because I'm the one who found you
        when you were an infant and handed you over to Polybus.

OEDIPUS:  You found me, Old Man?

OLD MAN:  On a wooded mountain near Cithaeron.

OEDIPUS:  What were you doing there?

OLD MAN:  I was herding livestock.

OEDIPUS:  How did you find me?

OLD MAN:  Those scars on your feet will tell you.

OEDIPUS:  Indeed! . . .  Those old scars I grew up with . . .  No one
        ever told me anything about them, of their secret or origin.

OLD MAN:  They are the marks of fetters.  You were shackled by
        your ankles!  I was the one who took off your fetters.  For
        this reason you were "Oedipus" — that is, Swellfoot!

OEDIPUS:  By heaven . . . who did that to me?  Was it my mother
        who gave birth to me or my father who rejected me?

OLD MAN:  I don't know anything about that.  Ask the one who
        delivered you to me about that.

OEDIPUS:  Delivered me to you? . . .  Weren't you, then, the one
        who came across me?

OLD MAN:  No, another herdsman was the one who entrusted you to me and put you in my hands in that form.

OEDIPUS:  Another herdsman?  Who is he?  Can you inform us who that herdsman was?

OLD MAN:  I remember he said that day he was one of Laius' men.

OEDIPUS:  Laius? . . .  The former king of Thebes?

OLD MAN:  Yes, King Laius . . . That herdsman told me he was one of his servants . . .

OEDIPUS:  He had many servants, no doubt.  Is the servant you mean still alive? . . .  Is it possible for me to see him, question him, and learn from him?

OLD MAN:  This is a matter the people of Thebes can answer for you.

OEDIPUS:  People!  Inform me!  Hasn't any one of you heard anything about the servant we are speaking of? . . .  Hasn't one of you seen him in the city or in the fields?  Let one who knows among you speak . . .  Do not remain silent!  Here we have now reached the key to the secret . . . the secret of my birth and of my reality which I have for so long investigated and pursued.

CHORUS:  Ask Queen Jocasta . . .  perhaps she knows that servant in the household of Laius . . .

OEDIPUS:  My dear wife!  Don't you know anything about that servant?

JOCASTA (*her face drained of color*):  What servant are you talking about? . . .  I know nothing.  We ought not to know . . .  My husband, you are paying too much attention to what is being said . . .  Leave this matter.  Close this door.  You won't find anything of value behind it.

OEDIPUS:  How strange, Jocasta!  How can I close this door when it has begun to open on the secret I long to know?

JOCASTA:  No, no, Oedipus!  Don't do all this digging in search of a secret . . .  You are digging now the grave for your happiness!  I entreat you to desist . . .  I'm afraid . . .  An eternal curse is gathering to break over our heads . . .  For heaven's sake desist, Oedipus!

OEDIPUS:  Don't be afraid! . . .  I told you one day that you shouldn't be concerned about the truth of my birth . . .  Even if I were the child of your humblest slaves . . . would this frighten you . . . or cause you shame that would humiliate you or damage your self-esteem?  I will continue my search for my reality . . . that desire is stronger than I am.  No one can stand between me and my desire to know who I am and will be . . .

CHORUS:  Proceed on your course, Mighty King!  Remove the curtain from your birth.  Whatever your origin and birth, we are proud of you.

OEDIPUS:  I don't want to live in a fog, even if the price is the kingship.  I left Corinth and its throne to search for the truth . . .  Now that I have almost placed my hand on its key, should I recoil, draw back and desist? . . .  That shall never be! . . .  That shall never be.

CHORUS (*turning towards the back*):  What's with this herdsman in back of the crowd who is slinking away like a person wishing to flee?

OEDIPUS:  Which herdsman?

CHORUS:  The one who was in Laius' retinue.

OEDIPUS:  Seize him and bring him forward!  He must know

something.

(*Some of the people push the HERDSMAN forward to the place where OEDIPUS stands.*)

CHORUS:  Why are you fleeing, Herdsman?

HERDSMAN:  I wasn't fleeing . . . But I saw no cause for me to stay.

OEDIPUS:  Your departure in this way must be for a reason we shall now learn . . . Perhaps you know the person we seek.

HERDSMAN:  I don't know anyone . . . or anything.

OEDIPUS:  First, bring him close to the messenger from Corinth. Messenger, examine his face carefully.  Perhaps that may lead to something . . .

(*The HERDSMAN is pushed near the OLD MAN.*)

CHORUS (*looking at the two men*):  Two feeble old men . . . They seem to be the same age.

OLD MAN (*shouting after staring at the HERDSMAN*):  He's the very one . . . the very one!

OEDIPUS:  Who? . . . Who?

OLD MAN:  The herdsman who handed me the infant.

OEDIPUS:  Do you hear, Herdsman?

HERDSMAN:   I haven't understood anything this old man said.

OEDIPUS:  Haven't you previously met this old man any place?

HERDSMAN:  I don't remember.

OEDIPUS:   How is it he can remember?

OLD MAN:  Allow me, Oedipus, to sharpen his memory . . .  I don't think he has forgotten those days when we worked near each other in the region of Cithaeron.  He was herding two flocks and I was herding one.  Three seasons from spring to fall passed in succession until winter came.  I drove my flock away returning to Corinth and he drove his two off returning to Thebes . . .  Didn't we do that, Herdsman?

HERDSMAN:  Yes . . . this is truly what we used to do . . . but that was many years ago.

OLD MAN:  Yes . . . many years have passed, but that doesn't prevent you from remembering that nursing infant which you put into my arms one day, imploring me to raise him as if he were my son.

HERDSMAN (*trembling*):  What do you mean? . . .  What do you want me to say?

OLD MAN:  I simply want you to look in front of you, Old Friend . . .  This is your nursing infant! (*He points to OEDIPUS.*)

JOCASTA (*unconsciously emitting a whisper like a rattling in her throat*):  Enough! . . .  Enough!

(*She starts to dart off toward the palace, but OEDIPUS prevents her.*)

OEDIPUS (*shouting*):  Where are you going, Jocasta?

JOCASTA:  Oh God!  Mercy!

OEDIPUS:  Stay a moment to hear with your own ears the truth of my origin.

JOCASTA:  I can't stay another moment . . . I can't . . . can't.

OEDIPUS:  You can't endure the blush of shame tinting your face when you hear in front of this crowd from whose womb your husband emerged! . . . I have never compelled you to do anything before, but I compel you now to remain where you are to learn about me what the assembled people will learn at this time . . . even if there is in that some humiliation for your royal majesty and wound for the glory of your ancient family.

CHORUS:  Stay with us, Queen!  Hear what we hear . . .  Nothing will harm you.  Oedipus is our king because of his heroism, not because of his lineage.

JOCASTA (*hiding her face with her veil*):  Have mercy, Heaven!

OEDIPUS (*to the HERDSMAN*):  Now, Herdsman!  Give us a frank and straight answer with no twist to it about the real facts concerning that infant you delivered to this comrade of yours.

HERDSMAN:  This comrade of mine, your Majesty, doesn't know what he is saying.  He is no doubt mistaken.

OEDIPUS:  Beware, Herdsman!  If you refuse to answer when asked nicely, we know how to force you to talk!

HERDSMAN:  Be gentle, your Majesty, with an old man like me.

OEDIPUS:  If you desire gentle treatment, speak!

HERDSMAN:  What more do you want to know than you know already?

OEDIPUS:  That infant of whom your friend spoke—are you the one who handed him to him?

HERDSMAN:  Yes, your Majesty . . . I did . . . and I wish I had died that day.

OEDIPUS:  I will treat you to death today, if you refuse to reveal the truth.

HERDSMAN:  Alas for me!  This truth is death for me, and what a death!

OEDIPUS:  Haven't you ceased trying to shirk and evade?

HERDSMAN:  There's no longer any way for me to . . .  Haven't I confessed that I gave him the infant?  What more to you want from me then?

OEDIPUS:  Where did you get that infant? . . .  From your own house or someone else's?

HERDSMAN:  Not from my house . . . rather . . . from someone else's.

OEDIPUS:  Whose?

HERDSMAN:  Woe!  Alas!  I entreat you for heaven's sake to desist from questioning me!

OEDIPUS:  Answer . . . answer.  If you refrain from answering now, I will subject you to every form of torture and have you killed in the worst possible way . . .  Speak!

HERDSMAN:  That infant was from the house of Laius.

OEDIPUS:  Was he the son of one of his slaves? . . .  Speak!

HERDSMAN:  Can't you spare me from saying it?  Your Majesty, have pity on me!

OEDIPUS:  You must speak . . .  I must hear.  Otherwise, I will crush  your white head mercilessly and pulverize your feeble body.

HERDSMAN:  The infant was his . . . own son.

OEDIPUS:  Whose?

HERDSMAN:  The son . . . of Laius!

OEDIPUS:  The son of King Laius?

HERDSMAN:  Yes!

(*There is commotion among the people . . . OEDIPUS sways . . . but he is able to regain his composure.*)

OEDIPUS:  What you say is hideous, Man.  It's hideous what you are saying!  My mind can scarcely believe . . . Beware, Man, that there be in your words any lie or fiction . . . I understand now the reason you were fleeing from me . . . In actuality, you are the real source of the story . . . The temple priests no doubt learned it from you!  For no secret is buried in the chest for seventeen years without an aroma spreading from it into the air.  You are the origin of the Delphi oracle!  Take care that you don't trump up a lie against me or give inspiration to a falsehood!

HERDSMAN:  But it's the truth . . . It's in your power to ask Queen Jocasta, for everything took place in her presence and with her knowledge . . . They gave me the child to destroy, but my heart did not dare . . . so I gave him to this man to take to his country and to have for his son.  He took him and in that way saved his life.

OEDIPUS:  Was it a son Queen Jocasta bore?

HERDSMAN:  Yes, your Majesty.  It was said at that time it was necessary to destroy him . . . because of an unlucky prophecy attached to him . . . that this son would kill his father!

OEDIPUS (*screaming*):  Laius! . . . Jocasta!  Heaven!  Heaven!  The fog has dispersed from around me.  I have seen the truth . . . How repulsive is Truth's face!  What a curse!  Never before

has a person been subjected to one like it! Tiresias! . . .
Tiresias! But you are motionless, like a statue . . . I sensed
the specter of disaster and my chest was oppressed by it,
before it struck . . . but I never imagined it would be so
hideous . . . You also were disturbed by it, Jocasta . . .
Jocasta!

(*JOCASTA, who seems to have been standing erect but in a daze all this time, falls to the ground in a swoon.*)

CHORUS (*shouting*): Hasten to the Queen . . . Queen Jocasta sinks
under the weight of the catastrophe! Help her . . . Give her
first aid. Take her into the palace!

(*People gather around the Queen. They carry her gently. OEDIPUS assists them, stunned by the misfortune. They take her into the palace, leaving TIRESIAS where he stands.*)

TIRESIAS: Take me far away from this place, Boy . . . For heaven
has been pleased to make it a playground . . . Yes! For God
is as play, creating art, shaping a story . . . a story based on
my thought. With respect to Oedipus and Jocasta, it is a
tragedy. With respect to me a comedy. You who rule this
palace must shed tears. I am obliged to laugh! (*He laughs hysterically.*)

**Act Three**
**Scene One**

*In the palace . . . JOCASTA is in her chamber, stretched out on her bed.*
*OEDIPUS and the CHILDREN surround her apprehensively.*

OEDIPUS (*whispering*): Keep back from her a bit, my children, and
  don't be alarmed. She's sleeping.

ANTIGONE: Her eyelashes are moving, Father!

OEDIPUS: Yes, she's coming to . . . Take care not to let her see
  your anxiety . . . It's just a passing illness which will soon
  vanish.

(*JOCASTA sighs and opens her eyes.*)

JOCASTA: Where am I? . . . Are you here, my children? . . . Is this
  you, Oedipus . . . Woe is me! Woe is me!

OEDIPUS: Have courage, Jocasta!

JOCASTA: Am I still alive then? . . . Hasn't the earth swallowed
  me? Haven't I ceased to exist?

OEDIPUS (*in a lowered voice*): No more of this talk in the presence
  of our children.

JOCASTA: Our children . . . our children . . . How repulsive your
  words are!

ANTIGONE (*alarmed*): Mother!

OEDIPUS: Antigone, you go along with the other children . . .
  Don't disturb your mother now. (*He gently shows them out of*
  *the room.*)

JOCASTA (*as though speaking to herself*): Our children! . . . Our
  children!

OEDIPUS (*returning to her*): Jocasta! . . . Darling! Have pity on yourself and on me!

JOCASTA: Our children! . . . From whose womb did they come . . . all of them including you, Oedipus! . . . A single womb carried them and you . . . You will never say after today that they are your children . . . rather they are also your brothers and sisters. You will not say I am your wife from now on, I am also at the same time your . . . I am also your . . . What? . . . What am I to say?

OEDIPUS: Don't say anything, Jocasta!

JOCASTA: Has the world ever known an offense like this before? Has the earth's face been defiled by a sin like this? Has anyone ever suffered a curse like this? . . . And in spite of that I am still alive. Alive and breathing . . . speaking . . . and seeing my children . . . All of my children . . . all of them! (*She weeps and tears her hair.*)

OEDIPUS: Have pity on yourself and on me.

JOCASTA: Oedipus! . . . My husband and . . . my son! Why did heaven do that to us? What crime necessitated this punishment for us? . . . Do you think it was my crime the day I left you, a babe, to your destruction . . . My son and husband! Is this possible? . . . Is it possible for a human being to suffer this without being afflicted by insanity . . . or instantly struck by a thunderbolt! I must die, Oedipus! . . . I must die!

OEDIPUS: You will not die, Jocasta! I will protect you like an enraged beast . . . I will stand in the way of anyone who tries to touch a hair of you. I will defy heaven's thunderbolts with you . . . and the blows of fate . . . and the curses of human beings. You will not die! . . . You will not die!

JOCASTA:  What value does life have now, Oedipus?  What value does our life have? . . . Our enemies are not in heaven and not on earth.  Our enemy is within us.  Our enemy is that buried truth which you dug up with your own hands and uncovered leaving no way to escape it . . . except by ending our lives . . . I must die if I am to stifle the repulsive sound of that repulsive truth deep inside me.

OEDIPUS:  You will not die . . . I will destroy every enemy you have. . . even if it is inside you!

JOCASTA:  No, Oedipus!  Don't do it! . . . In that way, you extend my torment.  You don't relieve me.  The matter has been decided and the curse of God and of the people has settled on us . . . Wherever we go, looks will follow us like stones thrown at us.

OEDIPUS:  Take heart and be brave like me . . . Endure everything to face the actuality.

JOCASTA:  Which actuality can we face after today?

OEDIPUS:  Our unitary being . . . our united family . . . our loving hearts . . . our souls filled with affection and strengthened by compassion.  Who would be able to destroy this edifice?  What power could demolish this tower built of love, affection, and compassion?

JOCASTA:  Oedipus! . . . My . . . I don't know what to call you.

OEDIPUS:  Call me anything you like, for you are Jocasta whom I love.  Nothing will change what is in my heart . . . So let me be your husband or your son . . . Names or epithets cannot change the love and affection rooted in the heart.  Let Antigone and the others be my children or siblings.  These terms cannot change the affection and love I harbor for them in my soul.  I will confess it to you, Jocasta, that when I received the blow I almost collapsed under it . . . But that was not in any way able to make me change my feelings for you a single moment . . . For you will always be Jocasta. No matter what I hear of your being my mother or sister, this will never change the actuality at all . . . For you are always Jocasta to me!

JOCASTA:  Oedipus!  You whom I cherish more than myself. Don't try to lighten the effect of the catastrophe on me . . . The actuality is as you described it, but the truth, Oedipus . . . What shall we do with the screaming voice of truth?

OEDIPUS:  The truth? . . . I have never feared its face a day . . . nor been alarmed by its voice.

JOCASTA (*as though addressing herself*):  For how long have I cautioned you against that . . . I have worried about it for you . . . you who have spent your best days chasing after it . . . from city to city in order to grasp its veil . . . until she turned on you at last, bared a little of her terrible face, and screamed in her resounding voice.  It devastated the palace of our happiness and brought us to the state you see . . . the wreckage of a family to which no family term applies and for which there is no human description.

OEDIPUS:  It was necessary for me, Jocasta, to know the truth.

JOCASTA:  Now that you know it . . . do you feel relieved?

OEDIPUS:  I truly wish I didn't know it . . . Could I have imagined it would be so terrible? . . . Did it occur to me that it could destroy my bliss?  I have realized that only now . . . after it has taken revenge on me for playing with its veil.

JOCASTA:  It took revenge on all of us, Oedipus, with a vengeance from which we can never recover.

OEDIPUS:  Don't say that, Jocasta.  We are capable of recovering. Rise with me . . . Let's put our fingers in our ears and live in actuality . . . with the life which throbs in our hearts overflowing with love and compassion.

JOCASTA: I can't, Oedipus! I can't remain with you . . .   Your love for your family has blinded you . . . You are not thinking of people. What would they say if we were to continue this abnormal life after today . . . I am no longer fit to stay. Darling, there is only one solution, for me to go.

OEDIPUS: You will not go! I will compel you to live. I will guard you night and day. I will not permit anything to destroy our happiness and demolish our family. I will abandon the kingship and the palace. We will travel together with our young ones outside this country.

JOCASTA: Travel together? . . . Certainly not. Rather, I will travel alone.

OEDIPUS: Jocasta! Take care you don't proceed with a matter which will bring despair to my heart . . . You know I can't bear to be parted from you. Take heart and rise to meet life with me . . . Rest assured that so long as we have hearts, we are fit to remain.

JOCASTA: We are no longer fit to remain together . . .

OEDIPUS: What is this force which is to separate us?

JOCASTA: You can't overcome it, Oedipus . . . not even with that heroism of yours that vanquished Father Terror.

OEDIPUS (*as though addressing himself*): What a destiny! I am a hero because I killed a beast they claimed had wings. I am a criminal because I killed a man they showed to be my true father . . . I am neither a hero nor a criminal . . . I am just another individual upon whom the people have cast their fictions and heaven its decrees. Must I suffocate under the burden of these cloaks that have been thrown over me? . . . This heart of mine still throbs. I am alive. I want to live. I want to live, Jocasta, and want you to live with me. What is this chasm which separates us now? What hidden enemy and concealed foe rises between us like a giant? . . . Truth?

What power does this truth have? If it were a savage lion with sharp claws and teeth, I would kill it and throw it far from our path. But it is something found only in our minds. It is a figment of the imagination, a ghost. My blow does not penetrate its vitals. My hand does not seize its being. It truly is a winged beast, lurking in the air. We can't reach it with our weapons. It kills our happiness with its riddles . . . Jocasta! You are trembling at a ghost, Jocasta. The actuality in which we now live must endure. We must not allow anything we can't see to destroy it. Free yourself from the truth we heard, Darling! Listen to the throbbing of your heart right now. What is it saying to you? Is it telling you that something has changed? Has your love for your young ones changed? Has your love for Oedipus changed?

JOCASTA:  No . . . This love will never change . . . Never, never. But . . .

OEDIPUS:  What are these tears in your eyes? Say you want to live for our sake.

JOCASTA:  Oedipus!

OEDIPUS:  Why are you looking at me this way as though I were your child . . .

JOCASTA:  Oedipus!

OEDIPUS:  What's come over you, Dear Jocasta? . . . You feel sorry for me. My tenacity for our lost bliss fills you with sorrow. I see pain and torment in your face. Give vent to your pain a little . . . rather plunge into the pain, for the greatest forces have collaborated to destroy this happy family. All the powers! . . . Man's rebellious thought, God's ironic planning, the people's traditions, and human fictions . . . Everything conspires to torment us. Even my intellect which spent years searching for my destruction . . . until I brought out into the open for us that ghost which firmly established itself in empty space . . . to disrupt our smiling life, rock our lovely actuality, and prevent us from communing in a nest we have built from the feathers of our mutual regard over a long period of time . . . Jocasta! Let's accept the pain of the flow of the disaster which has overcome us. Our souls were both oppressed by it when it neared . . . Don't you remember? But let's not surrender to what has befallen us. Everything will pass so long as we protect our home. The heart's warmth will melt away all sins, even the intellect's sins and errors. I believe in the purity of your heart and mine, for we did not sin deliberately. We did not will any of this evil the consequence of which we suffer. There is no way anyone can reproach us. No power has the right to request an exorbitant price from us for crimes we made no effort to commit. If we must pay a price, let it be this glory, sovereignty, and wealth . . . But you, Jocasta, and our children . . . No, no, no.

JOCASTA (*whispering*):  Our children! . . . Our children . . .

OEDIPUS:  What are you whispering?

JOCASTA:  Nothing . . .

OEDIPUS:  I see something in your eyes . . . I am afraid, Jocasta.

JOCASTA:  Have no fear . . . It's just a little fatigue . . . Leave me now.

OEDIPUS:  I think you are worn out.

JOCASTA:  Yes.

OEDIPUS:  If you would sleep a little . . . If you sank into a long slumber, Darling . . .

JOCASTA:  This is my resolve.

OEDIPUS:  But I won't leave you now until you promise me we

will travel together from this country to a distant place . . .

JOCASTA (*as though speaking to herself*):  To a distant place . . .
     Yes, I promise you!

OEDIPUS:  I will request that at once from the people and from
     Creon.  Have a rest now and don't think about anything
     until I return.

JOCASTA:  Go along . . . Oedipus!

OEDIPUS (*looking at her for a time*):  I won't leave you alone.  I'll call
     the children to remain by your side till I return.  (*He calls.*)
     Antigone! . . . Antigone!

(*ANTIGONE appears at the threshold.*)

ANTIGONE:  Father!

OEDIPUS:   Come in with the other children.  Look after your
     mother.  Cheer her up until I return.

(*He puts his hand on the necks of his children.  JOCASTA gazes at them
while they are joined in this fashion.  OEDIPUS leads them to their
mother.*)

ANTIGONE:  Father, you are the only one who can cheer up
     Mother.  All you have to do is to tell her the story of Father
     Terror.  Mother, as you know, always loves to hear it from
     you.

OEDIPUS:  The people are waiting for me, Antigone.  You take
     care of this for me.  You do a better job of telling the story
     than I do.  I entrust your mother's care to you until I come
     back.  Take care not to leave her at the mercy of her
     thoughts.

(*OEDIPUS goes out followed by the distraught glances of JOCASTA.*)

JOCASTA (*whispering*):  My husband! . . .  My son!

ANTIGONE:  Mother!  You truly seem to be thinking about
     something sad.

JOCASTA:  That won't last long, Daughter.

ANTIGONE:  Why are you looking at me this way?

JOCASTA:  You love your father a great deal, Antigone.  I am sure
     you will always be at his side . . . if I were fated to go one
     day to a distant place . . .

ANTIGONE:  Mother, are you going to a distant place?

JOCASTA:  That may happen one day.

ANTIGONE:  What distant place do you mean?

JOCASTA:  A distant place . . . where the heart lives free . . . like a
     peaceful dove.  That bird with wings and claws which preys
     on love does not fly in the sky there.

ANTIGONE:  I don't understand what you are saying, Mother.

JOCASTA:  Never mind.  Don't try to understand now.  All I ask of
     you is to take care of your father if one day you see him all
     alone . . .  I leave him to your care, Antigone.  For he
     deserves all our love.  If one day you see his tears flowing
     from his eyes, then with your pure little hands, wipe away
     those tears.

ANTIGONE:  Why are you saying this to me, Mother?

JOCASTA:  Because I don't want your father to suffer.  He must
     live bright-eyed and find solace in you for everything.

ANTIGONE:  Are you weeping, Mother?

JOCASTA:  I entrust him to you, Antigone!  I entrust him to you!

(*She embraces her daughter for a long time.*)

### Scene Two

*In the square in front of the palace . . .  The CHORUS is assembled as before.  The PRIEST and CREON have taken their places in the crowd.*

CHORUS:  Who would have imagined that these alarming things would be disclosed?  Who would have thought that Oedipus would fail to know these things about his reality?  This hero who has persevered in his research and was proficient at solving riddles was blind to his situation.  He did not notice which woman was in his bed, which child he fathered, or which man he killed . . .  It seems that this man who grasped more of what is secret than was necessary for him missed the minimum a person ought to know.  He dared to attack even Father Terror to wrest away his secret and shrank from knowing what was hidden in his own house and in his past.  How miserable is this man who began to drill into the depths, for nothing burst up at him except the spring of his sorrows . . .  What do you suppose he is doing now?  What has become of Jocasta?  Has she regained consciousness?  What do you suppose they can do now?  This palace encompasses them in its belly like an animal with unclean and decaying matter in its intestines . . .  We don't know whether to pity Oedipus or be angry at him . . .  In spite of everything, he is more our king and hero than he is one who has sinned against his own truth and that of his relatives.

PRIEST:  That's enough talk from you, People, concerning Oedipus.  Leave his suffering now and busy yourselves with yours.

CHORUS:  What stratagem do we have at our disposal?  Ask Oedipus.  He's the one who always sees what must be done for us.

PRIEST:  You haven't stopped putting Oedipus up where you raised him.  You still imagine him with the same qualities you knew from him.  You are not able to get free quickly from the enchantment of an idea you have grown accustomed to nor to make any sudden change in it.  For that required an ability for quick perception . . .  How stolid your thought is, People.  How slow your hand is to put the statue where it belongs.  But I draw to your attention that Oedipus now has sufficient concerns of his own.  He has an affliction which saps, a trial submerging him, and work which turns him away from having time for you.

CHORUS (*looking at the palace gate*):  Here is Oedipus!  He has appeared.

OEDIPUS:  It is difficult for me to show myself to your eyes after disgrace has covered me and dishonor has enveloped me.  But I have come to receive the verdict of the citizens on me, People.  Have a little mercy for me, if your verdict delivered just now in my absence is harsher than I can bear.

PRIEST:  They have not delivered judgment on you, Oedipus.  Don't expect them to, but remember that you promised to deliver your verdict on the killer of Laius . . .  So do not go back on your promise.

OEDIPUS:  I will not go back on my promise, Priest.  What punishment did I decree for you when I accused you and Creon?

PRIEST:  Death or banishment?

OEDIPUS:  I am not brave enough for death now, because I love my family . . . so let it be the latter, Priest.  Allow me to travel with my family from this land . . . not to return!

CREON:  Oedipus, you ask too much!  What is your family but mine?  How can we allow you to wander off with the family to foreign parts . . . to take them never to return?

OEDIPUS:  And can this land support us after today?

CREON:  No one here has the right, Oedipus, to authorize this departure for you . . . We are not able to issue any ruling for it before we ask God's guidance.

OEDIPUS:  What's this you say, Creon?  Aren't you the one who brought the oracle from the temple at Delphi?  Didn't it tell you to cleanse this land of the person who defiled it with pollution?

CREON:  What you request, Oedipus, is too serious for me to grant without permission . . . The oracle is sometimes obscure for us.  There must be some hesitation in your case.  It is not easy to have the family of Laius leave its place of origin . . . It's an outcome over which there can be no haste or speed.

CHORUS (*turning*):  Here is Tiresias approaching . . . Perhaps he has an opinion.  He is able to understand the oracles.

OEDIPUS:  Come here, Tiresias, and settle our disagreement.  You know the events which have taken place and the calamities which have landed on my head.  Here I am proposing to give up this kingship which is plunged in mud and blood.  I wish to flee from this land with my family, but these people refuse to shorten my torment and humiliation.

TIRESIAS (*pushing his boy away from him*):  Get away from me, Boy. I see my path now.  God has struck my eye and I can see.

OEDIPUS:  Tiresias! . . . Listen to me.

TIRESIAS:  Who is this calling me?  Is it a human being or a god?

OEDIPUS:  I'm Oedipus.

TIRESIAS:  Oedipus? . . . Who is Oedipus?

OEDIPUS:  Don't you know now who Oedipus is?  Allow me to

remind you of him. He is the one on whom you brought down all these misfortunes. You are the person so stupid he wished to interfere in something beyond his power . . . You are the blind man who thought he could see better for people than heaven could. You are the one who willed, and your will was a curse on the innocent. Had you allowed matters to run the course intended for them according to the designated laws, I would not be a criminal today . . . You wished to challenge heaven. You banished young Oedipus from the kingship and place on the throne a man of your making. But this man you put up is the very same Oedipus you banished. For a long time you have prided yourself on your free will . . . Yes, you truly had a free will. I have witnessed its effects. But it was always operating, without your knowing or sensing it, within the framework of heaven's will.

CHORUS: We don't understand anything of this strange speech Oedipus is uttering.

PRIEST: Allow Oedipus to say whatever he wishes, for he would like to appear in the garb of the innocent and throw the crime on the shoulders of this blind old man. This old man was simply the bearer of a divine oracle . . . and the prophecy has been borne out.

OEDIPUS: Yes! It was correct. This is something causing amazement. It amazes him in his soul . . . this old man who was the bearer of the prophecy. When I uttered that statement just now I did not wish to appear innocent. I have never defended myself before you. It's a statement only Tiresias understands. It is of no significance for you. If you learned, People, what I mean, you would be filled with amazement. And you, Priest . . . Who knows? Perhaps you were, unconsciously, for Creon what Tiresias was for me . . . Man is man. He must act, will, and proceed according to the motivation of his aptitudes and conceit. His shortsightedness does not distinguish between his will and God's.

TIRESIAS:  What is this clamor around me?  I hardly hear anything people say.  My ear is filled with laughter coming from above.

OEDIPUS:  Yes!  Heaven wished to make a laughingstock of you . . . You who thought to wage war and tried to make your will a sword.  You selected this palace with its peaceful residents as the battlefield!  You struck your blow, but God had only to mock you and strike your blind eye.  Then you saw your stupidity and conceit . . .  The palace, however, has been razed to the ground with its inhabitants by your stupid blow and heaven's irony . . .  Although it would have been more chivalrous, Tiresias, to think a little about the victims.  Speak and give the judgment you think just . . .  I ask only to depart with my family from this land, carrying away our disgrace.  Perhaps in another land we will succeed in restoring our fortunes.

TIRESIAS:  Boy! . . .  What is buzzing from the depths of silence?  The drone of an insect deep in the mud?

OEDIPUS:  It's a creature which killed its father, married its mother, and fathered children who were its siblings.  Insects deep in the mud do that, because they're blind.  I did that, because since I came into existence a blind man has wished to guide my destiny . . .  You are the true criminal.  If your blood were pure, I would shed it and wash my wounds with it.  But it was fated that you live respected and deceive people, while I pay the price of your errors and wear the ignominy of your crimes.

PRIEST:  Have pity on the old man, Oedipus!  Have pity on the old man!

CHORUS:  Bear your destiny alone, Oedipus, as befits a hero!

OEDIPUS:  You're right, People.  It's foolish to dispute the destinies allotted us.  Perhaps some of it is of our own making.  Do you hear, Tiresias?  Your closed eye could not see God's hand in this existence . . . This system ordained for things is so straight a path that everyone who strays from it finds pits to fall into. You have a path you can proceed down according to your will, or you can stop. But you are not to challenge or deviate. You did, Tiresias, and you fell. But you swept us along with you. The fall affected you only in your pride. God used it to put you back in your place. We, however, were hit in our hearts. No one can give us assistance now. Not even you . . . You keep silent except to prate and babble. No hope remains for us save the people's hearts. We ask them to have some mercy on us . . . Now get away from me, Old Man. From now on you are good for nothing, in my opinion. Take him far away, Boy.

TIRESIAS (*to the BOY*): Take me to God so I can ask him when He prepared and planned His mockery — before creating us . . . or after our deliberation? Take me up to heaven, Boy. Bring me to God. I would know whether He truly is laughing at me just now . . . or whether He does not know me or care about me . . . Has He laughed in advance, since the beginning of creation . . . since He created this jest and shot it off into time to strike anyone who opposes it? It envelopes anyone who challenges it and clings to anyone who stands in its way . . . Take me up to heaven, Boy, so I may know. If I find God laughing at me, I too will laugh in His presence . . . like this . . . and this . . . (*He pushes the BOY in front of him. While he laughs, they depart.*)

CHORUS (*watching TIRESIAS leave*): What has happened to noble Tiresias today? It seems the events have made him oblivious to us and have unbalanced him.

PRIEST: Let him go. I think he's out of sorts today.

(*A scream resounds from inside the palace. Everyone turns towards the portal. Then ANTIGONE appears screaming.*)

ANTIGONE: Father! Father!

OEDIPUS:  What's happened?  What's happened?

ANTIGONE:  Mother . . .  Hurry to Mother!

(*OEDIPUS leaps up the steps and enters the palace, terrified, with his daughter behind him.  The crowd stares at them, motionless from alarm, like statues.*)

CREON (*recovering from the surprise and beginning to move*):
What's happened to my sister?  (*He starts to go to the palace.*)

PRIEST (*catching and restraining him*):  Stay, Creon!  Your place now is with these people who have been left by their guardians. Their protectors are too preoccupied to care for them . . . We can guess the pain you suffer and the sentiment filling you . . .  For you are a branch of this ruling tree and a member of this unhappy family.  You are shaken by the tempests and losses which toss it . . .  Your loyalty to Oedipus and your sister inspires us to request you to put your hand to the tiller of this ship before it sinks with all of us.  So rise before this anxious and apprehensive people. Fasten their vessel to a safe shore.

CREON:  Who grants me this sovereignty?

PRIEST:  The encompassing circumstances and the tyranny of events give you the right to look after the people's welfare. In the same way, waves washing over a ship give the resolute sailor the right to hoist the burden and establish tranquility, stability, and safety when the captain is down.

CREON:  Didn't you see how I was accused of desiring the throne?

PRIEST:  That accusation against you was dropped, because the truth was on your side.  Never listen to any voice except that of your duty.

CREON (*shouting into his ear*):  Hush!

(*Screams ring out from inside the palace.*)

CHORUS:  What are the frightening sounds coming from inside
the palace?

PRIEST (*turning towards the palace*):  Not so fast.  Here is a servant
coming to us from the palace.

CHORUS:  Look at this person coming from the palace.  His eyes
show signs of alarm.

SERVANT:  People of Thebes! . . . Queen Jocasta is dead.

CHORUS:  Dead?

CREON:  O Sister! (*He rushes into the palace.*)

CHORUS: Speak . . . speak.  Tell us what happened!

SERVANT:  We did not see anything at first, but we heard
Antigone screaming, "Where's Father?  Where's my father?"
When we asked her what was the matter with her, she said
that her mother had risen from her bed and kissed her and
the other children.  She pretended that she was overcome by
fatigue and that she wished to sleep for a long time.  She
drew them outside her room.  Then she entered it and
blocked the door from the inside.  Her eyes flashed in a way
to arouse fear and awaken anxiety . . . After that, the young
ones heard through the cracks of the door only suppressed
cries and choking moans . . . Then there was a dreadful,
pervasive silence . . . and Antigone rushed outside to you as
you saw to tell her father . . . Then Oedipus hastened after
her to the locked room, banging on the door as though
crazed.  There was no answer.  He bellowed like a
frightened animal and attacked the door with his shoulder
until he knocked it down.  And here we saw a sight which
froze the blood in our veins . . . Queen Jocasta hanged by
her neck from a rope.  She was dangling in the air with
everything around her quiet as a tomb.  Oedipus had

scarcely seen her in this state when he rushed to the rope and pulled it down. Then the queen's corpse fell cold to the floor . . . At that time, our eyes saw the most hideous sight observed by the human eye. Oedipus became quite crazed. He bent over Jocasta's body rubbing his cheeks against her and wiping his head against her feet. He shouted: "They are slow to bring me a weapon of death too . . . I have no need for the sword. Here's something more hideous than death, more violent and painful!" He stretched out his hand like a hawk's talon to the breast of the royal robe which Jocasta wore. He tore off its gold brooches and plunged them violently into his own eyes, saying: "I will weep for you only with tears of blood!" He proceeded to tear his eyelids and rip his eyelashes with the brooches. Blood flowed from his eyes in streams, dyeing with its dark color the surface of his cheek like black lines from the judgment of a stern fate.

CHORUS (*including women's voices*): Enough! Enough!

PRIEST: Where is this wretched king now?

SERVANT: He is stumbling about inside the palace writhing from his pain.

PRIEST: Hasn't anyone been quick to attend to him?

SERVANT: Of what use would an attempt to care for him be now? . . . Look, I see his arms beating the air, groping for the way out of the palace.

(*OEDIPUS appears, blinded, with blood on his face and clothes.*)

CHORUS (*shouting in alarm*): Woe!

OEDIPUS (*stumbling while he advances*): Where have my feet led me?

CHORUS: Why did you do this to yourself, Oedipus? It hurts to look at it.

OEDIPUS:  This is you, Generous People.  I seek your pardon and
forgiveness for me . . .  I did not wish to hurt your eyes with
a distasteful sight.  But I am searching for the only path left
to me.

CHORUS:  What path is this, Oedipus?

OEDIPUS:  The path of death . . .  There beyond the walls of
Thebes.  I will wander aimlessly through the countryside
until I encounter a beast to devour me.  Then the birds will
land to feed off the remains of my body.

PRIEST:  We won't allow you to go to your destruction.

OEDIPUS:  Have mercy on me.  Don't bar the way before me any
longer.  You refused us exile until it was too late . . .
Nothing remains for me but to meet death.

PRIEST:  You will not walk to meet it.

OEDIPUS:  Who will prevent me?

PRIEST:  God . . . if He thinks your time has not yet come.

OEDIPUS:  What interest does God have in drawing out my
torment?  Hasn't He fully exercised His right to punish me
yet?

PRIEST:  Perhaps He wishes you well . . .

OEDIPUS:  What good can happen to me after today?  The light
around me has been extinguished . . . all light in my eye and
in my heart.  An eternal darkness has blotted out my life.  It
seems a cloak of mourning which will never be lifted from
me.

PRIEST:  If you wish to draw near to God and light a lamp to Him
in your soul, it will give you light on your darkest nights.
But you have preferred to light candles in your intellect

which have all gone out in the first gust of wind.

OEDIPUS:  Don't scold me, Priest, and don't take revenge on me.  I truly lit these candles to search for Truth.  Tiresias cautioned me one day against letting my fingers touch its face and come close to its eyes.  It does not like anyone to look at it more than is necessary.  Yes, these fingers have come closer to it than they ought, until I have put out my eyes . . .  It has taken revenge on me, so don't you be hard on me, Priest.  I need your pity and compassion.

PRIEST:  What good will my compassion be to you when all these mishaps have befallen you?  But I will ask heaven's mercy for you.

CHORUS:  Here's Creon coming pale-browed out of the palace . . .

OEDIPUS:  Creon is coming?  Ask him to help me and to lighten my pains.

CREON (*when he has appeared*):  Why did you do this to yourself, Oedipus?  What do you wish from me to alleviate your pains?

OEDIPUS:  Allow me to go far away from Thebes.  Expel me from your land like a curse.

CREON:  Don't ask that of me, Oedipus.

OEDIPUS:  I shall not ask you, Creon, to take my family with me . . . as I requested at first.  The circumstances have changed now, as you know.  I shall go alone, leaving my children with you.  You take care of them; you are an excellent father for them.  I entreat you to take good care of the two girls, Creon . . . and Antigone in particular . . . She has been very attached to me.  She will have greater need for your affection . . . So you can see the matter is easy for you to consent to, for I have committed to you my family and yours, that is what remains of it.  So far as I'm concerned, it

is of no use for me to remain.  I am no longer fit to remain
. . . Dear Jocasta was right.  I vainly encouraged her to live.
She resisted as I did, but something stronger and more
violent was victorious.  With the departure of Jocasta, I
perceived the power of that thing which compelled her
death.  I understood that my life as well was completely
futile.  Then I immediately wrapped it in darkness.

CREON:  Do you have a last request, Oedipus?

OEDIPUS:  Yes! . . .  Don't forget to have the appropriate funeral
rites performed for the burial of that one who lies shrouded
in her chamber.  She is your sister, and I am confident that
you will do your duty well . . .  I have no request beyond
that except to commend my children to you once more . . .
And I appeal to your generosity, Creon, and ask you to send
for them now so that I can touch them with my hand.

CREON (*gesturing to the servant near the palace gate*):  I had thought
to spare them these painful sights . . .

OEDIPUS:  For a time which may be the last . . . if you allow it,
Compassionate Creon, I would touch their innocent faces
with my fingers.  I would imagine their features and
contemplate  their images in my head . . .  What's this I hear?
That is the sound of their little feet and that the sobbing of
Antigone which I know.  They are coming.  I wonder
whether you have had mercy on me, Creon, and sent to
fetch them?

(*ANTIGONE comes out of the palace leading the other children.*)

CREON:  I ordered them brought to you, Oedipus, for I know how
much you love them.  Here they are, close to you!

OEDIPUS (*stretching his hand out in the air*):  Thank you, Creon!
Where are you, my children?  I don't see you.  My eyes will
never see you again.

ANTIGONE (*holding back her tears*):  Never mind, Father.  So long as I have eyes, they are yours.  You shall never be alone.  I will be by your side wherever you are . . .

OEDIPUS:  Antigone, my daughter!  My heart is not pleased to drag you with me down the road of suffering.  Your place is here beside your uncle with the other children.

ANTIGONE:  The only place for me is next to you, Father.  I will see for you.  Don't you remember that I aspired one day to see things with your eyes . . . to see them as you see them.  I will try to observe things the way you would.  I will not let you feel for a day that you have lost your sight.

OEDIPUS:  To the contrary, I was the one who aspired to see existence, pure and clean, through your eyes, but I am no longer worthy of that.  Stay far from me, Daughter.  Your radiant youth is yours, not mine.  I will not take it from you and thereby commit another crime . . . Live life, my children.  Keep your hands clean of me.  For I am nothing to you but a blot.  I am nothing but a burden on you.  My ill-omened shadow which will attend you on the morrow will be enough of me for you to bear.  You will be a proverbial example, a tidbit for mouths and toy for tongues.  So long as people need fictions to fill the emptiness of their days, you will be a legend for people.  The only hope for you is your uncle Creon.  Make him your father.  You will find affection and sympathy in his care.  He has pledged to care for you.  Here I extend my hand to you to confirm the pact . . .
Where is your hand, Friend?

(*CREON takes OEDIPUS' hand and presses it without speaking.*)

OEDIPUS:  Young Ones, make Creon your example and model . . . This man is even-tempered and pure-hearted, with a believing soul.  Take care . . . take care not to make your father a model.  Rather, take a lesson from his fate.

(*ANTIGONE's tears fall on OEDIPUS' hand with no sob or sound.*)

OEDIPUS:  What are those tears on my hand?  Whose tears are these?

ANTIGONE (*exploding*):  Don't say that, Father!  I will never take anyone for a model besides you . . . Never . . . You are the hero of Thebes!

OEDIPUS:  This is you, Dear Antigone . . . You still believe your father a hero?  (*He weeps*.)  No, I am no longer that today, Daughter.  Indeed, I never was a hero at all.

(*ANTIGONE brushes away OEDIPUS' tears with her hands.*)

ANTIGONE:  Father!  You have never been the hero you are today!

# THE TRAGEDY
# OF OEDIPUS

by Ali Ahmad Bakathir

Translated by Dalia Basiouny
and Marvin Carlson

### Translator's Introduction to Bakathir's *Oedipus*

"A real translation is transparent; it does not cover the original, does not block its light, but allows the pure language, as though reinforced by its own medium, to shine upon the original all the more fully."

Walter Benjamin, "The Task of the Translator"

Professor Marvin Carlson was interested in the Arab dramatists' attraction to the myth of Oedipus, as he explains in his introduction to this volume. He wanted to collect some Arabic Oedipus plays and make them available to English language readers. Ali Ahmad Bakathir's *Oedipus* was a cornerstone of this project, and since it was not translated in English, we embarked on translating it. We started the translation project in the Fall of 2003 as a team. It was an ideal translation team as both of us had some knowledge of both languages, Arabic and English, and each of us had one of them as a mother tongue.

We tried different methods of cooperating on the translation. First I translated segments of the play and sent the rough drafts to Professor Carlson for revisions, then we met and discussed the revisions in relation to the original text, until we agreed on the words which had the same shades of meaning or the phrases which evoked the same feelings. We worked for one year using this method, meeting every few weeks, and were able to translate half the play. As the deadline for publication approached Professor Carlson suggested a new method for translation, in which we would work on the first draft of translation and revision at the same time. Hence we started weekly sessions of translation/revision where I orally translated the text, Professor Carlson revised it and then wrote it down. Later we revised the whole text to check for continuity, consistency, and language accuracy. Indeed, the new way of working proved to be more time efficient and allowed for a more collaborative process and immediate revisions and re-revisions.

This translation project marks a distinctive moment in my professional and literary translation work. Previously, I translated news, short stories, a play (Timberlake Wertenbaker's *The Love of the Nightingale*) and other texts from English to Arabic, and various texts from Arabic to English. Co-translating Bakathir's *Oedipus* with Professor Carlson was a unique experience for me as it allowed me a larger sense of freedom and experimentation in playing with the language, knowing that I have the expertise, support and language resourcefulness of my collaborator. Negotiating shades of meaning of words and phrases opened my eyes to new ways of connecting both languages, Arabic and English.

As a text, Bakathir's *Oedipus* poses a number of challenges for translation: archaic phrases and expressions, old forms of Classical Arabic, the Qur'anic language (especially that of Tiresias) and Bakathir's use of some old stylistic devices. Some of the recurring examples are the words "Waylak" and "Wayhak" that start many dialogue lines. These old forms of address in Arabic often, but not always, indicate warning or lamentation. There is no direct translation for either of them. We considered using "Alas!" as an equivalent but we decided against it as it did not carry the range of meanings conveyed in the Arabic words, and it created a sense of estrangement and distance when heard on stage. Instead, we used various words or phrases to translate these expressions, depending on the meaning in each sentence, such as: woe, oh, oh my, stop, how dare you, curse you, damnation, damn you.

Another example is Bakathir's abundant use of the Arabic stylistic device of using two words with overlapping meaning for empahsis. It was not an easy task to find pairs of words in English which carry the same shades of meaning. A third challenge was Bakathir's choice of the language Tiresias uses, which is closely connected to the Qur'an and to philosophic/religious debates about fate and destiny. We chose to stay as close as possible to the original Arabic, even if the English translation departed from everyday English usage. We also decided to keep some phrases that sounded unfamiliar in English as they also were unfamiliar in the Arabic original (e.g. the way the word "Temple" is used). Recalling Benjamin's discussion of "Fidelity and freedom" in translation, striking a good balance between being true to the original language and having the freedom to carry it into the new mode the host language allows, I think we found a good balance in this dance between Arabic and English expression.

I believe that Bakathir's choice of unfamiliar language could be deliberate to create a distancing effect for his readers and audience, emphasizing the Greek roots of the Oedipus myth. It's interesting to compare the language of Bakathir's play to that of his contemporary al-Hakim. Both playwrights use Classical Arabic, but al-Hakim's language seems distinctly less archaic.

Though written in the first half of the twentieth century, Bakathir's *Oedipus* is extremely relevant at the beginning of the twenty-first century. The playwright uses the story of Oedipus to present his ideas and beliefs about religion and the meaning of true religion and to counter the claims of atheism in his time. This version of the tale has earthly explanations and provides reasonable justification for many of the details of the Greek myth. Bakathir's main focus is to expose the manipulation of religion by those in power. Currently religion is more than a backdrop to the global wars, worldwide tension and the good-evil dichotomy dominating political discourse. Religion is being used and misused by many to reach their political and financial goals. Reading Bakathir's *Oedipus* today, we can see Oedipus as a modern man trying to counter the attacks of those using religion to control people's lives, and make financial gains with no concern about how many people and nations they destroy in the process.

Dalia Basiouny

# THE TRAGEDY OF OEDIPUS

## OEDIPUS

A Play in Three Acts
by Ali Ahmad Bakathir
1949

# CHARACTERS

OEDIPUS, King of Thebes

JOCASTA, Queen of Thebes

CREON, the Queen's brother

ANTIGONE and ISMENE, Oedipus' daughters

POLYNICES and ETEOCLES, Oedipus' sons

TIMONE, the Queen's chambermaid

TIRESIAS, a reforming priest

LUCASIUS, the High Priest of the Temple at Delphi

MENSAS and LAMYAS, priests

POLYBUS, King of Corinth

MEROPE, Queen of Corinth

NIKOS, Laius' servant

BETAKORAS, a Corinthian shepherd

PONTUS, a friend of Oedipus from Corinth

THE SPHINX, one of the priests

CHIEF ELDER, a representative of the people

THEBAN ELDERS

## Act One
## Scene One

*Scene: A large luxurious hall in the royal palace in Thebes, leading on the right to a large balcony, overlooking the palace square. The hall has three doors, the downstage right door leads to the outside, two other doors backstage right and left lead to inside the palace. At the far left is a small chamber. Center stage is occupied by a large throne, surrounded by other chairs.*

*Time: Early afternoon*

*The curtain rises on JOCASTA and CREON, sitting on the large throne.*

CREON:  Did you talk to him yesterday, Jocasta?

JOCASTA:  Yes, I spoke to him yesterday before bedtime and again this morning, but I don't think he is convinced.  I don't think he is going to change his mind, Creon.

CREON:  What are we going to do?  The plague is growing worse; every day it claims new victims—men, women, and children.  The people are suffering.  Those who do not die of the plague are dying from lack of food.  The people are crying out their complaints.  The Elders of Thebes are urging me every day to speak to Oedipus, to convince him to listen to the pleas of the people and to do what they wish, and I don't know how to respond to them.

JOCASTA:  You can only repeat what Oedipus said when they kept appealing to him about this.

CREON:  Oedipus himself could not convince them with his response, so how can I convince them, when I am not convinced myself?  Ah!  What would he lose if he did what the people wanted and sent someone to the temple at Delphi to ask the oracle about this calamity so that God would remove our affliction.

JOCASTA:  I wish he would, Creon.  That might relieve him from the agony of trying to think of some way out of this crisis.  I am worried about the consequences of his continuous thinking until all hours of the night.  He has enjoyed neither food nor sleep since this calamity has befallen us.

CREON:  I am worried that the people will lose their trust in him if they see him insisting upon his own opinion and not responding to their request, which they think is easily fulfilled.

JOCASTA:  Yes, but the real danger is greater than that.  It's the High Priest, Creon.

CREON:  Yes.  I am surprised that Oedipus dared to appropriate the Temple's wealth and property, without considering the dangers of this act to himself and his kingship.

JOCASTA:  That is Oedipus.  He would do anything that he thinks would benefit his people.

CREON:  But a word from the High Priest could turn the people against him.  I do not know how Oedipus could ignore such an obvious thing.

JOCASTA:  This is the problem, Creon.  Shhhh.  Here he comes.

CREON (*getting up . . . says quietly*):  O Heavens.  Guide me; help me in my task.

(*Enter OEDIPUS, looking exhausted and troubled.*)

OEDIPUS:  You are here, Creon.  So what are you talking about?

CREON:  What else would we talk about but this calamity?

OEDIPUS (*with a faint smile*):  So, have you found a solution better than mine?

CREON:  We do not have any other solution than the one that the people want.

JOCASTA:  My dear husband, what is the harm in responding to the people's request?

OEDIPUS:  Oh, have mercy on these poor people. They still believe in the Temple, and the Temple is the source of their problems.  What can the Temple do for them?  The Temple is interested only in its possessions, and that distracts it from caring about the misery of the people.

CREON:  Oh, Oedipus! Don't say this in front of anyone.  The people would not accept on the throne a leader who does not believe in the Temple.

OEDIPUS (*angrily*):  And I can't bear to see my people in this great distress, for which I know the true cure.  I can't allow them to force me to consult the Temple, knowing that the Temple is the source of their misery and suffering.

CREON:  But how will you convince the people?

OEDIPUS:  I don't think I could convince the people, while I couldn't convince my own household.  They will have to see for themselves the results of what I am planning to do.

CREON:  Their suffering hasn't left them with any patience.

OEDIPUS:  I won't make them wait for long.

CREON:  And the Elders of Thebes, Oedipus, what should I tell them?  They sent me to you to ask you to follow the wishes of the people, and they are waiting for me to bring them your response.

OEDIPUS:  Promise them that all will be well!  Tell them I know what they are going through.  Tell them each of them is suffering his own pain, and I suffer for all their pains.

CREON:  I told them similar things before and this didn't satisfy them. They don't want words, they want action.

OEDIPUS (*angrily*):  Beware Creon! What is consulting the Temple but merely words from some powerless person to a God even more powerless than he is. Do you call this action and call what I plan to do words?

CREON:  I am only saying what they would say.

OEDIPUS:  So tell them this from me. Tell them I have found the cure, and soon the suffering will be over. Will you follow my orders, Creon?

CREON:  I will follow your orders, your majesty. (*He exits from the first door.*)

OEDIPUS (*sighing*):  Oh, how my heart aches! I see the path so clearly in front of me, and not one eye around me can see it. Even you, Jocasta, you let me down and don't help me!

JOCASTA:  Oh, darling! How can I help you do something that makes my heart tremble when I think about its consequences? Creon worries about you and he doesn't even know what I know. So what do you expect from me, Oedipus? I wish some fear would enter your heart.

OEDIPUS:  Do not wish things you do not like on those you like.

JOCASTA:  My darling, you are braver than you should be. Courage is blind, and fear has sharp eyesight.

OEDIPUS:  No, fear is blind, Jocasta, and courage sees clearly. One fears what one does not know, not what one knows.

JOCASTA:  If courage were not blind, you would have been able to see the great danger in your path, that threatens you and us with you. The High Priest is watching us closely. If you attack him, wouldn't he strike back with the sharp weapon

he has?  Oh dear!  What will become of us if he
announces the horrible truth to the people?

OEDIPUS (*shaking*):  What truth, Jocasta?

JOCASTA:  What's wrong with you, Oedipus?  You know what I
mean.

OEDIPUS (*eagerly*):  What do you mean?  What do you fear?

JOCASTA:  I fear that he will tell the people that you killed Laius.

OEDIPUS:  Is that all that you fear?

JOCASTA:  Of course, my darling.  Isn't that enough to make me
shake with horror?

OEDIPUS:  Calm down, my dear Jocasta.  This is not serious.

JOCASTA:  This courage of yours, darling, does not allow you to
see the danger that is threatening you.  But I am a woman,
moved by fear to be cautious and avoid trouble.  Do you
think I would have presented the Temple with those
offerings and sacrifices if I didn't fear that the High Priest
could reveal our secret?

OEDIPUS:  Oh, calamity!  Your offerings and sacrifices were one of
the reasons for the famine attacking the people.  You used
the treasury's money to satisfy the Temple, until the priests
gathered up all that money and nothing was left for the
people.  I can no longer live with you, Jocasta, unless I
return their money and property to the people.

JOCASTA:  Then the priest will announce that you killed Laius.

OEDIPUS:  Let him do as he pleases; the people won't prefer Laius
over me if he does.

JOCASTA:  Yes, you have became closer and dearer to the people than Laius was, but still they will not hesitate to follow the orders of the Temple and its oracle.

OEDIPUS:  Damn the Temple, its oracle, its gods and its priests.

JOCASTA:  Don't let the Temple make you forget your own good and overlook the danger that threatens you and threatens me along with you.  Oh, I fear the day when the priest tells the people of Thebes that I married the man who killed their king, knowing that he killed him.

(*OEDIPUS is silent.  His face seems worried.*)

JOCASTA (*sweetly, in a flirtatious tone*):  If what I said worried you, then you understand my meaning.  But if it made you mad at me, please don't be.  I cannot stand for you to be mad at me.

(*OEDIPUS remains silent.*)

JOCASTA:  Oedipus.  Say something.  What's wrong?

OEDIPUS:  Tell me, Jocasta, how old are you today?

JOCASTA:  How old?  What do you mean by asking about my age?  Do you think I am not young anymore?  Alas!  Has my love diminished in your heart?  Is the passion between us dying?

OEDIPUS:  No Jocasta, nothing like that.

JOCASTA:  So why this strange question that you are asking me for the first time?

OEDIPUS:  It was only a passing thought.

JOCASTA:  It must be the mention of Laius that led you to this thought.  I want you to know, Oedipus, that Laius married me before I reached puberty.  Do not think he was close to me in  age.

OEDIPUS:  Yes, Jocasta, I know that.  But how many years did you
　　　spend with Laius?

JOCASTA:  What is it to you, darling?  Other husbands can't stand
　　　the mention of their wives' ex-husbands. Let's stop talking
　　　about Laius.

OEDIPUS:  Do you hate his memory, Jocasta?

JOCASTA:  Yes. I don't like to remember him.

OEDIPUS:  Why not?

JOCASTA:  Because he disturbs our peace.

OEDIPUS:  Disturbs our peace . . .  How so?

JOCASTA:  Oedipus, you are different today.  Did you feel jealous
　　　at the mention of Laius?  Do you think I loved him?  I
　　　wonder at you, Oedipus.  You saw him yourself; how would
　　　you think that an old man like him would have a place in
　　　my heart like yours?

OEDIPUS:  You didn't answer my question yet.

JOCASTA:  Which question?

OEDIPUS:  How does he disturb our peace?

JOCASTA:  Because he reminds me of my fear that the High Priest
　　　would reveal to the people that you are his killer.

OEDIPUS:  Didn't his death sadden you at all?

JOCASTA:  Of course it did.  I was sad for a while, till fate brought
　　　me someone better.

OEDIPUS:  Didn't you feel any distress in marrying the person who killed him?

JOCASTA:  Why all these questions, Oedipus?

OEDIPUS:  Answer me, Jocasta.

JOCASTA:  This was my destiny; what could I do about it?  Who knows, maybe fate wanted to punish Laius for killing his innocent baby out of fear that the child would kill him and marry me, as that insane oracle predicted.  So as a punishment someone killed him and married his wife.

OEDIPUS:  Do you think that child was killed?

JOCASTA:  Yes, I've told you many times, Oedipus, that Laius gave the baby to his servant to kill him in the wilderness.

OEDIPUS:  Did the servant kill him?

JOCASTA:  Would a servant dare disobey his master?

OEDIPUS:  Where is this servant?

JOCASTA:  This is the fourth time you've asked me about the servant.  What do you want from him, Oedipus?

OEDIPUS:  I want to know!  Where is he?

JOCASTA:  I don't know where he went.

OEDIPUS:  Jocasta, do you remember the last time you saw him?

JOCASTA:  Yes.  It was the day you killed the Sphinx and took Laius' place.  I have not seen him since.

OEDIPUS:  Did he tell you that he killed that child?  Did you hear him say that yourself?

JOCASTA:  Yes Oedipus.  I heard him with my own ears.  What are all these questions?  You frighten me with your questions.

OEDIPUS (*his face brightening*):    Do not worry, my darling, you won't hear them again.  I am certain now that the Temple priests lied in the oracle they gave me.

JOCASTA:  What did the Temple priests tell you, Oedipus?

OEDIPUS:  It's an old lie.  It doesn't deserve repeating.

JOCASTA:  Tell me anyway. I don't want you to keep anything from me.

OEDIPUS:  I will tell you, so that you can laugh at it.  The High Priest claimed that Laius' child was not killed by the servant. Instead the servant gave him to a shepherd from Corinth, who in turn gave him to Polybus and Merope, and that I am that child.  Have you ever heard a lie more foolish than this?

JOCASTA:  But you have never told me about this before!

OEDIPUS:  Why would I tell you such a thing?  I wouldn't have told you about those lies now if you didn't insist.  I wish all those deceived by the priests could hear this.  Then they would know the truth about what they believe in.  Darling, you look concerned, what is wrong?

JOCASTA:  Now you frighten me even more, Oedipus!

OEDIPUS:  Oh, Jocasta!  Do you believe those lies?

JOCASTA:  No, Oedipus.  But I am worried that the High Priest would mention this and the people would believe him. Beware of angering the High Priest, darling.  You should change your plan completely.

OEDIPUS:  Oh, who would believe these enormous lies?

JOCASTA:  All of Thebes would believe them.

OEDIPUS (*sighing*):  Ah . . . I wish I knew who my parents are!
    Then I could prove to the people the lies of the priests by
    undeniable proof.  If my lineage were known, the priests
    wouldn't have dared make up such lies.  Oh, Jocasta, how
    miserable I am not knowing who my parents are!

JOCASTA:  Don't be disturbed, my sweet Oedipus.  I am sure your
    parents were noble people, or they wouldn't have given
    birth to such a noble person as you.

OEDIPUS:  Does it bother you, Jocasta, that you are married to a
    man who doesn't know his father or mother?

JOCASTA:  No, I swear by your precious life, and by how much I
    honor you, that this never occurred to me.  I am content to
    have married you, a king so handsome and generous, like
    no one else.  I'd sacrifice myself for you, Oedipus.

OEDIPUS:  Thank you, Jocasta darling.  Your love is my only
    solace, but I would still like to know who my parents are.

JOCASTA:  Do not wish to know something that fate decided to
    hide.  Who knows, maybe it is better that you don't know.

OEDIPUS:  Are you worried that it might be discovered that I am
    from a humble background that would not suit your noble
    birth?

JOCASTA:  God forbid, Oedipus!  Kind fate brought you to me, I
    married you, and loved you, and enjoyed you and having
    children together.  You are my lord and king, whatever your
    background is.

OEDIPUS:  So why do you want to deny me the desire to know my
    parents?

JOCASTA:  I don't want you to worry about something that doesn't matter at all.

OEDIPUS:  But it matters a great deal, Jocasta.  If I knew who my parents are then I could prove to all the people of Thebes and Hellas the lies of the priests they believe in.

(*Enter CREON, looking concerned as if is he bearing important news.*)

OEDIPUS:  What do you bring us, Creon?

CREON:  Important news, Oedipus.

OEDIPUS:  Maybe the Elders of Thebes did not like my response. Don't worry about them.  I know what I am doing.

CREON:  This is a more serious matter, Oedipus.  Tiresias came asking to meet you.

JOCASTA (*terrified*):  Tiresias.  The banished priest?

CREON:  Yes.

OEDIPUS:  Tiresias, the old priest the Temple expelled?

CREON:  Yes, him.

OEDIPUS:  Where is he? Let him come in.

JOCASTA:  No, Oedipus, don't let him in.  The Temple priests cursed him and banished him from Thebes.  How could you allow him in your palace?

OEDIPUS:  This makes me even more eager to welcome him.  If he were not a good man the priests wouldn't have banished him.  Let him in, Creon.

JOCASTA:  Oedipus!  Listen to me, Oedipus.  Do not let him in.  If the High Priest knew you allowed him into your palace, he would stir up the people against you.  I wonder how this cursed man dared to enter Thebes, and why the people didn't stone him to death.

CREON:  He came in disguise.  No one knows he is here but myself and the boy guiding him.

OEDIPUS:  Don't worry now, Jocasta.  No one will know about his presence in the palace.  Bring him in, Creon.

CREON:  He wants to meet you alone.  Be careful with him, he is not to be trusted.  (*He exits.*)

JOCASTA:  Don't meet him alone.  Let Creon stay with you.  He is blind.  He would not know.

OEDIPUS:  No, Jocasta, I would not deceive my guest.  And why are you so frightened of an old blind man?

JOCASTA:  He is terrifying.

OEDIPUS:  He won't be more terrifying than the Sphinx.

JOCASTA:  They say he is very cunning.

OEDIPUS:  Then I hope he can help me with his cunning.  I have longed to see the banished priest, and here he comes to me.

JOCASTA:  My heart tells me he brings evil.

OEDIPUS:  What terrifies you about him?  Do you know him, Jocasta?  Have you ever seen him before?

JOCASTA:  Yes.  I saw him when he came here after the priests cursed and banished him.  I heard him scream at Laius, so Laius ordered him out and banished him from the city. People followed him, screaming at him "The cursed! The cursed!" while he laughed like a mad man.  He looked so frightening, and his laughter was terrifying.

OEDIPUS (*jokingly*):  Is this what frightens you?  I don't think he came here to laugh.

JOCASTA:  His visit to the palace was a bad omen, after which disaster after disaster came upon us, till you arrived.  (*She looks at the first door and jumps up in terror.*)  Beware, here he comes.  (*whispering*)  Take care, Oedipus.

OEDIPUS (*smiling*):  Do not worry, Jocasta.

(*JOCASTA exits from third door.  Enter TIRESIAS led by CREON.*)

TIRESIAS:  Am I in the presence of his majesty King Oedipus?

CREON:  Yes.

TIRESIAS (*moving towards OEDIPUS as OEDIPUS stares at him*):  Blessings and greetings to you, great king.

OEDIPUS (*shaking hands with him*):  And the same to you, noble priest.

TIRESIAS (*looking pleased*):  Noble priest!  Then I had the right intuition about you!  I wish to stay in your palace, Oedipus.  If you allow me that, I can order my guide to leave.

OEDIPUS:  With pleasure, Tiresias.  (*He takes his hand and seats him.*)

TIRESIAS:  Thank you, Oedipus.  Would you allow me to speak to you alone?

OEDIPUS:  I grant you that.  (*He sits next to TIRESIAS.*)

TIRESIAS:  Would the honorable Creon tell my guide to leave?

OEDIPUS:  Tell him that, Creon.

CREON:  Of course, Oedipus.  (*He looks suspiciously then leaves from the first door.*)

TIRESIAS (*after a short silence*):  Excuse me, Oedipus.  As you know, I can't see who is around. Is there . . . ?

OEDIPUS:  Yes, say what you want.  There are only the two of us.

TIRESIAS:  Remember, Oedipus, that God is here listening to what we say.

OEDIPUS:  God!  Do you believe in this lie that the priests created to take people's money?  I thought that you'd know better than that, since they cursed and banished you, but you are still the same.

TIRESIAS:  Come, Oedipus.  No one denies God but an ignorant or a proud man.  I hope you are not either of those.

OEDIPUS:  I don't care if you call me this or that.  But leave my palace, and return from where you came.  I don't think you can do any good.

TIRESIAS:  Be careful, King.  Don't send me away until you hear what I have to say.

OEDIPUS:  What good can you do?  I have enough to worry about concerning myself and Thebes without listening to your lies.

TIRESIAS:  I am not like those priests, Oedipus!

OEDIPUS:  How so?  Don't you believe in God?

TIRESIAS:  Yes, and that is why they banished me from the Temple and cursed me.

OEDIPUS:  Beware, don't think I am feeble-minded like the mob, believing everything I hear.  If they really banished you, it must be because you wanted more than your share.

TIRESIAS:  No, Oedipus.  They expelled me because I was condemning their greed, and their love of money.  I am here today only to support your intention in appropriating the Temple's property, and confiscating its money to distribute it to the suffering people.

OEDIPUS:  Come now!  How did you know this is my intention? Who told you that?

TIRESIAS:  The High Priest already knows about your plans, and he is ready to resist.

OEDIPUS:  And how do you know?

TIRESIAS:  I have eyes in the main Temple and all the other temples.  They tell me about all the plotting and planning that takes place.

OEDIPUS:  This is a secret I confided only to the Queen and her brother Creon and told them not to reveal it.  How did it leak to the Temple?  Are you sure, Tiresias, that what you say is true?

TIRESIAS:  Isn't telling you enough proof for you?

OEDIPUS:  Yes, you are right, Tiresias.  I am the one to blame for entrusting others with such a secret.

TIRESIAS:  Maybe there is good in that.  It's the reason I decided to come to you.

OEDIPUS:  What good is your visit if the High Priest already knows about my plan, and is ready to resist it before I am ready to implement it?

TIRESIAS:  Do not worry, Oedipus, the priest will not be able to prevent you if you insist on your decision.  I am here, and won't leave, till you do what you planned, in spite of them, or I perish for this cause.

OEDIPUS (*seeming pleased*):  Then you are an atheist like me, Tiresias.  So why did you say earlier that you believe in God?

TIRESIAS:  I am a true believer.  I am not an atheist and you shouldn't be an atheist.  I am also here to return you to the flock of the believers.

OEDIPUS:  I only believe in my mind and my will.  So invite others to believe in your rash God that inspires his priests and temple keepers to evil-doing and sin.

TIRESIAS:  No, Oedipus.  The true God does not inspire evil, he inspires good deeds.

OEDIPUS:  Enough of this!  I don't like pointless arguing.  But tell me, is it a good deed for one to kill his own child?

TIRESIAS:  No, Oedipus.  This is a great evil and a great sin.

OEDIPUS:  Your God inspired that evil when his oracle told my predecessor Laius that he would have a child that would kill his father and marry his mother.  That made him get rid of his child.  Don't you know about that?

TIRESIAS:  Yes, Oedipus.  This is what I am here to clarify.

OEDIPUS:  Enough of that!  I don't need your clarification.  Only tell me, what do you think about this evil oracle?

TIRESIAS:  It is a false oracle, made up by the High Priest to force Laius to get rid of his child, so that he'd remain childless.

OEDIPUS:  What do you mean, a false oracle?  Not from God?

TIRESIAS:  The Wise God would not inspire such evil.  Attributing this falsehood to God is what I fought Lucasius about.  That made him expel me from the Temple and describe me as an atheist and nonbeliever.

OEDIPUS:  So what led him to make up this oracle?

TIRESIAS:  His greed for money.

OEDIPUS:  How?

TIRESIAS:  He received 20 thousand Obols from the king of Corinth.

OEDIPUS:  From Polybus?

TIRESIAS:  Yes.  He was the enemy of Laius and his rival for the rulership of Hellas.  He was worried that his opponent would have an heir while he didn't.

OEDIPUS:  I can't believe that Polybus, that good old man, would do such a thing.

TIRESIAS:  Polybus cannot be blamed.  He was only a king worrying that his kingdom would fall to his rival.  The blame rests on this charlatan priest who for the sake of money made up such a false oracle and claimed it was from God.

OEDIPUS (*after a short silence*):  Are you sure, Tiresias, that it was a false oracle?

TIRESIAS:  Of course.  I advised Laius then not to believe in it, but he didn't listen to me.  Instead he insulted me and banished me from Thebes.  He then continued to follow the advice of this charlatan priest until he pushed him to his death at the hands of the child he tried to get rid of.

OEDIPUS (*terrified*):  Come now!  How can you say it's a made-up oracle, and then claim that the one who killed Laius was his son?

TIRESIAS:  This is the responsibility of the High Priest.  He made up this oracle and then worked on fulfilling it, until it came true through his manipulations and cunning.

OEDIPUS (*in real horror*):  Came true!

TIRESIAS:  Yes.

OEDIPUS:  Curses!  What are you saying?  Do you mean that what the false oracle foretold did take place?

TIRESIAS:  Yes.

OEDIPUS:  Do you know the meaning of this "Yes" you are uttering?  Do you know what that means?

TIRESIAS:  Yes, Oedipus.

OEDIPUS (*furious*):  Yes!  Yes!  Don't you have anything else but this word?  Doesn't your accursed tongue know anything besides this accursed word?

TIRESIAS:  Don't curse my tongue, Oedipus; it never uttered anything but the truth.

OEDIPUS:  Then it deserves more curses.  I would have preferred that I were on your tongue instead of this accursed word, and be struck by lightning from the sky, and burn on your tongue before you uttered me.

TIRESIAS:  Mercy on you, Oedipus.  I am only trying to reveal to you this horrible matter to rescue you from the state you are in.

OEDIPUS:  What are you saying?  Do you think I believed you?  What  do you take me for?  Do you think I believe everything I hear?  Everything you have said is false.

TIRESIAS:  No, Oedipus, this is true, not false.

OEDIPUS:  I have evidence which proves to me that you are lying.

TIRESIAS:  No.  I am not a liar, Oedipus: I know nothing of lying.

OEDIPUS:  Then you are mistaken in what you claim you know. Don't deny that, too.  I don't want to accuse you of lying.  I am accusing you of being mistaken in believing what you thought was the truth without having any evil intention. Understand me, I know you had no evil intention.

TIRESIAS:  No, Oedipus.  I am not disillusioned or mistaken about the truth.

OEDIPUS:  Beware!  You don't know the terrible matter that lies behind your words.

TIRESIAS:  But I do know.

OEDIPUS:  Curse you, don't argue about what you don't know.  If you knew Laius' killer you wouldn't have said that.

TIRESIAS:  Yes, I know him, Oedipus, as well as you know him, and the High Priest knows him and Queen Jocasta too.

OEDIPUS:  Who is he?

TIRESIAS:  You!

OEDIPUS (*He is surprised for a moment, but then composes himself.*):  Now I know you.  I accuse you.  They sent you here to threaten me and warn me.  You all are very cunning. Yes.  I killed your king Laius.  I killed him and sat on his throne and married his wife.  Tell this to the people, I don't care.

TIRESIAS:  Oedipus!

OEDIPUS:  I will seize your Temple's money and property and distribute it to my people, even if the skies collapse on me.  I challenge all your gods to stop me from pursuing my plan.

TIRESIAS:  Oedipus!

OEDIPUS:  Go back to those who sent you, and spread the news
that I am the killer of Laius.  It won't stop me from doing
what I intended to do.

TIRESIAS:  Slow down, Oedipus.  I am here to support you in
pursuing your plan, so how can you accuse me of taking the
side of the Temple's priests against you?

OEDIPUS:  I am sure you are conspiring with them, and that they
told you what you said to me.

TIRESIAS:  Don't hurry to accuse me about what you don't know.
And let me rescue you from the sin this charlatan priest
pushed you into, a sin no man has ever committed before.

OEDIPUS:  Come now, what sin do you mean?

TIRESIAS:  That of killing your father and marrying your mother.

OEDIPUS:  This is the false oracle the High Priest gave me before.

TIRESIAS:  It is the truth, Oedipus.  It's true that Lucasius made
up this oracle, but then he worked with cunning and
planning to make it happen, until everything he predicted
took place.

OEDIPUS:  You, blind man, are making a huge claim.  If you don't
make it clear to me how Lucasius managed to do that, I will
add the darkness of your grave to the darkness of your eyes.

TIRESIAS (*angrily*):  You rogue!  You taunt me with my blindness?
Alas, the blind man is not the one who has lost his eyes, but
the one who has lost his vision.

OEDIPUS:  Stop that, and quickly tell me what I asked you to
explain.

TIRESIAS:  The blind man is the one who was blinded for
      seventeen years about the disgrace he has lived in, until the
      seer tells him about it.  Then he becomes arrogant and says
      you are the blind one and I can see.

OEDIPUS:  Hurry, curse you!  I feel the earth is shaking
      underneath me and as if its mountains are falling on me.
      Hurry, before I pounce on you and destroy you.  The devils
      of evil are moving from my heart to my body and are about
      to move my body to attack you.

TIRESIAS:  Control your anger, Oedipus.  You will not understand
      with anger.

OEDIPUS:  Tell me!  How did the High Priest manage to do what
      you say he did?

TIRESIAS:  I will explain it to you step by step.

OEDIPUS:  No, tell me everything.

TIRESIAS:  Do not be in a hurry, Oedipus.  Soon you will know
      everything.  Lucasius invented this oracle for Laius.

OEDIPUS:  Yes, I know that.

TIRESIAS:  Laius gave his child to a shepherd to kill him in the
      wilderness.

OEDIPUS:  I know that too.

TIRESIAS:  The High Priest convinced the shepherd not to kill him,
      but to give him to a shepherd from Corinth.

OEDIPUS:  Then what?

TIRESIAS:  The High Priest convinced that shepherd to give him to
      Polybus.

OEDIPUS:  Ah, and then what?

TIRESIAS:  Polybus adopted him and he grew up thinking he was Polybus' son.

OEDIPUS:  Then what?  Hurry, curse you!

TIRESIAS:  Then the High Priest inspired Pontus . . .

OEDIPUS (*very troubled*):  Who is Pontus?

TIRESIAS:  Did you forget him, Oedipus?  Did you forget that man who angered you while you were drinking and insulted your lineage so that you were forced to consult the oracle of Delphi?

OEDIPUS:  Yes.  Now I remember him.  Oh, calamity!  Then what?

TIRESIAS:  The High Priest told you that you are the son of Laius and Jocasta, and that you would kill your father and marry your mother.

OEDIPUS:  Yes.  That's true.  But how did you know?

TIRESIAS:  Didn't I tell you before that I have eyes in the Temple, who tell me everything?  I know every word the High Priest told you.

OEDIPUS:  So tell me, what did he do after that?

TIRESIAS:  He went to you to warn you against going to Thebes, to tempt you to go.

OEDIPUS:  Tempt me?

TIRESIAS:  Yes, because he knows how stubborn you are.  So you went to Thebes to challenge the oracle, and gain your father's blessing, instead of killing him.

OEDIPUS:  Yes, that's true.

TIRESIAS:  But Laius met you on the way.  Do you know why he met you?

OEDIPUS:  No, I don't.  But Lucasius told me that Laius would do that.

TIRESIAS:  He sent someone to tell Laius how you survived and grew up in Polybus' palace, and that you were heading to Thebes to kill him, fulfilling the oracle.  He said that if he wanted to avoid that destiny he should meet you before you reached Thebes and kill you before you killed him.

OEDIPUS:  Calamity!  Now I know why Laius insisted on attacking me after I told him I was his son and that I wanted his blessing.

TIRESIAS:  So you went back to Corinth and were even more frightened that the second part of the oracle would come true.

OEDIPUS:  Yes, but I didn't believe in it at all.

TIRESIAS:  I know that.  You wanted to challenge the oracle, so the High Priest warned you against going to Thebes, or else you would marry your mother.

OEDIPUS:  I wish I had obeyed his orders that day.

TIRESIAS:  If you had obeyed him, you'd have disobeyed him.

OEDIPUS:  What do you mean?

TIRESIAS:  He only warned you to tempt you, like the first time.

OEDIPUS:  The damned priest.  Now I know why he was describing Jocasta's beauty, and warning me that if I saw her I would definitely fall in love with her.

TIRESIAS:  So that he would set in your heart the roots of what you fear, which would make it easy for you to succumb.

OEDIPUS:  Oh, I wish Laius' men had killed me where the road forks into three routes in Phocis, and used my bones to create a sign for the traveler.  I wish I had not killed the Sphinx, and that he had devoured me instead.  I wish someone else had killed him, to gain the accursed prize Thebes had decided on.

TIRESIAS:  That would not have been possible, Oedipus.  The prize was planned for you and you alone.

OEDIPUS:  How?

TIRESIAS:  The High Priest suggested to Creon to announce that prize for the one who would rescue Thebes from the Sphinx, because he knew that no one would conquer the Sphinx but you.

OEDIPUS:  How did he know that I would be the one to kill the Sphinx?

TIRESIAS:  You didn't kill him, Oedipus.

OEDIPUS:  What are you saying, Tiresias?  How can you deny what everyone knows?

TIRESIAS:  I have explained to you, Oedipus, things that the people don't know.  The truth is not proven by people's knowledge or denied because they don't know it.

OEDIPUS:  Curse you, do you deny that I rescued Thebes from that monster that was attacking people at the gates of the city and devouring them if they couldn't solve his riddles?

TIRESIAS:  This monster doesn't exist at all, Oedipus.  It was a creation of the priests, hiding one of them inside it to move it and speak the riddle.

OEDIPUS:  But he was devouring those who didn't solve his
　　　　riddle.

TIRESIAS:  The priests spread this news, to scare the people.  So
　　　　when someone met the Sphinx they'd faint from fear, and
　　　　the priest inside would kill that person.

OEDIPUS:  But when I solved his riddle, he fell dead.

TIRESIAS:  He dropped down as his superior ordered him to.  The
　　　　High Priest ordered him to die when he met you, and he
　　　　obeyed so that you would get the prize and earn the throne
　　　　and marry . . .

OEDIPUS (*crying out*):  My mother.  Ah!  Ah!  Oedipus is cursed
　　　　for eternity.  (*He jumps from his seat like a madman, pulling out
　　　　his hair and his beard.*)  People of Thebes, kill me.  Oh skies,
　　　　fall on me!  Oh Gods, curse me!  Snakes of the earth, come
　　　　out of your caves, curl around me and eat me alive!  Oh
　　　　hungry beasts that live on rotten meat, run to me, I am the
　　　　most rotten ever.  (*He beats his chest and head with both hands
　　　　and cries out.*)  Woe!  Woe!  Woe!  I am the cat of Corinth
　　　　that bit his father and attacked his mother.  The cat of
　　　　Merope who took his mother from his father.  Kill me.  Kill
　　　　the cursed cat.  Rip him apart.  Rip him apart.

(*CREON enters from the first door, JOCASTA from the second door, and
Oedipus' four CHILDREN followed by the chambermaid TIMONE rush
in from the third door.*)

JOCASTA:  What's wrong, Oedipus?

CREON:  What has happened to you?

OEDIPUS (*looking at JOCASTA with fear, and hiding behind
　　　　TIRESIAS*):  Help me, Tiresias.  Help me.  (*He faints on the
　　　　floor next to TIRESIAS.*)

JOCASTA (*throwing herself on OEDIPUS*):  Oedipus!  Oedipus!  My darling Oedipus.  My husband!  My lord!

(*OEDIPUS doesn't answer.*)

THE CHILDREN:  Father!  Father!  Answer, Father!  What's wrong
    with him, Mother?

JOCASTA:  This cursed priest did that to him.  Alas!  What did you
    do to him, you accursed priest?  What did you do to my
    husband?  What did you do to the king?

TIRESIAS:  Be calm, Jocasta, he is all right now.  He was asleep and
    he woke up.

JOCASTA (*angrily*):  He is all right now?  Curse you, you hurt him,
    then mock him.

TIRESIAS:  No, Jocasta, I didn't hurt him and I don't mock him.

JOCASTA (*scolding him*):  What did you do then?  (*She turns to
    CREON*)  Why are you standing there so quietly?  Did you
    see what he did?  Did you hear what he said?

CREON:  What do you want me to do, sister?

JOCASTA:  Kill him, Creon.  Kill him.  If you can't kill him, expel
    him from here.

CREON:  I can't do this without the orders of the king.

JOCASTA:  Oh!  I told you not to let him into the palace, and you
    didn't listen to me.  (*Shaking OEDIPUS*)  Oedipus!  Oedipus!
    Oh my husband.  Oh my beloved!

CREON:  What did you do to him, Tiresias?  What's happening to
    Oedipus?

TIRESIAS:  He is all right, Creon.  He just fainted.  Take him to his
    bed; he will wake up soon.

(*CREON carries OEDIPUS.  JOCASTA and TIMON help him as the curtain begins to slowly descend.*)

TIRESIAS:  Poor Oedipus.  He moved with open eyes when he was asleep; when he woke up he closed his eyes.

## Curtain

## Scene Two

*Scene: Same place*

*Time: Noon the following day*

*As the curtain goes up, TIRESIAS is sitting in the same place. OEDIPUS is sitting next to him, collapsed, his face full of sadness.*

TIRESIAS:  Hold on, Oedipus.   However great the crisis is, there are people who can deal with it.  These are the heroes, Oedipus.  The bigger the troubles they deal with, the greater their nobility and heroism.

OEDIPUS (*seemingly distracted from what TIRESIAS is saying*): What a horrifying truth!  Ah!  Did all of that really take place?  How could I be alive after that?  Why was I not struck by lightning strong enough to have broken a mountain?

TIRESIAS:  There are men, Oedipus, who have hearts that are stronger and mightier than mountains.

OEDIPUS (*leaving his seat, dazed, and walking back and forth*):  Ah!  Why did I wake up yesterday?  I wish it were the end of me.  I wish I could sleep forever, so that my eyes would never see this light full of sin, and my lungs would not breathe this air reeking with sins and filth.  (*He begins to shake and moves backward as if he is seeing something terrible in front of him.*)  But then I would be on the other side, where my father is.  How would I face him?  Oh!  Miserable me!  Even the door that those who can't face life head towards is closed to me.

TIRESIAS:  Stop it, Oedipus.  Never contemplate suicide.  That adds more sin to those you have already committed.

OEDIPUS:  If my fear were only of committing a sin, I would have done it.  There is nothing that could worsen my sin.  It's my embarrassment at meeting my father after I took his place in my mother's bed.  What a rejected outcast I am, expelled from this world and not accepted in the next!  What a miserable ostracized creature!  I am stretched out on the rack.  I cannot stay and I cannot leave.

TIRESIAS:  Mercy on you, Oedipus.  I don't know which is greater; your sin or your misery.

OEDIPUS:  Let's not go into that, Tiresias.  Just tell me how to get out of this?  Where can I go and what can I do?  Will you help me find a way out?  Help me find the path? (*He moves closer to TIRESIAS.*)  Tell me, Tiresias, by the God that you believe in, who gave you your knowledge and wisdom, is there in His vast kingdom a third place for those who can't live in the world of the living, and are terrified of moving to the world of the dead?

TIRESIAS:  Come now, Oedipus, the Universe has only those two dwellings: the dwellings of the living and the dwellings of the dead, the place of work and the place of reward.

OEDIPUS:  Oh, what a pity for me!  If it occurred to that God in His eternity that there would be a poor person like me for whom there is no place in either world, He might have created a third place, Tiresias.  Ah!  My calamity is greater and mightier than your God could have imagined.

TIRESIAS:  Oedipus, don't return to atheism after you found your way to faith.

OEDIPUS:  This is not atheism, Tiresias, I am not blaming your God, I am trying to find excuses for Him.

TIRESIAS:  That is atheism, Oedipus!  Humans shouldn't blame
God or excuse Him.  You can only excuse those whom you
can blame.

OEDIPUS (*rubbing his forehead as if looking for an answer to a
problem*):  Shh!  I have found it, Tiresias.  I have found the
answer.  I'll pluck my eyes out, to live the rest of my life
without seeing this existence that was stained by my shame,
making it filthier than the stables.  And if I die and go to the
world of the dead I won't see the face of Laius, and the
sneering faces of those around him, pointing to him and me.

TIRESIAS:  Beware, Oedipus, beware of extinguishing the light that
was given to you to find your path.

OEDIPUS:  This light did not lead me to my path; it diverted me
from it.

TIRESIAS:  No, Oedipus, don't do it.  As you see, I am deprived of
this blessing, and no one can tell you the value of something
like the one who is deprived of it.

OEDIPUS:  This blessing was damnation to me.

TIRESIAS:  How dare you, Oedipus?  You kept your eyes when
you were rolling in sin and filth, and now you want to pluck
them out when it is time to use them to repent your
sins, and cleanse Thebes from its corruption, and save its
people from this torture.  No, Oedipus, today your eyes are
not yours alone; they belong to the people.

OEDIPUS:  What would a miserable king do for this miserable
people?  What good is left in me?

TIRESIAS:  Not so fast, Oedipus.  The people have never needed
you more than today, and you were never in a better
position to serve them than you are now.

OEDIPUS:  And the misery I am in?

TIRESIAS:  Calm down, Oedipus.  For every problem there is a
solution.

OEDIPUS:  How dare you!  The earth is shaking beneath me, the
skies are about to collapse on me, and you sit here telling me
to be calm!

TIRESIAS:  Do not worry, you won't have to face more than what
you have already faced.  The deep agony in your heart that
stirs up every drop in your blood is proof that God will have
mercy on you and accept your repentance.

OEDIPUS:  God will have mercy on me.  Don't push me to an
atheism worse than my previous one.  Where was your God
when He let that criminal priest commit all those sins and
inflict disasters on me and my family?  Did He exist then or
not?

TIRESIAS:  Oedipus, respect your God, and do not say that about
Him.

OEDIPUS:  How dare you, Tiresias?  Do you deny the one who
suffered injustice a few words to ease his suffering, while
you don't blame the One who inflicted him with pain,
pouring it on his head and the heads of his family?

TIRESIAS:  The one who was unjust to you is the High Priest, but
you also did yourself injustice, Oedipus.  God does not
inflict injustice on anyone; people do that to themselves.

OEDIPUS:  I can't absolve the One who could have relieved me
from injustice but did not.

TIRESIAS:  Slow down, Oedipus, and consider what I am saying.
If what you say were true, it would not have been a matter
of justice or injustice.  There would have been no sin, no
charity, no aggression.  But the wise God, whose wisdom

can't be fathomed by anyone else, created good and evil. And He gave us the mind to discriminate between them, and the will to choose which one to follow so that He can reward us for our good deeds.

OEDIPUS: Didn't this wise God know that the evil priest would commit such crimes?

TIRESIAS: Yes, Oedipus.

OEDIPUS: So how could the priest have avoided what he was destined to do?

TIRESIAS: You are defending the criminal with arguments he would not dare use to defend himself. I swear that if you asked him whether he felt that he was pushed to do what he did or whether he did it out of his free will, he would answer you—if he answers honestly—that he had the choice. So how can you, Oedipus, deny him the responsibility for his crime and lay the responsibility on God?

OEDIPUS: How about me, Tiresias? How can you say I did myself injustice? What is my guilt in what happened? The net was placed around me when I was a fetus in my mother's womb; then the traps were set in my path, without me seeing them or knowing who set them, or even that they were there, so I fell in one trap after the other until all of this happened. So what is my guilt? What is my guilt?

TIRESIAS: Oedipus, you cannot deny that God gave you a mind and a will.

OEDIPUS: What use is my mind or will? How could I have avoided what I didn't know about—this sophisticated plan to make me come to Thebes, take its throne, and marry its widowed queen?

TIRESIAS: You could have, actually should have told the people the truth about yourself. You could have said that the High

Priest claimed such and such, but you didn't know much about your lineage. You could have said "So what do you say, people of Thebes? You agreed that I become your king, and gave me the right to marry the widowed queen. There is nothing to stop me from accepting the throne, but I cannot marry the queen until I know for sure that I am not Laius' child who was given away to be murdered. You, people of Thebes, look into that matter and bring me all the witnesses you can find."

OEDIPUS: Have mercy on me, Tiresias. Your words are like butchers' knives cutting through my body. Wouldn't the people of Thebes have killed me if they knew I killed their king Laius?

TIRESIAS: Stop, Oedipus. Isn't that less serious than committing this great sin, the sin of violating your mother's honor?

OEDIPUS: Yes, Tiresias, yes. I wish they had killed me that day, and stained the palace square with my blood, and scattered my body in Thebes, before I committed that terrible transgression.

TIRESIAS: No, Oedipus, you could have avoided that destiny. You could have defended yourself and said that you came seeking peace and good, but Laius and his men attacked you, so you did what you did without prior intention. The people of Thebes wouldn't have killed you that day, because your father attacked you, and especially since you saved them, as they believe, from the monster who was killing them.

OEDIPUS: Oh! I wish I had done what you say, that day. But believe me, Tiresias, I was not able to do that.

TIRESIAS: I ask you by God who knows all secrets, didn't you know then that you were able to do it?

OEDIPUS: Yes, Tiresias. By the God that you made me swear by, I

tried that day to do some of what you said, but the palace
servants surrounded me, one washing me, another
perfuming me, a third combing my hair, a fourth dressing
me with luxurious clothes, each of them singing the praises
of the queen's looks.  The beauties of my mother, Tiresias!
Ah, I wish their mouths were filled with the wild bees that
roam the mountains . . . (*his breath growing faster*)  Then I was
taken to her, a beautiful maiden, as if she were still a virgin,
and any trace of a possibility that she could be my mother
was erased from my heart.  I only saw a vision of Merope as
if blaming me by saying, "Would you marry this beautiful
maiden without inviting me to your wedding?"  Ah!  How
could I have found a way out, Tiresias?

TIRESIAS:  One often deceives oneself, Oedipus.

OEDIPUS:  Have mercy one me, Tiresias.  Do not blame me for the
trap that was so well planned for me to fall in.  Do you want
me to carry the guilt for this crime, and not the ones who
pushed me into it?

TIRESIAS:  No, Oedipus.  I told you that most of the guilt falls on
the sinful Priests, and only some of it is yours.

OEDIPUS:  Some of it!  This "some" is enough to make me feel that
I am the most sinful person ever born.  No, that won't heal
my soul, Tiresias, I want you to tell me that I am not
responsible at all for what happened.

TIRESIAS:  Stop it, Oedipus.  This is not in my hands.  God alone
is the one who would judge you.  He is the one who knows
what's in people's hearts.  Sin has ways that are lighter than
illusion and deeper than secrets.  Only God, the knower of
the unknown, can understand it.

OEDIPUS:  Oh calamity!  Oh helpless me!  Oh, Oedipus!  Oh,
Jocasta!

TIRESIAS:  Don't forget, Oedipus, that the doors of repentance are
open before you.

OEDIPUS:  What shall I do?  What shall we do?

TIRESIAS:  You and your mother should get out of the position
   you are in now, and repent to God, the merciful, who
   accepts repentance.

(*ANTIGONE appears from the second door.*)

OEDIPUS (*wiping his eyes with his sleeves*):  Antigone!  Come in,
   Antigone!

(*ANTIGONE beckons to him to come closer to her, while looking at
TIRESIAS in fear.*)

OEDIPUS:  What is the matter?  (*He gets up and goes to her.*)

(*ANTIGONE whispers in his ear while pointing to TIRESIAS.
OEDIPUS answers her in whispers, shaking his head and comforting her.
He kisses her compassionately on the cheek.  She kisses his head and runs
back inside.  The smile disappears from his face as he sees his daughter
leave, then he walks to where TIRESIAS is.*)

OEDIPUS (*muttering*)  What is her crime?  These innocent children,
   what is their crime?

TIRESIAS:  Did your daughter leave, Oedipus?

OEDIPUS:  Yes.  Tell me, Tiresias, what is the crime of these
   children?

TIRESIAS:  They have committed no crime.

OEDIPUS (*sighing*):  So why should my shame follow them all their
   lives, so that they can't hold up their heads in front of
   people?

TIRESIAS:  This is the rule of life, Oedipus.  You transgress against
   me one day, but you don't transgress against me alone, and

you are good to me another day, then you are good to others along with me. This is not injustice, Oedipus. A good deed and a bad deed in the earthly scales is reflected in the heavenly scales. Look at the crime the High Priest committed against you and others.

OEDIPUS: Yes, Tiresias. But what do I have to do with this sinful priest? Consider what will happen to my children if I confess to the people that their mother is no longer my wife, that she is my mother? How could we face the people with such a scandal, Tiresias?

TIRESIAS: There is no other way, Oedipus. The penance should be as great as the sin.

OEDIPUS: Can't we cover it up, Tiresias, and live in the palace as if we were husband and wife in front of the people, and mother and son in the eyes of God?

TIRESIAS: The priests won't let you. They will tell the people of Thebes to turn them against you, unless you follow their will and stop confiscating the Temple's money.

OEDIPUS: So what can I do, Tiresias?

TIRESIAS: Continue with your plan, and don't worry about them. It is better to anger the priests than to anger God. And this scandal you are worrying about would be the penance for you and your mother.

OEDIPUS: And Jocasta, how would I tell her this terrible truth? How could I tell her that she is my mother, and I am her son, her children are my children and my siblings, and she is their mother and grandmother?

TIRESIAS: There is no way out, Oedipus. Every moment that passes without you telling her this truth, you are a sinner content with your indulgence and sin.

OEDIPUS:  How would she feel if she knew about this horrible matter?

TIRESIAS:  She would be no worse off then than now, not knowing that she is letting her son take the place of his father in her bed.

OEDIPUS:  What a disgrace!  What a horrid sin!

TIRESIAS:  Would you prefer that you hadn't known about this truth,  and continued to sleep with your mother and have a fifth and a sixth child with her?

OEDIPUS:  Stop!  How dare you!  The sound of the hissing snakes of hell is easier to hear than what you are saying!

TIRESIAS:  And the entwining of those snakes around you and your mother is less horrifying than the sin you are dwelling in.

OEDIPUS:  You are right, Tiresias, and I was hoping you were not. I will tell Jocasta now, and whatever will be will be.  May all the snakes of hell curl around me, and dig their black fangs into my mouth and nose.  May all the lions of the earth rip me apart with their teeth, and the eagles tear off my head, and pluck my eyes out with their beaks.  May the heavens rain their thunderbolts on my head, and all the gods heap their anger upon me!  All of this would not stop me from telling Jocasta about the sin we have been living in.

TIRESIAS:  May you be blessed, Oedipus.  Now my heart is comforted, knowing that Thebes will be freed from this plague.  You will have victory over those lying priests, and will cleanse the Temple from their sins, and God will cover you with His mercy and forgiveness.

(*Loud noises are heard outside the palace, sounding like a group of people entering.*)

OEDIPUS:  What is this noise?  (*He looks out from the balcony.*)
There are a group of people coming towards us, I wonder
what they want?

(*CREON enters from the first door.*)

CREON:  The people of Thebes are here, Oedipus, led by the elders
of Thebes.

OEDIPUS:  What do they want?  Did they know that Tiresias is in
here?

CREON:  How would they know, Oedipus?  This is a secret only
we know.

OEDIPUS (*in a reproachful voice*):  Maybe this news reached them
the same way the High Priest knew I am planning to
confiscate the Temple's money.

CREON:  Oh God!  Did he know about that?

OEDIPUS:  Yes, and he is already planning to resist and plot
against me.

CREON:  He must have known through the Oracle.

OEDIPUS (*sarcastically*):  The Oracle!  The Oracle is your answer to
everything.  Can't you suspect your Temple and priests for
once?

CREON (*suppressing his anger*):  Oedipus, remember our pact; you
leave me to my beliefs and I leave you to yours.

OEDIPUS (*after a short silence*):  So what is wrong with those
people?  What brought them here?

CREON:  They came to plead with you to send me to the Temple
of Delphi to ask its assistance in dealing with this plague
that ruined everything in our land, dropped the fetuses from

pregnant women, and prevented the living from burying their dead.  May God relieve us from it.

OEDIPUS:  Curse you, didn't you tell them what I ordered you to say?

CREON:  They didn't like my answer, Oedipus.  They agreed that the only way out of this suffering is to consult the Temple.

OEDIPUS:  Let them dwell in their darkness.  I know my way.

TIRESIAS:  No, Oedipus.  It is wise to respond to their demands today, until you have a chance to implement your plan.

OEDIPUS:  Is this your advice, Tiresias?

TIRESIAS:  Yes, and it might be better if you tell them that yourself.

CREON:  Yes, that's better, Oedipus.

(*OEDIPUS moves to the balcony overlooking the people.*)

PEOPLE (*outside*):  Help, Oedipus!   You who saved us from the Sphinx, rescue us from this torture.

OEDIPUS:  Beloved people of Thebes, I will respond to your demands, and send Creon to consult the Temple of Delphi.

PEOPLE (*from outside*):  Long live Oedipus!  May the Gods protect you, Oedipus!  May you reign long, Oedipus!

OEDIPUS (*returning from the balcony*):  Creon, get ready to go to the Temple of Delphi.

CREON (*looking happy*):  I hear and obey, Oedipus.  Now you have calmed my soul.

OEDIPUS (*taking TIRESIAS' hand*):  Let me take you to your room, Tiresias.  No one should see you here.

TIRESIAS:  Thank you, Oedipus.

(*OEDIPUS leads him out of the third door.  JOCASTA appears from the second door, checking the room before she enters.*)

JOCASTA:  Creon!

CREON (*turning to her*):  Jocasta!

JOCASTA:  What is this, brother?  What am I hearing?

CREON (*cheerfully*):  Be comforted, Jocasta.  Your husband is responding to the people's demand and is sending me to the Temple of Delphi.

JOCASTA:  Would you leave me alone, Creon?

CREON:  What worries you, sister?

JOCASTA:  Didn't you see what happened to Oedipus yesterday?

CREON:  That was the result of his troubled thoughts and lack of sleep because of this problem.  Now he is sending me to consult the Temple, so calm down, Jocasta, he will not feel that way again.

JOCASTA:  How can I calm down while this cursed priest is here in the palace?

CREON:  Don't be angry at him, sister.  It was his advice that made Oedipus respond to the wishes of the people.

JOCASTA:   I am afraid, Creon.

CREON:  Come, my sister, what are you afraid of?

JOCASTA:  Of everything . . . of the oracle you will bring, of this Tiresias, and of Oedipus.

CREON (*surprised*):  Of Oedipus?

JOCASTA:  Yes, he looks at me strangely.

CREON:  What are you saying, Jocasta?

JOCASTA:  As if he couldn't bear to look at my face.

CREON:  You are imagining this, Jocasta.

JOCASTA:  No, my brother.  This is not my imagination.

CREON:  I think I know the reason.  Oedipus learned today that the High Priest knows about his intentions to confiscate the Temple's property, and he thinks one of us must have revealed that secret, since he doesn't believe in the Oracle, as you know.  This must be the reason he was looking at you in a different way, because he is blaming you.

JOCASTA:  No, Creon.  I know my husband, when he is happy and when he is suspicious.  This is neither.  This is something strange I have never experienced before.

CREON:  If you had remained faithful to the Temple, and not followed your husband's atheism, you would have the peace of mind that would protect you from these worries.

JOCASTA:  Come now, Creon.  The Temple is the source of my fears.  How can I believe in it when it is what threatens my happiness and the happiness of my husband and children?  If you meet the High Priest, Creon, tell him Jocasta begs him to hold his wrath and she promises him that she will try to convince Oedipus not to do what could anger him.  Promise me, Creon, that you will give him my message.

CREON:  It will be my pleasure and my honor, Jocasta.  I wish you could really convince Oedipus to reconsider his plan.

JOCASTA:  Tell him also that we haven't been sending offerings and sacrifices because the Treasury is empty, and once these hard times are over we will continue our customary offerings.

CREON:  I will tell him that, Jocasta.  Goodbye, my sister.  Don't become trapped by your illusions and worries.  (*He embraces her and then exits.*)

JOCASTA (*standing alone, confused*):  What oracle will you bring us back, Creon!

(*OEDIPUS appears at the third door, hesitating to enter.  He then gains more courage and enters from behind JOCASTA.*)

JOCASTA (*feeling his presence and turning to him*):  Oedipus!

OEDIPUS (*in a trembling voice*):  Jocasta . . .  My mother!

JOCASTA:  Your mother!  What about her, darling?  What about your mother?

OEDIPUS (*lowering his voice, mumbling*):  I miss seeing her, Jocasta.

JOCASTA:   I don't think she misses seeing you, or she would have visited us, at least once.  You invited her often, and she never came.

OEDIPUS:  Who do you mean, Jocasta?

JOCASTA:  I mean your mother, Merope.

OEDIPUS:  You are aware that Merope is not my mother.  You are, aren't you?

JOCASTA (*in horror*):  What, Oedipus?  I am what?

OEDIPUS (*stammering*):  You are . . . you are aware of that, Jocasta!

JOCASTA (*sighing in relief*):  Yes, of course I am.  I wish I knew her.  I would love her as I love you, darling.  I love her now, even without knowing her, Oedipus.  I can picture her in my mind.  She is beautiful and noble.  She is fair, with some gray hairs that make her look even more beautiful and dignified.

OEDIPUS:  No, Jocasta.  She is still young, with no gray hairs.

JOCASTA:  Do you think she still is, my darling?  It's possible, if you are her first child.

OEDIPUS:  Yes, I am her first child, Jocasta.  She married my father before her first period, and soon after she was pregnant with me.

JOCASTA:  Come now, my darling, what are you saying?  You knew about your parents and never told me all those years?  Did you worry that if you told me about them it might change my love for you?  No, I swear to you on your precious head and clear vision that it wouldn't change, even if they were shepherds in the mountains.  Tell me everything now, darling, and don't worry about a thing.

OEDIPUS:  I can't tell you, Jocasta.  Every time I try, I become tongue-tied.

JOCASTA (*tenderly*):  Come now, my darling.  Then you can keep it a secret if you like, for as long as you want.  I only care about you, and your happiness.  You are my husband, and the father of my children, and I am happy and proud of you and of them.  You and the children are all that I have.

OEDIPUS (*touched by her tenderness, but not giving in*):  Where are they now, Jocasta?

JOCASTA (*happily*):  In the garden playing.

OEDIPUS (*as if talking to himself*):  My poor children!  They are playing in the garden, unaware of what threatens Thebes and their father.

JOCASTA:  You didn't see them today, Oedipus.  Even when I sent Antigone to check on you, she returned quickly.  I will call them now.  May their presence lighten your mood. (*She leaves hurriedly from the middle door.*)

OEDIPUS (*alone*):  Oh!  I could not tell her the truth.  (*Throwing himself on the chair*)  It is as if something stops me.  Am I deceiving myself?  Tiresias told me "One often deceives oneself."  But, no, no.  I really want to repent, and I cannot accept this sin one more moment.  So why couldn't I tell her?  "Every moment that passes without telling her makes you a sinner who accepts his sin and evil doing."  This is what Tiresias told me.  But he did not tell me how to break the news to her.  How?  How?  Oh, calamity!  Is it predestined that I will not ever tell Jocasta?  (*He jumps to his feet.*)  No!  I don't think that is possible.  Yes . . . Yes . . . today, now.  This hour I must choose!  I can tell her, or not. So which one is destined?  If I tell her, then this is destined, and if I don't tell, then that is destined.  But I don't know now.  I don't know which is destined.  No, I do know. Destiny is in my own hands!  I can make it yes, or no.  I will tell her the truth, and make that destiny.  I shall tell Jocasta this hour "you are my mother.  You, Jocasta, are my mother, the mother who gave birth to me from the seed of Laius." (*He goes to the second door,  calling in anguish.*)  Jocasta! Jocasta!

JOCASTA (*her voice approaching*):  Yes, Oedipus.  I brought the children.

OEDIPUS: (*He moves back until he falls on his chair, looking at the heavens.*)  You great and powerful God, give me some of Your power!

(*JOCASTA enters with ISMENE and ETEOCLES in front of her, and POLYNICES and ANTIGONE behind her.  OEDIPUS opens his arms to embrace them, with tears in his eyes and a smile on his lips.*)

OEDIPUS:  Come to me, my children, come to me, my little precious ones.  (*They throw themselves in his arms; he showers them with hugs and kisses.*)  I missed you.  It's as if I haven't seen you in years.  Where have you been?

CHILDREN (*in one voice*):  Playing in the garden.

OEDIPUS (*in a playful tone*):  You naughty children!  Why didn't you even say good morning to me?

ISMENE:  The terrifying blind man was here.

POLYNICES:  When will he leave?

ETEOCLES:  Why don't you throw him out of the palace, father?  If you wish I can throw him out for you!

ANTIGONE (*scolding them*):  Stop it!  You have no business with him.  Don't you know he is your father's guest?

OEDIPUS (*embracing her*):  Do you like him, Antigone?  So why were you frightened of him earlier?

ANTIGONE:  No father, I don't like him.  But if you want him here, we all want him.

ISMENE:  No, we don't like him and we don't want him.

ETEOCLES:  Yes, don't like him, don't want him.

POLYNICES:  Mum too doesn't like him and doesn't want him.

ANTIGONE:  Now, shut up!

ISMENE AND ETEOCLES:  You shut up!

JOCASTA (*laughing*):  Come now, children, do not fight in front of your father.  (*To OEDIPUS*)  They do not like him, Oedipus, because he has taken you away from them . . . and from me.

OEDIPUS (*looking at her tenderly and with compassion*):  It's all right, Jocasta.

POLYNICES:  Yes, father!  Whenever we want to see you, Timone says you are busy.

OEDIPUS (*gathering his children in his arms*):  No, my darlings, nothing would take me away from you.

JOCASTA (*overwhelmed by tenderness, leans over his head and kisses it and touches him with her hands, as if she had found a valuable thing she was about to lose*):  Oedipus!

OEDIPUS (*touching her without looking at her*):  Jocasta!

### Curtain

## Act Two

## Scene One

*Same scene as Act I*

*Time: Before dawn. It is quiet in the palace, everyone is asleep.*

*As the curtain rises, JOCASTA is standing confused with a candle in her hand.*

JOCASTA:  Oh, me, what should I say to him?  How do I open a conversation with him?  Should I warn him, or ask for his sympathy?  My anger at him tempts me to be violent with him, and yet I wish to be gentle, in order to get what I want from him.  But time is short and there is a lot to say.  I wish I had two tongues to tell him both desires of my heart at the same time.  Ah, me!  It seems to me that all that I had in my mind is gone. (*A scream is heard from a distance.*)  What do I hear?  It is Thebes wailing for its dead.  Night and day they are dying, night and day they weep and wail.  You restless plague that never closes its eyes, are you like me?  Has your beloved deserted you, and this keeps you awake at night?  What is this desolate silence?  I feel the wind of death in this hall.  And this sad candle reminds me of the night my mother was dying and we were gathered with candles around her.  What do I tell Tiresias?  Oh, dear!  I am anxious and terrified.  When he approaches me in this dark hour, it will be like the ghost of Laius coming out of his grave to say to me: How dare you, Jocasta!  How could you marry the person you know has killed me? (*She moves towards the second door as if she is going out, but she does not.*)  No, Jocasta, this is a chance that might not come back.  What terrifies you about him?  What is behind him is even worse and more terrifying.  Remember you are the Queen of Thebes, and he is only an outcast priest. (*She moves back to the middle of the hall.*)

(*TIRESIAS enters from the third door led by TIMONE.*)

TIMONE:  Here is her majesty the Queen.

TIRESIAS:  Hail Queen!

JOCASTA:  Have him sit by you, Timone, then stand by your
    Lord's door, and let me know when he wakes up.

TIMONE:  I hear and obey, your majesty.  (*She seats TIRESIAS on
    the chair and leaves from the third door.*)

TIRESIAS:  You asked for me, Jocasta?  I hope you have realized
    my sincerity and are willing to welcome me.

JOCASTA (*moving towards him*):  No, I won't welcome you until
    you make right what you ruined.

TIRESIAS:  I am here to make right what others ruined.

JOCASTA:  You are the one who ruined it for us.  We were living
    in happiness and bliss before you came to our palace and
    you turned it to a hell.  You turned my husband against me,
    and made him desert my bed, and believe in this myth that
    he often rejected before your arrival.

TIRESIAS:  But it is not a myth, Jocasta, it's the truth.  Oedipus
    rejected it before, but now he accepts it, since he has seen
    proof.

JOCASTA:  It is false!  You made it up, just as your friend the High
    Priest made up that senseless oracle.  You priests are all
    lairs.  Your only interest is hurting people, ruining their
    lives, and demolishing their happiness with the lies that you
    make up.

TIRESIAS:  My Lady, if you considered a little you would have
    realized that I did not make up anything.  Oedipus knows it
    is true because he experienced it himself.  I only showed him

how the High Priest manipulated the situation, to save you from the sin you live in, and to save Thebes and its people from the priests' manipulation of religion and their misleading of the people.

JOCASTA:  How dare you!  They will stir up the people against Oedipus and me and announce our scandal in front of everyone.

TIRESIAS:  It's their scandal before it is yours.  Let them announce it if they wish, but then the evidence would be against them and we would win.

JOCASTA:  What would we gain if they are exposed after we are ruined?  Do you want to drown us in order to drown the priests?

TIRESIAS:  There is no way out of this harsh penance.  It would mean repentance and purification for you, and punishment and shame for them!  This is God's will, Jocasta.

JOCASTA:  You lie!  The God of the Temple would have left us in peace, as He did before, if it were not for you.  You pushed Oedipus to challenge the priests and anger them to avenge yourself, after they expelled you and banished you.  Curses on you!  You came here to use Oedipus to revenge yourself on your enemies!

TIRESIAS:  The true God is mightier than what the priests claim.  I don't think that you, Jocasta, would believe in a God that would accept your sin so long as Oedipus did not threaten the priests' money.  Then, when he does threaten to confiscate it, God would show His anger.

JOCASTA:  If we have to believe in a God, then I would believe in a God who has more sympathy on me and Oedipus than your God does.

TIRESIAS:  Do not fool yourself, Jocasta.  You do not believe in that false God the priests are promoting.  You just want to believe in Him today to keep what you should give up.

JOCASTA:  Then I do not believe in either God.  I am an atheist!  Get away from me and my husband and children, all of you priests of evil!

TIRESIAS:  No, you believe in your heart in the true God, who cannot accept sin, but you are trying to refuse Him to keep your fleeting fortune, and to hang on to your false happiness.  Know, Jocasta, that your desires do not create what is not there, or deny what is there.  The sun is shining even if the blind like me cannot see its light.  It still shines even if someone who can see, like you, chooses to cover her eyes to block its light.

JOCASTA:  How dare you!  Ah, me!  How can you want me to lose the husband I love, and who loves me?

TIRESIAS:  Yes, you would lose a sinful husband, who killed his father and allowed himself to lie in his mother's bed, and win a virtuous son who would stop the corruption spreading in this country, save the people from the famine, the state from destruction, cleanse the Temple from the evil priests, and replace them with a priesthood of good and truth.  Instead of being the wife of the one who usurped his father's bed, you would be the mother of a good king, who would eliminate evil and suffering from his father's land and his father's people.  Choose, Jocasta, which one would you prefer?

JOCASTA:  No, No.  I won't let you make me lose my beloved husband to add a son to my four children.

TIRESIAS:  Holding on to him will make things worse and add to your son's suffering.

JOCASTA (*shouting*):  Stop this!  Don't say my son, you evil priest!  He is my husband, and will remain my husband, in spite of you and your God.  Listen, you, if you don't stop turning my husband against me, I will let the priests seize you, drag you away, and finish you off.  Do you think that the High

Priest does not know that you are in the palace?

TIRESIAS:  I know that he knows, and I know that you are the one
who informed him.

JOCASTA:  Curses on you!  Do you want to tell my husband that,
to turn him against me even more?  Do whatever you want,
I don't care.

TIRESIAS:  No, Jocasta, I will keep this a secret, so don't tell him
yourself.

(*TIMONE enters.*)

TIMONE (*anxiously*):  I heard my lord's voice, your majesty.  I
think he just woke up.

TIRESIAS (*leaving his chair*):  Timone, take me to my room.  Don't
let your lord Oedipus know that I met your Queen.

(*TIMONE leads him out of the third door.*)

JOCASTA (*wiping away her tears*):  Oh, what misery!  I didn't get
anything from him.  I wish I hadn't met with him.

(*She blows out the candle in her hand, as daylight fills the hall, and moves
towards the second door, then she returns quickly and puts the candle on
one of the shelves.  OEDIPUS enters from the second door.*)

OEDIPUS:  Good Morning dear . . . dear Jocasta.  What woke you
up early today?

JOCASTA:  Ask me if I slept at all last night, or the nights before?
Ask me if was able to rest my body throughout all those
nights?

OEDIPUS:  Mercy on you, Jocasta.  Why can't you sleep?

JOCASTA:  You are deserting me, and ignoring me through no

fault of my own.  Since our marriage I don't remember that we were separated for even one night, and now it has been ten nights since you started sleeping away from me.  Now you ask me why I can't sleep?

OEDIPUS (*tenderly*):  Believe me, Jocasta, what you feel is only part of what I suffer.  Continuous insomnia is easier than what I suffer.  But do not worry, we will soon get used to this, and enjoy deep sleep.

JOCASTA:  Ah, me, are you planning never to share my bed again?  Is it true, Oedipus, that we will never be in one bed again?

OEDIPUS:  It's hard for me, Jocasta, but this is what will happen.

JOCASTA:  This is all Tiresias' fault.  You deserted me, Oedipus, because of that banished priest.  For him you betrayed my love, my happiness, and the happiness of your children. You betrayed everything.  (*She falls on the chair, crying.*)

OEDIPUS (*leans over her, consoling her and touching her shoulders*):  Be easy on yourself, Jocasta.  You are the dearest and most treasured person to me!  We have to bear this with courage.

JOCASTA:  There is no way to bear this.  What a crisis this is!  This is a calamity beyond all calamities.

OEDIPUS:  Yes it is, Jocasta, but we can only bear the pain patiently, hoping that we will feel comfort and happiness afterwards.  Be patient with the first shock, then things will become easier.

JOCASTA:  No, Oedipus, my beloved husband, I can't lose you.  I don't know how to bear that.  If you hated me because of a problem in me, or if I hated you because of a fault in you, it would have been easier.  But when you love me, and I love you, how can you suddenly ask me to give you up forever?  If you left me to go to Corinth to visit your mother Merope and your father Polybus and left me behind, I would wait till your return.  If you left me to lead your army into the battlefield, I would wait, hoping you would come back to me safe and victorious, and if you returned wounded, I would nurse you and wait by your bed until you recovered.  If there were a new Sphinx, more fierce than the old one, attacking the people, and you went to fight him and liberate Thebes from his evil, I would hope that you would conquer him like you conquered the first one, and return to me a greater hero in the eyes of the people.  But when I wake up one morning and find you in front of me, but not my husband anymore, and your bed is not my bed, this is what I cannot bear, and it would be easier for me to be dead.  (*She weeps.*)

OEDIPUS (*in pain, pleadingly*):  Dear God in your heavens, give me something of Your powers.  Release the knot in my tongue to be able to give Jocasta this heavy news.

JOCASTA:  What is the heavy news you haven't yet given me, Oedipus?

OEDIPUS (*with much effort*):  Mother . . . oh dear mother!

JOCASTA (*exploding*)  No!  Don't speak!  How dare you go back to this cursed word?  Didn't I tell you when you first uttered it never to repeat it again?  (*In a softer tone*)  If it is hard for you, Oedipus, to call me your wife or your beloved, you can just call me by my name, without insults.  Call me Jocasta; it's the name my parents gave me.

OEDIPUS (*gathering up his courage*):  Listen to me, Jocasta.  We shouldn't lie to ourselves anymore.  I obeyed you and went along with you that day because of my compassion for you until the effect of the shock was gone, and you were calmer.  Now you have to face the truth as I faced it before you.  You are my mother, Jocasta.  My mother who gave birth to me from the seed of Laius.

JOCASTA (*screaming*):  No!  I am not your mother, not your

mother.  (*She begins crying.*)

OEDIPUS:  Please, mother.  Help me in this plight.

JOCASTA:  Call me "dear wife" or "my beloved" as you used to.  Don't call me mother.  I have four children calling me that, but I only have you to call me beloved.

OEDIPUS:  But I am your son, mother.

JOCASTA:  No, you are not my son.  My sons are Polynices and Eteocles.

OEDIPUS:  They are your sons from me, I am your son from Laius.

JOCASTA:  No, my son from Laius was killed as a child.  The shepherd killed him.  Laius gave him to a shepherd and asked him to kill him in the wilderness.

OEDIPUS:  But you know that the shepherd didn't kill me, instead he gave me . . .

JOCASTA:  Yes, he didn't kill you, Oedipus, he killed my child from Laius.

OEDIPUS:  I am your child from Laius.

JOCASTA:  No . . . No . . . You are my husband, Oedipus.

OEDIPUS:  Yes, I was your husband before I knew that I was your child, but today . . .

JOCASTA:  Today is just like yesterday.  You are my husband yesterday, today, tomorrow, and the day after and forever, Oedipus.  You are my husband forever.

OEDIPUS:  But now I know for sure that I am your child from Laius.

JOCASTA:  No, you are not.  I gave birth to that poor child, and I know him better than you or anyone else.

OEDIPUS:  You don't know what happened to him after they took him away from you.

JOCASTA:  Neither do you.

OEDIPUS:  Yes, but those who witnessed what happened know that I am that poor child.  There is Tiresias, Polybus, Merope, and the High Priest himself.  Ask them and they will tell you that I am your son from Laius.

JOCASTA:  No, even if the heavens and the earth said so, if the mountains, seas, animals, and trees said so, if all the people said so, if all the gods said that you are my son from Laius I would not believe any of them and you will always be my beloved husband Oedipus.  Please, Oedipus.  I beg you by my rights on you.  And by my love for you, and our four children, and by the wonderful years we spent together, and sweet memories that no power on earth or heaven can erase, that you should not believe them either.  Stay my beloved husband Oedipus forever, and I will stay Jocasta, your loving faithful wife forever.

OEDIPUS:  I wish that were possible, Jocasta!  But we cannot live in an illusion.

JOCASTA:  We lived in what you call an illusion for seventeen years, the best years, Oedipus.

OEDIPUS:  Yes, Jocasta, and we ended up with this fate.

JOCASTA:  You created this fate when you believed Tiresias' fantasies.  Can't you refuse to accept his lies just as you refused to accept the lies of the High Priest before?

OEDIPUS:  How can I do that?  I told you how the Priest made up that oracle, claiming it came from Apollo, and how he worked on making it happen, through his plotting and scheming until everything he predicted took place.

JOCASTA:  This is all lies.  This is all made up.

OEDIPUS: Why don't you want to listen to this?

JOCASTA:  This is beyond Lucasius' ability.  This is not the work
of a human being.  This could only be the work of God, if
God exists.  This is a fable that the banished priest made up
to set you against his enemy Lucasius.  Tiresias is using you
to avenge himself, to take revenge on his old enemy.  Expel
him from your palace, Oedipus, and deny his lies.

OEDIPUS:  No, Jocasta!  How can I deny what I know for certain is
the truth?  How can I refuse to believe?

JOCASTA:  No.  If you still loved me you'd have done anything for
me.  But you don't love me anymore, Oedipus.

OEDIPUS:  No, by your life, Jocasta, I love you and honor you.

JOCASTA:  I don't want your honoring.  I just want your love,
Oedipus.  I want it for myself alone, not sharing it with
another woman.

OEDIPUS:  What are you saying?  What woman?

JOCASTA:  You now see me as older.  The prime of my youth is
gone, and you want to replace me with a younger woman.

OEDIPUS:  If this is what concerns you, don't worry.  I will not
marry after you.  I will be yours alone with no other love in
my heart.

JOCASTA:  No.  I can't believe you.  You are like Laius.  You want
to behave like him.  You want me to die of despair so that
you can marry a young woman after me.  This is what Laius
did with his first wife.  He kept on blaming her and
accusing her, not because she did not bear him a child, as he

claimed, but because she was getting old.  Finally she died of despair, and he was able to marry the young, beautiful Jocasta.  This is what you men do.  You use us when we are young, then throw us away to enjoy another young woman.

OEDIPUS:  I told you I will not marry after you.

JOCASTA:  No, I won't believe you.  You desire my death, so that you can marry again like Laius.  But beware, Oedipus, I am warning you, and you will see the truth in what I say.  This young woman you will marry after me will never love you.  She will hate you as I hated the old Laius, and wished I could replace him with a young shepherd.

OEDIPUS:  Jocasta!

JOCASTA:  Remember what I said.  The young woman that you will marry after me will see herself as a captive in the prison of your age.

OEDIPUS:  Jocasta!

JOCASTA:  But what a shame!  You are still young.  You are a young man, a beautiful, beautiful boy.  Ah, wait for me a little, Oedipus.  Give me a few years, till I say goodbye to my youth, then forsake me and find another.  No, just wait two years, or one, or less.  I am going to die soon, Oedipus, very soon.  I don't have much more time.

OEDIPUS:  Mother . . . Mother!

JOCASTA (*not hearing him*):  And when I die, lay me down in my grave, then find the young woman you want before you even wash the dust of my grave from your hands.

OEDIPUS:  Oh, mighty God, help.  Oh merciful God, have mercy and pity my mother.

JOCASTA:  Oh, Oedipus, are you asking your God to take me and bring my end sooner?  No, beloved Oedipus, I don't want to die today.  I still have a little bit of youth.  Anxiety turned my face pale, and took away my youth in a few nights . . . these long horrible nights.  But when you accept me again, and call me your beloved wife, I will regain the freshness of looks and youth.  Please, Oedipus, please!  I don't want to die.

OEDIPUS:  No, mother, you won't die.  You will live a long life with me, mother.

JOCASTA:  Won't die.  Why not?  This word alone, this accursed word is enough to shatter me and crush my heart.  When you call me your mother, it is as if you are feeding me poison.  I will drink the poisonous cup if this pleases you.  Ahhhh . . . ahhhh . . .  (*She faints, falling to the floor.*)

OEDIPUS (*catching her*):  Timone, Timone!

TIMONE (*entering hurriedly*):  Your Majesty!

OEDIPUS:  Help me, Timone!  (*She helps him in laying JOCASTA on the big chair.*)

TIMONE (*rubbing JOCASTA's feet and fanning her face*):  Don't worry, your Majesty.  This fainting happens to her often these days.

OEDIPUS (*looking at TIMONE in heavy sadness*):  Do you know about our plight, Timone?

TIMONE (*in deep pain*):  Yes, your Majesty.  I know everything.  Have mercy on her and pity her, she is . . . (*She chokes with tears.*)

OEDIPUS:  Tell me, Timone, would it please you if you had a son, and he married you?

TIMONE:  God forbid, your Majesty.

OEDIPUS:  And you love your queen, Jocasta.

TIMONE:  I'd sacrifice my life for her, your Majesty.

OEDIPUS:  Would you want your queen to stay married to the child she gave birth to?

TIMONE:  Please, have mercy, your Majesty.  I don't know how to answer you.

OEDIPUS:  You have to help me, Timone, to convince her to endure this plight.

TIMONE:  I am at your service, your Majesty.  But you know that I cannot anger my queen.

(*JOCASTA moves, and opens her eyes.*)

OEDIPUS (*in a quiet voice*):  Thank God!

TIMONE:  I hope you are well, your Majesty.

JOCASTA (*She cannot see OEDIPUS, who is standing behind her*):  Where am I?  What are you doing here, Timone?

TIMONE:  I was rubbing your feet, your Majesty.

JOCASTA:  Oh me, how came I to sleep in the hall?  Ah, I had a strange dream just now, Timone.  I saw my husband Laius come back as a young man.  Why are you looking behind me?

TIMONE:  My master is there, your Majesty.

JOCASTA:  (*She sits up, and turns to see OEDIPUS.  She is very surprised, as if she cannot believe her eyes.*)  Laius, my beloved husband!  It's really you, returned to your youth!  Then it was not a dream.  Look, Timone, look!  Your master Laius became a young man, full of youth.  Oh, dear Laius.

May God return me to my youth like you!

(*OEDIPUS, confused, cannot find words.*)

JOCASTA: What's wrong with you, Laius? Did you forget me? Did you forget your wife and beloved?

OEDIPUS (*in pain*): Oh . . . mother!

JOCASTA (*astonished and surprised*): Mother!

OEDIPUS: I am Oedipus, don't you know me?

JOCASTA: Oedipus!

OEDIPUS: Yes, did you forget Oedipus?

JOCASTA: This is the name of our son, who they claim has survived. Do you want to take his name, Laius? Why do you want to change your name, my beloved? There are children who are named after their fathers, but no one has ever heard of a father taking the name of his son!

OEDIPUS: What are you saying, mother? I am your son Oedipus!

JOCASTA: You are my son Oedipus?

OEDIPUS: Yes, you are my mother Jocasta.

JOCASTA: Are you joking, Laius?

OEDIPUS: No, mother. I am not joking.

JOCASTA: Then you are making fun of me!

OEDIPUS: No, mother.

JOCASTA: Look, Timone, at this deceitful husband. Never get married, Timone!

OEDIPUS:  Mother, what's wrong with you, mother?

JOCASTA (*angrily*):  Curses on you, Laius!  Is it fair that you make
 fun of me like that because you returned young, and found
 me older than you?  Remember when you married me, I was
 a young woman, and you were an old man, and I accepted
 you and had patience with you, and never made fun of you.
 Will you accept me now, when my youth is gone, and your
 youth has returned, as I accepted you before?

OEDIPUS:  Mother, return to your senses, mother!

JOCASTA:  Shame on you, Laius.  Don't turn my happiness into
 gloom and misery with your restored youth.  (*Changing her
 tone*)  Please, dearest husband, do not make fun of me.  I
 need your tenderness and compassion.

OEDIPUS:  I swear by your life, mother, that I am not making fun
 of you.

JOCASTA:  So why do you call me "mother"?  You were as old as
 my father when I married you, and I never called you
 "father."  I always called you husband.  Now do you call me
 "mother" because I look old enough to be your mother?
 You are cruel, Laius!

OEDIPUS:  Mother, when will you return to your senses?  I am not
 Laius, as you think.  I am your son, Oedipus.

JOCASTA:  Don't try to delude me.  You are Laius, as he was in his
 youth.  You are the young beautiful Laius, who was loved
 and dreamt of by the women of Thebes.

OEDIPUS (*turning to TIMONE*):  Timone, why are you silent?  Tell
 your mistress that I am not Laius.

TIMONE:  Yes, my dear Queen, this is my master Oedipus, not my
 master Laius.

JOCASTA:  Even you, Timone, are taking his side.  Oh, poor me, can't I find one person to support me?

TIMONE:  Oh, my dear mistress, Jocasta.  My master Laius died a long time ago.  Don't you remember when they brought you the news of his death?  Don't you remember that day?

JOCASTA:  Ah, me!  How can I forget that day?  What do you think of me, Timone?  Do you think I am crazy?

TIMONE:  God forbid, your Majesty.  Maybe you did forget.

JOCASTA:  No, I didn't forget that day he died.  But God returned him to me, a young man.  I wished for that one day, when I was with him in the Temple, and God responded to my prayer, and fulfilled my wish.  Oh, how I wish that I had asked Him to keep my youth too.  It didn't occur to me that my youth would vanish one day, Timone.

TIMONE:  My mistress, Jocasta!

OEDIPUS:  Mother!

JOCASTA:  How dare you?  You don't believe me?  Curse you, you are both cruel!  Is it fair to give me the old Laius, and take away the young Laius from me?  You were generous with his bleak winter, but when it becomes a warm lively spring are you becoming miserly?

OEDIPUS:  I am your son, Jocasta.  I am your son, mother.

JOCASTA:  No, you are my husband . . .  My husband . . . husband.  Remind him, Timone, that he is my husband.

TIMONE:  Yes, your Majesty . . . but . . .

JOCASTA:  But what, curse you?

OEDIPUS:  But today I became your son.

JOCASTA:  Became my son!  Do you mean to say that you were my husband, then became my son?  Who could believe what you are saying?  Is it possible that the husband becomes a son?  This is impossible!  This is sheer madness.

OEDIPUS:  It's hard to believe, but it is what happened!

JOCASTA:  No, Laius.  This is impossible.  God can make the old younger, as He did with you, but can't make the husband into a son.  If all the gods gathered to do this they would fail.

OEDIPUS:  Wait a moment, mother.  Listen to me.

JOCASTA:  No, you listen to me.  What are you saying?  How can you speak this nonsense, that even the most crazy person wouldn't accept?  Remember our four children!  Did you forget our children?  Did you forget Antigone, Polynices, Eteocles, and Ismene?  Aren't they your children, from me?

OEDIPUS:  Mother!

JOCASTA:  Timone, hurry and call them!  Maybe their father will remember them when he sees them.

TIMONE (*hesitant*):  Your Majesty!

JOCASTA:  Hurry, curse you!

TIMONE:  I obey, your Majesty.  (*She leaves from the second door.*)

JOCASTA:  You will see them now, and remember.

OEDIPUS:  I remember them, mother.

JOCASTA:  Aren't you their father?  Am I not their mother?

OEDIPUS (*in pain*):  Yes.  They are my children, and my siblings, and you are their mother and their grandmother!

JOCASTA:  Who can believe that?  Children and siblings at the same time?  Mother and grandmother at the same time?  Is everyone going crazy?  Are all the gods mad?  Are all the laws of existence breaking down?  Did all the rules of life fail?  Are all the boundaries gone?  Are all the balances imbalanced, and is everything mixed up?  I am their mother and grandmother, and you are their father and brother!

OEDIPUS:  This is the disaster that fell upon us, mother.  This is our calamity!

JOCASTA:  The disaster is in the mind that believes in the disaster.  You, mad of the earth, everywhere, if you want to be considered sane, believe that your brothers are your mothers' husbands, and that your mothers are your fathers' mothers.  No, be even saner and say that the grandchild is the grandmother, and the grandfather is the grandchild.  You mad people, be merry today!  You are no madder than anyone else.

OEDIPUS:  Jocasta, listen to me, Jocasta.  We lived for seventeen years not knowing that we were living in sin and evil.  Our eyes were clouded, Jocasta, and now the cloud has lifted and we can see this horrifying, gruesome truth.  There is no way out of this but to repent and do penance, so let us face it with courage, and repent to God and ask His mercy and forgiveness.

JOCASTA (*as if waking up*):  Repenting . . .  Penance . . .  Now I remember.  Tiresias!  He is behind all this.  This banished priest came to destroy our happiness, and pull down this palace on our heads.  (*She stands up with determination.*)  Where is the accursed Tiresias?  Where is the outcast priest cursed by the gods?  I swear by the sacredness of the Temple, who expelled and banished him, that I will ruin him!  No, by the heavens and by the gods, I will not stand still while he is destroying my home.  (*She runs towards the third door.*)

OEDIPUS (*trying to stop her, in vain*): Jocasta, what are you doing? Jocasta!

JOCASTA: Let me go! Let me go! (*She leaves followed by OEDIPUS.*)

JOCASTA (*her voice offstage*): I will destroy this blind man. I will tear him apart!

OEDIPUS (*his voice offstage*): Jocasta! What's in your hands? Drop this, Jocasta! No, no, don't do it, Jocasta!

JOCASTA (*her voice offstage*): Let me! Let me! Ah, where are you, brother? Where are you, Creon?

(*TIRESIAS enters from the door, in a hurry, led by a young priest, MENSAS.*)

TIRESIAS: Take me to the chamber. (*He moves towards the chamber.*)

JOCASTA (*her voice from the direction of the second door*): You will not escape, you cursed priest!

(*JOCASTA enters, with OEDIPUS, who is trying to convince her, while holding to one side of the iron bar she is carrying.*)

JOCASTA: Let me! Let me! (*She sees the young priest leading TIRESIAS and stops in shock.*) Mensas! How dare you! Even you, Mensas, are siding with the outcast priest? Ah, if the High Priest knew that you support the man expelled from the Temple! (*Her grip loosens on the iron bar, and Oedipus pulls it away from her.*) Oh, you are all with Tiresias against me. All of you! All of you! There is no one supporting me. Oh, poor Jocasta! All the earth is plotting against you, and all the heavens are against you. (*She collapses on the ground. OEDIPUS catches her, and takes her out of the second door.*)

TIRESIAS: Poor Jocasta! The shock was too much for her! She couldn't face the truth.

MENSAS:  It seems to me that she has gone insane.

TIRESIAS:  If she does not go insane, she will not be able to live. (*Praying*) Dear merciful God, have mercy on Jocasta, and strengthen Oedipus' heart! (*He sits down. MENSAS sits beside him.*)

MENSAS:  Are you worried that Oedipus' resolve will weaken?

TIRESIAS:  No, my son. I am asking God to give him more strength.

MENSAS:  Aren't you worried about Jocasta's influence on him?

TIRESIAS:  No, there is no fear of that now. Oedipus has faced the fiercest storm. Don't worry about him after that.

MENSAS:  And Lucasius, don't you worry about his effect on Oedipus? He would give him the choice between yielding to him or exposing his scandal to the people. Aren't you worried that Oedipus might change his mind if the High Priest confronts him and threatens him with circulating the new oracle?

TIRESIAS:  Be comforted, my son; facing Jocasta was the most daunting obstacle Oedipus had, and he survived it today with strength and courage. What comes next is easier for him, and he is braver and more capable.

MENSAS:  Are you sure of that?

TIRESIAS:  Yes, as I am sure of myself. Don't forget, Mensas, that he decided to confiscate the Temple's property on his own, before I even contacted him. I only supported his decision, which increased his determination and strength.

MENSAS:  I am still anxious, Tiresias.

TIRESIAS:  Don't worry about that, and tell me, didn't Creon ask them about the new Oracle?

MENSAS:  Yes, and they said no one should hear it before
     Oedipus.

TIRESIAS:  Did they tell Creon of their intention to have him take
     over Oedipus' throne if Oedipus doesn't change his mind
     about confiscating the Temple's property?  Did they talk
     with Creon about that?

MENSAS:  As far as I know they didn't discuss that yet.  Here is
     the King coming.

(*MENSAS and TIRESIAS stand up.  OEDIPUS enters from the second
door, depressed, dragging his feet.*)

OEDIPUS:  Sit down, my friends.  (*He sits, then they sit.*)

TIRESIAS:  What did the Queen do, Oedipus?  How is she now?

OEDIPUS:  I am confused by the way she is.  I don't know if she is
     unconscious or awake, sane or mad.  When I took her to bed
     to lay her down, I was sure she was unconscious, but she
     asked me to take her to my bed to lay her there!  I am really
     worried about her, Tiresias!

TIRESIAS:  Do not worry, Oedipus.  God is with you.  However
     hard the penance seems, its reward will be greater.
     (*Hopefully*)  God will have mercy on the Queen.

OEDIPUS:  Forgive her, Tiresias.  She is not aware of what she is
     doing.  Don't hold anything against her.

TIRESIAS:  Of course, Oedipus.  I only have pity and sympathy for
     her.

OEDIPUS:  Pray for her good, Tiresias.  Pray for her, for my sake.  I
     used to worship her as a wife, now I worship her as a
     mother.

(*Sounds are heard from the second door.*)

ANTIGONE (*offstage*):  Don't anger your father.  Wait till I ask his permission for you to enter.

ISMENE (*offstage*):  No, we will not wait.  You are not better than we.

OEDIPUS:  Antigone!  Let them in, Antigone!

(*The three CHILDREN enter, followed by ANTIGONE, apprehensive, and not happy with what they are doing.*)

OEDIPUS:  What do you want, children?

ETEOCLES:  We want to throw this blind priest out of the palace!

POLYNICES:  Yes, father.  He is the cause of mother's illness.

ISMENE:  Throw him out, father, and throw this other priest out too.

ANTIGONE:  How dare you?  How could you say this to your father?  Come on, let's get out of here.  (*She tries to push them out.*)

OEDIPUS:  Let them be, my dear daughter.  (A*ddressing the other three*)  Oh, dear children!  The priest Tiresias is here to treat your mother for her illness.  He is a very skillful doctor.

ISMENE:  But mother says that he is the cause of her illness.

ETEOCLES:  And he wants to end her life.

OEDIPUS:  Your mother says that because she does not like the bitter medicine he treats her with.  Don't you fear the doctor and cry when he gives you bitter medicine?

POLYNICES:  I don't cry, father, and I don't fear the doctor's medicine!

OEDIPUS:  Because you are brave, my son, but your mother fears it like Eteocles and Ismene.

ETEOCLES:  No, father!  I will not cry about the medicine again. Give me that bitter medicine.

OEDIPUS (*smiling*):  Not now, my son.  You are not sick now, and I don't give medicine to those who are not sick.

ETEOCLES:  Then tell me, father, that I am brave, and that I don't fear the doctor or his bitter medicine.

OEDIPUS:  Yes, today you are brave, Eteocles.

ETEOCLES (*proud of himself*):  I will show you, if I fall sick and the doctor comes to give me medicine, I will drink the whole bottle.

(*OEDIPUS and the two priests laugh.*)

POLYNICES:  Don't believe him, father.  He will start screaming as soon as he sees the medicine.

ETEOCLES:  Liar!  Tomorrow, you will see that I am braver than you!

OEDIPUS:  Dear children, run to your mother and tell her to be patient about the bitter medicine, until she recovers.

(*The three youngest children leave quickly, while ANTIGONE stays behind, as if she doesn't believe what she heard.  Her face seems very sad.*)

OEDIPUS (*looking at her tenderly and in sympathy as if he can see what troubles her*):  Come here, Antigone, my dear daughter. (*She throws herself onto him crying.  He embraces her tenderly.*) What is wrong, my beloved daughter?  Why are you crying?

ANTIGONE (*burying her face in her father's lap*):  Tell me, my dear
    father . . . is it true . . . that . . . you are . . . the son of . . .

OEDIPUS (*tears run down his face*):  Yes, Antigone!

ANTIGONE:  Then . . . then I am . . . I am your . . . daughter . . .
    and your . . . sister?

OEDIPUS:  Yes, Antigone . . . You are my daughter and my sister.

ANTIGONE:  And today you want to . . .

OEDIPUS:  To repent to God, the merciful.  Don't you think this is
    better for me and your mother?  You are wise, Antigone.

ANTIGONE:  All that you do is good, my father.

OEDIPUS:  And that wouldn't change your love for me, Antigone?

ANTIGONE:  No, father.  Nothing could change my love for you.
    I will always love you.

OEDIPUS:  I am so happy to hear that, Antigone.  I know it's a
    very bitter medicine.

ANTIGONE:  What cures you and my mother, I will also take with
    you, father, and its bitterness will be sweetness in
    Antigone's mouth.

OEDIPUS:  Bless you, Antigone. (*He gently moves her from his lap.*)
    Come on.  Let the priest Tiresias bless you, and pray for
    you!

TIRESIAS:  Come to me blessed, brave daughter. (*She moves closer
    to him, and he puts his hands on her head.*)  May God bless
    you and protect you.

OEDIPUS:  Now go to your mother, Antigone.  Cheer her up, and
    don't leave her side.

ANTIGONE (*wiping away her tears*):  I will, father.  (*She exits.*)

OEDIPUS (*looking at MENSAS*):  You, young priest, haven't I seen your face before?

MENSAS:  Yes, your Majesty.  You have seen me here, in the palace.

OEDIPUS:  Did you carry the Queen's offerings to the Temple?

MENSAS:  Yes, your Majesty.

OEDIPUS:  He is too young to have been with you in the Temple, Tiresias.  How does he know you?

TIRESIAS:  He is a follower of my followers, Oedipus.

OEDIPUS (*after a short silence*):  There is still good in this world (*sighs*) even if my share of it is so little!

(*A knock is heard on the first door, then a GUARD enters.*)

GUARD:  Your Majesty!

OEDIPUS:  Come in.  What's happening?

GUARD:  My master, Creon, just entered the gates of the city, your Majesty.  He is accompanied by the High Priest, who wants to meet your Majesty before he announces the Oracle of Apollo to the people.  (*He moves backward to exit.*)

OEDIPUS:  Wait by the door till I call you.

GUARD:  I obey, your Majesty.  (*He stands by the first door.*)

OEDIPUS:  What do you think, Tiresias?

TIRESIAS:  This young priest informed me that the High Priest wants to bargain with you, Oedipus.  And I am sure that you will refuse!

OEDIPUS:  Yes, Tiresias.

TIRESIAS:  I think you should call three of the Elders of Thebes, and hide them in that chamber, so that they can hear what the priest says when he negotiates with you, and then be witness to what he says in front of the people.

OEDIPUS:  This is a very wise plan.  (*He calls the Guard, who approaches him.*)  Summon three of the Elders of Thebes, to come here at once.

GUARD:  I obey, your Majesty.  (*He exits.*)

VOICES (*heard from a distance*):  Welcome, Creon!  Creon has returned.  The Oracle of Apollo is here.  Welcome!

OEDIPUS:  I wished, Tiresias, that Creon's return could have been delayed till the arrival of Polybus, King of Corinth.  Do you think Polybus will come?  I am worried, Tiresias, that he might not come.

TIRESIAS:  Of course he will come, Oedipus.  He loves you, and appreciates you.

OEDIPUS:  I often asked him to visit us, and he never did.

TIRESIAS:  Didn't I tell you that before coming to your palace I conferred with Polybus?  He is coming.  He promised my men in Corinth, and he wouldn't break his promise.

(*The sound of crowds of PEOPLE approaching, and their cries to CREON and the HIGH PRIEST are clear.*)

PEOPLE:  Welcome, Creon!  Welcome, High Priest!  Welcome Oracle of Apollo!

(*GUARD enters.*)

GUARD:  The Elders of Thebes you asked for are here, your
    Majesty.

OEDIPUS:  Let them in.

(*Three of the ELDERS of Thebes enter. The GUARD exits.*)

THE ELDERS:  Hail to the Great King!

OEDIPUS:  Welcome!  (*The ELDERS are surprised to see TIRESIAS.*)
    Do not worry.  This is Tiresias, the noble priest.  God sent
    him to us to save Thebes from its plight.

ONE OF THE ELDERS:  But, Oedipus, this priest was banished
    from the Temple, and cursed by the High Priest.

OEDIPUS:  You will see today which of them deserves banishment
    and curses.

TIRESIAS:  You are from the notables of Thebes, and represent the
    people, and our noble King thought of involving you in his
    plan, so be generous with your advice.  Follow his orders
    now, and then decide later what should be done.

THE ELDERS:  Our king deserves our respect and obedience.

(*Sounds of the people are heard approaching.*)

OEDIPUS:  Here they are approaching the palace.  Enter the
    chamber, so that you can hear what takes place between me
    and the High Priest.  Then give me your advice on what to
    do afterwards.

(*They all exit to the chamber, leaving OEDIPUS alone in the hall.  A
GUARD enters.*)

GUARD:  My master, Creon, is here, with the High Priest.

OEDIPUS:  Let them enter.  (*The GUARD exits.*)  Dear God, you who are strong and powerful, give me some of your strength, and turn my heart toward what is good for me, my people and my country.

(*Enter CREON and the High Priest, LUCASIUS.*)

LUCASIUS:  Hail great king!

OEDIPUS (*greeting them*):  Welcome to the bearers of Apollo's oracle!  Come in, sit down.  (*He sits down, they follow.*)

CREON:  Our High Priest thought it better that he deliver the oracle to you himself.

OEDIPUS:  This is good.  I have heard that the oracle of Apollo is not to be carried by any one person.  What did the temple say regarding this crisis, Creon?

CREON:  I don't know anything, Oedipus.

OEDIPUS:  Don't know anything?

CREON:  The High Priest will tell you himself.

OEDIPUS:  Let him say what he has to say.  I am listening.

LUCASIUS (*controlling his annoyance at OEDIPUS' not addressing him*):  It is better, Oedipus, that no one else hears Apollo's oracle but you.

OEDIPUS:  Not even Creon?

CREON (*standing up*):  It's time to leave you two alone now.

OEDIPUS:  No, stay where you are, Creon . . . you are part of my family, and my secrets are your secrets.

LUCASIUS:  You must listen to it alone first, Oedipus.

OEDIPUS:  The whole nation is waiting to hear the oracle, so why do you want me to hide it from Creon?

LUCASIUS:  This is for your own good, Oedipus.

OEDIPUS:  My own good!  I only consulted the Temple for the good of the people.

LUCASIUS:  The good of the people is based on the good of whoever is on the throne.

CREON:  There is no problem, Oedipus.  I will go inside to see my sister.  I heard she is not well.

LUCASIUS:  Give the Queen my regards, Creon.

(*CREON exits from the second door.*)

OEDIPUS:  Now tell me your oracle.  There is only the two of us.

LUCASIUS (*looking around him*):  It is the oracle of Apollo, Oedipus.

OEDIPUS:  Let Apollo convey it to me.

LUCASIUS:  I am his messenger, and the carrier of his oracle.

OEDIPUS:  Deliver it then.  What is stopping you?

LUCASIUS (*looking around*):  First, I would like to advise you, Oedipus.

OEDIPUS:  What is your advice?

LUCASIUS:  Do you remember, Oedipus, when you were in Corinth, and came to consult me about the oracle in Delphi.  Then I warned you not to go to Thebes or else you'd kill your father, Laius.  You didn't follow my advice and what I warned you  about happened.

OEDIPUS:  Yes, I remember that.

LUCASIUS:  Then I warned you one more time not to enter
        Thebes, or else you would marry your mother, Jocasta.  You
        disobeyed me again, and what I warned you about
        happened.

OEDIPUS:  Yes, this took place.

LUCASIUS:  Beware of disobeying me a third time.  This would be
        worse.  Apollo's oracle says that Thebes' suffering will not
        be relieved until its people avenge the killing of their king
        Laius,  and cleanse Thebes of the sinner who killed his own
        father, and violated his own mother.

OEDIPUS (*trying to control his anger*):  Did your God know before
        today that I killed my father and married my mother?

LUCASIUS:  What is this question?  God knows everything.

OEDIPUS:  It has been seventeen years, so why didn't He urge
        Thebes to take revenge on me before now?  Was He content
        with what I did before, and now has become angry?  So
        what motivated His anger today?

LUCASIUS:  This is the business of God.  Only He knows.  Maybe
        you aroused His anger when you stopped the offering to
        His Temple and then planned to confiscate the Temple's
        property.  Then, as if this were not enough, you opened
        your palace to His enemy, the banished priest, Tiresias.

OEDIPUS:  So, what do you advise me to do?

LUCASIUS:  Reinstate the offerings as they were, change your plan
        of confiscating the property, and hand Tiresias over to us, to
        be tried for his conspiracy.

OEDIPUS:  And how will I be rewarded if I accept your offer?

LUCASIUS:  If you accept, you will stay on your throne, and your secret will be hidden from the people.

OEDIPUS:  And if I refuse?

LUCASIUS:  We will announce the oracle to the people, and they will revolt against you, and dethrone you.

OEDIPUS:  Do you promise me that you will keep this oracle from the people if I accept your offer?

LUCASIUS:  Yes, Oedipus, I promise you that.  Obey me this time, Oedipus.  Follow my advice.  I am your good counselor.

OEDIPUS:  Listen to me well, Lucasius.  Do you promise to keep the oracle of God from the people?

LUCASIUS:  Yes, trust my promise, Oedipus.

OEDIPUS:  Then . . . (*He moves his lips without a sound.*)

LUCASIUS:  Excuse me, Oedipus.  I didn't hear what you said.

OEDIPUS:  Then . . . (*He repeats the same thing.*)

LUCASIUS:  Then what, Oedipus?

OEDIPUS:  What is wrong with you?  Are you deaf?  Or are you playing deaf to break the promise you made me?

LUCASIUS:  No, Oedipus.  I am still keeping my promise and would not go back on it.  I did not hear what you said.  I only you heard you say "Then," and nothing after that.

OEDIPUS:  I will repeat it now, and raise my voice . . . beware, don't play deaf, because I will not repeat it again.

LUCASIUS:  Speak, Oedipus, I am listening to you.

OEDIPUS (*loudly*):  Then . . . (*He moves his lips without a sound.*)

LUCASIUS:  Then what?  I didn't hear!

OEDIPUS (*screaming at the top of his voice*):  Then announce your
    oracle to the people!  I do not believe in any oracle that a
    charlatan priest like you could hide when he wants and
    reveal when he wants.

LUCASIUS:  Calm down, Oedipus.  Listen to my advice.  It's better
    for you, before your scandal and your mother's are
    announced to the people, and you lose your throne and your
    head as well.

OEDIPUS (*loudly*):  How dare you, you traitor!  It's better to lose
    my throne and my head than to have my people suffer this
    plight.

LUCASIUS:  You are the cause of this plight because you angered
    the gods.

OEDIPUS:  Then, let my head roll, and let my scandal and my
    mother's be announced if this is what the gods want, as you
    claim.  Get out of here and announce your oracle.

LUCASIUS:  I have to hear Queen Jocasta's opinion on that.

OEDIPUS:  You have no business with her.  Her opinion is the
    same as mine.

(*A movement is heard at the second door.*)

LUCASIUS:  Do you think Jocasta will accept that her scandal be
    announced to the people?

OEDIPUS:  This is not your business.

(*JOCASTA enters suddenly, followed by CREON, as if he wants to stop
her from entering.*)

JOCASTA:  No, Oedipus. I don't want to the people to know about my scandal.  What will your fate and my fate be?  What will be the fate of our innocent children, Antigone, Ismene, Eteocles and Polynices?

LUCASIUS:  Yes. Counsel your husband, Jocasta.  Talk to your brother-in-law, Creon.  Restore him to his senses.  Let him know  what's good for him and for his family, and his people.

CREON:  Oh, what am I hearing?  I don't understand anything.

JOCASTA:  Do what you want, Oedipus.  Consider me your wife or your mother, but don't disgrace me in front of the people.  Obey the High Priest and expel Tiresias from the palace!

OEDIPUS:  It's hard for me, mother, not to answer your request.

CREON (*to himself, surprised*):  Mother!

JOCASTA:  And our scandal, Oedipus, do you accept that?

OEDIPUS:  And the people's famine, mother, do you accept that?

JOCASTA:  Is the famine our fault?

OEDIPUS:  Yes, if we allow him and his followers to take over the people's land, while the people are falling between its two fierce enemies, hunger and the plague.  One weakens them and the other destroys them.

JOCASTA (*in tears*):  Oedipus!  Have mercy, Oedipus!  Have mercy on your children!  Have mercy on your little ones!  Have mercy on your self!  Don't you hear me?

OEDIPUS:  Yes, mother.  But the heavens are crying out, "Oedipus, have mercy on your people!"  Don't you hear the heavens, mother?

JOCASTA:  Creon, talk to him, Creon.

CREON:  What do I tell him, sister?

JOCASTA (*to the High Priest*):  Lucasius!  Have mercy on me,
    Lucasius!  Don't reveal my scandal to the people.  Do this
    for me.

LUCASIUS:  This is Apollo's oracle, Jocasta.  I cannot keep it
    hidden.

OEDIPUS (*angrily*):  Get out now, damn you!  What are you
    waiting for?  Get out and announce your oracle, before I
    silence you with my own two hands forever!  Get out!

LUCASIUS (*going to the balcony, and calling at the top of his lungs*):
    Elders of Thebes.  People of Thebes.  Prepare to hear the
    oracle!  I am coming out to announce it to you.

(*He leaves from the first door. TIMONE appears from the second door.
JOCASTA collapses against her, confused.*)

JOCASTA:  You will regret what you have done, Oedipus.  You
    will regret this action.

(*She leaves with TIMONE.  TIRESIAS and MENSAS appear from the
chamber with the three ELDERS.*)

OEDIPUS:  Did you hear that, Elders of Thebes?

ELDERS:  We heard and we could not believe it.  How great are
    you today, Oedipus.  Forgive us, Tiresias.

TIRESIAS:  You are not to blame.  Now, Mensas, go to our friends
    and let them prepare what I explained to you.  Do you
    understand?

MENSAS:  Yes.  (*To OEDIPUS*)  Allow me to go, Master.

OEDIPUS:  Go, do what Tiresias asked you to.

ELDERS:  Give us permission to leave, Oedipus.

OEDIPUS:  If you wish.

TIRESIAS:  Leave with them from the back door, Mensas.

MENSAS:  Let us go.  (*He leaves and takes the ELDERS with him from the third door.*)

LUCASIUS (*heard from outside the palace*):  Now hear the Oracle of Apollo.  In the palace of your king is a man who killed his father (*sounds of repulsion*) and he is the killer of your late king Laius (*sounds of anger*).  The plague won't be lifted from Thebes till you take revenge on the killer of Laius.  Avenge your late king, and purify your city from this sinner (*mixed sounds*).  Now go, spread this oracle everywhere in Thebes.  Tell every man and woman.

(*The sounds of the crowd dispersing everywhere.*)

OEDIPUS:  Damn this cursed priest.

TIRESIAS:  He won't stop negotiating with you, so be firm and do not give way.  God will support you.

OEDIPUS:  I will stop him from negotiating with me.  I will close every door for that, until my heart is at peace, Tiresias.

TIRESIAS:  I have confidence in you.

OEDIPUS:  But I don't have confidence in myself.  Fate is unclear to me, Tiresias.  The unknown is hidden from me, and I am worried that a fate I do not want will overtake me.  (*To CREON*)  Stay here with Tiresias.  Don't let anything harm him.

CREON (*dazed*):  I obey, Oedipus.

(*OEDIPUS exits from the second door.*)

CREON (*moving closer to TIRESIAS*):  Help me, Tiresias.  I am going crazy.  I don't understand anything about what is going on today in this palace.

TIRESIAS:  Oh, Creon!  What is not clear to you?

CREON:  Everything!  I did not understand anything about what went on.  It seems to me that either I went crazy or those around me have gone crazy.

TIRESIAS:  No, Creon.  You are not going crazy, nor are those around you.  This is waking up, Creon, waking up from a long slumber.

CREON:  What slumber and what waking up?

TIRESIAS:  The slumber of ignorance, and the waking up of truth.

CREON:  Now you are making things more mysterious, and adding to my confusion.  What is the meaning of what the High Priest announced?

TIRESIAS:  Why didn't you ask the one bearing the oracle, when you came with him?

CREON:  He didn't tell me anything.

TIRESIAS:  Now he has announced it to everyone, and you have heard him.

CREON:  Yes, but who is the sinner the oracle means?

TIRESIAS:  One of two, either me or Oedipus.

CREON:  It's one person, so which one of you?

TIRESIAS:  Only two people can decide, either Lucasius or Oedipus.

CREON:  Curse it!  I want you to tell me, not give me riddles.

TIRESIAS:  I told you as much as I can, I didn't give you any riddles.

CREON:  These are riddles I don't understand, curse you.

TIRESIAS (*controlling his anger*):  These are not riddles.  The problem is in your mind that sees clear things as riddles.

CREON (*angrily*):  You atheist priest, stop confusing me!  You are exhausting my patience!

TIRESIAS:  You, believer in the Temple, stop your stupidity.  My mind is becoming fogged.

CREON:  Are you ridiculing me for being a believer, damn you?

TIRESIAS:  Just as you ridiculed my atheism.

CREON:  My belief is not a fault, as your atheism is.

TIRESIAS:  My atheism is not a fault, as your belief is.

CREON:  The Temple didn't expel you for nothing.

TIRESIAS:  The Temple didn't deceive you for nothing.

CREON:  It was right that the heavens erased your eyesight.

TIRESIAS (*exploding in anger*):  It was right that they erased your vision.  Go away from me, you foolish, corrupt man.  By the heavens, if it weren't for the likes of you, this charlatan priest wouldn't have been able to claim that he spoke for heaven and to do with the people as he pleased, while they believed in him, and praised him.

CREON:  You rejected blind man, consider who are you talking to!

TIRESIAS (*more angry*):  If you didn't already have enough blindness to cover you and all the bats of the world, I would have asked God to blind your eyes.  I know who I am talking to.  I am talking to a marble statue, decorating Oedipus' palace, crafted by the artist to show human stupidity.

CREON:  Oh, if only Oedipus hadn't asked me to protect you.

TIRESIAS:  I relieve you from that.  Go and open your eyes, first, and look at the pit that the Temple dug for you and your family, the Temple you believe in as the old folks do.  Then come back after that to protect me, if you think I deserve your protection.

CREON:  If there is a pit, then it could only be you who dug it for us.  You, the one condemned by the gods, inflamed the anger of the Temple by coming to this palace.

TIRESIAS:  You stupid, stupid man, how can I speak to you so that you will understand?  These people are suffering their plight because of the Temple, and you do not know it.  Oedipus is suffering the worst of pain because of the Temple and you do not know it.  Your sister, Jocasta, is thrashing about like a dying bird, and you do not know it.

TIMONE (*off stage*):  Help!  Help!  My master, Oedipus!  My master, Creon!  (*He enters from the second door, running.*)  Help!  Help!  My master, Creon, where is my master, Oedipus?

CREON (*jumping up*):  What happened?  What happened, Timone?

TIMONE:  Hurry!  Hurry!  Help my mistress, Jocasta.  She locked herself up.  She wants to . . .

TIRESIAS (*crying out*):  Help her, Creon.  Aid her, hurry.

CREON (*running to the door*):  Where is she?  Go before me, hurry.

(*They exit, running.*)

TIRESIAS (*muttering*):  Oh, dear God.  She must have done
    something.  I wish she had more patience to wait until the
    storm subsided.  Oh, mercy on Jocasta.  She couldn't bear
    this crisis, and she couldn't calm her mind.  No wonder she
    collapsed!  Oh, merciful God, have mercy on her and on
    Oedipus.

(*CREON enters, carrying JOCASTA, with TIMONE screaming and the
CHILDREN following them, dazed.*)

JOCASTA (*in a dying voice*):  Take me to Tiresias.  Where is Tiresias,
    where is he?

CREON:  Here he is, sister.  Here is Tiresias.  (*He lays her down on
    the big chair.*)

TIRESIAS:  I am sorry for you, Queen Jocasta.  Here I am, Tiresias,
    at your command.  What is happening to you?

JOCASTA:  Listen to me, Tiresias, before I die.  Take care of
    Oedipus.  Protect him from the cunning of the Priests.  May
    the true God help you to prevail.  (*She faints.*)

CREON (*crying*):  Jocasta!  Jocasta!  My dear sister.  Ah, Jocasta,
    why did you do this to yourself?

TIMONE (*wailing*):  My Queen!  My Queen!  I wish I had died
    before you!  My Queen!  My Queen!  I wish I had died
    before you.  My Queen!  My Queen!

THE CHILDREN (*screaming around their mother*):  Mother!  Mother!
    Talk to us, mother.  Don't die, mother.  Mother!  Mother!

(*OEDIPUS rushes in from the third door.*)

OEDIPUS:  Oh, God!  What do I hear?  Oh God, what do I see?
    Jocasta!  (*He falls on her, kissing her.*)  Jocasta!  Jocasta!

Jocasta!  Oh God, what happened to Jocasta?  (*Looking to those around him*)  Curse you, what happened to her?  What happened?  What took place?  (*Growling*)  Curse you, why don't you speak?  Answer me, Creon.  You answer, Timone.  Curse you, answer.

TIMONE (*her limbs shaking, her lips trembling*):  Oh, my master.  I wish I had died before this day.

OEDIPUS  (*screaming*):  Tell me what happened.  Weren't you with her?

TIMONE:  Yes, my master.  I was with her in your chamber, while she was lying in your bed, hugging your pillows, kissing them and wetting them with her tears.  I was keeping her company, rubbing her feet, these beautiful feet.  (*She cries.*)

OEDIPUS:  Continue, Timone, continue.

TIMONE (*wiping her tears*):  As we were there, we heard the voice of the High Priest pronouncing the oracle.  As he finished it, my mistress rose, like a storm, slapping her cheeks and pulling her hair.  I tried to calm her down, but she broke away from me, ran to her room and locked the door.  I tried to open it with all my force but I couldn't.  I called my master, Creon.  Oh, my master, I wish I died before her.  I wish I could have been sacrificed instead of her.  I wish the gods . . .

OEDIPUS:  You speak, Creon.  Why didn't you hurry to rescue her?  Why didn't you fly to her, like you flew to the Temple of Delphi.  Speak.  Speak!

CREON:  Yes, Oedipus.  I flew to her like a madman.  I found the door locked.  I broke it and entered, and I found my sister.  Oh, the horror I saw.

OEDIPUS:  Continue, curse it!

CREON:  Oh horror!  I found her hanging from the ceiling with a big rope around her neck, and she was trembling, quavering, and groaning.

OEDIPUS (*growling like an irritated lion*):  And you didn't do anything to help her?

CREON:  Yes, I jumped to the rope and cut it with my knife.  As I released it from her neck, she said in a failing voice: "Take me to Tiresias.  Where is Tiresias?"  I carried her here without thinking . . .  Oh, Oedipus!

OEDIPUS:  Was she able to speak then?  What did she say?  Who did she speak to?

CREON:  To Tiresias, Oedipus.

OEDIPUS:  What did she say, Tiresias?  Have you forgotten what she said?  Don't you remember anything she said?

TIRESIAS:  Yes, Oedipus.  She only asked me to take care of you.

OEDIPUS:  She asked you to take care of me, I who made her suffer all of this, and you who pushed me to do it.  What a sinful criminal I am!  I killed my father, then I killed my mother and my wife.  (*He throws himself on JOCASTA again.*)  Jocasta! Jocasta!  Talk to me, I am your husband, Oedipus.  Jocasta! Jocasta!  (*He turns to TIRESIAS.*)  I wish I had listened to her.  I wish I had obeyed her and ignored you, you, expelled by the temple, cursed by the heavens, and damned by the gods.

TIRESIAS:  May God forgive you, Oedipus.  The plight you are in should not distract you from what you are about to do.  You are Thebes' only hope.

OEDIPUS (*throwing himself on JOCASTA*):  Jocasta! Jocasta!  Jocasta!  My wife.  My beloved.  I am calling you the way you like me to call you.  Answer me, Jocasta.   Answer me.

Talk to me, my beloved, my wife.

(*JOCASTA moves and opens her eyes.*)

OEDIPUS: Jocasta!

JOCASTA: Oedipus! Thank God. I get to see you, my son, before I die.

OEDIPUS: No, you will not die, Jocasta. You will stay with me. You will live for me.

JOCASTA: No, my son. Your mother has finished her time. Today I die, pleased with you and your brothers and sisters. (*The CHILDREN gather around her, kissing her and wetting her with their tears.*) I am going to your father Laius. I ask you to take care of your brothers and sisters. They have no one but you, Oedipus. You are their elder brother. You are in their father's place.

OEDIPUS (*bitterly and in pain*): But I am their father, Jocasta.

JOCASTA: Yes, you are their father, as they have no other father.

OEDIPUS: And I am your husband, Jocasta, your husband and lover.

JOCASTA: Yes, my dear son. You were like a husband to me, since your father Laius died, and you were like a father to my children. You were so good to me that you didn't get married so that another woman would take you away from me and my children, or annoy me like some daughters-in-law do to their mothers-in-law. Thank you, my son.

OEDIPUS (*sighing in pain*): Oh, Jocasta. If this were the whole matter it would have been easy.

JOCASTA: Oh, Oedipus, do you regret that you wasted your youth for the sake of your mother and siblings? I thought we were happy with the way things were, or else I wouldn't have let you remain without a partner to keep you company.

OEDIPUS:  No, Jocasta, that is not what I meant.

JOCASTA:  Don't think I am blaming you, Oedipus.  You sacrificed a lot for us.  But don't worry, my son, you are still in the prime of your youth, and any virgin princess would desire you.  When your father married me he could have been the age of your father today.

OEDIPUS:  No, Jocasta, that is not what I meant.

JOCASTA:  Do not worry, my son.  I don't deny that my possessiveness affected you.  So forgive me, Oedipus.  Forgive your mother.  I do not want to die while you are displeased with me.

OEDIPUS:  No, you will not die, Jocasta.  You won't die.

JOCASTA:  Don't be in agony, my son.  Death is the end of every living being.  What would your young brothers and sisters do if they saw you, their elder, show all that agony?  I ask you to take care of them, Oedipus.  (*Looking at the four children*)  And you, my dear children, my little ones, obey your brother Oedipus as you would obey a father.

CHILDREN (*screaming*):  Do not die, mother.  Don't go, mother.  Don't leave us, mother.

JOCASTA (*turning to CREON*):  And you, Creon, my dear brother.

CREON:  Yes, sister!

JOCASTA:  I ask you to take care of Oedipus.  He is your nephew, Creon.  He is my son.  So be faithful and honest to him as you have always been.  (*She is out of breath.*)  Tiresias.  Where is Tiresias?

TIRESIAS:  Yes, Jocasta.  I am here with you.

JOCASTA (*with a failing voice*):  Protect my son, Oedipus, from the cunning of the priests.  Don't desert him, Tiresias, and may God help you to prevail.  Ah!  Ah!  (*She dies.*)

OEDIPUS (*screaming*):  Jocasta!  Jocasta!  My Mother!  My Wife!  Don't leave me!  Wait for me, Jocasta!  (*He jumps to take his sword.*)

CREON (*stopping him*):  Oedipus!  What are you doing?

OEDIPUS:  Let me!  Let me!  Who do I live for after Jocasta?

TIRESIAS (*in a loud voice*):  For the people of Thebes, Oedipus.  Did you forget your people?  You are their only hope, Oedipus.

(*VOICES of the people are heard outside the palace.*)

VOICES:  Throw the sinner to us, Oedipus.  The sinner is in your palace, Oedipus — the sinner who killed his father, and married his mother.

OEDIPUS:  Curse you, Tiresias!  Are these the people you want me to live for?  They want to kill me.  (*He pushes CREON to take his sword.*)  Let me, Creon!  I am the sinner they are after.

CREON (*pulling at him strongly*):  No, Oedipus.  Don't do it.  Don't do it.

TIRESIAS (*finding his way to them, till he embraces both OEDIPUS and CREON*):  Beware, Oedipus, beware!

VOICES:  Throw the sinner to us, Oedipus.  The sinner is in your palace.

OEDIPUS:  Curse you!  Let me rid them of myself.  I am the sinner they want.

TIRESIAS (*in his loudest voice*):  No, Oedipus.  You are the cleansing river that will wash the sin from Thebes, and relieve the pain of its people.  This is your day, Oedipus.  This is the day of judgment.  This is the day of decision.  This is the day of Thebes.  This is the day of God.

### Curtain

**Act Three**

**Scene One**

*Setting:  In front of the royal palace.  The HIGH PRIEST is sitting on the right, surrounded by the priests, the ELDERS of Thebes and the nobles of Thebes.  On the left, OEDIPUS on his chair.  Around him are TIRESIAS, CREON and Guards.  Behind them is the main entrance to the palace and two side doors.  The PEOPLE of Thebes are moving about in front, weeping and wailing.*

PEOPLE (*weeping and wailing loudly*):  Oh, calamity!  Oh, disaster!  Thebes is weeping for you, Jocasta.  Our crisis is great and we will mourn long.  Oh dear Queen!  Oh, Jocasta! . . . Oedipus, our King, our hearts go out to you in sympathy and we would sacrifice our souls for you.  Good-by, Jocasta.  Good-by, dear Queen.  May the Gods have mercy on you, Jocasta.  Heaven will welcome you, Jocasta.

CHIEF ELDER (*who represents the people, stands in front of Oedipus*):  In your name and in the name of Thebes . . . (*The crowd becomes quieter.*)  Oh, Oedipus, noble King, it was hard for us to come to you today to ask you to remove the cause of our suffering, that the high priest made known to us.  Instead, we now hear this terrible news of your great loss.  All the people are saddened by Jocasta's death.  Our grief is increased because it comes the same day that we had a spark of hope to escape the suffering we have been enduring.  You told us, Oedipus, and we trust you, that each of us feels his own pain and you feel the pain of all of us.  Today, Oedipus, know that the great loss that occurred in your palace made each of us suffer the same pain as you.  This is how we show our gratitude to you.

OEDIPUS (*wiping away his tears*):  Dear people of Thebes, my noble people, if there is anything that could console me for the loss of Jocasta, it would be the sincere feelings that you show me.  I can only thank you from the depths of my sad heart.

CHIEF ELDER:  We would like to leave you today to mourn your loss and put off our request to another time, but the problems of Thebes are too great to be delayed, and Apollo's oracle revealed the reason behind our suffering.  It is in your hands to relieve it, and you are too merciful and too generous not to do that, however occupied you are.

OEDIPUS:  People of Thebes, believe that however occupied I may be, I will not be distracted from your suffering.

CHIEF ELDER:  You are blessed, Oedipus!  This is what we always believed of you.  People of Thebes, hail your king!

THE PEOPLE:  Long live Oedipus!  May the Gods smile upon you!

OEDIPUS:  Now, say what you want.  What do you wish me to do for you?

CHIEF ELDER:  We plead with you to give over to us the evildoer that Apollo's oracle said could be found in your palace, so that God will relieve our suffering.  Give us the man who killed his father and married his mother and who killed our former king, Laius.

OEDIPUS:  What if I alleviated that suffering?  Would you still ask me afterwards to give you that man?

CHIEF ELDER:  There is no way, Oedipus, to remove the suffering except by purging the city from this evildoer.  This was the exact text of the oracle.

OEDIPUS:  Do you know of whom the oracle was speaking?

CHIEF ELDER:  No, Oedipus, we only know that he is in the palace.

OEDIPUS:  Wasn't the oracle given to the High Priest?

CHIEF ELDER:  Yes.

OEDIPUS:  Then ask him to tell you who he is.

CHIEF ELDER:  You are right, King Oedipus.  Oh, High Priest, carrier of Apollo's oracle, we beg you to identify the person the oracle meant.

LUCASIUS:  Your King Oedipus knows this person better than I do.  And the God asked me to let Oedipus tell you who he is.  (*He indicates TIRESIAS.*)

OEDIPUS:  People of Thebes, witness that your Priest is pressing me to claim that this person is Tiresias, but I will never do that.

LUCASIUS: People of Thebes, Oedipus is being merciful to this evil man but is not being merciful to you, who are dying by the hundreds every day from hunger and sickness.

OEDIPUS:  No, people of Thebes.  I have mercy on you, more than I do on myself and my family.  Because of that I angered this priest and his followers.

LUCASIUS: No, by God, I am not angry at Oedipus.  I only delivered the oracle to save you from heaven's wrath, that brought this suffering on you.

CHIEF ELDER:  Yes, Oedipus.  If you know this person, tell us who he is and purge your palace and the city from his evil.

OEDIPUS:  People of Thebes, I am asking you to tell me the truth since only the truth will save us today.  What do you think of me?

CHIEF ELDER:  You are a good king, who does good.  You saved us from the Sphinx.  Then you ruled us justly and wisely.  Your reign has been a blessing to us with safety and abundance until we were struck by this devastating famine.

THE PEOPLE:  Yes, Oedipus, this is true.

OEDIPUS:  Did I ever deprive you of anything I could have given you?

PEOPLE:  Never, Oedipus, never.

OEDIPUS:  You know that the Treasury is empty today.  If it were full, would I have kept it from you and from relieving your troubles?

PEOPLE:  Never, Oedipus.

CHIEF ELDER:  We do not blame you, Oedipus, for anything.  You tried everything you could to lighten our burden yet it was greater than you could lift.

OEDIPUS:  If I tell you that I can lift it from you, would you believe me?

PEOPLE:  Yes, yes.  You saved us before from the sphinx.

OEDIPUS:  So if I refuse to lift it from you because I fear the anger of this High Priest, would you forgive me?

PEOPLE:  No, that would be no excuse.

LUCASIUS:  Does King Oedipus want to tell us that he does not think that this suffering comes from God's wrath, as the oracle said?

OEDIPUS:  No, I think this suffering comes from God's wrath and I am the one who deserves to suffer.

PEOPLE:  No, Oedipus, never.

OEDIPUS:  Yes, people of Thebes, I am the one who deserves to suffer because I could have ended this famine earlier and I did not.  And today I made penance for my sins.

LUCASIUS:  But the suffering hasn't ended.

OEDIPUS:  It will end today, people of Thebes.

CHIEF ELDER:  Today?

OEDIPUS:  Yes, today I will feed your hungry, cover your nakedness, heal your sick, and enrich your poor.  Do you know, people of Thebes, what caused God in his wrath to send this suffering to us?

CHIEF ELDER:  It was because of the evildoer that the oracle mentioned.

OEDIPUS:  No. This evildoer was here before, while the famine only occurred this year.  It is because I let the money of the nation accumulate in the hands of those priests, who kept it from you while you were dying of hunger.  This is the reason for your suffering, and today I decided to confiscate the Temple's money and distribute it equally among you.

LUCASIUS:  People of Thebes, the Temple's money is the gods' money, and Oedipus does not believe in the gods you believe in.  He wants to confiscate it so that more suffering will come upon you.

OEDIPUS:  Would you, Tiresias, answer that for me?  You know more about these issues.

TIRESIAS (*rising*):  People of Thebes, you heard this priest describing your King as an atheist because he tried to improve your condition and relieve you from this plight. This priest tried to do the same with me and he expelled me from the temple when I tried to improve it and stop the corruption brought about by him and his men.

LUCASIUS:  Beware, people of Thebes.  Don't believe the words of this accursed wretch!

TIRESIAS:  People of Thebes, God created you and gave you the mind to evaluate right and wrong and discriminate between good and evil and know what is helpful to you and what is harmful. Do not stop using your mind because of whatever a priest or King says. I don't want you to believe Oedipus because he is the king, but because he is telling the truth, and I don't want you to disbelieve Lucasius because he is a priest, but because he is lying. Lucasius is telling you that this is God's money. I want you to know that we are all God's servants and all that we own, and not just the money in the temple, belongs to God. But you also know that God does not eat or drink and He gave us material things for our benefit and not for the priests to keep for themselves, claiming that these belong to God. (*The PEOPLE give sounds of approval.*)

LUCASIUS: People of Thebes, do not listen to the words of this atheist. He doesn't believe in God and he misled your king, Oedipus. They both plotted against the temple to avoid revealing the evildoer that the oracle asked us to get rid of. God is asking you to take revenge on the person who killed your previous king and these two men want to ignore God's orders. They are taking revenge on me because I proclaimed the oracle that revealed this heinous crime and this evil that all of the water of the two rivers cannot wash away. Can you accept, people of Thebes, that the man who killed his father and married his mother, who killed your previous king, Laius, would live in the royal palace?

THE PEOPLE: No! No!

LUCASIUS: Then ask Oedipus to give you this evildoer so that you can kill him and cleanse your city so that God can alleviate your suffering.

CHIEF ELDER: Our Lord, if you know this evildoer, surrender him to us so that we can purify our city.

OEDIPUS: Yes, I know him, people of Thebes. He is this priest, Lucasius.

(*The PEOPLE utter sounds of surprise.*)

LUCASIUS (*with a false smile*):  See, people of Thebes, how your
     king despises me because I proclaimed the oracle and didn't
     cover it up.  I want you to know that the oracle said the
     evildoer lives in this palace and Lucasius does not live here.

OEDIPUS:  Then let him tell you who he is.

LUCASIUS:  King Oedipus must reveal him himself.

OEDIPUS:  People of Thebes, I know how to make this priest
     reveal who he means.  Know that I confiscated the Temple's
     money before you gathered in this square.  The Temple's
     money is now in the hands of my men and I will distribute
     it among you before the sun sets.

LUCASIUS:  It is not surprising, people of Thebes, that Oedipus
     would take the money from the temple because he is the
     evildoer that the oracle meant.  He is the person who killed
     his father and married his mother and killed your king,
     Laius.

CREON (*rises, angrily*):  Now everything is clear to me.  The clouds
     have lifted from my eyes.  People of Thebes, if this oracle is
     from God, then the God that you worship is a false God and
     the temple that you look toward is a false temple.

LUCASIUS:  Slow down, Creon.  You were a true believer.  What
     happened to you today?

CREON:  As a believer, I was deceived.  Now I renounce that belief
     because I know the truth about you.  People of Thebes, I
     accuse this priest of killing your queen, Jocasta, my sister.
     He made her believe his false oracle, that she was the
     mother of her husband, Oedipus, so she committed suicide
     in her fear of shame and scandal.

PEOPLE (*in shocked disbelief*): Suicide! The Queen committed suicide?

CREON: Yes, people of Thebes. Your Queen killed herself. She hanged herself with a thick rope.

OEDIPUS: Stop, Creon.

CREON: Oedipus, let me reveal the truth to the people. If Jocasta was your wife, she was also my sister and what affects her honor touches me more deeply than it does you. This priest drove Jocasta to commit suicide and ruined her reputation and the reputation of my noble family with this oracle that he made up to convince you not to take the temple's money. Look, people of Thebes. Didn't you see how this priest refused at first to name the person that the oracle meant, since he was hoping that Oedipus would change his mind, and give up Tiresias as the evildoer. But when Oedipus announced that he had already implemented his plan there was nothing for the priest to negotiate. He then announced that Oedipus was the evildoer. Is this a God's oracle, or the lies of a charlatan priest?

LUCASIUS: Stop this, Creon! If you deny the truth in what the oracle said, your sister Jocasta did not deny it, or else she would not have committed suicide

CREON: How dare you, charlatan! You deceived her with your false oracle, which she took as true.

LUCASIUS: You know that your sister, like her mate Oedipus, had little belief in the temple. So why would she commit suicide if she didn't know that the oracle was true?

CREON: Would her lack of belief in the temple make much difference? She realized that the people would believe your false oracle even if she herself did not believe it. Oh, poor Jocasta! She is a victim. Her bad luck placed her between Lucasius and Oedipus. Between the priest who makes up oracles for his own purposes and the king who lets nothing prevent him from working for the good of his people and his kingdom. Even if this meant his damnation and the damnation of his family, and creating scandal for them all. People of Thebes! For your sake Oedipus sacrificed himself and his family, so do not sacrifice Oedipus and his family for this charlatan priest!

LUCASIUS: People of Thebes! Do not blame Creon. His grief for his sister has driven him out of his mind and made him disbelieve the oracle that Oedipus himself cannot deny. If you doubt this, here is Oedipus in front of you. Ask him! (*All eyes turn toward Oedipus.*)

OEDIPUS (*after a short silence, during which the people stand breathless*): Yes, people of Thebes. What Lucasius has said is true. I am the person who killed his father and married his mother. I killed Laius, who is my father and married Jocasta, who is my mother.

CREON: Oedipus!

OEDIPUS: Kill me, people of Thebes! I am the evil you are seeking. Kill me and throw my body to the hungry lions and vultures! There on top of Mount Cithaeron where I was supposed to die thirty-five years ago.

CREON: People of Thebes! Don't believe what Oedipus is saying! He is saying this because he cannot bear living after Jocasta's death. He tried to kill himself when he saw her breathing her last, but I stopped him and Tiresias reminded him that his life is not his own alone but is for his people. So Oedipus agreed to continue living to serve you, people of Thebes, and save you from the suffering you are in. And now he feels that he has paid his debt to his people after he confiscated the temple's money which is going to be distributed among you. So he wants you to kill him, to end the life which has become a burden to him after Jocasta's death.

OEDIPUS:  Yes, people of Thebes.  What Creon said is true and what the High Priest said is also true.

CREON:  Don't believe Oedipus.  He wants you to believe what the Priest fabricated because he has despaired of his life after Jocasta's passing.  How would he know that he is Laius' child with no proof of it but this false oracle?

CHIEF ELDER:  We are torn between Oedipus' words and Creon's. Can the High Priest shed any light on what he knows about this matter?

LUCASIUS:  Yes, I know the whole matter.  An oracle from Apollo came to us thirty-five years ago that Laius would have a child who would kill his father and marry his mother and everything the oracle predicted came to pass.  Laius tried to escape this destiny so he sent his son with his shepherd to kill him in the wilderness, but fate was stronger than Laius and this wretched child lived until he killed his father and married his mother.  This wretched child is none other than Oedipus!

CREON:  No, don't believe this lying priest!  Laius' son was killed by the shepherd then.

(*OEDIPUS is about to speak. TIRESIAS pulls his robe to silence him.*)

LUCASIUS:  Creon is speaking nonsense.  He is trying in vain to defend his nephew, lest you follow the new oracle and purify the city of him, but his defense does not change the truth.  If you are unsure of the oracle, luckily Laius' shepherd is still alive.  Come, Nikos, where are you?  Where are you, Nikos?  (*An elderly man walks from behind the priest and stands in front of the crowd.*)  No doubt a lot of you know this face.

THE PEOPLE:  Yes, yes.  This is Laius' old servant.

LUCASIUS:  Tell them the story of Laius' son.  You must speak the truth.  You are in front of a people's tribunal and in the hands of almighty God.

CREON:  You killed him as your master ordered, didn't you, Nikos?

NIKOS:  No, sir.  I didn't kill him.  I gave him to a shepherd from Corinth.

CREON:  How can we know what the Corinthian shepherd did with him?  Maybe he adopted him and he died there or maybe he is still alive, herding sheep like the father who adopted him.

LUCASIUS:  Luckily the Corinthian shepherd is also still alive. Come here, Betakoras.

(*BETAKORAS moves forward.  He is as elderly as NIKOS.*)

LUCASIUS:  Do you know this man, Nikos?

NIKOS:  Yes, this is Betakoras, the Corinthian shepherd to whom I gave the child.

LUCASIUS:  So tell us, Betakoras.  What did you do with the child?

BETAKORAS:  I gave him to Queen Merope and King Polybus, who adopted him.

CREON:  People of Thebes!  In such a serious matter, we should not rely on the word of a senile shepherd or trust him.  How do we know that this Corinthian shepherd might not have given the king of Corinth some other child, not Laius' son?

LUCASIUS:  Creon, you're trying in vain to contradict what the oracle foretold.

CREON:  I don't believe the oracle that you invented.

LUCASIUS:  Do you know of any identifying marks on this child, Nikos?

NIKOS:  Forgive me, master.  Old age doesn't leave much of my memory that I can trust.

LUCASIUS:  Remember, Nikos, (*threateningly*) remember.  The mark that you know could not be forgotten.

NIKOS:  Forgive me.

LUCASIUS:  Speak up.

NIKOS:  I only remember that in his feet at the back of the heel were two deep scars like a horseshoe — the mark of the rope we used to bind them.

OEDIPUS: (*eagerly, in concern*):  Did you do that to him?

NIKOS (*terrified*):  No, my master.  It . . . it was Laius.  Laius is the one who bound the child's feet and gave him to me like that.

LUCASIUS:  And you, Betakoras, do you remember anything about this mark?

BETAKORAS:  How can I forget, master?  I am the one who named him Oedipus because of the swelling in his feet.

LUCASIUS:  Oh, people of Thebes.  The great God is showing you one of his manifestations so that you can witness with your own eyes the truth of his oracle and so that Creon can stop attacking what he doesn't understand.  Creon challenged the oracle.  Let Oedipus show him his feet.

OEDIPUS (*exposing his feet from beneath his robe*):  Yes, people of Thebes.  This is the mark of the rope that Laius bound my feet with.

CREON (*closing his eyes*):  Oh, calamity!

LUCASIUS:  Do you believe now that the oracle doesn't lie?

CREON (*silent for a while as if stricken by deep sorrow, then he shakes suddenly as if he remembers something he had forgotten*):  Damn you, Nikos!  You are the only one who survived from Laius' followers on that fatal trip and you are the one who brought back the news of his death.  I remember that clearly.

NIKOS:  Yes, master, that is true.

CREON:  And you were in Thebes the day Oedipus entered it after he killed the Sphinx.

NIKOS:  Yes, master.

CREON:  Why didn't you tell us then that Oedipus had killed Laius?  Then my sister would not have married  and this disaster would never have happened.  Curse you, you evil servant!  (*To the PEOPLE*)  Elders of Thebes, Jocasta's honor is my honor and this shepherd caused it to be sullied and degraded, and this led her to her death.  So it is my right to ask you to condemn him to the harshest punishment.

PEOPLE:  Yes, Nikos has to be punished.  Nikos must suffer death.

LUCASIUS:  Not so fast, people of Thebes!  Let's hear what Nikos has to say.

CREON:  Speak up!  Why didn't you tell us that he killed Laius?

NIKOS:  I told Queen Jocasta and she told me not to reveal this to anyone else.

CREON:  Did you tell her that he was Laius' son?

NIKOS:  No, master.  I didn't tell her that.

CREON:  Curse you!  Why didn't you tell her?

NIKOS:  Because my master Laius had me swear by all the gods
never to tell my mistress Jocasta that his son was still alive.

CREON:  When did he have you swear this?

NIKOS:  The day he summoned me to accompany him on that fatal
trip.

CREON (*in a trembling voice*):  Oh, dear Jocasta!  Death has sealed
your lips forever.  There is no way to question you about
what this sinful shepherd is saying.

NIKOS (*with tears in his eyes*):  My master, Queen Jocasta was good
and generous to me.  Even after she believed that I killed her
son, her heart didn't change toward me.  If I would lie to
everybody, I would never lie to her.

CREON:  What a calamity!  What a scandal!  I wish the earth had
swallowed me up before I saw this day.

LUCASIUS:  People of Thebes, do you see how Apollo's oracle
revealed its terrible truth?  Have you ever seen or heard of
any sin worse than this?  Is it any wonder that God pours
out his tortures on this country and afflicts you with this
famine and this plague?  Don't you see that this is justice
from the heavens?

PEOPLE:  Yes, this is justice from the heavens.

LUCASIUS:  Are you willing to have someone on the throne of
your country who killed his father, married his mother,
polluted your sacred temple and kept in his palace this
atheist priest who was banished by the temple and cursed
by the gods?

PEOPLE:  No, no!

LUCASIUS:  What are you waiting for?  This is the sin I ordered
you to cleanse your city from.  Are you willing?  Shout after

me.  Down with Oedipus, the sinner!

PEOPLE:  Down with Oedipus, the sinner!  Down with the house
of Laius!  We will no longer be ruled by a sinful house.

LUCASIUS:  Not so fast, people of Thebes!  Do not mix the guilty
with the innocent.  This is your Prince Creon. As you know,
he has a spotless reputation.  And if he recently spoke
against the Temple, still in his heart he is a believer with a
sincere belief. If you wish, you can make him the King of
Thebes.  He is worthy.  Do you agree?

PEOPLE:  Yes, yes!  We want Creon to rule us.  You are our King,
Creon!

CREON (*shouting in anger*):  Curse you!  What are you saying?
This is a betrayal of King Oedipus.  I can't accept this
betrayal by you or by myself.  People of Thebes, I should
have hidden out of shame because of what happened in my
family, not to appear in front of you or utter a word.

LUCASIUS:  You are innocent, Creon.  You are not to blame.

PEOPLE:  Yes.  You are innocent, Creon.

CREON:  But Thebes is my country and it is my duty to advise you
and speak the words of truth.  Fate decided that Oedipus
would be the husband of my sister and also her son and that
I would be his brother-in-law and also his uncle.  But neither
the throne of Thebes nor that of any other country has ever
seen a better king in his reputation, justice, generosity,
nobility, love for his people and dedication to their service.
Do you deny that?

PEOPLE:  No, no!  This is true!

CREON:  Then you and I both owe it to him to ask God to forgive
him and have mercy on him, since he did not know when he
killed Laius that he was his father or when he married

Jocasta that she was his mother.  The tragedy that has befallen him deserves your sympathy, not your anger.

PEOPLE:  Creon speaks the truth!  This is the truth!

LUCASIUS:  Yes, Creon spoke well, yet if Oedipus had done what he did to his parents without knowing that they were his parents, then the oracle of the gods wouldn't have considered him a sinful person who must be cleansed from the city.

CREON:  No, Oedipus couldn't have known.  That is impossible.

LUCASIUS:  Here is your nephew, Creon.  Ask him yourself.

CREON (*overcome by anguish*):  Oh, calamity!  I do not dare to ask him!

LUCASIUS:  Then I will ask him myself.  Tell the truth, Oedipus.  You are standing before the judgment of the people and in the hands of the all-knowing God, who knows all secret and hidden things.  Didn't you know, when you were in Corinth, that Laius and Jocasta were your parents and that you would kill your father and marry your mother, as the old Apollonian oracle predicted?

OEDIPUS:  Yes, I heard but I did not believe this untruthful oracle and I wanted to challenge it, to prove its falseness.

LUCASIUS:   Did you hear, people of Thebes?  Oedipus did kill his father and marry his mother to prove the oracle false, to challenge God.

PEOPLE:  Oh, abomination!  What a terrible crime!  What a horrible sin!

LUCASIUS:  Come, now.  What are you waiting for?  Carry out heaven's command!  The suffering will not be lifted from you until you cleanse the city from this sin, from the sinner who killed his father and married his mother to challenge God.  (*A great disturbance among the crowd.*)

PEOPLE:  Down with Oedipus!  Down with the sinner!

OEDIPUS:  People of Thebes!  My life is in your hands.  Kill me if you choose and no one from my family will seek revenge, or banish me from your land if it is hard for you to kill me, but do not forget that the money my men confiscated from the temple is yours by right.  Divide it fairly among you, since my worst fear is that the city would be cleansed from my sin, but the torment would remain.

LUCASIUS:  Do not be deceived by what this sinner is saying.  He wants to soften your heart so that you will keep him.  Tell him, "You sinner, this is not your business."

PEOPLE:  You sinner, this is not your business.  Down with Oedipus!  Down with the sinner!

TIRESIAS (*standing up and shouting*):  People of Thebes!  People of Thebes!  You heard what the high priest said.  Now listen to what I have to say.

LUCASIUS:  This atheist priest wants to defend the sinner.  Silence this blind one.

PEOPLE:  Silence, Tiresias!  We don't want to hear you.

TIRESIAS:  People of Thebes . . .

PEOPLE:  Silence, blind one, may the gods silence you as they blinded you.

TIRESIAS (*angrily*):  Curse you!  Do not deny the wisdom of the heavens!  They took my eyesight so that I see no evil and allowed my tongue to say the truth.  People of Thebes, hear one word from me.  I will not say another unless you ask me.

CHIEF ELDER:  Let's hear what he has to say.

PEOPLE:  What does he have to say?

TIRESIAS:  Don't you see that Oedipus committed a major sin, since he killed Laius and married Jocasta after he was told they were his parents?

PEOPLE:  Yes, yes!

TIRESIAS:  Then know that this was my one word.  Do you want to hear the other?

PEOPLE:  Yes.  Say what you want.

TIRESIAS:  Did you know about this major sin before today?

PEOPLE:  No, we did not.

TIRESIAS:  Did anything like this ever cross your mind before today?

PEOPLE:  No, it never crossed our mind.

TIRESIAS:  Isn't it for your own good and for the good of Thebes that such sin is revealed to you so that you can cleanse your land?

PEOPLE:  Yes.

TIRESIAS:  Wouldn't you like me to reveal to you other sins that are greater and worse, to cleanse your city from all sins and not just some of them?

PEOPLE:  Yes.  Say what you want.  We are listening.

LUCASIUS:  Beware, people of Thebes!  Don't let this rejected priest who was cursed by the gods mislead you.

TIRESIAS:  This priest is worried that if I reveal these, he would become the object of your wrath as did Oedipus, his partner in this sin.

LUCASIUS:  Am I his partner in this sin?!

TIRESIAS:  Yes, and you know it well.

LUCASIUS:  A lie!  No one can believe it!

TIRESIAS:  Then why would you worry if I reveal this matter to the people?  People of Thebes, if you are content that I do not reveal the whole truth to you, then you will assume the burden of my silence.

PEOPLE:  No!  Say what you want.  Let him, Lucasius.  We need to know everything.

TIRESIAS:  Do you know, people of Thebes, why this priest expelled me from the temple and banished me?

LUCASIUS:  Because you turned away from God and became an atheist.

TIRESIAS:  No, people of Thebes.  It is because I tried to stop sins like those Oedipus committed.

LUCASIUS:  Just look at this clever atheist!  See how his skills have failed him and his lies have been revealed to you.  You all know that I expelled him from the temple during the reign of Laius, not in Oedipus' time.  How can he say I expelled him because he tried to stop Oedipus' sin?

TIRESIAS:  Wait a moment, people of Thebes.  Soon you will know everything and this tragedy will reveal to you the strangest thing you have heard today.  Oedipus and Jocasta sat under the shadow of the tree of sin, and ate from its forbidden fruit for a long time.  That tree was planted in the time of Laius.  Do you know who planted it and watered and tended it until it grew, flourished, and branched out?

PEOPLE:  Who? Who?

TIRESIAS:  This priest who is worried now that I might reveal to you the whole truth of which you know only a part.

LUCASIUS:  Don't believe him, people of Thebes.  He is a lying atheist!

TIRESIAS:  Did you see me interrupt the speech of this priest when he revealed to you the crime of Oedipus and his mother?

PEOPLE:  No, no!

TIRESIAS:  Didn't you see me keep silent until he finished his speech?

PEOPLE:  Yes, yes.

TIRESIAS:  Then ask him not to interrupt my speech before I have revealed to you the whole truth.

PEOPLE:  Don't interrupt him, Lucasius.  Let him finish his speech.

TIRESIAS:  The elders among you know about the animosity and rivalry between your previous king Laius and Polybus, the King of Corinth.  When Jocasta became pregnant, jealousy gnawed at Polybus' heart and he worried that his kingdom would be inherited by Laius' heirs if he died childless.  So do you know what our high priest did then?

PEOPLE:  What did he do?

LUCASIUS:  Do not believe this atheist.

PEOPLE:  Let us hear the rest of his speech.  Don't interrupt him.

TIRESIAS:  This priest contacted Polybus and promised him that he would have a curse placed on Laius and his hiers if Polybus pledged twenty thousand Obols to the Temple. Then he made up this old oracle to make Laius kill his son, and become heirless.

CREON:  Then this was a plot of our enemy Polybus, king of Corinth.  What a scheme!  It could shake mountains!  Ah, if only Laius knew, he wouldn't have tried to kill his son, and this terrible catastrophe wouldn't have happened.  Ah, if I can only take revenge on Polybus for the shame and disgrace he caused me and my sister.

OEDIPUS:  Remember, Creon, that Polybus is now a friend.  There are friendly relations between our kingdoms.

CREON:  How could we have a friendship with him after what he has done?

TIRESIAS:  This is not Polybus' fault, he was Laius' enemy, and what enemy wouldn't want to see his foe going through such misfortune?  What king who envies his rival for having an heir wouldn't want that heir to move to his own palace, for him to rear, knowing that this baby is going to grow up to kill his father and marry his mother?  I swear that if Laius was in the place of Polybus, he wouldn't have hesitated in giving this priest any sum of money, to cause this catastrophe to his enemy.  The criminal is not king Polybus, it's the priest Lucasius.

CREON:  What a terrible evil!  What great cunning!

LUCASIUS:  This is a calumny on me and the king of Corinth.  If Polybus were here he would have denied this.

TIRESIAS (*says something to his follower, who goes quickly inside the palace*):  Be witness, people of Thebes, to what this priest is saying.

LUCASIUS:  No, be witness to a great king, who is a good ally of

Thebes and a friend of its people.

TIRESIAS: People of Thebes, you will hear now the testimony of this great king himself. The King and Queen of Corinth arrived today in your city, and are the guests of your king Oedipus.

CREON: Oh, my God. What am I hearing? The wicked enemy and his wife are here?

OEDIPUS: Be careful, Creon.

CREON: People of Thebes. This is your enemy, who came from his country to see the outcome of his doing, and to gloat over you and your royal family.

OEDIPUS: Creon, do not let your anger run away with you. Polybus who is visiting Thebes today is not the Polybus who was our enemy in Laius' time. Remember that he is our guest today and we should not insult a guest even if he is an enemy. Polybus came to support Thebes in its plight. He is bringing three thousand wagonloads of food that are on their way to us.

PEOPLE: What a generous king!

OEDIPUS: Kind people of Thebes. Here are our noble guests. Give them the greeting of great kings.

(*Enter POLYBUS and MEROPE with their retinue.*)

PEOPLE: Welcome, King and Queen of Corinth. Welcome Merope and Polybus. Long live Polybus and Merope!

POLYBUS (*greeting them*): Thank you, thank you, good people of Thebes. The Queen and I thank you for this warm welcome in spite of your troubles. We would have liked to have visited great Thebes at a happier moment and in more prosperous times.

CHIEF ELDER:  The people of Thebes would like to thank your
  majesty for your sympathy and generosity.

TIRESIAS:  And they hope to hear your testimony.

LUCASIUS:  Your majesty, Polybus the Great, will you tolerate this
  cursed atheist Tiresias accusing you in front of the people
  who love you and honor you, saying that you bribed me to
  make up this oracle to Laius about his son?  Deny this lie in
  front of the people, Polybus.

POLYBUS:  Kings should not lie to their people, neither should
  they repudiate their own past actions.  Are you worried,
  Lucasius, that if I tell the truth, my son Oedipus and his
  kind people would have a change of heart and the pure
  friendship that connects our countries and our people would
  be harmed?  No, I will not deny that I was Laius' enemy as
  he was mine and that led to animosity between Thebes and
  Corinth, but merciful God changed our hatred into
  friendship and war and discord into peace and harmony in
  spite of those who were working to fan the flames of hatred,
  in order to fill their boxes with the gold of our offerings and
  sacrifices.  And you, Lucasius, know who I mean.

TIRESIAS:  This is the day of judgment and the people want to
  know everything, so would you tell them who were
  disrupting the peace between you and Laius?

POLYBUS:  This High Priest and his men.

TIRESIAS:  The people want to hear your testimony, Polybus,
  about Laius' child.

PEOPLE:  Yes, good Polybus.  We want to hear your testimony.

POLYBUS:  When I heard that Queen Jocasta was pregnant by
  Laius I was very jealous so I went to the temple asking God
  to give me what they gave Laius and I received an oracle
  saying that the one of us that would die without an heir

would lose his kingdom to his rival. I was very troubled and when this priest saw that he comforted me and asked me what I would offer the Temple if we asked the gods not to let Laius enjoy his son. I offered him 20,000 Obols. A few days later the priest gave me the oracle regarding Laius' son.

LUCASIUS: I don't think, my Lord, that you mean that I invented this oracle myself. You saw how the oracle was fulfilled in every detail. If it was not from the God Apollo it would not have come about in that way.

POLYBUS: I did not say that you invented that oracle.

LUCASIUS: Then bear witness to the people, my Lord, that I did not invent it.

POLYBUS: I cannot bear witness to something I do not know.

TIRESIAS: Tell the people, Polybus, how Laius' child ended up in your palace.

POLYBUS: Lucasius came to me one afternoon to inform me that the gods had decided that Laius' child should grow up in my palace until adulthood. Then he would kill his father Laius and marry his mother Jocasta.

LUCASIUS: Didn't what I told you about come to pass? Didn't Laius' child come to you and didn't you raise him in your palace?

POLYBUS: Yes, Betakoras the shepherd brought him to me. We were very happy with him and the Queen and I adopted him.

CREON: You adopted him and raised him in animosity so that he would kill his father and marry his mother when he grew up.

OEDIPUS: Creon!

POLYBUS:  I do not deny, noble Creon, that this was my intention to begin with, but Merope and I came to love Oedipus and we felt as if he were our own son.  Later, I sincerely wished that he had not done what he did, but this was beyond my control.

LUCASIUS:  Listen carefully, people of Thebes, to what Polybus the great is saying.  If I had made up the oracle as Tiresias claims, the child would not have survived the killing to grow up in Polybus' palace and committed the acts he did.

TIRESIAS:  Luckily, the shepherds Nikos and Betakoras are still alive.  Let's hear their testimony.  Bring Nikos the shepherd.

LUCASIUS:  What do you want from Nikos?  He has already given his testimony.  Do you want to make him change what he said earlier?

TIRESIAS:  Order this priest to be silent.  He is worried that Nikos will testify against him.

(*NIKOS steps forward.*)

TIRESIAS:  Tell me honestly, Nikos.  Who gave you Laius' child?

NIKOS:  My master Laius.

TIRESIAS:  Did he order you to kill him?

NIKOS:  Yes.

TIRESIAS:  Did you kill him?

NIKOS:  No, my master.  I did not.

TIRESIAS:  Then you disobeyed the order of your king and master, as you have testified yourself.  You must be punished today for disobeying this royal order.

NIKOS (*fearfully, pleading*):  But, my master, I could not have killed him, even if I wanted to.

TIRESIAS:  What could have stopped you?

NIKOS:  The heavens' oracle, that said this child is not to be killed.

TIRESIAS:  Who told you about that oracle?

NIKOS:  The High Priest himself, my master.  Ask him if you wish.

TIRESIAS:  Where did the High Priest meet you?

NIKOS:  On my way to Mount Cithaeron.

TIRESIAS:  What did he tell you?

NIKOS:  He told me that I could not kill him because the oracle declared that he should live and that I should give him to a shepherd from Corinth.  I did what the oracle foretold and I gave him to Betakoras.

TIRESIAS:  Now bring me Betakoras. (*BETAKORAS steps forward. To NIKOS*)  Did you tell Betakoras when you gave him the child that he was Laius' son?

NIKOS:  Yes.

TIRESIAS:  Did you know, Betakoras, when you took the child to your king Polybus that he was the child of Laius, king of Thebes?

BETAKORAS:  Yes.

TIRESIAS:  People of Thebes, punish this shepherd who kidnapped the son of your king Laius and gave him to his enemy.

BETAKORAS (*frightened*):  But I am a citizen of Corinth and not a citizen of Thebes.

TIRESIAS:  Today you are in Thebes and you are subject to its
    laws.

BETAKORAS:  My king Polybus the Great, protect me from them.
    I am one of your subjects.

POLYBUS:  I cannot protect you from the laws of Thebes while you
    are here.

BETAKORAS:  You, High Priest, save me.  I only did what you
    ordered me to do.

LUCASIUS:  Liar!  I didn't give you any order.

BETAKORAS:  You told me it was an oracle, so how could these
    people punish me for carrying out what the heavens' oracle
    foretold?

LUCASIUS:  Yes, you should not punish him for carrying out the
    oracle from the heavens.

TIRESIAS (*laughing*):  The heavens' oracle!  Laugh with me, people
    of Thebes, at Lucasius' so-called oracle.

LUCASIUS:  Laugh at the oracle if you wish, since you are an
    atheist, but the people of Thebes are believers.  Their faith
    keeps them from ridiculing the oracle.

TIRESIAS:  I am asking them to ridicule the oracle you invented.
    Now I ask them to admire your skill and talent in authoring
    this tragedy, more strange and monstrous than anything the
    world has ever seen.  How skillful you are, Lucasius.  You
    made up this oracle, and then you carried it out through
    your cunning plans.  You brought suffering on Laius and
    denied him the greatest pleasure in life, the pleasure of
    having a child.  You turned this blessing into a curse on him
    and made him commit this terrible crime, to give up his

innocent child to be killed and you didn't even stop at that.
Instead of ending the tragedy by killing the child, you were
enjoying the pleasure of authorship so much that you added
more acts to the play. You refused to let the child be killed
and encouraged Nikos to give him to Betakoras and had
Betakoras take him to Polybus. And you told each of them
that he was fulfilling an oracle from heaven, abusing their
belief in God and in the Temple to execute your plan and act
in your farce.

LUCASIUS:  However convincing you are in misleading the people
and causing them to doubt their faith in the Temple and in
God, you cannot deny the truth of this oracle. If I, as you
said, encouraged those people to place this child in Polybus'
palace where he grew up, how would you explain the
fulfillment of the rest of the oracle? Can you, the one
expelled from the Temple and cursed by the gods, claim that
I insinuated that Oedipus kill his father and marry his
mother?

TIRESIAS:  Yes, using the same style in which you wrote the first
act, you continued creating the tragedy. People of Thebes,
this great author wishes to hide from you the way he wrote
this brilliant tragedy. The good creator usually hides the
secrets of his trade, lest others follow him and compete with
him. I will reveal to you the technique of this author and
share with you the secret of his brilliance. Not that I would
like any of you to follow his example. It is enough for the
people of Thebes, of Hellas, no, it is enough for humanity to
have one man who excels in this art as this priest does, to fill
the earth with evil, tragedies and crises that would rend the
heart, shake the body and fill the heavens and earth with
uproar. I will reveal to you the secret so that no one after
you will be deceived by a charlatan like him who abuses the
sacred and trades on the faith of believers and uses God's
love, which is one of the noblest feelings, as a tool to
manipulate people to commit the worst of crimes and the
most horrible sins.

LUCASIUS:  Do not try to tempt these listeners with your rhetoric. Answer me.  Can you claim in front of the people that I encouraged Oedipus to do what he did against his mother and his father?

TIRESIAS:  People of Thebes.  It is our good fortune and the misfortune of this skillful author that the people he chose for his tragedy are real people who are still alive among us. They can tell us what he is trying to hide from us.  They can testify for or against him in this difficult day, this day of judgment.  I will not judge him.  This is the people's right.  I will only draw back the curtain to reveal his tricks and machinations.  I am only one of the characters in his tragedy and I explained to you my role as did Polybus and Nikos and Betakoras in the first act of the tragedy.  Now let us call upon the characters of the second act to tell us about the work of this author and the roles he created for them, which they acted out in this theatre of life in this suffering country. Would King Oedipus reveal to us the truth about the role that was given to him?

OEDIPUS (*standing*):  People of Thebes.  If it is easy for others of the characters of this tragedy as Tiresias calls it to tell you about their roles, it is very hard for me to tell you about my role, as I will be cursing myself in front of you.  Would you please absolve me from testifying?  I have already been humiliated enough.

TIRESIAS:  Oh, great Oedipus!  You were brave when you chose rather for that priest to expose you and scandalize your family, than to give up the reform you wanted for your people.  Don't let anything stop you from revealing the circumstances that caused you and your family to fall into these tragic events.  Let the people know the root of the problem that caused all these pains and crises.  Tell them how you grew up in Polybus' palace and how you ended up killing your father Laius and marrying your mother Jocasta.

OEDIPUS:  I found myself in the royal palace in Corinth enjoying

Merope's tenderness and Polybus' generosity.  For all that I knew, they were my parents and I was their only child. Polybus raised me well and entrusted me to good teachers who taught me everything that a king's son ought to know.

TIRESIAS:  Do you remember if either of them ever hurt you or humiliated you?

OEDIPUS:  No, except for one day when my mother Merope hit me lightly.  I wouldn't have remembered but for the fact that it was connected to an event that still makes me troubled and uncomfortable.

TIRESIAS:  What is it, Oedipus?  Tell us, tell your people everything.

OEDIPUS:  I was then about seven years old and in the palace there were two cats, who bore a little kitten.  My mother Merope loved and pampered them.  One day I saw the two male cats fighting over the female, so I hit the kitten to prevent him from mounting his mother.  Then Merope hit me and scolded me, saying  "Don't you have any sympathy for this weak animal?  Do you want to kill him when he is innocent?"  So I told her with tears in my eyes that he bit his father and attacked his mother.  So she picked me up to console me and said, "This is an animal who cannot reason. You cannot blame him."  Alas for my sin.  I have lived to see myself behave worse than this animal.

TIRESIAS:  Look, people of Thebes, how this reveals Oedipus' true. nature.  He refused even when he was a child to accept that this animal attacked his father and assaulted his mother. Don't you see that he wouldn't have committed as an adult what he rejected as a child, except that the author of this tragedy forced him to play this horrible role and deviate from the true nature that gracious God gave him.

LUCASIUS:  What has this to do with me?  This atheist priest wants me to bear the guilt for Oedipus' sin, but with no proof.

TIRESIAS:  Oedipus is going to present the proof.  Go on, Oedipus, with your story.  Tell us what made you then travel to Thebes?

OEDIPUS:  I had heard about Thebes and its king Laius, but they didn't mean any more to me than any other Greek cities and their kings until I was seventeen years old.  One night I was drinking with a group of friends.  We got drunk and I got into a quarrel with another young man.  He angered me and I cursed him.  He took me aside and told me that Polybus and Merope were not my parents and that I was a foundling with no known father or mother.  The blood was boiling in my head and I was about to kill him for his insult but he told me to consult the oracle at Delphi and if I found him a liar I should kill him then.

TIRESIAS:  Didn't you tell Polybus and Merope about what you heard?

OEDIPUS:  Yes, I told them and they denied this.  They claimed that this was all a result of drinking and they consoled me and comforted me.  But I was still suspicious so one day I sneaked out and went to the Temple of Delphi to ask about my true ancestry and this High Priest told me that I was the son of Laius and Jocasta, the King and Queen of Thebes and recounted to me how Laius gave me up to be killed in order to escape the fate the oracle had foretold.  But fate made sure that I lived and grew up in Polybus' palace to fulfill my destiny.

TIRESIAS:  Did this young man tell you how he knew about that secret?

OEDIPUS:  No, he didn't tell me and I didn't ask.

CREON:  Maybe our honorable guest, King Polybus, is the one who suggested it to the young man.

POLYBUS:  The honorable Creon is against me because of my old animosity with his relative Laius.  I want you to know, Creon, that I did not know up until this day who that young man was.

CREON:  Didn't you ask Oedipus about him then?

PLOYBUS:  Yes, I asked him then and he refused to tell me his name.

OEDIPUS:  I promised him that I would not punish him or reveal his name unless the Temple of Delphi denied what he said.

POLYBUS:  Would you tell us his name now, Oedipus?

OEDIPUS:  And would he be safe from your wrath?

POLYBUS:  Yes.

OEDIPUS:  He is here among us.

POLYBUS:  Here?

OEDIPUS:  Yes, among your retinue.  If he wishes to reveal himself, he should do so and I guarantee his safety.  (*One of POLYBUS' men stands up.*)

MAN:  I am here, my master.

POLYBUS (*regarding him fiercely*):  You, Pontus?

PONTUS:  Yes, my master.  Forgive me, great Polybus, for the sin I committed.

TIRESIAS:  Oh, God, thou art just.  You have allowed all the secrets of this tragedy to be revealed to us.  Tell us, young man— Excuse me, I am blind.  I don't see you.  You must have grown older since—Tell us, Pontus, who told you that secret?

LUCASIUS:  Beware, Pontus, lest your tongue wrong the Temple.

PEOPLE:  Be silent.  Let us hear what he has to say.

PONTUS:  This High Priest is the one who told me to goad
    Oedipus and tell him what I told him.

PEOPLE:  What a horrible plot!  What a crime!

TIRESIAS:  How could you agree, Pontus, to do this task?

PONTUS:  He claimed to me that this was Apollo's oracle and he
    had chosen me to be the person to reveal this secret to
    Oedipus.  I had no choice but to follow his orders.

TIRESIAS:  What do you have to say about that, Lucasius?

LUCASIUS:  I only told him what the oracle said.  How can I be
    blamed?

TIRESIAS:  The High Priest is still defending his oracle.

LUCASIUS:  Why wouldn't I, a believer, defend the oracle when an
    atheist like you attacks it?

TIRESIAS:  The best answer we can give you is to listen to the rest
    of King Oedipus' story.

OEDIPUS:  I returned from the Temple of Delphi with my faith in
    the temple and the gods shaken.  I asked myself how could I
    believe in such an arbitrary God, who destined me for this
    horrible fate?

LUCASIUS:  Now you can hear for yourselves how Oedipus
    confesses his disbelief and atheism.  Do you think it is was
    too much for a person like him to be struck such
    punishment from heaven?

TIRESIUS:  Look, people of Thebes, at this weak logic.  Oedipus was a believer and went to the Temple to consult the gods about his true ancestry, but this priest shook his belief and planted in him the seeds of doubt and atheism.

OEDIPUS:  Yes, people of Thebes.  I doubted then the wisdom of God.  Then I doubted his existence, but I never doubted my own mind and free will.  I said to myself, I am a human being who has choices.  I can do something or not do it.  At that time I was addicted to wine to help me deal with my problems.  I would line up the cups in front of me, throw some of them on the ground to break them and leave the others in place unbroken.  I used to tell myself, "This cup in my hand, I can break it if I want or leave it whole."  I did not doubt my ability to do this and my free will.  No one could force me to break a cup or leave it whole, so how could these priests claim that I would kill my father and marry my mother?  Then I decided to challenge this rash oracle.

LUCASIUS:  Look, people of Thebes, how this wretched person believed in his own mind and will and did not believe in the God who created him.  He wanted to challenge his fate.  I advised him against that and he rashly refused to listen to me.

OEDIPUS:  Yes, this priest summoned me and when I met him he told me not to challenge the God's oracle.

TIRESIAS:  He summoned you?  I wonder who told him about your intention.

OEDIPUS:  I do not know.

POLYBUS:  I informed him.  I became suspicious that Oedipus was shutting himself off, becoming addicted to wine, breaking glasses and talking unintelligibly to himself.  And when I asked him to tell me what was going on in his mind, he swore on my honor that he would go to Thebes and kiss the head of his father and comfort the heart of his mother to prove that the oracle was untrue.  I was concerned for him about the results of that, so I spoke to the high priest so that he might bring him back to reason.

TIRESIAS:  In fact, the priest brought about his suffering and calamities.

LUCASIUS:  This is all fabrications and lies.  I strongly warned Oedipus against going to Thebes and advised him as best I could.  He did not accept my warning or my advice.  Let Oedipus deny this if he can.

OEDIPUS:  Yes.  It is true that Lucasius warned and cautioned me and when I insisted on going he described Laius to me in such detail as if I could see him and claimed that he would block my path to Thebes.

TIRESIAS:  Listen, people of Thebes.  He described Laius to Oedipus in great detail and told him he would block his path.

LUCASIUS:  I meant for Oedipus to recognize him when he saw him, to avoid approaching him and so avoid killing him, if he could.

TIRESIAS:  No, you described him so that Oedipus would recognize him and kill him.

LUCASIUS:  You lie!  If I wanted that, as you claim, I wouldn't have warned him against going to Thebes.

TIRESIAS:  No, you warned him in order to tempt him with what you were warning him against.  Since you knew how headstrong he was, the more you warned him the more you tempted him.

LUCASIUS:  If you believed in God, you wouldn't go to such extremes in denying His oracle and you would have deduced from this the truth of the oracle, since my warning did not prevent it from taking place. Or else tell me how Oedipus would have killed his father when he was planning to kiss his head, as he claimed?

TIRESIAS:  Tell us, Oedipus, how you killed Laius.

OEDIPUS:  I headed for Thebes until I reached where the three roads  met.  There I met Laius with his retinue in a carriage preceded by a powerful runner.  I knew it was Laius as soon as I saw him so I directed my horse toward him shouting "Do not fear me, father.  Do not believe that false oracle. Here I am, coming to kiss your head and obey your orders."

TIRESIAS:  How did he answer you?

OEDIPUS:  He did not answer me.  He did not give me time to answer.  He and his retinue attacked me with their swords. I tried to protect myself with my sword and in a cursed moment — I do not know how it happened — I found my sword dripping blood and saw my father and four of his men dead and the fifth running away.  I didn't want to follow him and I changed my direction and returned to Corinth.  I was cursing the hand that struck down my father. I reached for my sword to cut off that hand and I realized that I had broken my sword on my saddle and thrown it down on the road. (*He is overcome by tears and cannot speak.*)

PEOPLE:  Oh, poor Oedipus.  Mercy on Oedipus!

TIRESIAS:  People of Thebes, this priest must have told Laius about Oedipus' journey and described him to his father. Or else how would Laius have known that this rider was Oedipus and known the time he left Corinth?

LUCASIUS:  Liar!  Liar!

TIRESIAS:  Then tell me.  What made Laius leave Thebes on that accursed day?

LUCASIUS:  How would I know?  I am neither his keeper nor his confidant.

TIRESIAS:  Creon, do you know anything about that?

CREON:  No.  Laius didn't tell me anything that day, which offended me.

TIRESIAS:  Bring me Nikos the shepherd.  He might know something.

LUCASIUS:  How would a shepherd know about the king's intentions, when his brother-in-law and confidant didn't?

TIRESIAS:  Do you want to prevent the shepherd's testimony to the people?  Come on, Nikos.  You saw how God has exposed this priest in front of everyone.  He will not be able to harm or help anyone after this.  Tell the truth and do not be afraid.  Did your master Laius tell you why he was leaving Thebes that day?

NIKOS:  Yes.  He left in order to stop Oedipus and kill him before he reached Thebes, hoping to survive the cursed oracle because if Oedipus was able to get into Thebes then Laius would be a dead man.

TIRESIAS:  Who informed your master about that?

NIKOS:  A messenger from the High Priest.

LUCASIUS:  Do not believe this shepherd.  He only said that at the atheist Tiresias' prompting.

TIRESIAS (*laughing*):  How could I prompt him when he was with you and you brought him here to testify for you?  See, people of Thebes, how this criminal priest planned everything in order to push Oedipus into killing his father.

LUCASIUS:  People of Thebes.  Anyone who has eyes can see.  The

blind Tiresias planned all of this to absolve his master
Oedipus from the crime of killing his father.  He wanted to
find a justification for this heinous crime.

TIRESIAS:  Yes, the blame for killing Laius does not fall on
Oedipus, as you have heard yourself.  It falls on this priest
who carefully planned this crime and pushed Oedipus into
it without leaving him any chance to escape.  Tell me,
people of Thebes, would any one of you dare to claim in
front of the people's tribunal and in front of almighty God
that he would have been able to escape from this tight net if
he were in Oedipus' place?  If there is any one of you who
can claim that, let him come forward.

PEOPLE:  No, no!

TIRESIAS:  Then the killer of your king, Laius, is not in fact his son
Oedipus but this sinful priest.

PEOPLE:  Down with the sinful priest!  Death to Laius' killer!

LUCASIUS:  It is hard for me, People of Thebes, to see that you
could  be deceived by the words of this banished atheist.  He
was able to make you accept Oedipus' crime of killing his
father.  I fear that he will drag you into accepting him
marrying his mother as well.  This would be a grave
disaster.

TIRESIAS:  The one who pushed Oedipus into killing his father is
the same person who pushed him into marrying his mother.
Listen to your king Oedipus telling you how it all happened.

OEDIPUS:  I returned to Corinth with my worry increased, fearful
that the second part of the oracle would come true just as
the first part did, but I never lost my belief in my will and
my freedom of choice.  I said to myself that Laius and his
people attacked me with their swords and forced me to
defend myself.  Laius was killed without my planning or
premeditating it.  But to marry my mother, who gave birth

to me, would be impossible for me even if there were a
thousand oracles from a thousand gods.

TIRESIAS:  People of Thebes, think about what Oedipus is saying.
Wouldn't this be how any of you would have felt if he were
in Oedipus' place?

OEDIPUS (*continuing his speech*):  But the image of Laius dying,
covered in blood, kept haunting me, increasing my feelings
of guilt.  I often thought about killing myself, but I was
suspicious about whether I was truly descended from Laius,
and what strengthened this suspicion was how he met me
and the evil look he gave me, which could not be that of a
father toward his son, who never wronged him.  But this
suspicion did not alleviate my suffering, since it led me to
another question.  Who really was my father and who was
my mother?  Oh, People of Thebes, if you only knew how
much pain and suffering a person who doesn't know
his parents feels.

PEOPLE:  Mercy on you, Oedipus.

TIRESIAS:  Continue your story, Oedipus.  Tell us how you met
this priest after that and what he told you.

OEDIPUS:  He summoned me after my return from Corinth and
blamed me for going to Thebes and told me, "Beware of
going there again or else you will marry your mother."  This
angered me so I swore to go and challenge this rash oracle.
So he started describing to me how young and beautiful
and attractive Joscata was and insisted that if I saw her I
would definitely marry her.  This increased my anger and
increased my determination to challenge his oracle.  I left
him feeling that I was swimming in a dark sea of worries
and troubles and I doubted everything.  I doubted the earth
and the sky, the mountains and the stars, the people and the
gods, but one thing I could not doubt.

TIRESIAS:  What is that, Oedipus?

OEDIPUS:  If Jocasta were really my mother, I would not marry her.

TIRESIAS:  Do you see the guilt of this priest, in how he burdened Oedipus with all these sorrows?

LUCASIUS:  He brought it on himself.  He testified before you that I warned him and threatened him.  Neither the warning nor the threat worked and he was overcome by his unhappy fate.

TIRESIAS:  By now you know the skill of this priest in using temptations disguised as warnings.

LUCASIUS:  Don't you wonder at this atheist, who wants me to bear the guilt of Oedipus even after Oedipus confessed it himself?  You heard Oedipus say that he doubted everything except for marrying Joscata if she were really his mother.  Now it has been proven that she was his mother and he married her and had four children with her.  How do you think this happened if the oracle wasn't from Apollo, whose oracles never fail?

CHIEF ELDER:  Yes, how did this happen, Oedipus?

PEOPLE:  How did this happen, Oedipus?

TIRESIAS:  Have you forgotten, People of Thebes, the story of the Sphinx that Oedipus saved you from?

PEOPLE:  No.  No, we haven't.  What about it?

TIRESIAS:  Tell them, Oedipus.

OEDIPUS:  When I reached the gates of Thebes, this strange creature barred my way.  I was about to strike him with my sword, but he asked me his riddle.  As soon as I answered it, he fell on his face, motionless and dead.  A crowd of people carried me on their shoulders, cheering and dancing and throwing flowers until they put me down in this palace, where the servants surrounded me, one washing me, another perfuming me, a third dressing me in luxurious garments, another combing my hair. Meanwhile all of them were describing to me the beauties of Jocasta and how I was more suitable for her than the elderly Laius because we were both still in the prime of our youth. During this, I tried to tell them, "Stop this, curse you, Jocasta is my mother. I am the son of Laius." But my tongue was tied and those words died on my lips. I said to myself that maybe she was not my mother and maybe Laius was not my father. (*He sighs painfully.*) Oh, how miserable I am!

TIRESIAS:  Then what, Oedipus?

OEDIPUS:  Still singing her praises, they took me to her. I saw among the decorations a beautiful young woman who looked like a virgin maid and in my mind I heard my mother Merope blaming me: "Wicked Oedipus! How dare you marry away from me without me witnessing your wedding and enjoying your happiness." At that moment, any doubt I had that she could be my mother disappeared from my mind and I was sure that I had not killed my father and I was able to calm down. And there she was, in my arms, and I was kissing her, our nuptial kiss. Oh, I wish lightning from the heavens had struck my head at that moment, before my hands touched her. Have mercy on me, People of Thebes, I am the most miserable person who ever existed. (*He collapses on his chair.*)

PEOPLE:  Oh, Oedipus. You are truly the most miserable person who ever existed.

LUCASIUS:  Slow down, People of Thebes. How can you pity a man who committed a sin so enormous that the water of the two rivers could not wash it away? He is the sinner who angered the heavens against you. Your suffering will not be lifted unless you cleanse your city from him. God ordered you to cleanse Thebes from his sins, not to cry for him and pity him.

PEOPLE:  Yes, this is a great sin.  The water of the two rivers could not wash it away.

TIRESIAS:  If Oedipus' sin is grave, then Lucasius, who pushed him toward it, has committed a graver sin.  You saw how this priest set the trap and wove the plan, while Oedipus was still a fetus in his mother's womb and how Oedipus tried to escape from the trap that he did not know had been set for him, although he couldn't.  Do not lie to yourself, people of Thebes.  God knows what is within you.  I do not presume that any one of us could have avoided falling into the trap Oedipus fell into if we were in his place.  Remember well that when he was taken to the palace he still had suspicions that Jocasta was his mother.

LUCASIUS:  Perhaps this is so, but shouldn't he have checked the matter to be sure she was not his mother?

TIRESIAS:  This is what Oedipus did.  He came to Thebes after receiving what he did from this priest.  He doubted everything in the universe except that he would not marry his mother.  When this tight, devilish plot took him to Thebes, he believed that Jocasta was not his mother and he believed that all along until I contacted him recently.  When he learned from me the terrible truth, he almost killed himself from the horror of what he had learned.  He then avoided his mother's bed, repented his sins and sacrificed his reputation and the reputation of his mother and his family as penance.  Oedipus repented, People of Thebes, but the one who was behind all these crimes and sins did not repent.  He is still indulging in sinful behavior as you see.  Here is the sinner you are seeking.

CREON:  People of Thebes, what are you waiting for?  Declare your wrath against the chief sinner who dragged us and you and Thebes into all these crises and calamities.

PEOPLE:  Down with Lucasius, the criminal!  Down with the chief sinner!  Death to Lucasius!

LUCASIUS:  Beware, People of Thebes, beware.  I am worried that this blind priest will mislead you and the heavens will inflict on you worse suffering than you now endure.  Now that what I have been worried about has already occurred, you may expect that great suffering, expect the horrible Sphinx. I see him advancing on you, mouth agape.

TIRESIAS:  Do not fear, People of Thebes.  You did not renounce God, you only renounced this charlatan priest.  The one who truly believes in God does not fear the unknown.

LUCASIUS:  Look out!  Here he is!  The atheists are doomed. (*Everyone looks in the direction he is pointing.  The people are terrified, screams and howls are heard.  People push each other to get out of the way of the SPHINX.*)  People who believe in the Temple should not be afraid.  The Sphinx came to punish the athetist Tiresias and whoever follows him. Those who agree that Oedipus should confiscate the Temple's money are the athetists that the Sphinx will kill and devour and those who refuse to agree with this should not be afraid.  (*The SPHINX appears.*)

PEOPLE:  Have mercy, Oedipus!  Return the Temple's money, Oedipus!  Do not subject us to the fury of the gods!

TIRESIAS:  People of Thebes . . .

PEOPLE:  Be silent!  We renounce your atheism and disbelief!

TIRESIAS:  My curses on you!  Didn't Oedipus save you from this beast before?

PEOPLE: Yes.

TIRESIAS:  He could save you today as well.

LUCASIUS:  No, people of Thebes.  God allowed Oedipus to conquer him before so that his oracle might be fulfilled. Today is different.  People of Thebes, if you wish to survive the Sphinx, revolt now against this atheist priest and this sinful king.  Revolt against Tiresias and Oedipus!

TIRESIAS:  Calm down, people of Thebes.  Here is your king Oedipus.  He will attack him and conquer him as he did before.

OEDIPUS (*approaching the SPHINX*):  People of Thebes, the weakest person amongst you can conquer this beast.  Let any of you approach him.  You will be able to conquer him.

LUCASIUS:  Look, people of Thebes.  Your hero is afraid.  He wants to push one of you to meet his death instead of him.

PEOPLE:  No, Oedipus.  None of us will approach him.  You kill him if you can.

OEDIPUS:  Don't let this artificial figure frighten you.  I will teach you his riddle and the answer to his riddle.  He does not know any others.  He will ask you "What is the creature that walks on four in the morning, on two at noon and on three at night?"  Tell him, "It's a human being.  He crawls on four as a baby, then he stands up and eventually, as he ages, he relies on a stick."

LUCASIUS:  Beware, People.  The Sphinx has endless riddles.  Do not expose yourselves to death based on the suggestion of this arrogant sinner.

PEOPLE:  No, Oedipus.  None of us will approach him.

OEDIPUS:  Then this is the proof.  (*To the SPHINX*)  You, tell me your riddle!

SPHINX (*after a short silence while everyone holds their breath and he moves his head and waves in wings in anger*):  What is the creature that walks on four in the morning, on two at noon and on three at night?

OEDIPUS:  It's a human being.  He crawls on four as a baby, then he stands up and eventually, as he ages, he relies on a stick. (*A cry of horror is heard from the SPHINX and he falls to the ground.*)

TIRESIAS (*laughing very loudly, to the surprise of the crowd of people*):  Ha ha ha!  He he he!

LUCASIUS (*looking in turn at his priestly followers, angrily.  Then he locks eyes with his assistant LAMIAS, who consoles him and then turns to the people*):  People of Thebes, do not think that the Sphinx is dead.  He only gave Oedipus the riddle that he knows to tempt him, to increase his arrogance.  Now he will get up and give Oedipus a riddle he does not know.  He will then kill him and kill thousands of you who rejected their God and believed in this wretched sinner and his atheist priest.  (*The SPHINX moves and slowly rises, until he is as upright as before.*)  Look here, he has arisen!

OEDIPUS:  Believe me, people of Thebes, he does not know any other riddles.  If any of you approaches him, you will conquer him.

LUCASIUS:  Beware, people of Thebes!  If you wish to survive the Sphinx, revolt against this sinner and his banished priest.

(*TIRESIAS laughs loudly.*)

OEDIPUS:  You!  Ask me your riddle.

SPHINX (*after a short pause while everyone holds their breath*):  What is the creature that walks on four in the morning, on two at noon and on three at night?

LUCASIUS (*angrily, looking harshly at his priestly entourage*):  What is this, curse you!

(*TIRESIAS laughs loudly.*)

OEDIPUS:  Any of you can approach him and answer him.  (*A MAN from the people approaches hesitantly.*)

SPHINX (*approaches him.  The man moves back.*):  Answer!  Answer!

MAN:  It's a human being!  (*A cry of horror is heard from the SPHINX and he falls to the ground.*)

(*Uproar from the crowd, though which TIRESIAS' laughter is heard.*)

LUCASIUS (*angrily*):  This is a false Sphinx!  Thebes, beware of God's anger!  There are traitors among the priests!  There are atheists even in the Temple!  (*TIRESIAS laughs.*)  Damn you, Lamias!  You traitor!  You planned this with Tiresias!  Curse you!  You will be banished from the Temple as he was.

LAMIAS (*standing up and shouting at the top of his voice*):  No, damn *you*, sinful charlatan!  You are the guilty one who polluted Thebes and its king and his mother Jocasta and his father Laius before.  You are the sinner who angered the God against Thebes so that He poured out His wrath upon it.

LUCASIUS (*stammering and shaking all over*):  Look at this traitor!  He is with Tiresias!

LAMIAS:  You priests!  Those of you who choose to stay with this charlatan have only yourselves to blame for the punishment that will befall this great criminal.  Otherwise you should renounce him now!

PRIESTS (*in unison*):  We renounce Lucasius and his sins!  We all support Tiresias!

LUCASIUS:  Curse you!  You are all traitors!  You are all atheists!  (*TIRESIAS laughs.*)  People of Thebes, don't you see how this colossal atheist is laughing at you and at your temple and your God!

TIRESIAS:  Forgive me if I laughed a great deal today.  I have not laughed for a long time.  Do you remember, people of Thebes, the day I was expelled from the temple how you all rejected me and drove me out of the city?  That day I was laughing at you for believing the lie of this charlatan.  After that, I spent thirty years without a smile, because I was so saddened about Thebes and your condition.  Today I have the right to laugh as I witness this chief criminal with his keen eyesight falling into the pits that he dug one after another.  Ha!  Ha!  Ha!  Ha!

LUCASIUS:  All the priests have conspired with this atheist and plotted against God, bringing you this false Sphinx.

LAMIAS:  Ask him to bring you the true Sphinx, if it exists.

PEOPLE:  Bring us the true Sphinx.

LUCASIUS:  Have you all become non-believers and followed these atheists?  If the true Sphinx comes, he will destroy you all.

LAMIAS:  You saw how the Sphinx was overcome and destroyed.  Now do you want the secret of how this happened?

PEOPLE:  Yes, yes.

LAMIAS:  Remember that it killed dozens of innocent people when it appeared during the reign of Laius.  If you want its mystery to be revealed, appeal to your King Oedipus to forgive the Sphinx.  It only committed those crimes by order of the chief criminal.

PEOPLE:  Forgive him, Oedipus!  Grant him your forgiveness, Oedipus!

OEDIPUS:  I forgive him.

LAMIAS:  Now come out of your apparatus.  (*The body of the SPHINX opens up and a priest comes out with a knife in his hand.*)

MAN:  Thank you for urging the King to pardon me.  People of Thebes, witness that I renounce this charlatan and his sins and follow Tiresias in worshipping almighty God.

LUCASIUS:  People of Thebes, do not be deceived by those traitors and liars.  The true Sphinx killed people with his riddle.  This fake one did not do anything.

PEOPLE:  Yes, the true Sphinx killed people.

MAN:  It is hard for me to admit to my brutal crimes in front of you.  I used to stop people outside the walls of Thebes.  When I confronted any one of them, he would be stunned and fall on the ground in terror.  I would slay him with this knife and disembowel him.

PEOPLE:  How horrible!

MAN:  Do not forget that I was only carrying out the orders of the High Priest, who claimed to me that I was fulfilling God's oracle.

CHIEF ELDER:  Then how did Oedipus overcome you when he met you?

PEOPLE:  Yes, how did Oedipus overcome you?

MAN:  Don't you understand the mystery yet?  This priest created me for Oedipus and ordered me to be overcome by him, as I did today in front of you.

PEOPLE:  Didn't you give him your riddle?

MAN:  Yes, I gave him the riddle the same way that you heard today and he answered me just as you heard.  Then I fell to the ground the same way that you saw.  (*The PEOPLE laugh*.)

CHIEF ELDER:  But how did Oedipus know the answer?

PEOPLE:  Yes, how did Oedipus know the answer?

MAN:  I do not know.  Here is our King, Oedipus.  Ask him.

OEDIPUS (*with a continuing expression of deep sorrow on his face*):
At the time, I did not know how I was inspired with this answer.  Recently, I remembered  that I heard this riddle and knew its answer from my mother, Queen Merope.

LUCASIUS (*triumphantly*):  Queen Merope is not your mother!
Your mother is Jocasta whom you married and impregnated with four siblings!

OEDIPUS:  Not so fast, you!  Everyone now knows this fact; I confessed it in front of them.  It is true that my mother is the one who killed herself in grief and regret but Queen Merope adopted me and raised me and there is no reason not to call her mother.

CREON:  What am I hearing?  Was our honorable guest conspiring with this colossal criminal in plotting this tragedy that ruined our royal family and tainted it forever?  (*Angry murmurs from the PEOPLE.*)

MEROPE (*rising from her chair*):  People of Thebes, do not be angry with me until you hear what I have to say.  Believe me, Oedipus' People, I love you all as I love him.  I learned this riddle from this charlatan priest who claimed that the Sphinx would kill my son Oedipus if he did not know it, so I taught it to my son to protect him without knowing the priest's evil intentions.

PEOPLE:  What great cunning!

CREON:  Forgive me, honorable Queen, for misjudging you.

MEROPE:  Do not be concerned, my son.  We are all suffering the same calamity.

LUCASIUS:  Do not believe this Queen.  She and her husband are in league with Tiresias, the atheist.

POLYBUS:  Yes, People of Thebes.  I and all my people support Tiresias, who is the only one who could reform our temple.  It has been defiled by this charlatan priest, who has made it a source of evil and sin instead of being a source of goodness and morality.  Don't you think that any of the sins committed by this charlatan priest would be enough to justify his condemnation and his expulsion from the Temple?

CHIEF ELDER:  Yes, he should be expelled from the Temple and punished for his sins.

PEOPLE:  Punish Lucasius!  Expel him from the Temple!  Curses on Lucasius!

POLYBUS:  What if I tell you that he wrote to me inciting me to attack your city, occupy it with my soldiers, and adding it to my own kingdom, arguing that since Thebes was distracted by famine and plague, attacking it would be easy and occupying it would be effortless?

PEOPLE:  Treason!  What a corrupt traitor!

LUCASIUS:  These are all lies and fabrications!

POLYBUS:  What are you thinking?  Has your reason left you?  If I wanted to lie, I would not announce my lie in front of everyone.  What honor would I have left after that?  Look, People of Thebes, this is his letter to me, in his own handwriting, sealed with the Temple's seal (*handing the letter to the CHIEF ELDER*).

CHIEF ELDER (*looking attentively at the letter*):  Yes, what treason!

Its proper punishment is death.

PEOPLE:  Kill the traitor!  You must kill the traitor!

TIRESIAS:  If you kill him, you relieve him from the pain of regret
    and humiliation.  He does not deserve this relief and the
    decision after all is for our king Oedipus to make.

OEDIPUS:  No, people of Thebes.  I stand in front of you to be
    judged by you, not to judge others.  I can no longer be your
    leader after what I have done.  Chose another for your
    throne.  Here is Creon; he is strong and honest.  He is the
    best suited to rule your country.

CREON:  No, Oedipus.  Thebes will not accept another ruler, and
    no one can lead it but you.  Whatever happened, happened.
    You purified yourself with penance and the great sacrifice
    that only you could bear.  As for me, I swear by God that I
    would rather be dead than sit in your place.  I will always be
    your servant and ally.

(*The three ELDERS of Thebes stand and one of them begins speaking.*)

ELDER:  Allow us now to give our testimony.

LUCASIUS (*becoming excited*):  Yes, people of Thebes.  You
    representatives of the people.  May all the gods bless you.
    Now testify to the truth.  All the others testified falsely.

ELDER:  The three of us were in Oedipus' room when Lucasius
    came to the palace to tell him about the alleged oracle from
    Apollo, so we heard what took place between him and
    Oedipus.

CHIEF ELDER:  What did you hear?

ELDER:  We heard this priest's negotiations with Oedipus.  He
    promised not to reveal the oracle to the people if Oedipus
    would agree to change his mind about confiscating the

Temple's money and turn over Tiresias to him.

PEOPLE:  What treason!  What a traitor!

ELDER:  Do you know how Oedipus responded?  He screamed in his face, "Curse you!  Do you want me to betray my people?  Go and announce your oracle!"

PEOPLE:  How great Oedipus is!

ELDER:  Do you think, People of Thebes, that Oedipus should give up his throne after he sacrificed his name and his family's honor for you and for Thebes?

PEOPLE:  No, no.  You are our king, Oedipus!  We have no king but you!

OEDIPUS:  People of Thebes, if you still love me, please relieve me from this matter to have time for myself.  I wish to spend the rest of my miserable life on this earth in regret and penance, hoping that the gods will forgive some of my guilt.

PEOPLE:  No, Oedipus.  Don't forsake us, Oedipus.  We have no one but you!

TIRESIAS:  If you wish for the gods' forgiveness, Oedipus, then spend the rest of your life serving your people.

CHIEF ELDER:  Accept, Oedipus, accept the pleas of your people.  They have no one but you.

OEDIPUS:  If you will not accept anyone else, then I will follow your wishes.

PEOPLE:  Blessings on you, Oedipus!  May the gods grace you, Oedipus!

TIRESIAS:  Now tell us your decision concerning the sham priest.

OEDIPUS:  Take him to the top of Cithaeron mountain and leave him there until his death.

CREON:  Soldiers, carry out the king's order!

LUCASIUS (*shouting as the soldiers are pushing him out*):  Kill me, Oedipus!  Have mercy on me, Oedipus!

PEOPLE:  Be damned, Lucasius.  Be damned, you consummate villain!

OEDIPUS:  I appoint Tiresias head of the Temple.

PEOPLE:  Long live Tiresias, the benevolent!  Long live Tiresias, the High Priest!

OEDIPUS:  Let the Temple's property and money be distributed equally among all the people.

PEOPLE:  Live, Oedipus!  May your days be long, Oedipus!

(*A MESSENGER appears from inside the palace.  He walks toward CREON and whispers something to him.*)

CREON:  Good news, people of Thebes!  The supplies have arrived from Corinth.  Three thousand wagonloads of food!

PEOPLE:  Long live Polybus, king of Corinth!  Long live Polybus and Merope!

POLYBUS:  People of Thebes, if I offer you another gift, would you accept it?

PEOPLE:  What you have given us is more than enough, Polybus. We thank your generosity and bounty.

POLYBUS:  People of Thebes, you see I have grown older and weaker, and I do not have any heir but your king Oedipus. He is my son and I bequeath to him my throne of Corinth.

Here are representatives of my people to testify to you that the Corinthian people accept this decision.

(*One of the CORINTHIAN representatives arises.*)

CORINTHIAN:  Yes, people of Thebes, all of our people accept this decision.

POLYBUS (*to OEDIPUS*):  So, my dear son, please accept this gift from your mother and father and from the Corinthian people, who love you.  (*He opens his arms to OEDIPUS. OEDIPUS embraces him.*)

TIRESIAS:  People of Thebes, raise a cheer for Corinth and its king and queen, Polybus and Merope!

PEOPLE:  Hurrah for Corinth!  Long live Polybus and Merope!

POLYBUS:  People of Thebes, this is the happiest day of my life, as I see Corinth and Thebes united under one throne.  Cheer for Oedipus, king of Thebes and Corinth!  Cheer for Oedipus the Great!

CROWD (*in unison*):  Long live Oedipus, King of Thebes and Corinth!  Hurrah for Oedipus the Great!  Long live Oedipus the Great!

**Scene Two**

*Time: The waning hours of the night.*

*Scene:  On the right side of the stage, part of the main portico of the palace, lit by moonlight, showing the two doors leading inside the palace. Also to be seen is the top part of the marble stairs leading from the portico to the outside to the left of the stage, in darkness.  When the curtain is raised, OEDIPUS appears from the far door, on tip-toe, until he reaches the end of the portico, between the huge columns, looking at the sleeping city.*

OEDIPUS (*his face drawn in misery*):  Enjoy your sleep tonight, dear Thebes!  As the plague that kept you awake so long is finally lifted.  Do not worry about its remains, since tomorrow everything will be over.  Sleep, sleep!  Sweet dreams!  Now that this horrible nightmare is over.  I envy you, Thebes, because your troubles are over but I am not jealous of you.  I would not wish that your plight was like mine, since there is no way to relieve mine; rather I wish that my plight would be like yours, present for a while and then gone.  Jocasta, oh, Jocasta.  How many moonlit nights have we stood here enjoying the night breeze and whispering quietly about our future desires and the memories of our happy past.  Oh, who could have thought then that a hidden disaster was lying in wait, about to pounce on us, sending my beloved Jocasta, covered in shame, to her grave, and leaving me here alone, the most miserable creature in the universe.  Oh, this portico is the same portico.  The moon is the same moon.  The breeze is the same breeze.  But where is Jocasta, and where is Oedipus?  (*He is overcome by tears.  Then, recovering*) Oh, what sorrow!  How can I cry over a past that is full of sin and evildoing?  Oh, wretched me!  I turn to my past and I am appalled by my sin and shame!  I look into my present and I find only regret and grief.  I look into the future and I find only desperation and hopelessness.  (*Looking at the palace*) You horrid palace!  You are the place of suffering and misery!  If you were not in sacred Thebes and if my children were not inside you, I would have summoned the heavens' curses upon you.  But this is the end between us. (*Looking toward the city again*)  Oh, Thebes!  Oh, my kind people!  Do not be sad if you wake up tomorrow and find Oedipus' palace without Oedipus in it.  Farewell, Thebes, my precious country.  Farewell, my loyal, kind people.  Farewell to the dear departed in her new resting place.  Farewell, my young children.  Farewell, Antigone.

(*ANTIGONE appears from behind him, carrying a sack.*)

ANTIGONE:  No, father, I am going with you wherever you go.

OEDIPUS (*surprised*):  Antigone!  (*Embracing her*)  What woke you up at this hour of the night, my daughter?

ANTIGONE:  I did not sleep at all tonight.

OEDIPUS:  So you were awake earlier on when I kissed you and your brothers and sisters?

ANTIGONE:  Yes, father, I let you think I was asleep to see what you were up to.

OEDIPUS:  Why didn't you sleep like the others, Antigone?

ANTIGONE:  I felt that you were about to do something, so I decided to stay awake and when I felt the tears on my cheek after your kiss, I realized that what my heart was telling me was true.  I implore you, in the name of my love for you, to take me with you, father, and do not leave me behind.  I can not live apart from you.

OEDIPUS:  Oh, this is a long journey, Antigone.

ANTIGONE:  I know that, father.

OEDIPUS:  A young girl like you cannot bear these difficulties.

ANTIGONE:  I will bear everything with you.  I will bear the hunger and thirst, the hardships and troubles, the heat and the cold, the darkness, the wind, and the rain.  All of this is easier than you being away from me.  I will support you, father; I will not be a burden.

OEDIPUS:  Oh, my dear child!  I will wander in the mountains and the wastelands and I might meet my end on the road.

ANTIGONE:  That is no problem, father.  It is easier for me to meet my end with you than to die here from my sadness for you.

OEDIPUS:  And what is this in your hand?

ANTIGONE:  A sack with some supplies for us.

OEDIPUS:  You are very kind to your father.  It seems to me that you are not allowing me any choice but to take you.

ANTIGONE:  If you leave me behind, I will waste away from sadness and grief.  (*Whispering*)  Oh, I hear someone coming!  It might be my uncle Creon!  Don't tell him about my intention or else he might prevent me from going away with you.  I will wait for you behind those trees.  (*She descends the marble stairs until she is covered in darkness.*)

(*Enter TIRESIAS, feeling his way.*)

TIRESIAS:  Oedipus!

OEDIPUS:  Who is it?  Tiresias, what brought you here at this hour?

TIRESIAS:  I am here to prevent you from what you are planning to do.

OEDIPUS:  Impossible, Tiresias!

TIRESIAS (*moving closer*):  Think of your people, Oedipus. Remember the people of Thebes who love you and whom you love.

OEDIPUS:  I will never forget them, Tiresias.

TIRESIAS:  They have no one but you, Oedipus.  To whom do you leave your people?

OEDIPUS:  To the One who created them and me, Tiresias.  Where is your belief in God?

TIRESIAS:  And how about your promise to the people that you will stay for their sake?

OEDIPUS:  I don't think that they would blame me in their hearts if they knew my reason.

TIRESIAS:  They might excuse you, Oedipus, but you should not excuse yourself when you know how much they need you and depend on you.

OEDIPUS:  Curse you, Tiresias!  Do not keep me standing here telling you what you already know.  Thebes will not lack a king that will take care of it better than I did, without having my misery and without suffering my shame.  I am the past, Tiresias, and he is the future.  I represent despair and he represents hope.

TIRESIAS:  Thebes would never find a king who has your mind and reason.

OEDIPUS:  Reason?  I can no longer reason, Tiresias.  When did I ever use reason?

TIRESIAS:  My ears have never heard a voice more reasonable than yours.

OEDIPUS:  Tell me, what is the difference between the one who has reason and the one who has lost it?

TIRESIAS:  Wisdom, Oedipus.  In words and deeds.

OEDIPUS:  I swear by God almighty, Tiresias, that I often feel like trampling on you and strangling you until I see you shaking and gasping, until you die.  Is this wisdom in words and deeds?

TIRESIAS:  No, Oedipus.  You will not attack me unjustly.

OEDIPUS:  Curses!  How can you blame an insane person for his deeds?

TIRESIAS:  You are far from insane, Oedipus.

OEDIPUS:  So is it perfect sanity, according to you, that I forsake my throne, my people, this grand palace and my young children to wander in the prairies and the wastelands, the dust my bed and the sky my canopy, not knowing where my feet might take me or what my fate might be?

TIRESIAS:  Mercy on you, Oedipus.  I feel sympathy for you and your unknown fate.

OEDIPUS:  Would you sympathize with the kind people of Thebes, ruled by an insane king like myself?

TIRESIAS:  No, Oedipus, you are not insane.

OEDIPUS:  If you consider my departure wise and sage, why are you trying to dissuade me from it?  (*Laughing a quiet, hysterical laugh*)  Aren't you afraid that in some unguarded moment I might order that you be hanged in the square and return Lucasius to his post at Delphi and return the money and property to the Temple, then rush to Jocasta's grave, awaken her from her sleep and tell her, "Do not fear, my beloved.  Everything we experienced was only a nightmare. It is over as if nothing has happened."  Ha, ha, ha!

TIRESIAS:  When do you plan to leave, Oedipus?

OEDIPUS:  Damn you, priest!  Are you expelling me from my palace?

TIRESIAS:  No, Oedipus, I only wanted to know when you are leaving.

OEDIPUS:  If you did not encourage my madness with your talk of sanity, or my sanity with your talk of madness I would already have been wandering in the wilderness far away from you and this wretched palace.

TIRESIAS:  Oh, Oedipus, don't you want to say goodbye to your children?

OEDIPUS (*tenderly*):  My dear children!  I said goodbye to them earlier.  I kissed them on their beds as they slept.  (*Sharply and angrily*)  Why aren't you, evil man, asleep like everyone else?  Why are you spying on me?

TIRESIAS (*gently*):  Is it gracious of you to depart without saying goodbye to me?

OEDIPUS:  Yes, I forgot to kiss you goodbye.  Let me kiss your forehead, you reverend priest.  (*Moves closer to TIRESIAS and holds his throat with both hands.*)  Ha, ha, ha!  I wish that my hands could . . .

TIRESIAS (*terrified*):  Oedipus!  What are you doing!

OEDIPUS:  Nothing, Tiresias.  I only want to kiss your head.  (*Kissing his head.*)

TIRESIAS:  Would you please remove your hands from my throat?

OEDIPUS:  Damn them!  What brought them to your throat?  (*He removes his hands from TIRESIAS' throat.*)

TIRESIAS:  Are you angry with me, Oedipus?

OEDIPUS:  How could I be, Tiresias?

TIRESIAS:  Don't you love me as I love you?

OEDIPUS:  How can I not love you, when you are the one who saved Thebes from its suffering and saved me from sin? You sent Jocasta from this palace where she used to dine in sin and sent her to where worms now dine on her.  Do me the same favor you did her.

TIRESIAS:  What do you want me to do for you, Oedipus?  Order me and I will obey.

OEDIPUS:  I only want you to leave me alone.

TIRESIAS:  Where are you going, Oedipus?

OEDIPUS:  To where nobody knows me and I do not know anyone.  Give me your hand, Tiresias.  (*OEDIPUS takes TIRESIAS' hand and puts it on his sword.*)  Do you know what this is?

TIRESIAS:  This is a sword, Oedipus.

OEDIPUS:  Do you know what I will do with it?

TIRESIAS:  Protect yourself from the beasts and the robbers.

OEDIPUS:  No, the beasts do not want me and what would the robbers find on me?  I will use it to kill anyone who dares to follow me and dissuade me from my plan.  Do you understand?

TIRESIAS:  Yes, Oedipus.

OEDIPUS:  Tell Creon that (*in a softer tone*) and ask him to take care of my children.

TIRESIAS:  Will you be well, Oedipus?

OEDIPUS:  Yes, yes, I will be well so long as Thebes is well. Goodbye, Tiresias.  Goodbye, High Priest.

TIRESIAS:  Goodbye, Oedipus.

OEDIPUS (*descends the staircase slowly until he is covered in darkness, while speaking to himself in a dazed manner*):  Phocis . . . Cithaeron . . . Cithaeron . . . Cithaeron . . . Phocis . . . Pontus . . . Sphinx. . . Sphinx . . . Pontus.

(*CREON appears from his hiding place behind the door.*)

CREON (*with tears in his eyes*):  Mercy on you, Oedipus!

TIRESIAS:  Did you hear?  Who would you leave your country to?

CREON:  Yes, I heard everything.

TIRESIAS:  It is not possible to dissuade him.

CREON:  Yes, it is impossible.

OEDIPUS (*his voice is heard chanting*):  Laius . . . Lucasius . . . Lucasius . . .Laius  . . .  Nikos . . . Betakoras . . . Betakoras . . . Nikos.

CREON:  Listen to that!

TIRESIAS:  Oh, poor Oedipus!

CREON:  He must have gone crazy, Tiresias.

TIRESIAS:  I don't know, Creon.  I am not sure.

OEDIPUS (*chanting*):  Polybus . . . Merope . . . Merope . . . Polybus . . . Oedipus . . . Joscasta . . . Jocasta . . . Oedipus.  Where are you, cat of Corinth?  Friend of my youth, where are you? We walked together on the road.  Let's finish the journey together.

TIRESIAS:  Oh, mercy on you, Oedipus.

OEDIPUS (*quietly*):  Antigone, let's go, my beloved daughter.

CREON:  Listen to him, Tiresias.  He imagines that his daughter, Antigone, is with him.  Do you suspect his sanity after that?

OEDIPUS (*calling from a distance*):  Tiresias!  Tiresias!

TIRESIAS:  Yes, Oedipus!

OEDIPUS:  Can you hear my voice, Tiresias?

TIRESIAS:  Yes, Oedipus.

OEDIPUS:  Remember . . . after despair there is hope! After the past there is the future!  I am the past, Tiresias, and I am making way for the future.  I am despair, Tiresias.  I must leave for hope to come.  I am well, Tiresias, so long as Thebes is well.

(*TIRESIAS and CREON remain motionless.*)

CREON (*in pain*):  He left, Tiresias.

TIRESIAS (*regretfully*):  And he will never return.

CREON:  Do you want to return to your bed?

TIRESIAS:  Thank you, Creon.

(*CREON leads TIRESIAS solemnly toward the door.*)

**Curtain**

# THE COMEDY OF OEDIPUS

## YOU'RE THE ONE WHO KILLED THE BEAST

by Ali Salim

Translated by Pierre Cachia
and Desmond O'Grady

# THE COMEDY OF OEDIPUS

## YOU'RE THE ONE WHO KILLED THE BEAST

A Play in Three Acts
by
Ali Salim
1970

## CHARACTERS

OEDIPUS, a young man whose precise provenance is unknown, living in Thebes

JOCASTA, Queen of Thebes

HORIMHEB, High Priest of Amon and President of the University of Thebes

ONAH, President of the Chamber of Commerce and of the Municipal Council of Thebes

AWALIH, Chief of Police in Thebes

CREON, Commander of the Guard in Thebes

TIRESIAS, the same personage, with the same well-known characteristics, as in ancient Greek literature

KAMI, a friend of Oedipus

SENEFRU, a Theban playwright

NEFER, Senefru's wife

CHILD of Senefru and Nefer

KA'IT, a citizen of Thebes

POLICEMAN

CHORUS of Theban inhabitants

PEOPLE of Thebes

## Act One

## Scene One

*The Scene: Thebes — the Egyptian, not the Greek Thebes. Its high ramparts, onto which the populace has climbed to watch in great apprehension something taking place at a distance. On the left is the balcony of the pharaonic temple of Thebes, around which are some ram-headed sphinxes, as if guarding the access to it. All around the place are semicircular graduated stone benches, and in the center is a round stone table with four seats round it — these are reserved for sessions of the Municipal Council, the stone benches being for the inhabitants of Thebes. To the right and at the front sit two persons, OEDIPUS and his friend KAMI, engrossed in a peaceful game of chess. From the depths of the stage, which is bathed in soft lights, comes TIRESIAS leaning on a stick. He advances to the front of the stage, where he becomes clearly visible.*

*The Time: A long time, a very long time ago.*

TIRESIAS:  Gentlemen — you who live in this city, let me tell you
the story of another City.  The story of Thebes — Thebes, the
bride of the Nile, the capital of the ancient world; Thebes of
the great temples, of flourishing trade . . .  The Thebes of
today is wretched and sad.  For the first time in its long life,
poverty and  misery have cramped my beautiful city.  (*After
a moment of silence.*)  At a spot not far from Thebes, on the
only way to the lands of the North, there has appeared a
strange beast.  It is said to have the head of a beautiful
woman and the body of an enormous animal.  They call it
"The Sphinx."  This beast poses a riddle to travelers and
kills those who do not know the answer.  During the last
three months, it has done away with all the men in the
caravans coming to Thebes by land, and those coming by
way of the mighty Nile.  Many have ventured out to
solve the riddle and earn the prize, but none have returned.

Reprinted from *Modern Arabic Drama: An Anthology*, edited by
Salma Khadra Jayyusi and Roger Allen.  Copyright © 1995 by
Indiana University Press.

Now, at last, Professor Ptah has gone — the Professor of Creative Rational Studies and Surgeon of the Royal Skull . . .

(*At the other end of the stage, OEDIPUS is speaking with his friend.*)

OEDIPUS:  And the Municipal Council has set the prize at . . . how much?

TIRESIAS (*continuing*):  Fifty thousand gold Theban pounds is what Professor Ptah will get if he solves the riddle.

(*TIRESIAS exits quietly.  At the same time the Queen JOCASTA appears on the balcony.*)

JOCASTA (*calling*):  Creon!

CREON (*answering from his place on the ramparts*):  Yes, my Lady?

JOCASTA:  Has he got there?

CREON:  He's on his way, my Lady.

(*Voices rise among the populace, "He's there!  He's there!"*)

ONAH (*raising his voice*):  He's there, my Lady, he's there!  He's standing before the beast thinking, clutching his head . . .

OEDIPUS (*quietly*):  Can't he think without clutching his head?

(*Voices are raised among the people to encourage Professor Ptah.*)

VOICES:  Speak, Ptah, speak!  Talk!  Solve the riddle!  He's about to speak!  He's going to talk! (*There is a sudden wild shout among the people, then a deep silence.*)

A MAN (*wailing*):  The beast has got him by the neck!

CREON:  He's dragged him behind the hill . . . We can't see him.

A MAN:  An arm!  An arm was thrown in the air!

ANOTHER:  A leg!

A MAN:  Maybe it's not the Professor's leg . . .  Maybe it's the leg
    of someone else before him.

ANOTHER:  Oh it's his alright!  I know it well.  He's used it many
    a time to kick me to study.

A MAN (*loudly, in a weeping voice*):  Oh God!  The man's been torn
    to bits!

(*The people climb down from the ramparts, obviously in deep sorrow.
They take their places on the stone benches, while members of the
Municipal Council make for the round table.*)

OEDIPUS:  Listen!  Do you hear that?

KAMI:  What?

OEDIPUS:  Like someone chewing something, crunching
    something . . .

KAMI (*straining to hear*):  Something like what?

OEDIPUS:  To be precise, a University Professor.  Now then, my
    good man:  Check!  Checkmate!  He could have solved the
    riddle if he'd gone out to solve the riddle.

KAMI:  What did he go out for then?  A walk?  You do have some
    strange notions, Oedipus.

OEDIPUS:  Not at all.  He went out thinking of the prize.  One
    cannot think of the prize and the riddle at the same time.

(*By the time OEDIPUS and the friend end their dialogue, the members of
the Municipal Council have taken their places at the table, and the
citizens theirs on the stone benches.*)

OEDIPUS:  Come on, let's sit among the people.  (*They do so.*)

HORIMHEB:   I told you from the start.  It's a plot to do away with the scientific wealth of Thebes—a beast that first eats the Professor of Mathematics, then the Professor of Rational Creativity.  This is why (*assuming an oratorical stance*) I, Horimheb, High Priest of Amon and President of the University of Thebes, proclaim that I will not allow any professor in the University to go and solve the riddle.  You may take this to be a decree.

ONAH:  Who, then, is to go?

HORIMHEB (*angrily*):  I don't know, Onah, I don't know.  It is not my responsibility . . .

AWALIH:  But it is your responsibility.  Riddles and conundrums and equations and things of that sort, they can be solved only by people who are good at thinking, and the people who are good at thinking are the university professors.

HORIMHEB:  That's true; but I cannot lower the status of my professors.  If the beast wants to challenge us over lectures, over M.A.s and Ph.D.s, I would have no objection; but riddles and trivialities of this kind—I refuse.

ONAH:  Well, then, go on refusing—until everyone dies of hunger.  Not one relief supply has gotten through in three months.

HORIMHEB:  So that's what's worrying you.  You, as President of the Chamber of Commerce, are concerned that trade should revive and your capital be enlarged.

(*The Queen comes forward on the balcony.*)

JOCASTA:  Are you going to quarrel?  Have I summoned you to think and relieve the people of the trouble they're in, or to spread out your dirty washing and make a display of yourselves?

AWALIH:  We are exchanging points of view, my Lady.

JOCASTA:  And do you, Chief of Police, have the nerve to speak out?

AWALIH:  Why not, my Lady?

JOCASTA:  Don't you know why not?  Where is his Majesty the King?  Where is your Lord and the creator of your prosperity, the King of Thebes?  If he were here, he would have solved the riddle in a minute.

ONE OF THE PEOPLE:  May God have mercy on his soul—he was another moron.

(*The people burst out laughing.  The Chief of Police gives them a threatening look, and they stop.*)

JOCASTA:  He was killed at the crossroads a mere five leagues from Thebes.  Right?  Who are the killers?  Where are the killers?  Have you looked for them, Mr. Chief of Police?  Answer me.

AWALIH (*stuttering*):  My Lady . . . the investigations . . . I mean . . . the confidentiality of the investigations . . .

JOCASTA:  Answer!  I command you to answer.

AWALIH:  There are certain secrets, my Lady, that I cannot reveal in public . . .

JOCASTA:  Please go ahead and answer in public.  Have you looked for the murderers?

AWALIH (*looks around with embarrassment, then leaves the meeting and approaches her.  In an aside to the Queen, nervously and in a low voice*):  What is all this, my Lady?  Didn't you tell me not to look?

JOCASTA: I said that?

AWALIH: Yes, you told me not to look—not very hard, that is. That was his fate, you said, and we're all destined to die . . .

JOCASTA: Well, then, I'm sorry, Awalih. I wan't being quite alert.

AWALIH: Won't you please make a point of it, my Lady? You nearly cooked my goose. (*Resumes his seat at the meeting.*)

OEDIPUS (*rises among the people and shouts in a loud voice*): Awalih—the Chief of Police. He's the one to go and solve the riddle.

THE PEOPLE (*in a voice like thunder*): Yes. He's the one to go and solve the riddle.

AWALIH (*thunderstruck*): Me? Why me?

OEDIPUS: You're the Chief of Police and you're supposed to be the cleverest man in the land. (*Addressing the people, in order to persuade them*) When any crime takes place, the Chief of Police applies his mind to it, and thanks to his cleverness he finds out who the criminal is. Any such case may be looked on as a riddle. The Chief of Police is expected to know how to solve any riddle.

CREON: That's sound talk. You're the Chief of Police because you're the cleverest man in Thebes.

THE PEOPLE: Hear! Hear! That's right!

AWALIH (*sensing that the noose is tightening around his neck*): What's right? Are you trying to get rid of me? What riddles and what crimes am I supposed to apply my mind to? In that kind of thing I'm the most thick-headed man in town.

HORIMHEB: What kind of talk is this?

AWALIH:  That's how it is.

OEDIPUS (*challenging him*):  If that's how it is, then how do you catch the criminals?

AWALIH:  I just arrest them.  I'm a very arresting man.  His Majesty the King—God rest his soul—he's the one who knew them one by one.  He used to give me lists of names and addresses: "Arrest these, let these go."  So I used to let those go and arrest these.  Simple.  (*Shouting, pleading*)  Does that make me a clever man?

THE PEOPLE:  It makes you a dummy.

AWALIH (*resuming his seat, muttering*):  A dummy let it be—just let me live.

KAMI:  I say, the son of a . . .

JOCASTA:  Please go on.  The problem has to be solved tonight!

AWALIH:  Good people, I want to warn you of something serious: the food available in Thebes will last us only a week.  After that . . .

A VOICE AMONG THE PEOPLE:  After that you will eat us!
    (*Loud laughter among the people.*)

(*TIRESIAS appears, calling out from some spot on the stage—it will be noticed that TIRESIAS appears and disappears at any time that suits.*)

TIRESIAS:  Good people, a little seriousness.  Merriment is a great thing, but the temples and mausoleums and great ramparts about you were not built by merriment.  It is admirable that one should face up to calamities laughing, but when laughter becomes a tomb in which to bury the future of the land, when jokes become demands that devour your sense of responsibility, when merriment becomes a shroud, when wretchedness and misery are called great fun—what is there

left to link you with life?  All is lost then, and what remains
is sure to be lost too.

ONE OF THE PEOPLE:  So what do you want us to do, Uncle
Tiresias?  Sit down and weep?

TIRESIAS:  You are in fact sitting down and weeping, and even
slapping your faces like women at a funeral.  What do you
think weeping is?  Tears running down one's cheeks?  Do
you understand what despair is?  (*Wanders among them as if
trying to implant his words into their depths.*)  Despair is empty
laughter.  It is naïve optimism.  It is senseless mockery of all
things.  This is the stupidity you have concocted in order not
to get to know the truth.  Senefru . . . Senekht . . . Aton . . .
Ka'it . . . and others . . . and others.  Not a household in
Thebes but one of its children has been devoured.  What are
you waiting for?

HORIMHEB:  Lord Tiresias, such emotional outbursts never solve
any problems.  There is no reason for resignation—or for
anger.  What is needed is calm thinking.

ONAH:  The basic problem, Lord Tiresias, is that there is a riddle,
and someone is needed to solve it.

AWALIH:  That's right—not a lot of talk about jokes and fun and
mockery.  Are you trying to depress people?  Leave people
to their own ways, brother.

HORIMHEB:  And if we find someone to solve this riddle, the
beast will go away and leave us alone.  That's the problem.

TIRESIAS:  That's a lie!  Nonsense!  That is not the problem!

AWALIH:  What do you mean?  That there's no beast and no
riddle?

TIRESIAS:  There is a beast, and there is a riddle—not the riddle
that you think, but another riddle that not one of you has

mentioned.  Good people: riddles are made up by philosophers and thinkers and the types of people who muse at night by the light of the moon.  Why should beasts pose riddles?  Why should beasts exercise their brains?  Beasts use their muscles and their fangs; they use their talons and their claws.  Have you ever heard of a serpent appearing to someone to pose him a riddle?  Have you ever heard of a lion intercepting someone to challenge him at hop-scotch?  Good people, use your brains!  The riddle is just an excuse.  The aim of the beast is very clear.  I am surprised that you cannot see it.

AWALIH (*sarcastically*):  So we can't see it, and you're the one who can?

TIRESIAS:  I am blind in the eyes only, Awalih.  The tables are turned on you, you who are blind in perception.  People of Thebes, listen!  The beast's purpose is very clear.  It is to devour all the clever people in the land one by one.  After that, the remaining foolish ones won't give him any trouble—he'll gobble them up wholesale.

OEDIPUS:  So what is the solution, Tiresias?

TIRESIAS:  Go out to meet the beast all together.  If the story of the riddle is true, surely one of you will be able to solve it.  And if it is a lie, then it is you who will be able to devour the beast.

A VOICE AMONG THE PEOPLE:  But what if he devours us?

TIRESIAS:  Let him, my good man!  Are you any better than those he has devoured already?  And in either case—whether he eats you or you eat him—your problem will be solved. (*Silence engulfs them all.*)  What have you to say?  Of course my words don't please you.  You don't like to hear talk of this kind.  You want somebody who will stand and tell you jokes, who will amuse you. (*With bitter sarcasm*)  O brave men of Thebes: every one among you is ready to cross many seas . . . to face up to crocodiles at the height of the flood . . . to wrestle with the gods . . . to sacrifice his life — all for the sake of hearing a new joke. May you wallow in a worse mess than you are in already! (*There are bursts of laughter among the people as TIRESIAS calmly exits.*)

AWALIH:  This man has no right to come and humiliate the people in the presence of the Municipal Council. We've let him get away with too much all along; but the difficulties we're going through won't allow us to let anyone disturb our thoughts or break our resolve. Having said that, I request that the Council allow me to arrest him.

CREON (*rising and shouting*):  I object! In my capacity as Commander of the Guard in Thebes, I will not allow anyone to be put under arrest merely because of his opinions. Regarding Tiresias in particular, no one can doubt his great love for the City. Tiresias was born with Thebes. Tiresias is Thebes.

PERSON NO. 1:  At the time we were born, he was already there.

PERSON NO. 2:  My father told me he existed even before he himself was born.

PERSON NO. 3:  My great-great-grandfather heard from his great-great-grandfather that he existed before any of them were born.

CREON:  If you imprison Tiresias, you'll be imprisoning the whole of Thebes. If you stop him talking, you'll be gagging the entire population of Thebes.

HORIMHEB:  We've strayed from the subject.

ONAH:  True. This is not the subject.

OEDIPUS:  Yes, it is the subject.

(*AWALIH rises, blazing with anger.  He moves toward OEDIPUS.*)

AWALIH:  What do you mean?  What are you hinting at?  Speak out plainly!

OEDIPUS:  You know what I mean.

AWALIH:  You mean that I'm placing freedom of speech under sequestration.  You mean that I'm preventing people from speaking their minds.

HORIMHEB:  That's enough, Awalih.  Are you going to blow this up into a quarrel?

AWALIH:  Oh, no!  I can't let this pass without clarification. (*Turning to the populace, and shouting menacingly*)  Have I prevented any of you from speaking?  (*Some of the policemen standing by move as if to encircle the public.*)  Speak out!  Is there anyone who has something to say and doesn't know how to go about it?  (*Stretches out his hand, gets hold of one of those sitting, and pulls him up.*)  Senefru—speak!  You're a playwright, and every year one of your plays is staged in the temple yard.  (*In a changed tone*)  It could have happened that nothing of yours was presented, couldn't it?

SENEFRU:  Yes.

AWALIH:  And yet all your plays have been presented and you say whatever you want to say—isn't that so?

SENEFRU:  Yes.

AWALIH:  And what was it you said in your last play?  Go ahead and speak so that Mr. Oedipus should know that we have freedom of speech here.

SENEFRU (*whispering*):  Which play?  The one you banned . . . ?

AWALIH (*in a low but rancorous voice*):  The one that was produced, you fool!

(*SENEFRU speaks out with confidence and assurance, with AWALIH's hand still on his shoulder.*)

SENEFRU:  In my last play I said . . . er . . . I said the boldest things it's possible to say . . .  I don't use symbols or project things back in history . . .  I write with great daring and I'm prepared to lay down my life for the sake of writing what I choose to write . . .  In my last play, I demanded that we try studying anew the myth of Isis in the light of the real needs of the people, and this without going too far, as some do, by disrupting the methods which are incompatible with our ability to bring civilization to fruition, especially in the period immediately following the flood of the Nile . . .

AWALIH (*shouting*):  Is there anything more daring than that, brothers?  Is there any country in the whole world that allows such words to be spoken on its stages?  Well, we do, with the sole restriction that they be spoken within an artistic framework.  Now there are things that are not spoken in a good artistic framework.  We're not the ones who ban these.  It's the responsible artists who ban them. (*Addressing himself to a section of the public dressing in bright clothes.*)  Isn't that so, responsible artists?

THE GROUP (*rising*):  Yes!

AWALIH:  Sit down! (*Addressing OEDIPUS*)  You must understand, brother Oedipus, that we're not savages.  We're civilized.  In fact, more civilized than the country you came from.

CREON (*very angry*):  That's enough—enough demagoguery. Thebes is facing a calamity, and our Lord Awalih can think of nothing  better than defending himself and displaying his oratorical skills.  Who will rid us of the beast?

AWALIH:  Why don't you?  You go and solve the riddle.  You're the Commander of the Guard, and you're responsible for repelling all outside threats.  You go and repel the beast!

CREON:  I'm a warrior.  I can make myself understood with the sword.  I know how to die below the walls of Thebes, facing any enemy that attempts to approach my city.  But riddles are something I know nothing about.

(*The Queen comes out on the balcony.*)

JOCASTA:  Are you still squabbling?  Haven't you found somebody yet with enough brains to solve the riddle?  When there are positions vacant that call for brains, you all come forward; but when there's a calamity to face, you all act stupid.  If within a quarter of an hour by the sandglass no one has come forward to solve the riddle, let the Municipal Council consider itself dissolved.  (*Addressing the populace*)  People of Thebes: let the wisest among you, the sharpest in understanding, the greatest in intellect, the widest in experience come forward to solve the riddle.

OEDIPUS:  Here am I, my Lady.

(*OEDIPUS steps out of the ranks of the common people and makes for the balcony on which the Queen is standing; he takes up a position where he can be seen by all.  Among the people, his name is echoed and reechoed: "Oedipus . . . Oedipus . . ."*)

JOCASTA:  Where are you from, Oedipus?

OEDIPUS:  It doesn't matter, my Lady, whether I'm from Methana or Babylon or any other place on earth.  All that matters to you is that I rid you of the beast.

JOCASTA:  Chief of Police!  What do you know of Oedipus?

AWALIH (*to one of his men*):  The Oedipus file!  (*He is given the file, opens it and reads.*)  Oedipus: color of eyes — brown.  Complexion — darkish.  Distinguishing marks — swollen feet . . .

JOCASTA:  Are you about to describe him when he's standing right here before me?  All right, go on!

AWALIH:  There are many rumors about him.  One is that he escaped from Methana after killing his father or having caused his death.  Another is that he is running away from a case involving alimony.  Mental ability—enjoys great mental powers; within one month of taking up residence in Thebes, was able to defeat all chess experts.  Degree of dangerousness—not involved in dangerous political activity.  Occasionally visits the temple of Amon before important chess matches . . .

OEDIPUS:  None of that is of any importance.  What is important is that I be able to solve the riddle.  What will you give me?

ONAH:  Solve the riddle and you will get fifty thousand pieces of gold.  And as President of the Chamber of Commerce, I undertake to pay you another fifty thousand out of its funds.

OEDIPUS:  O-ho!

HORIMHEB:  And we'll appoint you an assistant priest—that will be another hundred gold pieces a month, to say nothing of an allowance for acting.  And we'll promote you to full priesthood after two years.

OEDIPUS:  I didn't ask how much you'd pay me or what position you'd give me.  I'm asking: What will you give me?

HORIMHEB:  What do you want?

OEDIPUS:  Thebes!

THE PUBLIC (*in astonishment*):  Thebes . . . !

OEDIPUS:  Yes.  You have a King's position vacant.  Let me be appointed King.

THE PUBLIC:  King?

OEDIPUS:  Yes.  That's the only position I'm good for.

HORIMHEB:  What do you say?

AWALIH:  I say we agree.

ONAH:  And if he causes us trouble?

AWALIH:  No problem!  We'll make out that he's anti-Amon and bring about a coup d'état.

JOCASTA:  Why do you want to be King, Oedipus?  What are your qualifications for such an important position?

OEDIPUS:  My brilliance!  My genius!

CREON:  If only your qualification was love of Thebes . . .

OEDIPUS:  I have no love for anything that can be grasped by the hand.  I love principles, ideals, conceptions . . .

JOCASTA:  And if you succeed in solving the riddle, what do you intend to do for Thebes?

OEDIPUS:  I'll put it forward by five thousand years.  I shall realize for it all the inventions that Man is due to bring about over the next five thousand years.  The telephone, television . . .

ALL (*cries of inquiry arise from all present*):  What does it mean? . . . What does it mean?

OEDIPUS:  It means one thing:  let's not waste our time.  If I solve the riddle, I become the King of Thebes.  Do you agree?

AWALIH:  We agree.

OEDIPUS:  And the people?

AWALIH:  What have the people to do with it?  We are the
authority.

OEDIPUS:  It must be the people who agree to my appointment.
You're capable of appointing me today and dismissing me
tomorrow; but if the people appoint me, no one will know
how to dismiss me.  People of Thebes, do you agree?

THE PEOPLE:  We agree.

OEDIPUS:  One thing more.

PEOPLE:  What?

OEDIPUS:  I shall marry the Queen.  (*There is a moment of silence.*)

JOCASTA:  The impudence!  How dare you ask for a union with a
descendant of Amon?

OEDIPUS:  To me, my Lady, you are neither Queen nor a
descendant of the gods.  To me, you are the most beautiful
woman ever created by the gods.  (*JOCASTA hides her face in
embarrassment as he continues.*)  For many years, my Lady, I
have been wandering over hill and dale; I have sailed the
seas, I have crossed the ocean even to Mexico; all in search
of the mistress of this universe, the fairest of the fair, the
princess of princesses, the queen of queens.  Now I have
found you, my Lady.

JOCASTA:  I respect your point of view, and I can see that it's
worthy of discussion.  All the same, it doesn't give you the
right to marry a queen.  Don't forget that you're an ordinary
man, a son neither of Amon nor of Ra.

OEDIPUS:  So be it, my Lady.  I am at your command.  By the
same token, it had better be one of the sons of Amon or of
Ra who solves the riddle.

(*He moves away, but from the people rise shouts of protest and anger. AWALIH approaches the Queen and speaks with her in asides.*)

AWALIH: Consent, my Lady, consent! Oedipus is a lad who'll please you very much . . .

JOCASTA: How do you know?

AWALIH: My investigations . . .

JOCASTA: And if he proves a dud?

AWALIH: Impossible, my Lady. I am answerable for what I say . . . (*Resumes his place.*)

JOCASTA: People of Thebes! For the sake of Thebes, and only for the sake of Thebes, I shall sacrifice all our sacred traditions. More than that, I sacrifice myself in order to save Thebes. Oedipus, sir, I consent. (*The people break out in uproar and confusion.*)

HORIMHEB: A little order . . .

ONAH: There's no time for that. Do us the honor, Oedipus, sir!

CREON: Guard! Open the gate! Do us the honor, Oedipus, sir!

(*OEDIPUS advances among the populace as they shout and cheer. Suddenly TIRESIAS appears, barring their way.*)

TIRESIAS (*shouting in apprehension*): People! Good people! Good people! Wait! What is this you're doing? What are you doing? It may well be that Oedipus will solve the riddle and settle the problem of the beast. But what of the beast within you? Who is going to kill that—that stupid beast that makes you forever wait for the one who will solve your problems for you, in return for which you will concede him anything? Have you ever read before of someone who became king merely because he found the answer to a riddle-me-ree?  Think again, I beg you!  Think once and think twice before you do what you are about to do.  Suppose that Oedipus was not among you—what would you do then?

ONE OF THE PEOPLE:  He's at it—philosophizing!  Why should we suppose, when the man's right here and about to solve the riddle?

ANOTHER:  Why indeed?  He just likes to hear himself spouting.

TIRESIAS:  Good people, do stop making a joke of everything.

JOCASTA:  What's the matter, Tiresias?  Are you trying to convince us that we're all wrong and only you are right?

TIRESIAS:  Is it only a matter of numbers, my Lady?  What is right is right because it is right.  What is true is true because it is true.   If the entire population of Thebes were to stand up and say that the Nile does not exist, would it indeed be nonexistent?

SOMEONE:  Take it easy, old man—and spare us the noise!

(*The populace take no heed, but resume their rhythmic, modulated cheering: "Off you go, Oedipus!  On you go, Oedipus!  Out you come, beast of beasts . . ."*)

TIRESIAS (*in utter misery*):  Oh, people!  Good people!  Good people!  . . .  (*Exits.*)

(*OEDIPUS goes out of the city gate, and the populace crowds onto the wall watching him, still shouting and cheering.*)

SOMEONE:  The beast's behind the hill!

ANOTHER:  Can't see it!

ANOTHER:  Oedipus is still advancing . . .  Come out, beast!

ANOTHER:  Beast of beasts . . . Oedipus has got to the hill!

ANOTHER:  What a man!  He walks on without a care!

ANOTHER:  Behind the hill . . . Out of sight . . . can't see . . .

THE POPULACE (*all together*):  May god shield him!

SOMEONE:  Oedipus . . . He's reappeared . . . He's holding his
      hand high . . . He's running back . . .

ANOTHER (*in great joy*):  Oedipus has solved the riddle . . .
      Oedipus has killed the beast!

(*Shouts of joy burst out all over the stage.  The people dance with joy and
exchange kisses.  They meet OEDIPUS at the gate and carry him
shoulder high.  Flowers are showered on him from all sides.*)

OEDIPUS (*trying to raise his voice above the din*):  Sons of Thebes!
      . . . My children! . . . (*His voice is drowned by the crowd.*)

THE PEOPLE (*modulating their cheers*):  You're the one who killed
      the beast . . .

OEDIPUS:  Listen to me!

THE PEOPLE:  You're the one who killed the beast! . . .

(*OEDIPUS loses control over the populace.  TIRESIAS appears from the
wings, and he also shouts in despair.*)

TIRESIAS:  Listen to him . . . Let him speak . . . Let him speak . . .
      Good people . . .

(*The lighting is dimmed, and the shouting abates.  The stage sinks into
complete darkness.  Then the lights come on again, gradually, revealing
the throne room in the pharaonic palace.  OEDIPUS is on the throne,
wearing the royal mantle and the crown.  HORIMHEB comes in and
bows at great length.*)

HORIMHEB:  Good morning, my Lord!

OEDIPUS:  Good morning, Hor!

HORIMHEB:  The Supreme Council of the Priests of Thebes awaits your directions.

OEDIPUS:  Call a meeting for today, after sunset.  I want to talk to you about the new temple ritual, and about the new educational system I want to introduce.

HORIMHEB:  Yes, my Lord.

OEDIPUS:  Is there something else?

HORIMHEB:  Last night, as I was looking through the Amon and Ra documents that we keep in the Temple archives, I noticed that the name "Oedipus" occurs in seven papyri.  I was greatly surprised, my Lord, because these documents record only the names of the gods and of those descended from the gods.

OEDIPUS:  What are you driving at?

HORIMHEB:  What I'm driving at, my Lord, is that you are without a doubt a descendant of the gods.

OEDIPUS (*weighing his words*):  So—I'm a descendant of the gods, am I?  And this business is something you've discovered during the night?

HORIMHEB:  Yes, my Lord.

OEDIPUS:  What a wonderful man you are—you don't waste any time, do you?  Anyway, you may go now, and I shall give thought to this matter later on.

HORIMHEB:  We don't want to delay publicizing this matter too long, my Lord.  Scholarly integrity makes it incumbent upon me that I make it known.

OEDIPUS:  Scholarly integrity, is it?  A charlatan and a hypocrite—
must you be a braggart as well?  Off you go!  And don't you
dare raise this topic at present.

HORIMHEB:  As my Lord commands. (*Bows and exits.  Enter
AWALIH.*)

AWALIH:  May your morning be like a river in spate, my Lord.

OEDIPUS:  Welcome, Awalih!

AWALIH:  My appointment with your Majesty is at noon, but
there is a matter I discovered last night which I had to come
and lay before your Majesty.

OEDIPUS:  It seems that lots of people made important discoveries
last night.  So what is it, sir?

AWALIH:  The moment your Majesty demanded to be king, I sent
out my detectives to investigate your origins.  Forgive me,
my Lord; this was something I had to do.  It is my personal
responsibility . . .

OEDIPUS:  All right, all right!  Go on!

AWALIH:  The investigations made and the reports received, my
Lord,  prove that you are directly descended from divine
loins . . .

OEDIPUS:  You don't say?

AWALIH:  I swear it by the life of Horus, my Lord, by whom I
have never sworn but . . .

OEDIPUS:  And what is Horus god of?

AWALIH:  He is the god of police, my Lord.

*(OEDIPUS rises from his seat, gets hold of AWALIH and addresses him coldly.)*

OEDIPUS:  Listen, Awalih, I am a human, and the son of a human. Understand?  The true secret of my greatness is that I'm a man, the first human to rule over Thebes.  Understand?  Get that into your colleagues' skulls, and all of you try to help me realize the dreams of Thebes.  Understand?

AWALIH:  Why blame me?  This is what the investigations have yielded.

OEDIPUS:  Do you take me for a fool?  The investigations always yield what you want yielded.

AWALIH:  I'm sorry, my Lord.

OEDIPUS:  All right!  Off you go and see to your business.

AWALIH:  If your Majesty will be so good as to give me the lists of criminals . . .

OEDIPUS:  What criminals?

AWALIH:  Those who are opposed to your rule, my Lord.

OEDIPUS:  My rule?  Have I had the time yet?  I was appointed only yesterday.

AWALIH:  And is that a short interval, my Lord?  By now, half the city is against you — the envious, the resentful, the adventurers, the madmen — these are the ones that we term enemies of the regime.  If your majesty will have the kindness to give me the lists of their names and addresses, so we may arrest them . . .

OEDIPUS:  I know of nothing that may be termed "enemies of the regime," but there is something that may be termed "enemies of Thebes."  Those are your concern.  If anybody does anything against Thebes, it's your responsibility to stop him in his tracks.

AWALIH:  I see: each to his own style.  His Majesty the King who preceded your Majesty handed me his lists three days before he ascended the throne.  That's why he went on ruling for fifteen years without any enemies.  He was greatly loved.

OEDIPUS:  And that's why when he was murdered no one took the trouble to find out who killed him.  Isn't that so, Chief of Police?

AWALIH:  His fate will be known, my Lord.  Anyway, my Lord, I shall go on operating on the basis of the old lists.

OEDIPUS:  The old lists?

AWALIH:  Look here, my Lord.  Our family — the Awalih family — has held the post of Chief of Police for four hundred years.  I've noticed a strange thing: the lists of names of enemies of the regime are always the same.  They've been passed on from father to son — sometimes one or two names more, sometimes one or two names less.  But the lists have always been the same.

OEDIPUS:  Awalih, I have no time for this sort of thing.  You're supposed to know your business and your business is the maintenance of Thebes' internal security.  Out with you!

(*AWALIH bows and goes.  In comes KAMI, the friend of OEDIPUS who was playing chess with him in the first scene.*)

KAMI (*in a carefree, jocular mood*):  My, my!  What magnificence!

OEDIPUS:  Welcome, Kami.

KAMI (*laughing full tilt*):  Who would have believed it?  Give me a promise too, O Ra!  Now tell me, buddy — what job are you going to give me?

OEDIPUS (*perturbed*):  Kami, be serious!

KAMI (*still laughing heartily*):  Ho, ho!  (*Chanting*)  You're the one
who killed the beast!  You know, when you ran out to solve
the riddle, I was running behind you.  I hid behind the hill
to see how you were going to handle it.

OEDIPUS:  What are you driving at?

KAMI:  Nothing!

OEDIPUS:  Kami, that's enough clowning.  You are now standing
in the Royal Hall.  You'd better not speak this way.

(*KAMI bursts out laughing again.  At that moment, an arm stretches out
from behind the throne, seizes him by the throat, and drags him away.
OEDIPUS stares in amazement.  AWALIH appears from behind the
throne.*)

OEDIPUS:  What's brought you here, Awalih?  Where did you
come from?  How?  What's happening?

AWALIH (*coldly*):  These are inevitable measures, my Lord.  It's
true they're not very pleasant, but they're necessary.

OEDIPUS:  Necessary?

AWALIH:  You'll find out later on that they are necessary.  Excuse
me, my Lord.  This is my personal responsibility.

(*AWALIH bows and exits. The lighting diminishes, except on OEDIPUS,
who looks fixedly ahead, in bafflement and confusion. TIRESIAS appears
in a corner of the stage.*)

TIRESIAS:  The worst horrors and most intractable calamities
always begin thus: as the lord Awalih said, with things that
are unpleasant but necessary.  Only he hasn't told us why
they are unpleasant, or why they are also necessary.

(*The lighting fades as the curtain falls.*)

## Act Two

*The second act is made up of numerous quick scenes. This places a greater burden than usual on the producer and the stage manager. To ease the problem of quick changes, the producer had better resort to the puppet show technique: blackened stage, ultraviolet rays, projected shadows. It may be necessary to use actual puppets in the staging of parts of some scenes.*

## Scene One

*In the living room of SENEFRU's house. The furniture is semimodern, but with a pharaonic flavor. The same is true of the clothes worn by the characters. SENEFRU is sitting reading a magazine, turning the pages in a way that reveals annoyance. A small CHILD is playing with a toy. SENEFRU's wife, NEFER, is plucking at a large harp. In the living room is a large television set, a radio, and a telephone. The telephone rings.*

SENEFRU: Hello . . . Yes, this is Senefru . . . Listen to me, Ka'it . . . Later, later . . . We'll meet at night . . . Goodbye! (*Puts the receiver down with some violence.*)

NEFER: Be careful with the phone—you'll break it!

SENEFRU: Ka'it's a fool! I've told him a thousand times there are things not to be said on the telephone. And yet whenever he gets on the line he prattles on. I've told him a thousand times I have a household to look after, a son to bring up. The fool!

CHILD (*holding up his toy*): Daddy, please mend my toy.

SENEFRU: Bring it over, my pet; I'll mend it for you. You go and do your homework, and by the time you've finished that, this will be mended. (*The CHILD gets hold of a large book and settles down in a corner.*)

SENEFRU: What's this, Nefer? Can't you find any toy but this for the boy?  Does it have to be a beast with Oedipus killing it?

NEFER:  Where am I to get anything else?  All the toys on the
market are like this: a beast riding a bicycle with Oedipus
killing it; a beast on a plane with Oedipus killing it; a beast
playing ball with Oedipus killing it . . . (*SENEFRU reacts
with annoyance.*)

CHILD:  B-e-a-s-t beast; k-i-l-l kill.  Ramses, did you see the
beast?  Yes, Kamis, I saw it.

SENEFRU:  Ahmis, my darling, what are you doing?  What book is
this?

CHILD:  It's the beastly reading book, Dad!

SENEFRU:  All right!  Go and do your studying in your room.
(*The CHILD goes.*)  Even the children . . .

NEFER:  What's the matter with you?  Your nerves are frayed.  Is
anything wrong?

SENEFRU:  No, nothing at all.  We could do without the piece
you're playing just now.  (*This brings out the fact that what she
has been playing is "You're the One Who Killed the Beast."
SENEFRU gets up to turn on the radio.*)

FEMALE BROADCASTER'S VOICE:  You will now hear a
selection of sentimental songs, beginning with "You're the
One Who Killed the Beast" from the album of the same
name.  This will be followed by "Beastly is My Loneliness"
and "Bei mir Bist du Schön."  You will then hear that
moving artist, Camille Hoarse, in a rendering of a new song,
"My Love Is a Beast in His Passions."  The closing item will
be "If Thou Be-est My Love."  (*SENEFRU switches off.*)

NEFER:  Why did you switch it off?  Those are lovely songs.

SENEFRU:  I'd rather we looked at television.  There's a literary program on about now. (*Switches on and a woman BROADCASTER appears.*)

THE BROADCASTER:  Hello, we've received thousands of letters requesting a repeat of the comedy "Don't Be a Beast to Me and I Shan't Be a Beast to You." We're pleased to tell our viewers that we shall be showing it at the end of this evening's transmission.

NEFER:  That'll be good this evening. It's a wonderful play. Don't go out tonight. (*SENEFRU looks at her with distaste.*)

THE BROADCASTER:  Just now, we're in the company of the eminent critic Mahi Kah, in the program entitled "Questions and Answers." (*Professor MAHI KAH appears on the screen.*)

MAHI KAH:  The fateful and beastly struggle between Man and Beast, which is the subject of certain artistic works, besets us with sentiments best described as atavistic toward this bestial contest. I say this in connection with the publication this week of a book by Abwakh Kalt, to which he has given the title "Views on the Slain Beast." (*SENEFRU rises and switches off the television.*)

NEFER:  What are you doing? What's wrong with you? Why are you so upset? You want to smash the television, smash the radio, smash the telephone! Perhaps there is some sense in it. After all, you don't have to worry about anything. I'm the one who has to go to all sorts of trouble over the installments . . .

SENEFRU (*almost in tears*):  Please, Nefer; please shut up and leave me alone.

NEFER:  Have I come anywhere near you? What's the matter with you?

SENEFRU:  Nothing's the matter with me. It's just that everything has turned beastly . . . (*Correcting himself*) I mean, objectionable.

(*The lights are gradually dimmed.*)

## Scene Two

*Lecture hall in the University of Thebes. Dozens of students are sitting in the auditorium, only their heads showing. Before them stands HORIMHEB.*

HORIMHEB:  We dealt in the previous lecture with conditions in Thebes before the appearance of the beast.  In today's lecture, we shall give details of the main reference works relevant to this subject, wherefrom it will be definitively established that under no circumstances is it possible for man to solve the riddle posed by the Sphinx.  I say that no human could solve the riddle unless he was descended from the gods.  This is why Oedipus was able to do it.  I refer you to pages 15 to 340 of our own doctoral dissertation, in which we spoke at length of the divine origins of His Majesty Oedipus-Ra.  Let me return to the main theme of the lecture. This is how Oedipus did away with the beast and brought about in Thebes such efflorescence, such wealth, and such modern inventions as we enjoy today; this is how Oedipus made ours the greatest city in the world.

(*Gradual dimming of lights, as a large screen lights up, and on it appears the shadow of OEDIPUS, gigantic in stature, with tens of thousands cheering around him.*)

OEDIPUS:  My sons, sons of Thebes!  Today we celebrate the fifth anniversary of the slaying of the beast.

PEOPLE (*cheering in modulated fashion*):  You're the one who killed the beast . . .

(*Gradual dimming of lights.*)

## Scene Three

*In a narrow tomb inside a temple, AWALIH is interrogating KA'IT, one of the citizens of Thebes. KA'IT is tied to a stone pillar; beside him is a very young POLICEMAN.*

AWALIH: Our inquiries have established that you are spreading rumors to the effect that Oedipus did not solve the riddle and did not kill the beast. There isn't a place where you haven't said such things — in cafés, bars, graveyards, on the telephone . . .

KA'IT: I said no such thing.

AWALIH: What did you say, then?

KA'IT: I asked just one question: what was the riddle?

AWALIH: What business is it of yours? Why did you ask?

KA'IT: I want to know; and I believe there are many people who want to know.

AWALIH: Very good! We're getting to the point. Who, then, my dear sir, are those who want to know?

KA'IT: I swear by Horus . . .

AWALIH: Don't! Don't swear by Horus. Don't cut your own throat!

KA'IT: I swear by all the gods that I know of no one particular person . . .

AWALIH: Liar! How else would you learn that there are people who want to know? Is your Lordship a fortune teller?

KA'IT (*in great weariness, speaking with immense difficulty*): Listen, Awalih, I'm tired of this game. Every time a new king is enthroned, you get hold of me, beat me in the same say, and ask me the same damned questions. I want to know, good people; I want to know! I'm losing all faith—or perhaps one is better off dying . . . (*His head sinks to his chest.*)

AWALIH: Don't try to evade the question! Let's have no twisting and turning. How did you find out that there were people who wanted to know? Answer!

(*KA'IT does not answer. The young POLICEMAN raises KA'IT's head and then lets go, whereupon it again sinks to his chest.*)

POLICEMAN (*distressed*): He's dead!

AWALIH (*calmly*): So . . . And why are you so upset?

POLICEMAN (*greatly perturbed*): It's just that . . . he's dead . . . dead!

AWALIH: It's his choice, my man! Each one is free to do whatever he pleases. Tell me, how long is it since you were admitted to the force?

POLICEMAN: One week.

AWALIH: That's why. You'll get used to it tomorrow. Sit down and write the report.

(*The POLICEMAN gets hold of paper and pencil and writes, with a markedly trembling hand.*)

AWALIH (*continuing*): . . . and when the accused was confronted with irrefutable proof of his theft of the treasures of Ra . . . (*The young man stops and stares at AWALIH in amazement.*) Go on writing, young man—why do you stop? . . . his theft of the treasures of Ra stored in the temple . . . when confronted with proof . . . his resistance collapsed and he committed suicide by throwing himself out of the window on the fourth floor . . .

POLICEMAN:  But there are no windows on the fourth floor!

AWALIH:  So make it the fifth.

POLICEMAN:  There are none on the fifth floor either.

AWALIH:  Go on writing.  Don't bore me.  It's just a technical term.

POLICEMAN:  A technical term?

AWALIH:  It's not a window in the factual sense.  It's a symbolic one.  When you're a little more advanced you'll understand—and you'll get used to it.  Oh, that's enough. Close the report!  I have to go now.  An appointment for the cinema.  (*He looks at his watch.*)  Who-a!  I'm half an hour late.  (*He looks at the corpse.*)  Damn you!  Damn you!  I suppose you're pleased with this delay.  What will I tell my wife?  Well, by your leave . . .

POLICEMAN:  What will I do with this?

AWALIH:  He's not very heavy.  Take him and throw him off the roof.

POLICEMAN (*in great terror*):  Off the roof?

AWALIH:  Didn't you say there were no windows on the fourth and fifth floors?  (*Very angrily*)  Why do you have to complicate things for me?  Where else are you to throw him from?  How stupid can you get?

POLICEMAN (*totally rattled*):  I'm sorry.  Do go, Your Honor! Please go on to the cinema—or you might miss the Mickey Mouse cartoon . . .

(*Gradual dimming of lights.*)

**Scene Four**

*The Royal Throne Room. JOCASTA is pacing angrily; AWALIH stands alone.*

JOCASTA:  In his laboratory all day long and all night long.  His Lordship is busy with his inventions.  Since the day I married him, I haven't seen him more than four times.  It's true I'm a Queen, and a descendant of the gods as well.  But I'm also flesh and blood.

AWALIH:  How am I responsible for all this, my Lady?

JOCASTA:  Your responsibility is that you made me agree to marry him.  You're the one who advised me to consent.

AWALIH:  But, my Lady, I didn't know that this was how he was going to respond.

JOCASTA:   And since you're an ignoramus and know nothing, why did you make me agree? (*Imitating him*) "Consent, my Lady.  Oedipus is a lad who'll please you very much." "And if he proves a dud?" "I am answerable, my Lady . . ." Well now, sir—discharge your responsibility.

AWALIH:  What am I to do, my Lady?

JOCASTA:  You know, Awalih.  Do you want me to teach you your job as well?  You know what to do—the same as you did with his predecessor and the predecessor's predecessor. An accident  of the kind that takes place every day.  Who can be sure of his own life?

AWALIH:  I can't do it this time, my Lady.

JOCASTA:  What's different about this time?  You always managed before.

AWALIH:  Before now, people used not to ask.  The King is dead,

long live the King.  Goodbye Ahmes, hello Ramses.
Goodbye Mena, hello Thotmes.  It was no concern of theirs.
But with Oedipus, the situation's different.  The people are
the ones who appointed him.  Besides, he's made all these
inventions for them.  And even if we could cope with the
people, there's a very large group of Theban citizens who
make a living out of all this, and this group's very powerful
and influential.  The clearest examples are Brother Onah and
Brother Horimheb.  The moment Oedipus invents
something, they get hold of it, manufacture it, and sell it.
An awful lot of people are benefiting.  If anything happened
to Oedipus, they wouldn't keep quiet, and we, my Lady,
would be exposed.

JOCASTA:  And the solution?  There has to be a solution.

AWALIH:  Your arsenal, my Lady—a woman's arsenal.  It's more
powerful than the atomic bomb, which Oedipus is
intent on inventing.  See to your beauty, my Lady.  Certain
essences have come on the market these days that can turn
the head of the ablest of men; there are perfumes that can
turn the head of a monk, my Lady.

JOCASTA:  Perfumes, oils, ointments, powders—there isn't one I
haven't tried.  And still it's no use.  He's busy with his
inventions.

AWALIH:  All right, then.  Nothing's left but the traditional
method, the method our family's specialized in.  It's true it
takes time, but in the long run the results are guaranteed.

JOCASTA:  And what is the traditional method?

AWALIH:  Whenever he does something beneficial, he adds to the
number of people who love him.  So my task will be to add
to the number of people who hate him.  Of course you know
the rest.

JOCASTA:  How are you going to make people hate him?

AWALIH:  Nothing to it; it's very simple.  I shall make them love
　　　　him . . . (*pause*) by force!  That's our business, my Lady.
　　　　Don't you worry.  I only beg you by Isis that you intercede
　　　　for me so that Horus may be at my right hand.

JOCASTA:  I'll go this very night to pray in the Temple of Amon
　　　　and to call down blessings on you.

(*The Queen leaves the stage.  ONAH appears from the inner galleries,
holding some modern devices.*)

AWALIH:  Well, well, my good man!  You are busy!  All these
　　　　inventions are to be transmuted into gold.  And in the end
　　　　the gold will pour into the Municipal Council and the
　　　　Chamber of Commerce.

ONAH:  So what, brother?  You're a member . . .

AWALIH:  A fat lot I get out of it, worse luck!

ONAH:  You got an automobile, a yacht, and a helicopter.  Every
　　　　one of your children got a toy car.  And every month you
　　　　get you-know-what.  What more do you want?

AWALIH:  Nothing—but just keep an open mind.  All you've
　　　　mentioned amounts to crumbs in comparison with what you
　　　　get.

ONAH:  Is that all that's worrying you?  I'm at your service.  How
　　　　many Awalihs have we got?  You have only to say . . .

AWALIH:  It's no skin off your nose.  Our good friend invents, and
　　　　you make a profit.

ONAH:  You mean we do.  (*They chant together.*)  We're the ones
　　　　who killed the beast!

(*Both burst out laughing.  Gradual dimming of lights.*)

### Scene Five

*On the large screen: the PEOPLE of Thebes in silhouette are kneeling and chanting in voices filled with awe and devotion, as if praying. OEDIPUS stands before them.*

PEOPLE:  Oedipus-Ra . . . You're the one who killed the beast . . .
    Oedipus-Ra!

(*Gradual dimming of lights.*)

### Scene Six

*The Throne Room. OEDIPUS is sitting on the throne, and before him are AWALIH, HORIMHEB, CREON, and ONAH. OEDIPUS is greatly worked up.*

OEDIPUS:  What's happening behind my back?  How did all this
    business develop?  I want to know.

HORIMHEB:  Calm down, my Lord.  We're the ones who want to
    know.

OEDIPUS:  The people today were kneeling before me as the
    pharaonic bark sailed on.  The people today prostrated
    themselves before me in the temple as I prayed.

ONAH:  They respect you, my Lord.

OEDIPUS:  And didn't they respect me before?  Yet before today
    they used not to kneel before me.  Before today, they
    addressed me as Oedipus, plain Oedipus.  Now I have
    become Oedipus-Ra.  Awalih, have you issued a declaration
    saying I am a god?

AWALIH:  I have not, my Lord.  But it may be that the news
    leaked out.

OEDIPUS:  Leaked out?

AWALIH: Nothing can remain hidden, my Lord. Isn't it so, Horimheb? Speak out! Why do you stand silent?

HORIMHEB: In reality, my Lord . . . The truth is . . . As I see it . . . I mean, my point of view . . . would contend . . .

OEDIPUS: That means you're about to tell a lie. Since you mention reality and truth, it means you intend to lie.

HORIMHEB: No, my Lord. I'm not about to tell a lie. By now everybody knows that your Majesty is descended from the gods.

OEDIPUS: I warned you not to tell this tale.

HORIMHEB: We're not telling it, my Lord. We're studying it.

OEDIPUS: Studying it, are you?

HORIMHEB: Yes, in the various stages of the educational system.

OEDIPUS: I issued no orders to this effect.

HORIMHEB: Excuse me, my Lord. With all due respect to your Majesty this does not come within your Majesty's competence. This is a scientific fact, and scientific facts must be made known. Integrity makes it incumbent . . .

OEDIPUS (*rising from the throne and shouting*): Integrity? Is it integrity that you should lie?

HORIMHEB: I'm no liar, my Lord. It's not fitting that you should say such a thing to someone who is your father's age; nor is it fitting that you should shout in the presence of your elders. This matter is no lie; it's a fact. Isn't that so, Awalih?

AWALIH: Indeed.

OEDIPUS: Fact, is it? So you two know that I'm a god while I

don't—and you don't want me to shout?  Creon, why don't
you speak?

CREON:  Sorry, my Lord.  I'd better remain detached from any
political currents.  If the guard should interfere in domestic
or foreign policy, the outcome wouldn't be desirable.  I'm
under your orders, my Lord, in anything that relates to the
security of Thebes.

OEDIPUS:  So it doesn't matter to you whether the King of Thebes
be man or god?

CREON:  It makes no difference to me, my Lord.  And I have no
time.  I'm responsible for the training of the Guard in
relation to the defense of Thebes.  I have no time for
anything else.

OEDIPUS (*with genuine sorrow*):  Thank you, Creon.  You may go.
Goodbye!

(*CREON stiffens in a military salute and goes.*)

OEDIPUS:  Creon's an earnest fellow.  All he cares about is the
defense of Thebes.

HORIMHEB:  We too, my Lord; we care about the defense of
Thebes.

OEDIPUS:  That leaves one function unfulfilled.  I need someone to
protect me from you.

ONAH:  My Lord, you're looking at this matter in a very romantic
way.  You need to look at it from a realistic point of view.
The people of Thebes have been ruled by gods for
thousands of years.  The worship of Pharaoh isn't merely a
pious custom; it's a national tradition.  We can't all of a
sudden come and tell people that the king's an ordinary
man.

HORIMHEB:  Besides, the educational curricula at all stages assert this.  We can't change them.  The prayers also assert this. All our customs and traditions, our songs and tales, say the same thing.  It's a pyramid, my Lord, a pyramid of beliefs and concepts—and a very big pyramid.  This pyramid is erected on a very sound base.  This base says that Pharaoh is a god.  If now we come and say that Pharaoh is an ordinary man, everything will be confusion and chaos, and we'll all go down the drain—especially the priests of Amon.

OEDIPUS:  I have a different point of view.  We must make the people understand that there's something called the Law of Evolution.  You need to study this subject.  It's true that there were once kings who were gods, or the sons of gods . .

HORIMHEB (*interrupting*):  Do you believe this, my Lord?  Do you still believe that there were kings who were gods?  They were all wretched human beings like ourselves, and some of them, even, were beggars.  But we had to make them into gods.

OEDIPUS:  Why did we have to do that?  I don't see any necessity at all.

ONAH:  My Lord, you seem to think that this matter concerns you alone.

OEDIPUS:  Of course it concerns me alone.

ONAH:  Not at all.  It concerns us even more than it concerns you.

OEDIPUS:  How so?

ONAH:  All the organizations, the directorates, the departments, the institutions that function under the aegis of the Municipal Council, and which we are required to operate in the best possible manner—people respect us more when they know that at our head there's a god.  But if they knew that what makes us tick is a human, they'd become insolent toward us, and we wouldn't know how to make them function.

HORIMHEB:  It's a matter of prestige, my Lord.

ONAH:  Of course.  Do you think that if people know that Cheops wasn't a god, they would still have built him this pyramid?  They would scarcely have placed one slab above another.

AWALIH:  The truth is that your Majesty is still new at this trade and has no experience of pharaonic problems.  We're sparing your Majesty a great many calamities.

OEDIPUS:  Calamities?

AWALIH:  Of course.  For example, there are people who are skeptical about the story of the beast and the riddle.  They want to know what the riddle was.  What they're after is the riddle.  Their only concern is to demolish.  Just imagine: if people knew that you're just an ordinary man, they'd become insolent.  I tell your Majesty that we're sparing you a great many disasters, only one is reluctant to talk . . .

OEDIPUS:  What's so frightening about the riddle?  I'll tell you what it is, sir.  (*After a moment's consideration*)  What is it that walks on four in the morning, on two at noon, and on three at sunset?

AWALIH (*with exaggerated wonder*):  My, my!  It would be impossible for anyone in Thebes ever to solve this, my Lord.

HORIMHEB:  And what is the answer, my Lord?

OEDIPUS:  Man.

AWALIH:  Wonderful . . . Wonderful.  Bravo, my Lord, bravo!

ONAH:  And does your Majesty want to convince us that you are an ordinary man?  There's no way an ordinary human can solve this riddle. It's certain that your Majesty is of divine descent, or at least that the spirit of the gods is being incarnated in you.

OEDIPUS:  Do you think so?

ONAH:  Certainly.

OEDIPUS (*pleased*):  Thank you.

(*As he rises to leave, they bow to him.*)

HORIMHEB (*sarcastically*):  Ha! Is that the riddle?

ONAH:  Isn't that the riddle that was part of our curriculum in elementary school?  So why is it that no one could solve it?

AWALIH:  Any child in Thebes knows this riddle, and the answer.

HORIMHEB:  So how did the beast die?

AWALIH (*chanting*):  He's the one who killed the beast!  Why should we care, brother?  Our task now is to think up a somewhat difficult riddle to give out to the people, since some of them are beginning to ask.

HORIMHEB:  I'll tell you. (*He thinks.*)  What is it that walks on four in the morning, on two at noon, on three at sunset, on five at twilight, and the crawls on its belly at dawn?

ONAH:  And what is the answer?

HORIMHEB:  It's still Man.  (*Suppressing laughter.*)  Is anyone going to contradict us?

(*They burst out laughing as the lights are gradually dimmed.*)

## Scene Seven

*The great courtyard before Pharaoh's Palace, but with altered features: there is a multitude of shops before which people stand, selling the most modern devices, advertising them in modulated phrases. TIRESIAS appears, and the noise of the crowd abates.*

TIRESIAS:  The common voice now is Oedipus and the beast that was killed.  Everyone sings the same song to the new Pharaoh who has shortened the span of time by five thousand years.  The people of Thebes are benefiting from inventions which no one else shall see for a long, long time. The Municipal Council has made good use of these inventions to implant the desired tunes in the minds of the people — and, at the same time, to fill certain accounts with money.  Nor did the Municipal Council omit to put out a proclamation setting out the riddle and the solution which Oedipus offered to the beast.  The answer was: Man! Strange that Man has remained for thousands of years, and shall forever remain, the only answer to all riddles.  And man shall remain the correct tune, the one true, clear tune among all the bad tunes as age follows age.  Strange also that this truth, clear as the sun in a Theban day, often escapes the minds of many of the composers who make up the various peoples' music . . .

*(TIRESIAS disappears as OEDIPUS appears on the palace balcony, whereupon the PEOPLE in the courtyard crowd before it.)*

OEDIPUS:  Sons of Thebes, my sons! . . .  Today we celebrate the killing of the beast . . .

PEOPLE (*chanting*):  You're the one who killed the beast!

OEDIPUS:  I still remember that day as if it had happened yesterday, when I went out to the beast . . .

PEOPLE:  You're the one who killed the beast!

OEDIPUS: One thought was dominant in me, pervading all my perceptions. It was a supreme faith that this beast . . .

PEOPLE: You're the one who killed the beast!

(*AWALIH, holding on to SENEFRU, detaches himself from the masses and stands away from the crowd, at the front of the stage. OEDIPUS is still delivering his speech, but we no longer hear him.*)

AWALIH (*with murderous gentleness*): Senefru, why aren't you singing? I've been watching you. You've been standing there for an hour, not chanting.

SENEFRU (*picking up some courage*): You, sir, weren't singing either.

AWALIH: Senefru, I am the composer.

SENEFRU (*trying to make his voice sound hoarse*): It's just that my voice has gone hoarse today.

AWALIH: You don't say. Hoarse, eh? Well, then, whistle, or hum, show some response to the music! What are you made of — stone?

SENEFRU: To be frank . . .

AWALIH: Ah, yes! Do be frank!

SENEFRU: It's just that I haven't a musical ear.

AWALIH: I beg your pardon, Mr. Senefru, sir. The fact is that your ear is very musical indeed. It's just that it isn't clean, and I am going to clean it up for you.

SENEFRU (*pleading, in a low voice*): Awalih, I place myself under the protection of Amon . . .

AWALIH (*whispering*): Come with me, quietly — or do you want

people to know that your ear isn't clean?  It would be a
scandal . . .

SENEFRU:  I'll go home, wash my ears, and come back
immediately to sing.

AWALIH:  You won't know how.  This is a matter for a specialist.
It will take just one minute.  Come with me!

(*He goes out into the wings.  OEDIPUS' voice becomes audible.*)

OEDIPUS:  I thought of only one thing: Thebes must become the
greatest city in this world.  And for Thebes to become great,
what is needed . . .

(*SENEFRU dashes in, singing loudly and enthusiastically, and with true
harmony.*)

SENEFRU:  You're the one who killed the beast!

(*OEDIPUS stops, and the people look in amazement at SENEFRU, who
goes on singing with enthusiasm, but his wholeheartedness and
enthusiasm gradually change to bitter weeping.  He takes refuge in a
corner at the front of the stage, drops into sitting position, and weeps
quietly.*)

OEDIPUS:  So it was, my children, that the beast died.

PEOPLE:  You're the one who killed the beast!

(*OEDIPUS responds with a wave of his arms, and disappears inside the
palace.  At the same time, a huge howl rises of a man in torment.  THE
PEOPLE freeze where they stand in horror.  A man rushes in from the
gate in the wall, his face and body covered with blood.  THE MAN is still
uttering dreadful cries, then he drops to the floor among THE PEOPLE.*)

THE MAN:  A beast . . . A very great beast! . . . By the wall . . . It
devoured my leg . . . Ah! . . . I'm dying! . . .

THE PEOPLE:  A beast! . . .

(*THE MAN's movements cease.  THE PEOPLE, speechless, exchange glances.*)

SENEFRU (*through his tears*):  So the beast has come back!

(*AWALIH springs on SENEFRU.*)

AWALIH:  You wretch!  What beast has come back?  Weren't you singing a moment ago that Oedipus had killed the beast?

SENEFRU (*seized with terror*):  Yes, yes . . . It must be another beast . . . a different beast . . . The first beast was killed by Oedipus . . . Oedipus killed . . .

(*He tries to sing but cannot.  He goes on weeping silently, his whole body shaking in utter misery as down comes . . .*)

**Curtain**

## Act Three

### Scene One

*The same as at the beginning of the play: THE PEOPLE of Thebes are sitting on the stone benches, but they are now in gloomy silence. The members of the Municipal Council sit in the middle. AWALIH stands, holding a large sheet of paper from which he reads to THE PEOPLE.*

AWALIH:  People of Thebes!  The Municipal Council has entrusted me with the presentation of a report setting out the dimensions of the present situation regarding the beast's assault on the walls of the city.
　　**Item One:**  The Municipal Council asserts that this beast is a new one.  It also is in the semblance of a sphinx, but it is smaller in size than the previous one which was killed by Oedipus.  Such is the assertion of the experts in beasts, authenticated by Professor Horimheb.
　　**Item Two:**  The beast has attacked thirty-five persons, of whom thirty were devoured, and five have suffered lethal injuries from which they have since died.  Their consignment to the afterlife was carried out with due honors, this by debiting the account of the Chamber of Commerce — in consideration whereof the Municipal Council offers thanks to Brother Onah for this generous gesture.
　　**Item Three:**  We have no certain indication that the beast is posing riddles.  However, by analogy with the previous beast and in view of the fact that the new beast is of the same species and genus as the previous one, it is held to be almost certain that the new beast also poses riddles to travelers and demands solutions.
　　It has been decided to hold this plenary meeting of the inhabitants of Thebes to discuss the problem and arrive at a solution.  Long live Thebes!  Long live the people of Thebes, always and ever capable of killing beasts wherever they may be!  Long live Oedipus! . . .

PEOPLE (*chanting*):  He's the one who killed the beast.

AWALIH:  Promulgate at the permanent seat of the Municipal
        Council within the Temple of Amon.  Signed on behalf of
        the President of the Municipal Council: er . . . hmmm . . .
        Awalih.  Honored citizens of Thebes, in accordance with
        true democracy, we meet today in order to seek your views.
        How are we to get rid of the beast?

(*A member of the public speaks out, but we cannot spot him or ascertain
the source of the voice.*)

VOICE:  Oh, brother, what cheek!  What business is it of ours?
        You've always decided matters on your own — why the
        sudden change today?  What do you take us Thebans for —
        fools to be left out of every party and invited to every
        funeral?

AWALIH (*angrily*):  Who is it who spoke? . . . Let the speaker stand
        up . . . (*Even more angrily*)  Let the speaker stand up!  (*Then,
        trying to conceal his anger and to speak softly.*)  What need is
        there for anyone who speaks to be afraid?  Let him give his
        name so it may be recorded in the minutes . . . (*Leaves his
        place and wanders among the people.*)  Who was it who was
        speaking?  The voice came from over here . . . Who spoke?
        Anyone who wants to speak should put up his hand, ask for
        the floor, and give his name . . . Ever heard of something
        called democracy, you cattle? . . . (*Turns his back on the people
        and returns to his place.*)  A sorry lot without any feeling for
        democracy . . .

VOICE:  That's enough from you, Awalih, enough!  (*In a muffled
        voice*)  A curse upon your father's soul.

AWALIH (*springing up in horror and turning toward the people*):
        Who is it who used insulting words just now?  Who is it
        being rude?  (*Exploding*)  Oh, no!  I'm not going to be
        insulted by any of you!  Let him who was abusive stand up
        at once!  You don't want to tell?  (*Turning to the policemen*)
        Seize Thebes!

POLICEMAN: Thebes?

AWALIH: Yes, Thebes. All of it! The people, the Municipal
    Council, Oedipus, Jocasta . . . Everyone's under arrest.
    Everyone's under arrest until you produce the man who
    insulted me. (*In highly emotional tones, almost weeping*) Am I
    . . . Awalih . . . Am I to be insulted?

HORIMHEB: Calm down, Awalih.

AWALIH (*savagely*): Don't you open your mouth, sir! You are
    now under arrest. Such matters are not to be treated lightly.
    Don't utter a word until I bid you to. (*Facing the people*) Am
    I to have my father's soul cursed? A curse on the soul of the
    father of every one of you, no matter how big a mob! Who
    was it who uttered that insult? You don't want to talk? All
    right, here we stay. (*He squats down on the ground.*) There's
    no business to call us away, is there? No one's going home
    today. (*To the policemen*) Listen, my boys: if anybody
    moves, shoot—even if it's me. We'll see how I can be
    insulted. (*In a voice choking with emotion*) So, you tinkers,
    after all my services to you, you turn round and insult me.
    For years I've been working for you, day and night—and in
    the end I get abused. All right, I'm going to teach you a
    lesson.

TIRESIAS (*from among the crowd*): It's me, Awalih. (*It is clear that
    TIRESIAS was not the one who cursed.*)

AWALIH: Come on! Come up to me! Show yourself to me. Who
    are you? (*TIRESIAS stands up.*) Tiresias . . . Take him! (*Not
    one of the policemen makes a move, instead they stand in
    confusion.*) Men, obey your orders, one and all!

TIRESIAS: Don't be silly, Awalih. It's no good arresting Tiresias,
    my son. Have you forgotten? It's the first lesson you were
    taught when you were small. Have you forgotten? If you
    have, your policemen haven't.

AWALIH (*confounded*):  Isn't it shameful of you to insult me, Uncle
Tiresias?  I swear by Horus, if it wasn't that you're an old
man, this day wouldn't have ended well.

TIRESIAS:  Sorry, Awalih.  It slipped out in spite of me.  You know
that I utter insults only once every hundred years.  Never
mind; you just happened to be the butt this time.

AWALIH:  Only the last person you insulted did happen to be
my grandfather, Uncle Tiresias.

TIRESIAS:  That's how your luck runs.  I'm sorry.

ONAH:  Reconciliation is a blessing.  He's like your father, Awalih.

AWALIH:  All right: an amnesty.  An amnesty for Thebes.  I beg
you, good people: there are traditions we ought to maintain.
If there's anything anybody wants, let them speak out.  Only
let him say his name first.  We must have the name of
anyone who wishes to speak.  Otherwise our democracy
would crumble at the base, and the beast would eat us up.
Do you want the beast to devour us?  Of course not.  All
right, then.  No one is to speak a word until he's given his
name.  If he doesn't, it's up to anyone of you to give him
away.  That's settled, then.  Just allow me a word.  In my
view, the person responsible for doing away with the beast
must be the Lord Creon, since he's the person answerable
for guarding and defending Thebes.  Therefore I suggest he
be entrusted with doing away with the beast.

CREON:  If the purpose of the Lord Awalih is to do away with me
and with the Theban Guard, so be it; let's go and meet the
beast.  But if the aim is to kill a beast the size of which by
your own accounts is that of a pyramid, that has the face of
a woman and the body of an animal, then that will take me
a long time.

HORIMHEB:  What we understand from this is that you are afraid
to join battle with him at the present time.

CREON: Understand me well, Horimheb. I don't know the meaning of fear. But all the lessons and drills known to the Theban Guard are based on the assumption that the warrior is to encounter a warrior of his own ilk. The Theban Guard is capable of fighting with arrows and spears and war chariots. It can fence. It can wrestle. But the Theban Guard has never learned how to face up to a beast.

AWALIH: Attack him as if he was an army.

CREON: A brawl—is that what you want? There is a difference between warfare and brawling. What you're calling for is an act of collective suicide. To fight such a beast as this, we need to know what size he is; we need to know how thick his skin is, his range of vision, the parts of his body that are vulnerable; how he moves; how fast he can be; when he sleeps, and for how long. When we have all these data, we shall modify our training on the basis that our enemy is a particular beast whose characteristics are such-and-such, whose strong points are so-and-so and his weaknesses thus-and-thus. That is warfare. One might have expected the intelligence services run by the Lord Awalih to have supplied us with all this information, but it seems they were busy with other things. Such are the ways that I know. But then there is another, an easier way. It is that His Majesty Oedipus-Ra, just as he rid us of the first beast, should rid us of the second and no one else need trouble himself. (*This last sentence is spoken with bitterness mingled with sarcasm.*)

HORIMHEB: Pharaonic traditions forbid that Pharaoh be exposed to any possibility of danger.

CREON: But he did expose himself once before.

HORIMHEB: He hadn't become Pharaoh at that time.

ONAH: Pharaonic traditions must be respected no matter what dangers threaten Thebes. Traditions are our very life.

CREON:  Pharaonic traditions are your very life, are they, Mr. Onah, President of the Chamber of Commerce, sir?  Why don't you tell the truth just once in your life?  The truth is that you're afraid something may happen to Oedipus — you're afraid for the goose that lays the golden eggs.  If anything happened to him, the string of inventions would come to an end, and you would have to shut up shop.

HORIMHEB (*protesting*):  I will not allow such demeaning words to be spoken in the Municipal Council.

ONAH:  Nor I.

AWALIH:  Nor I.

CREON:  You don't say?  Why don't you arrest me, while you're at it?  Not so long ago, you had the whole of Thebes under arrest.

(*JOCASTA appears on the balcony.*)

JOCASTA:  What is this?  What's going on?  What's this gathering for?

CREON:  The beast has reappeared, my Lady.

AWALIH:  A different beast, my Lady; another one.

JOCASTA:  Have you alerted Oedipus?

ONAH:  The Lord Oedipus is in his laboratory, working on the most important of his inventions, my Lady.

JOCASTA:  Nevertheless, you ought to notify him.  He's the one who specialized in solving beasts' riddles and in killing them.

AWALIH:  Just so, my Lady.  That's sound talk.  Oedipus-Ra — he's the specialist.

HORIMHEB:  Bur pharaonic traditions, my Lady . . .

JOCASTA:  Forget about traditions.  The whole set of pharaonic traditions shrinks to nothing and becomes valueless when Thebes is exposed to danger.  (*Addressing the people*)  People of Thebes!  Experience has proved that Oedipus is the cleverest of men.  Therefore it is Oedipus who shall solve the riddle.

PEOPLE:  Yes . . . He's the one to solve the riddle!

A VOICE:  What do you make of that dame, brother?  She wants to do the fellow in!

(*AWALIH turns to face the people.*)

AWALIH:  Didn't we say that whoever wants to speak must give his name?  Why are you trying to annoy me?  Who was it that spoke?

PEOPLE:  We don't know.

(*OEDIPUS appears on the balcony, whereupon the people take to chanting.*)

PEOPLE:  You're the one to kill the beast!

OEDIPUS:  What's this?  What's up with you?  Is something the matter?

JOCASTA:  A second beast has appeared, my Lord; and the people have commissioned me to convey to your Majesty their wish that you go forth to solve the riddle and kill the beast.

OEDIPUS (*facing the people*):  You want me to kill the beast?

PEOPLE:  Yes!

OEDIPUS:  So be it!  I shall go and solve the riddle and kill the beast.  And if yet another beast appears, I shall go and solve its riddle and kill it.  But what then?  What will you do when I'm dead?

PEOPLE:  Dead? . . . Can Oedipus die?

OEDIPUS:  Yes, Oedipus shall die.

PEOPLE:  Oedipus is a god.

OEDIPUS:  No!  Oedipus is a human.

(*HORIMHEB intervenes in the exchange.*)

HORIMHEB:  It's true that Oedipus is human, but he's descended from the gods, and men descended from the gods don't die, but merely transfer to the other world, to rule there too. You are well aware that Pharaoh rules over this world and the next.  This is what my Lord means.  (*Firmly to OEDIPUS*) This is what you mean, my Lord.

OEDIPUS:  Listen to me!  We mustn't allow theories to impede our thinking.  We don't want words to tie us up in knots. Whether Pharaoh dies or transfers to the other world, whether he goes on to rule there or not—none of that matters to us.  We need to take heed of fact, of reality and its practicalities.  And the fact is that someday my heart will cease to beat; my lungs cease to breathe; my brain stop thinking; my blood stop flowing.  At that point, my existence comes to an end.  At that point, I shall be embalmed in the House of Death like any human among you.

AWALIH:  May you be spared, my Lord!

OEDIPUS:  Shut up, Awalih!  (*Turning again to the people*)  When that happens, what will you do?  What will happen to the entire civilization I've brought about?  To the paved roads? To the electric devices?  To the electronics?  To the motor cars and the airplanes?  The five thousand years that we've compressed into a few?  What will happen to all that?  Is all of this civilization to be demolished by some beast coming out of the desert?  I begin to feel that this massive edifice of civilization is a frail structure that any beast can destroy once I have passed to the other world.  I fear I shall be subjected to torment because I've bequeathed this civilization to those who are incapable of defending it. People of Thebes!  In the name of life I ask you to go out and confront the beast and do away with it — for your own sakes, for the sakes of those who will follow, for the sake of Thebes.

TIRESIAS (*springing up from among the people*):  At last we are back to our starting point.  This is what I said at the beginning. The people must undertake their own defense against the beast.  If there is to be a struggle, let the people go out and fight in its own defense.  Did we have to go through all that we have gone through so you should understand this plain truth?  Beasts do not pose riddles for their amusement. Beasts attack cities in order to devour them.  There are small animals — like snakes and wolves — that confront men individually, and there are beasts that attack entire societies. And then there is the Sphinx.  Now the Sphinx — understand this well, people of Thebes — devours whole countries and cities.  Should he leave Thebes alone now, he would return to it later, and then turn his attention to the remaining cities of the world.  People of Thebes, not for the sake of Thebes alone but for the sake of all cities, let us go out to encounter the beast.  The outcome, no matter what, will be a victory.  If we do away with the beast, we shall sing.  We shall rejoice for ourselves.  The people will sing for themselves alone. And if the beast destroys us, it will mean that we do not deserve life, but deserve our destruction.  A new age shall be born marking the end of humankind and the victory of the beasts.  People of Thebes . . . all together . . . to the beast!

PEOPLE (*thundering*):  To the beast! . . . To the beast! . . .

(*They rush together to the wall. JOCASTA leaves the balcony. OEDIPUS remains standing, looking proudly upon the people of Thebes who are leaving the stage with great enthusiasm, with only AWALIH remaining behind.*)

OEDIPUS:  Why don't you go with them, Awalih?

AWALIH:  And Thebes' Internal Security, my Lord?  Who would maintain security in Thebes?

OEDIPUS:  As I see it, the city's deserted.

AWALIH:  On the contrary, you will find it filled with the beast's supporters.

OEDIPUS:  I perceive no one but you and me . . . So it must be one of us.

(*Loud shouts are heard.  Dust is stirred, reaching across the walls.  There is fearsome roaring from the beast.  The sounds of battle rise.  Lights are gradually dimmed.*)

## Scene Two

*OEDIPUS is prostrate upon the throne, his head thrown back, his eyes closed – the very picture of wretchedness.  CREON stands before him, with spots of blood and mud on his clothing and face.*

OEDIPUS:  How could it be, Creon?  What exactly happened?

CREON:  I don't know, my Lord, nor is there anyone who knows.  All I do know is that we were defeated.  The Sphinx defeated the people of Thebes.  We couldn't stand up to him.  We didn't know precisely who or what we were fighting.  For the first time in Thebes' history, its people were unable to stand their ground in battle.  Thebes the magnificent, mother of heroes and of civilizations, could not stand firm in its struggle against the beast.

OEDIPUS:  It's your responsibility, Creon, the Guard's responsibility.  The Guard was in the forefront.  Surely there must have been some deficiency in the equipment, in the training of the Guard.

CREON:  Quite so, my Lord.  I am responsible for the defeat, as indeed every commander is for victory or defeat.  But why is it that I was defeated?

OEDIPUS:  Nothing can justify this defeat.

CREON:  I'm not trying to justify the defeat.  I'm carrying the full burden of my responsibility.  The question is of another kind; amid the cries of the wounded and the dying, in the thick of battle, before the terrifying roaring of the beast, I suddenly felt my mind calm and clear.  It's true that I'm answerable for weapon training; but weapons aren't what a man fights with.  Who trains the man?

OEDIPUS:  Trains him for what?

CREON:  For being a man.  To put it more clearly:  who's responsible for the making of human beings in this city?  We deployed our forces correctly.  We took up the correct positions.  Our weapons were powerful and sure.  Our zeal was great.  Our faith was strong.  Yet there was something wrong, and I don't know what it was.  I know the Thebans well.  The Thebans are very bold people.  They have no fear of death—to them death is merely a passing into another, a better life.  Why, then, were there so many who didn't hold their ground until either they died or we destroyed the beast?  Is it because we know nothing about this beast?  That's possible, but that's not sufficient reason.  Some pestilence has infected the people of Thebes, some strange disease.  What is it?  I don't know.  Who's responsible for it?  I don't know.  Something's wrong with the species of man in this place, and whoever's responsible for that flaw is necessarily responsible for the formation of man here.

OEDIPUS:  Defeat's turned you into a poet, Creon.  Thebes has lost
a commander and gained a poet.

CREON:  If your intention is to humiliate me, my Lord, I'm now
insensible to everything.  I can't feel shame.  There's
something wrong within me.  I also have been penetrated by
the pestilence to my very depths.

OEDIPUS:  So far as my responsibility goes for the making of
Theban man, you know what I've done, Creon.  I've done
the utmost that could be done.  I've hurried the evolution of
Thebes by thousands of years.  I've invented for people
what Man is yet to make in the future.

(*TIRESIAS appears.*)

TIRESIAS:  You are also, my Lord, the author of the worst
invention in  history — fear!  It is the one invention that ruins
the effect of all other inventions.  It is the most horrific of
human afflictions, more horrendous even than plague.  It is
the one disease that turns men into things.  All the afflictions
we know have clear and evident symptoms, but the
symptoms of fear are deceiving and misleading.  Let fear
worm its way into the heart of man and it mingles with his
blood, his intellect, his dreams.  Man and fear become one
and the same thing.  Man himself becomes fear itself
walking on two legs.  At that point, man is no longer man.
He becomes something brittle, and what's brittle easily
crumbles.

OEDIPUS:  Tiresias, what you are saying is momentous — and ugly.
My one concern was the happiness of man in Thebes.  My
one concern was to free him from fear.

TIRESIAS:  You were liberating him on the one hand, and others
were imprisoning him in fear on the other.  To all
appearances, your Majesty . . . What is that Awalih up to?

OEDIPUS:  I don't know.

TIRESIAS: It's your business to know!

OEDIPUS: Even if Awalih was spreading fear through the land —
and this I don't know for a fact — it still wouldn't be my
responsibility. Awalih was here before I became King.

TIRESIAS: But you allowed him to operate, and by the same
method his family has been operating for four hundred
years.

OEDIPUS (*in great torment and regret*): What method? I don't
understand anything. It's becoming evident to me at last
that I've been blind. (*Calling out*) Awalih!

(*AWALIH immediately appears from behind a curtain.*)

AWALIH: Yes, my Lord.

TIRESIAS: Awalih's like the air — always to be found everywhere.

OEDIPUS: What have you been doing to the people, Awalih?

AWALIH: Nothing, my Lord. You may ask them.

TIRESIAS (*sarcastically*): Ha! They'll say nothing happened. The
fearful always give the answer you want.

AWALIH: If what you're driving at is that some individuals
exposed themselves to . . . to . . . (*He fishes for the right
word*) to less than pleasant treatment, that involves only
some individuals, not the people of Thebes. And that had to
take place.

OEDIPUS: Why?

AWALIH: For the protection of Thebes, my Lord.

TIRESIAS: We are not speaking of traitors, evildoers, thieves,
criminals. These are all corrupt elements in the body politic.

What we are driving at is something else, Awalih.  You know what we mean . . .

AWALIH:  I don't know what you're driving at.  There are people who say that your Majesty didn't solve the riddle, and some who raise doubts about the solution.  Yet no one was with your Majesty when you encountered the beast.  There are also people who say that the second beast and the first were one and the same.  So we may have gone a little beyond the score with some.  It was necessary to stop people from saying such things, in order to preserve the dignity of the pharaonic system.

OEDIPUS:  And how did you stop them, Awalih?

AWALIH:  By all possible means, my Lord.

TIRESIAS:  By all possible means . . .  That means just one thing: torture — the crushing of everything within them, beautiful or ugly, then the wakening of the most repulsive thing in Man — rancor, the hatred of all things . . .

AWALIH:  It's clear that you want to get rid of me.  It's not as bad as all that.  If three or four expose themselves to treatment that is . . . that is . . .

OEDIPUS:  . . . less than pleasant . . .

AWALIH:  That's right — less than pleasant.  That doesn't mean that the entire population of Thebes was affected.

TIRESIAS:  Fear is not divisible, Awalih.  Fear is a common ill.  The people of Thebes is not a collection of individuals.  It is a living, self-consistent body, like any other society on the face of the earth.  And anything that happens to any part of this body affects the body of the society in its entirety.

AWALIH:  All right, then!  Sorry!

OEDIPUS:  What do you mean, "sorry"?

AWALIH:  I'm apologizing for my mistake.  It's just that I wasn't aware of this business of the social body.  The fact is that we've been operating all along by the same method and things were working out well.  No one ever complained about us.  Why suddenly now?

TIRESIAS:  You'll never understand, Awalih.  You belong to another world.

OEDIPUS:  Awalih, you'll have to be outside the city walls by sunrise.

AWALIH:  So be it, my Lord.  I'd anticipated something of the kind.  That's why I got myself a contract of employment in Babylon.  (*Brings a sheaf of papers out of his pocket.*)  To whom shall I pass on my trust, my Lord?

OEDIPUS:  What trust?

AWALIH:  The list of criminals . . .

OEDIPUS:  Take them with you.

TIRESIAS:  You know now,  Awalih, that fear is a social ill, don't you?  You too were afraid.  This is why you had in reserve a contract of employment in another country.

OEDIPUS:  If you stay one moment longer, I shall be giving out less than pleasant treatment.

AWALIH (*muttering angrily as he leaves*):  We've been operating all along in this manner, and nobody ever brought up that business of the social body.  Why now? (*Exits.*)

OEDIPUS (*in extreme despair*):  Creon!

CREON:  My Lord!  Command me as you will.  I am prepared to

sacrifice anything for the sake of Thebes, and for your sake, my Lord.

OEDIPUS:  Tiresias . . . Creon . . . The two persons dearest to me . . . Don't abandon me.  I don't know what to do.  For the first time, I feel that I'm blind.  You are now the eyes by which I see.  What are we to do?

CREON:  From a military point of view, we need to find out everything about the Sphinx, and we must remake Theban man.  Provide me with a well-made man, and I shall provide you with victory.

OEDIPUS:  Where are Horimheb and Onah?

CREON:  I never saw them during the battle.

TIRESIAS:  They aren't the kind to appear in battle.  But let there be some profit-making, and they'll soon appear and jump to action.

OEDIPUS:  And how are we to remake man, Tiresias?

TIRESIAS:  The people of Thebes love you, my Lord.  Let this be the starting point.  Let us preserve this love and foster it.  Whenever an attempt is made to hide the truth, people have to pay the price in the long run.  I don't know whether or not your Majesty killed the beast the first time around.  Whatever the truth of that may be, there is a truth that Thebes must understand.  You must make the Thebans understand that no matter how great the power or genius of an individual, he cannot forever be killing beasts on his own—even if you did solve the riddle, and even if you did kill the beast.  Come on, Oedipus.  We have no time to waste.

(*OEDIPUS goes out to the balcony, together with CREON and TIRESIAS.*)

OEDIPUS:  People of Thebes . . . My children . . .

(*The PEOPLE assemble.*)

OEDIPUS:  We've lost a battle, but a whole war still lies ahead of
　　　us.  And there are some truths I want to proclaim to you.
　　　Awalih has been banished from Thebes.  That means that
　　　there will no longer be a place for fear among us.  There will
　　　no longer be anything in Thebes to hinder the growth of
　　　Man's greatness and creativity.  And there is another truth
　　　which you must fully comprehend if victory over the Sphinx
　　　is to be won.  That is, no individual on his own can kill the
　　　beasts that attack cities.  I did not, on that first occasion, kill
　　　the beast . . .

PEOPLE (*chanting*):  You're the one who killed the beast!

OEDIPUS:  It's you who have asserted this.  I didn't say, on my
　　　return . . .

PEOPLE (*chanting*):  You're the one who killed the beast!

OEDIPUS:  Please . . .

PEOPLE (*chanting*):  You're the one who killed the beast! . . .

(*His voice is drowned by the chanting.  The lights are gradually dimmed.*)

### Scene Three

*Gradual intensification of light on a single spot near the front of the stage,
in which TIRESIAS appears.  The rest of the stage is in darkness.*

TIRESIAS:  It's easy to banish Awalih from Thebes, but it's
　　　impossible to expel him immediately from the hearts of the
　　　people.  I was well aware of this sad outcome, but it was
　　　essential that Oedipus see for himself what fear does to
　　　people.  It becomes possible for them to sing in celebration

of error. It becomes possible for them to develop a zeal for fakery. It becomes possible for the truth to be dispersed among them. Even the noblest impulses and traits, such as enthusiasm, daring, courage, can take shape as symptoms of this pestilence that is fear. The true starting point to the remaking of Man in a way that will release the creative potential within him is to free him of fear, free him from anxiety, and from doubt . . .

(*The lighting is gradually extended, revealing OEDIPUS and CREON in the throne room.*)

OEDIPUS:  But how, Tiresias, how?

TIRESIAS:  I know the answers to millions of questions, but this one question is the one that has confounded all philosophers. This is the true riddle. Whoever knows the answer shall create the greatest civilization on earth. The one who knows how to liberate Man from fear deserves to be recognized as the father of sages and philosophers. To put it simply, my Lord, he is the one who deserves the title of Ruler.

OEDIPUS:  How faint the light is in the palace tonight. I can't see very well.

(*CREON looks at him in puzzlement.*)

CREON:  Indeed, my Lord . . . the torches are not at full strength.

OEDIPUS:  It's strange. I can't see well at all . . .

CREON:  There is the first glimmer of a solution in my mind, my Lord.

OEDIPUS:  Don't talk about it, Creon! Carry it out with all the zeal of youth. You have Tiresias with you.

CREON:  And you, my Lord?

OEDIPUS (*rises from the throne*):  I shall go in search of the solution alone.  I've discovered at the peak of my glory that there are still things I don't know.  I shall leave . . . I shall set off on a long journey, in order to learn.  Take my hand, Creon; show me the door.  I thought it was the light that was faint . . . (*In distress*)  Ha! . . . I didn't know the world could hold so much darkness . . . You go back, Creon.

CREON:  My Lord . . .

OEDIPUS:  That's an order — the last order given by Oedipus. (*Exits.*)

CREON:  Everyone in Thebes will have to pay a heavy price.  With that price we shall buy Thebes . . . we shall buy life for Thebes — someone of great standing . . .

TIRESIAS:  Explain that.

CREON:  I shall explain in a practical way.

(*CREON goes out into the square, to which the light is gradually extended.  Proudly he marches through the square, and with his head held high, he goes out of the gate.  The people climb onto the wall.*)

ONE PERSON:  Creon's going out to meet the beast on his own . . .

PEOPLE:  On his own?  Alone?

ANOTHER PERSON:  Come back!  Creon, come back!

A THIRD:  He's approaching the beast sword in hand, his hand held high . . .

PEOPLE:  On his own . . .

SOMEONE:  He's getting information about the beast . . .

FIRST PERSON:  We must follow him!

*(A shout is uttered by the people. Some jump off the wall, and return carrying CREON on their shoulders, dead. The people gather round the corpse as the lighting is gradually restricted to a spotlight on TIRESIAS, at the front of the stage.)*

TIRESIAS:  Creon has paid the great price — the price of making people in Thebes understand that death must be met for the sake of life, that in death Man loses nothing except his fear, that annihilation is preferable to a life threatened by the Sphinx.  It is not important that we know what has happened to Oedipus.  He has become — someone said — a King of Poets.  Now Thebes will belong forever to its people, a people which has truly begun to know the solution. Thousands of years hence, any one of you who comes to visit Thebes, my beautiful city, shall see the great temples and other things that Man has made to endure, in defiance of Time, in defiance of the beasts of the desert.  And you people who live in this city and to whom I have told the story of my city, know that although you were provoked to some laughter as you listened to this story, I swear to you by all the gods that that was not my intention.

**Curtain**

# OEDIPUS

by Walid Ikhlasi

Translated by Admer Gouryh

# OEDIPUS

A Play in Two Parts
by Walid Ikhlasi
1978

# CHARACTERS

DR. SUFFIAN, a university professor of geography, in his late 40s, grave and sensitive.

ASMA, his wife, a little over 40 years old, firm and decisive in her human relationships.

YAZIN, their son, hope and pride of the family, still adolescent. He is idealistic and intelligent, an exemplar of a scientific and pragmatic generation.

SULAF, a beautiful girl, about 20 or a bit older, very intelligent, a secretary at the University Center for Electronics

DR. AL-BAHI, the head of the Department of Computer Science, professor of mathematics, about 50 years old, friend of Dr. Suffian. He is ambitious to discover the relation between science and man.

MUDER, SULAF's father, alcoholic, over 50 years old. Due to his job as a salesman, he is constantly traveling.

*The offstage CHORUS used in this tragedy is different from that of Greek tragedy. Here it is composed of inner voices representing human wishes, feelings and aspirations. The inner voices intervene with words and phrases that might shed more light on the scene or lend it additional dimensions. Furthermore, the inner voices are accompanied by modern music to make us much more familiar with the spirit of the age we live in.*

*The events of this tragedy take place in a noisy over-crowded city.  The city is the center of scientific and technological activities.  Traders and intellectuals compete to get to the top.  The time is close to the end of the twentieth century.  The characters seem to have almost the point of achieving their dreams.*

*The events of this play occur in three places:*
*1. A University Computer Center where we see different complicated machines, tapes, modern cabinets and various devices indicative of the technological advancements of this place.*
*2. Dr. Suffian's house, which is characterized by calmness and balance.  It also reflects his university career.*
*3. Sulaf's house, expressive of human warmth and feelings associated with old things.  Yet she is realistic and excels in her scientific studies.*

*Distinct from each other as these settings are, they are all permeated by one common and persistent feature:  the domination of technology over human life.  Thus, the role of science is not represented merely by a giant computer, it is expressed in the ceiling, the walls, the furniture, the floor, and every object, big and small.  Science should be presented as the source both of man's advancement and of his misery.  The décor of the settings should suggest the joy of our age through color and lines, but it should also suggest how we are weighed down by the age's complications and horror.*

## PART ONE

### The beginning of the week

### Scene 1
### Prophecy

*A room at the University Center.  It looks like an air conditioner in the trimness and elegance of its lines.  SULAF is seen filing papers in plastic boxes.  She is dressed in white and looks like a doctor.  She wears her hair upswept in a coil which lends her the gravity of a scientist.  After a little while, a side lamp lights up, indicating that someone has arrived.  She looks through a machine at one side to identify the person.  Her face glows with pleasure. She acts like a woman who has anxiously been waiting for her sweetheart.*

THE CHORUS (*hums*):  What do they want to know?  Everything indicates that life runs smoothly, all is in good order:  order, discipline, system, and significant power.  What do they want to know?  Prophecy belongs to the weather, to the ebb and flow of the tide, to those who fish in salty water.  But behold who comes!  Who comes!  Who comes!  (*SULAF's longing increases and she mumbles in a subdued voice.*)

SULAF:  My love has come . . . my love.  (*She looks at herself in the mirror, then goes toward the door.*)  What a surprise!  How lucky I am.

(*DR. SUFFIAN comes in with a serious look on his face and does not show any feeling for SULAF.  She too puts on an air of seriousness as her eyes glow with affection.*)

SUFFIAN:  I don't see Dr. Al-Bahi around.  Did he leave?

SULAF (*still serious*):  He is in his office.  He will be here in a little while to check out the results, sir.  Can I be of service to you, Dr. Suffian?  (*In a theatrical way*)  I am at your service, sir.

SUFFIAN (*looking around cautiously, then suddenly losing his sober air*):  Sulaf, you are beautiful.

SULAF (*still regarding him gravely*):  Do you want me to rush him, sir?

SUFFIAN:  You are naughty.

SULAF:  Shall I tell him it is a matter of great urgency?

SUFFIAN:  Tell him that I love you.

SULAF:  Then you have no objection to waiting for him.

SUFFIAN (*with affection*):  I want you to know that I am happy.  My happiness is without limit.  (*SULAF looks around, then both throw kisses to each other.*)

SULAF:  I have received your letter and I will keep it (*whispering*), my dear one.

SUFFIAN (*with affected anger*):  But you have not asked why I am happy.

SULAF (*thinking for a moment*):  Most probably because you have been appointed the head of the geography department.

SUFFIAN (*shakes his head disapprovingly, then takes an envelope out of his pocket and waves it*):  Guess.

SULAF:  You have become a part of the administration.

SUFFIAN:  You poor girl!  (*Slightly sad*)  Not even my wife would be as happy as you at the thought that I have become a department head or a dean.

SULAF (*happily*):  Then you have become the dean of a college.

SUFFIAN:  Such positions don't make me happy.

SULAF:  Then you must have seen me in your dreams.

SUFFIAN:  In my dreams and in every single moment of my life, Sulaf.  But you have not hit upon the truth.

SULAF:  I admit my ignorance.  Tell me, what do you have in that envelope?

SUFFIAN:  It is my medical report.

SULAF (*hugs him joyfully, then withdraws*):  I knew you were in good health.  This is what I want.  If I knew how to pray, I would always pray for your health.

SUFFIAN (*waving the medical report*):  No cholesterol, the percentage of uric acid has gone down, and the doctor told me that my heart is just perfect.

SULAF:  Like you.

SUFFIAN:  Everything indicates that the health of the man standing before you is no different from that of a young man.

SULAF:  But you are young.

SUFFIAN:  I don't need your flattery . . .  It is enough that you . . . (*Hesitant*)  Do you really love me?

SULAF (*imitating him lovingly*):  Do you really love me?

SUFFIAN (*seriously*):  Do you really love me?

SULAF:  Ask the computer.

SUFFIAN (*disapprovingly*):  That damned machine.  I hate it.

SULAF (*seriously*):  You hate it?!

SUFFIAN (*jokingly*):  You spend more time with it than you do with me.

SULAN:  Has Geography begun to be jealous of Technology?

SUFFIAN:  I am jealous of everything that touches you or comes close to you.  (*He moves closer, trying to embrace her.*)

SULAF (*withdrawing coquettishly*):  Aren't you afraid that somebody might see us?

SUFFIAN:  I fear only the moment in which I can embrace you, yet fail to do it.

SULAF (*staying away*):  Aren't you worried that the computer will record your attitude?

SUFFIAN (*getting closer to he*r):  I wish I could anger this silent monster.

SULAF (*chiding him*):  It is not a monster.  It can talk, if you want.

SUFFIAN:  It talks!  Does it know any language besides figures and solid facts?  Does it know anything about love?  Does it know how to love?

SULAF (*coquettishly*):  If an honest woman fell in love with it, it would speak.

SUFFIAN:  Does there exist an honest and loving woman besides you?

SULAF:  Is that true?

SUFFIAN:  It is the only true thing I know.

SULAF (*attracted to him*):  Does there exist a wonderful loving man except you?  (*She becomes aware of the arrival of DR. AL-BAHI and withdraws to speak more seriously.*)  Dr. Suffian, I think Dr. Al-Bahi will be here soon.

(*DR. AL-BAHI comes in with a restless, troubled look.  He gives SUFFIAN a nod as he sees him.*)

AL-BAHI:  Welcome to you, Dr. Suffian!  (*To SULAF*)  Today I don't want to keep any appointments.  (*To SUFFIAN*)  You look happy.  (*To SULAF*)  Give me the file of social figures, please.  (*Asking himself*)  Am I really tired?  (*To SUFFIAN*)  I will be with you in a moment.

SULAF:  The file is already here.

AL-BAHI:  You can leave.  I am sorry to have kept you here late.

SULAF:  On the contrary, it is still early.

AL-BAHI:  Then I must really be tired.  (*To SUFFIAN*)  I would like you to stay with me for a while.  (*SUFFIAN shows signs of displeasure.*)  Don't you notice how tense I am?  (*To SULAF*) I want you to finish the final report tomorrow.

SULAF:  I agreed to do it by the end of the week, not at the beginning.  Have you forgotten?

AL-BAHI:  I must admit that I am tired.  Then let it be the end of the week.

SULAF (*as she leaves*):  I'll be leaving now, unless there's something else I can do for you.  (*She looks at SUFFIAN silently.*)  Good night.  (*As she leaves, AL-BAHI leads SUFFIAN by the hand and seats him.*)

AL-BAHI:  Relax.  I want you to be a good listener as usual.  Do you know that you have mastered the art of listening very well?  (*To himself*)  Oh God, I am so tired.  (*In a louder voice*)  I should control it.

SUFFIAN (*jokingly*):  I hope you're not trying to control me.

AL-BAHI (*resuming*):  I have spent five years with this machine. Do you remember the day it was imported?  It was a red-letter day.  People said we had entered the age of technology . . . what a complicated civilization . . . but it is useful . . .

SUFFIAN:  At least, it is useful to you.

AL-BAHI:  I am trying to control it.

SUFFIAN:  Before it controls us.

AL-BAHI:  At this stage of history we are all frightened that it will control us.

SUFFIAN:  I'm not afraid of it.

AL-BAHI:  It's all around you but you're not even aware of it.

SUFFIAN:  Thank God I don't need your machine in my geographical research.

AL-BAHI:  You will need it some day.

SUFFIAN:  I will try to avoid it.

AL-BAHI:  And you will need my help to analyze the results of your research.  You know something?  I was afraid of it at first.  Despite my continuous studies in mathematics, this machine really frightened me.

SUFFIAN:  Our fathers were fearful when they first encountered a radio.

AL-BAHI:  But our children get used to television and space-ships.

SUFFIAN:  It is a question of habituation.

AL-BAHI:  As for me, it has never been a habit. (*Proudly*) Today . . . today, dear Suffian . . .

SUFFIAN:  Today is the first day of the week.

AL-BAHI (*occupied with his thoughts*):  True, today is the first day of the week, any week.  Yet today could be a memorable day in the life of our university, rather in the history of science.  Al-Bahi is able to control electronics and use it for the interest of mankind.

SUFFIAN:  The interest of mankind?

AL-BAHI:  All technology serves man's interest, because he created it.

SUFFIAN:  Bombs are also the creation of man, and so are intercontinental ballistic missiles.

AL-BAHI:  These are the outcome of man's insanity.  But this . . . this complicated machine will despise you if you don't try to understand it.  And now I am trying to understand it.

SUFFIAN:  You understand its language.  Does it understand yours?

AL-BAHI (*proudly*):  This, I believe, is what I have achieved.

SUFFIAN (*amazed*):  You mean it understands your language?

AL-BAHI:  Your language, too, and the language of everyone.

SUFFIAN (*jokingly*):  I understand your language, but I don't understand many other people's.

AL-BAHI (*showing SUFFIAN some papers and charts*):  Information . . . more information.  This machine takes the information and gives it back classified and arranged in the way you like.  You know that we use this machine to process thousands of university applications.  Through it we find the best ways of growing wheat and cotton.  This machine provides us with information about the weather and wind speed.  It also tells us where diseases lurk or where we can find oil.

SUFFIAN:  It is your conscious spy.

AL-BAHI:  That is true.  It helps us see through earth and space and around the corners of life.  It helps us understand unlimited mysteries.

SUFFIAN:  But it is not going to explore the depth of man's soul and it will never comprehend the dimensions of dreams and thoughts.

AL-BAHI (*triumphantly*): You are wrong and this is what I am going to prove.

SUFFIAN:  To prove what?  To explore man's inner life?

AL-BAHI:  Yes, I will prove to you that I can do it.

SUFFIAN:  Do you think those shining metal plates and tapes that run by themselves in some crazy way can penetrate the depths of man?

AL-BAHI:  I am sure they can.

SUFFIAN:  I don't understand.

AL-BAHI:  Feed this great machine with personal information and you will get answers.

SUFFIAN:  Personal information!

AL-BAHI:  Honest and detailed information.

SUFFIAN:  And the result?

AL-BAHI:  The more honest and precise you are, the deeper the computer's probing will penetrate.

SUFFIAN (*suspicious*): No . . . no.  I don't think I can comprehend these things.

AL-BAHI:  You will comprehend it when you see the wonderful results.

SUFFIAN (*addressing the machine sarcastically and loudly*):  My horoscope is Capricorn.  I am six feet high.  I live in an apartment on the 7th floor located on a street whose hustle and bustle annoy everyone.  Now, what is the temperature of this lovely night?

AL-BAHI: I know you are a serious man. Why do you ask the machine silly questions? Don't you believe me?

SUFFIAN: No, I don't, because . . . because your ideas remind me of fables.

AL-BAHI: Even you make fun of me, Dr. Suffian.

SUFFIAN (*gently*): I am sorry, but I don't believe in fables.

AL-BAHI (*determined*): All the imaginative ideas that men disapproved of once upon a time have become facts now highly respected by all. Abass Bin Farnes dreamed one day of flying and he did fly. And you . . .

SUFFIAN: Me!

AL-BAHI: In your geographical field something similar happened. Didn't the claim that the earth was a sphere cause people to consider scientists of the day lunatics?

SUFFIAN: I do believe in the sphericity of the earth.

AL-BAHI: But only after scientists of the past paid a high price. (*Resuming*) What about psychology? It was once considered an extension of magic and superstition. What do people say about psychology today? It has become part of objective facts. Even today's prophecies are likely to be future facts. We live in an age of wonders.

SUFFIAN (*with concern and eagerness*): I'm starting to get more interested in your thoughts.

AL-BAHI: You have always been interested in my ideas. Have you forgotten the days when we were studying together?

SUFFIAN: How could one forget them?

AL-BAHI (*sadly*): Those days have gone.

SUFFIAN (*recalling the past*):  I will never forget the intellectual puzzles you used to pose.

AL-BAHI:  And who can forget the Middle Eastern food you made then.

SUFFIAN:  You excelled over all of us.

AL-BAHI (*resuming his enthusiasm for his machine*):  My main concern lies in controlling it.

SUFFIAN (*slyly*):  You need somebody to help you to accomplish the dreams you talked about.

AL-BAHI:  Sulaf, my secretary, is a real treasure.

SUFFIAN:  Really!

AL-BAHI:  Sulaf has the kind of realistic mind that can't be found even among highly professional assistants.  (*Happily*)  And she was the first one who became interested in my project.

SUFFIAN:  Realistic mind and interested in an imaginary project!

AL-BAHI:  You will discover that it is not imaginary.  I am indebted to her.  She is active and creative.

SUFFIAN:  She is a woman of substance.

AL-BAHI (*suddenly*):  I don't understand why she respects you.  Probably because you are so serious with her.

SUFFIAN (*with a slight, mysterious smile*):  My gravity parallels her seriousness.

AL-BAHI:  But why you in particular?

SUFFIAN:  Maybe she likes geography.

AL-BAHI:  I don't know what she likes and dislikes.  I know she likes her job and this fantastic machine.

SUFFIAN:  Her future must be linked to the computer.

AL-BAHI:  Throughout the entire year she has never failed to be creative.

SUFFIAN: (*interrupting*):  A whole year and she has not learned to smile at me.

AL-BAHI:  A professor like you talking all day long about geography and oceans does not encourage one to smile. (*Both laugh.*)

SUFFIAN:  You've almost made me forget why I came to see you.

AL-BAHI:  I have also forgotten what I was going to ask you for.

SUFFIAN:  Then we're even.

AL-BAHI:  You must have some important news.

SUFFIAN:  I can't attend today's dinner party.  Please, convey my apologies to the president of the university.

AL-BAHI:  I'm not going to attend either.

SUFFIAN:  Then who will carry our apologies to the president?

AL-BAHI:  Who pays attention to their ceremonies?

SUFFIAN:  You said that you were going to ask me for something.

AL-BAHI (*imploring and insisting*):  I want you to be the first subject of my experiment.

SUFFIAN:  To be experimented with?

AL-BAHI:  With an intellectual man like you, I don't lose face if my experiment fails.

SUFFIAN:  What experiment?  I don't understand what you are
talking about.

AL-BAHI:  The human language of the computer that I have told
you about.

SUFFIAN:  What does the new human language of the computer
have to do with me?

AL-BAHI (*openly imploring*):  You have been my friend since we
were students and now I want you in particular to be
witness to my scientific capability.

SUFFIAN:  You have several colleagues at the university.

AL-BAHI:  Whom would you select, my friend?  They are
conceited men.  I don't trust anyone except you.

SUFFIAN (*shrewdly*):  What about Miss Sulaf?  Is she not worthy to
be trusted?

AL-BAHI:  To tell you the truth, I thought of her.

SUFFIAN:  Did she accept?

AL-BAHI:  Accept what?

SUFFIAN:  Becoming the rat of your experiment.  (*Both laugh.  As
they talk, THE CHORUS's voice rings out.*)

THE CHORUS:        You are heading for disaster.
Check your shaken position.
You have walked . . . you walk.
Your feet don't know where to land.
Stop . . . you are . . . you . . .
Well . . . the machine sharpens its teeth.

(*The two friends seem to have agreed to begin the experiment.*)

SUFFIAN:  How long does the experiment take? I have some important appointments.

AL-BAHI:  I have an appointment with the president but I don't care about that.

SUFFIAN:  All right, let's start the game.

AL-BAHI:  Let's start the revolution.

SUFFIAN:  Let's start the revolutionary game.

AL-BAHI:  It is a revolution, my dear fellow, not a game.  We are entering an age in which technology will serve man by exploring his depth and future.

SUFFIAN:  I am at your service.

AL-BAHI:  I want you to mention everything and the machine is going to record it.

SUFFIAN:  What shall I talk about?  An ordinary life of a simple man.  A life of a young man devoid of excitement and not worthy to be told.  A young man who wanted to be something in this crowded world.

AL-BAHI:  And your childhood . . . talk about it.

SUFFIAN:  A calm child . . . necessity taught him to watch and not to talk.

AL-BAHI:  Go ahead.

SUFFIAN:  He learned to fight for the sake of a small tribe of children and for a mother who would weave clothes out of shreds.  Feast days would pass without joy.

AL-BAHI:  Talk about joy.

SUFFIAN:  A girl died of diphtheria and a boy drowned in a shallow river.

AL-BAHI:  Who was the girl?

SUFFIAN:  My sister and the boy my younger brother.

AL-BAHI:  Are you still sad?

SUFFIAN:  No, I don't think so.  Forgetfulness is the balm of a distressed age.

AL-BAHI:  Are you forgetful by nature?

SUFFIAN:  I try to forget what is painful and enjoy happy memories.

AL-BAHI:  Don't you sometimes enjoy recalling and reliving painful memories?

SUFFIAN:  When I have time.

AL-BAHI:  Do you visit the graves of relatives or friends?

SUFFIAN:  I don't go to cemeteries and I don't expect anyone to visit my grave in the future.

AL-BAHI:  Death is not one of your problems!

SUFFIAN:  The problem is inside me; therefore it is not that important.

AL-BAHI:  Then you don't fear death.

SUFFIAN:  It is inside me, like an extinct volcano.

AL-BAHI:  But it may erupt at any moment.

SUFFIAN:  That is the crazy logic of volcanoes.

AL-BAHI:  Are you frightened of it?

SUFFIAN:  As much as I love life.

AL-BAHI:  Have you always loved it?

SUFFIAN:  Always, always, but only truly knew life when I knew love.

AL-BAHI:  When did you marry?

SUFFIAN (*after a moment of silence, attempting to ignore AL-BAHI's question*):  Anyway, as you and your intelligent machine see, death has not come yet.  The volcano is dormant.

AL-BAHI:  Again, what about childhood?

SUFFIAN:  My childhood or the childhood of death?

AL-BAHI:  We're talking about you.

SUFFIAN:  Childhood exists inside me, just as old age does.

AL-BAHI:  Does old age alarm you . . . frighten you?

SUFFIAN:  No, it does not.

AL-BAHI:  Early death frightens you.

SUFFIAN:  Death is death and one's time of dying is part of the plan of one's life.

AL-BAHI:  Do you sometimes weep?

SUFFIAN (*laughing*):  Only when I peel onions.

AL-BAHI:  And sadness!  Is it not associated with weeping?

SUFFIAN:  Sadness is linked with loneliness and loneliness is the most refined sadness there is.

AL-BAHI:  Are you sad by nature?

SUFFIAN:  I have experienced sadness in the past and I may experience it again in the future.

AL-BAHI:  And in the present?

SUFFIAN (*rapturously*):  In these days, I am no longer lonely.

AL-BAHI:  Then you are happy.

SUFFIAN:  It seems so.

AL-BAHI:  What about your youth?

SUFFIAN:  Working and studying.  I have forgotten that period.

AL-BAHI:  Was it a hard period?

SUFFIAN:  It was full of driving ambition.

AL-BAHI:  Then it was wonderful!

SUFFIAN:  One might call it my period of capital accumulation.  I made enough money.  Then I developed a plan for spending the interest.

AL-BAHI:  Do you regret the accumulation of money?

SUFFIAN:  Life has no place for regret.

AL-BAHI:  Is not regret a kind of catharsis?

SUFFIAN:  I want life for life's sake . . . (*He leaps like a happy young man as he repeats the last phrase.*)

AL-BAHI:  What about others?

SUFFIAN:  Others for life and life for others.

AL-BAHI:  Do you feel that you are doing your duty to others?

SUFFIAN:  What do you mean by "others"?  Who are they?

AL-BAHI:  Society, family, professional colleagues . . .

SUFFIAN:  I pay my debts regularly.

AL-BAHI:  Do you pay contentedly?

SUFFIAN:  What is contentment?  Doesn't it just mean behaving with a kind of compulsive politeness?  (*He jumps up, again breaking out of his seriousness.*)

AL-BAHI:  Relax, we have not finished yet.

SUFFIAN:  Is this an investigation or an interrogation?

AL-BAHI:  Have you gone through an investigation before?

SUFFIAN:  Not in the political sense.  But one day, a crime took place in our neighborhood.  I was still young.  A man murdered his young daughter and attempted to strangle his wife.  I was called to give testimony about what I had seen.  There, in the court, I began to ask the judge to acquit me.  I was screaming: "I am innocent!"

AL-BAHI:  Were you involved in the murder?

SUFFIAN:  My shouting was painful to me.

AL-BAHI:  Was there any evidence?

SUFFIAN:  And my shouting was full of pleading.

AL-BAHI:  Was there something that made them suspect you?

SUFFIAN:  And my tears nearly drowned my testimony.

AL-BAHI:  You pleaded guilty?!

SUFFIAN:  I confessed I was innocent.  (*He becomes emotional.*)
     The girl died, but the mother was rescued.

AL-BAHI:  Was the girl beautiful?

SUFFIAN:  Yes, she was.

AL-BAHI:  Did you desire her?

SUFFIAN:  She was older than me.

AL-BAHI:  Ripe as a bunch of grapes.

SUFFIAN:  Ripe as a bunch of grapes, but the fox said: "These
     grapes are sour."

AL-BAHI:  The fox must admit its failure.

SUFFIAN:  I was shy and I had no experience.  (*Laughing*)  The
     poor girl was murdered for no reason.  (*Silent*)  I think she
     had no experience, just like me.

AL-BAHI:  Did Europe offer you experience?

SUFFIAN:  It put my thinking in order.

AL-BAHI:  And your desires too.

SUFFIAN:  We were remarkable, you remember.  We were
     required to put everything in order.  In Europe one can't
     live in disorder.  We organized everything, even collecting
     the garbage.  There, we learned the value of discipline.
     Time crushes those who are undisciplined . . . I was

frightened of time.

AL-BAHI:  You feared it and you succeeded.

SUFFIAN (*puzzled*):  Succeeded?

AL-BAHI:  You triumphed over time.

SUFFIAN:  I triumphed over time? (*Laughing bitterly*)  And how?

AL-BAHI:  You achieved your ambitions.

SUFFIAN:  What about the heart which the doctor checks so regularly?  And the percentage of cholesterol in my blood? And the arteriosclerosis, which threatens me every moment? Dear computer . . . (*correcting himself*)  Dear Dr. Al-Bahi, my ambitious friend, I want you to listen with your ears, not with magnetized tapes.  We have not yet triumphed over time.

AL-BAHI:  Then you failed.

SUFFIAN:  Am I a failure?

AL-BAHI:  Yes, you are, because you have not achieved any success.

SUFFIAN:  But this does not mean I failed.

AL-BAHI:  Then what do you call it?

SUFFIAN:  I call it natural life.

AL-BAHI:  You surrender to life?

SUFFIAN:  I surrender to life's cruelty and happiness.

AL-BAHI:  Isn't surrendering a sign of weakness?

SUFFIAN (*bitterly*):  This sounds like a lawyer's interrogation.  The game is over.

AL-BAHI:  What game?

SUFFIAN:  Your electronic game.

AL-BAHI:  The machine does not play, friend.  It is time that toys with us.

SUFFIAN:  It is a tug of war and requires only our participation. We stand on one side and time on the other.  Come on, pull the rope, it is time that pulls against us.  Who has triumphed?  Time has, and we fell on the ground.  We get up.  Time is pulling on the rope again, but this round we are holding together.  Oh, what a disaster.  Time is both the enemy and the judge.

AL-BAHI:  Which time do you mean?

SUFFIAN:  The one we live.

AL-BAHI:  Do you live it as you should?

SUFFIAN:  I gain experience to live it.

AL-BAHI:  You are almost fifty years old and you are still experimenting.

SUFFIAN:  It seems that the true game lies in gaining endless experience.

AL-BAHI:  Do you think experimentation can come to an end?

SUFFIAN:  At any rate, being content with the experience we have gained is something of a triumph.

AL-BAHI:  What about a complete triumph?

SUFFIAN:  I haven't thought about it.

AL-BAHI:  Do you think someone could achieve a complete triumph in his life experience?

SUFFIAN (*after some thought*):  My son.

AL-BAHI:  Your son!  Is you son to gain total experience?

SUFFIAN (*after thinking*):  It is inevitable.

AL-BAHI:  It is inevitable!  I don't understand that.

SUFFIAN:  Because I believe in it.

AL-BAHI:  What evidence do you have?

SUFFIAN (*after thinking*):  I have strong faith in it.

AL-BAHI:  Is faith alone enough?

SUFFIAN:  As much as ignorance alone is enough.  (*AL-BAHI seems a little confused, but then resumes his questioning.*)

AL-BAHI:  Are you a believer?

SUFFIAN:  Believer!  What kind of belief do you mean?

AL-BAHI (*after a little confusion*):  The kind of mainstream belief most people have.

SUFFIAN (*thinking*):  I believe in myself and I am confident of that.

AL-BAHI:  To what degree?

SUFFIAN:  To the degree . . . to the degree . . .  (*He stutters, then becomes angry.*)  To the degree of refusing to continue this interrogation.  You act like some arbitrary authority.

AL-BAHI:  But I have no real authority to interrogate you.

SUFFIAN (*still angry*):  Like a horrible spy recording one's feelings without being seen.  I want to see the face of this machine.

AL-BAHI (*laughing*):  Are you really frightened of this? (*He points toward the computer.*)

SUFFIAN (*after his anger has subsided*):  I fear nothing.

AL-BAHI (*gently*):  Then shall we continue the experiment?

SUFFIAN:  Are there still things that the machine does not know about me?

AL-BAHI:  What does it know?

SUFFIAN:  My childhood, youth and feelings.

AL-BAHI (*interrupting*):  Nothing about your love life and hatred . . . we know nothing about the confidence you have in the spirit of this age, in the science you teach to your students.

SUFFIAN:  Love can turn into hatred and the unknown might bring you a beautiful love. (*Sadly*) Sometimes one thinks that he is only repeatng what he has been told and sometimes he feels that nobody responds to what he says. And there are moments when you are sure that what you say doesn't convey what you really know.

AL-BAHI:  You seem to be always looking for the best.

SUFFIAN:  I search for the most interesting things.

AL-BAHI:  The most interesting things in knowledge?

SUFFIAN:  In knowledge . . . in common matters . . . and in love. (*He suddenly stops talking.*)

AL-BAHI:  In love . . . then?

SUFFIAN:  Then nothing.  (*Almost angry*)  I will not go on.

AL-BAHI:  But you have not yet talked about love.

SUFFIAN:  I will not talk about love.  Turn off your machine and let us leave.

AL-BAHI:  The experiment is going very smoothly.  Please, don't spoil it.  Are you tired?

SUFFIAN:  Not exactly, but I have decided to put an end to this interrogation.

AL-BAHI (*hesitantly and sadly*):  I don't know if we have enough information to produce reasonable results.

SUFFIAN:  That is all I have to give.

AL-BAHI:  The computer needs more information in order to produce better results.

SUFFIAN:  The information would be sufficient for a psychologist.

AL-BAHI:  My machine is no less capable than a psychologist.

SUFFIAN:  I have never yielded to a psychologist.  I don't know what made me surrender to a blind machine that can't distinguish between me and a speck of dust.

AL-BAHI:  But dust does not love or dream.

SUFFIAN:  Then why don't you wait until I turn into dust myself and become rich in mystery?

AL-BAHI (*accusingly*):  Didn't you agree at the outset to help me conduct a unique experiment?

SUFFIAN:  I didn't know that I would be standing and having myself examined by a sightless eye.

AL-BAHI:  You don't hesitate to express your hatred for this electronic genius.  I'll give you odds that it does not know hatred.

SUFFIAN:  I respect your ingenuity, but that machine . . . I don't feel comfortable with it, not at all.

AL-BAHI (*jokingly*):  It won't feel comfortable either if you don't continue feeding it with information.

SUFFIAN:  Then let it punish me and condemn me to misery.

AL-BAHI:  It does not pass judgment on people.  It only analyzes the information given to it.

SUFFIAN (*moves as if to leave*):  You must have fed it before with some personal and social information besides what I have given.  I think that is more than enough.

AL-BAHI (*sighing*):  I am sure that it is not enough.

SUFFIAN:  Then you must have provided it with some preliminary information about me.

AL-BAHI:  Only with what the experiment requires.

SUFFIAN:  Then you did.

AL-BAHI:  To guarantee the success of the experiment.

SUFFIAN (*with sudden enthusiasm*):  Do you think it will succeed?

AL-BAHI:  That is what I wish; otherwise we will be forced to . . .

SUFFIAN (*interrupting*):  This experiment will not be repeated, regardless of the conditions or causes.

(*AL-BAHI goes toward the machine to press a button and get a tape out of it.*)

AL-BAHI (*happily*):  It has yielded a result.  (*Sharing his excitement with SUFFIAN*)  The experiment has become a fact.  It has become a true reality.

SUFFIAN:  I don't remember ever seeing you so happy.

AL-BAHI:  Don't you feel happy when a new child comes into the world?

SUFFIAN:  Your success doesn't surprise me.  You have always been creative.

AL-BAHI:  The results of long and hard effort.  Doesn't that make one happy?  (*He hands the tape to SUFFIAN.*)

SUFFIAN:  The results of my exam?

AL-BAHI:  Do you want to read what the computer says about you?  (*He reads the tape and suddenly looks at SUFFIAN with amazement.*)

SUFFIAN:  Bad news!

AL-BAHI (*confused*):  I don't understand.  I don't understand anything.

SUFFIAN (*sarcastically*):  Either I should be dying in a few moments or . . .

AL-BAHI:  I don't understand.  There is something wrong.

SUFFIAN:  . . . or I will be the dean of the medical school.

AL-BAHI:  You make fun of me while this confusing thing is tearing me apart.

SUFFIAN (*sympathetically*):  Don't tell me the experiment has failed.

AL-BAHI:  The confusing thing lies in its success, but . . . but I
don't understand anything.

(*SUFFIAN holds the tape and reads it silently.  He suddenly bursts into
laughter.*)

SUFFIAN:  Your computer is a prophet, but a prophet with a
sordid imagination.

AL-BAHI:  I have not comprehended the mystery yet.  It is really
strange.

(*SUFFIAN reads the tape again and begins to laugh, but less heartily
than before.*)

SUFFIAN:  Your machine has produced nothing but bad
prophecies.

AL-BAHI (*still confused*):  We should resume the experiment.

SUFFIAN:  To get more prophecies as trivial as those fabricated by
seers and palm readers?

AL-BAHI:  We need more information to get another result.

SUFFIAN (*thinking*):  Really confusing results, how did your
machine get them?  (*He reads the tape in a loud voice.*)  Results
of speciman X.  (*Sarcastically*)  Is that my new name or a
figure?

AL-BAHI:  That is to keep the experiment confidential.

SUFFIAN:  Is it true that my name has become X and my surname
zero . . . what a wonderful future!

AL-BAHI:  These are just symbols.  They don't mean anything.

SUFFIAN (*pointing to what is written on the tape*):  And this, doesn't it mean something?  (*Reading*)  You will get your daughter pregnant.  You will kill the one you love most.  You will wish death but in vain.  (*To AL-BAHI*)  Do you understand any of this?  I don't.

AL-BAHI:  It requires interpretation.  It must be interpreted.

SUFFIAN (*repeating a few words of the tape*):  Get my daughter pregnant.  Kill the one I love most.  (*Shouting*)  Your creative machine has made me an Oedipus and turned itself into a playwright, inventing all kinds of misery for men.

AL-BAHI (*regarding the tape with some doubts*):  Your daughter pregnant by you.  Your dearest one killed with your own hands.

SUFFIAN (*correcting him*):  The one you love most.  (*Resuming*) You will wish death but in vain.

AL-BAHI:  I am at a loss.  There must be an explanation.

SUFFIAN:  The only explanation is that your machine has a vivid but sick imagination.  We are entering the age of machines that create lies!

AL-BAHI (*shouting with rapture*):  Wait!  You say the machine has imagination.  Then the experiment is successful despite the faulty results, since this is only a temporary error.

SUFFIAN (*sarcastically*):  The lottery results came out, and everyone with the name of Suffian ends up like Oedipus.

AL-BAHI:  If the information was adequate . . .

SUFFIAN:  The results are adequate and deadly.

AL-BAHI (*repeating for himself*):  Imagination!  (*Shouting joyfully*)  I have found it!

SUFFIAN:  Would you please listen to something that will pour cold water on your joy?  Your machine is stupid!

AL-BAHI (*perplexed*):  Stupid?

SUFFIAN:  For several reasons:  First, my friend, as you know, although maybe you have forgotten, or you believe in your machine more than in me — I have no daughter.

AL-BAHI (*confused*):  That is true.

SUFFIAN:  And I have never once thought of killing even an insect.  Besides, I don't think a rational man like me could wish death.  Then how does your machine predict that my daughter will become pregnant by me?  In spite of my real self, your machine wants to make me a fictional character like Oedipus.  (*Decisively*)  With regret I must say that your experiment will not become popular except perhaps among writers of cheap and provocative stories.

AL-BAHI:  You really seem to be angry.

SUFFIAN:  Your machine is disgusting.  (*Annoyed*)  You will make your daughter pregnant!

AL-BAHI (*disappointed*):  Have all these efforts been useless?

SUFFIAN:  You played lots of roles when we were in school . . . the parties you threw were entertaining, but then, Oedipus had no place in your repertoire . . . and this little game of yours is no less . . . (*He controls himself.*)

AL-BAHI (*entreating*):  Help me just a little more.  Help me to finish this experiment and you will see the logical results.

SUFFIAN:  You know how much I admire you, but I want you to do me one favor.

AL-BAHI (*eagerly*):  What is it?

SUFFIAN:  Present my apology to the president for not attending tonight's party.  Being Oedipus has worn me out.  (*He goes to the exit.*)

AL-BAHI:  Please, don't leave.

SUFFIAN:  I will see you tomorrow.  We'll be in a better frame of mind to discuss all this.  (*He exits, leaving AL-BAHI alone and troubled.*)

AL-BAHI (*addressing the computer*):  You, too, act according to the logic of common superstitions!

THE CHORUS:    What happens is sheer superstition.
In vain you have worn your clothes.
The prophecy of prophesies lies in wires
That point at the ancient future.

**Darkness**

## Scene 2
## The Shredded Past

*It is night, a little while after the first scene, in the living room of Dr. SUFFIAN's house. The bookcase, maps, and a globe constitute an important part of the scene. ASMA, SUFFIAN's wife, is reading and their son YAZIN is talking on the phone.*

THE CHORUS:    The past is plotting . . . plotting . . .
A shred of rusted gold takes root.
The plot is plotting . . . plotting . . .
Hush . . . hush . . .

YAZIN:  I can't believe you would say something like that. (*He covers the receiver with his palm as he addresses his mother.*) It is Lina talking about luck.

ASMA:  That is the weakness of girls, son.

YAZIN (*resuming his talk on the phone*):  I don't believe in luck nor in coincidence. I study, therefore I pass my exams. Yes, what you just said is superstitious, dear. (*SUFFIAN comes n dressed, trying to fix his necktie.*)

SUFFIAN (*to YAZIN*):  You have not gone to bed yet? (*To ASMA*) Haven't you finished that novel?

ASMA:  I am re-reading the last chapter.

SUFFIAN:  It seems to be interesting.  What is it about?

ASMA:  It is a tragedy.

YAZIN (*on the phone*):  I'll help you tomorrow in mathematics provided you stop talking about luck and coincidence. So long. (*He hangs up and speaks to his father.*) You look very elegant tonight, Dad.

SUFFIAN:  It is a formal evening party. (*To his wife*) I am sorry, Asma, it's not a family party.

ASMA (*shrugging*):  Nobody blamed you for it not being a family party.

YAZIN:  Nor a party for young men!  We have no role to play.

SUFFIAN:  Your role will come in the future, when there is no room for the elderly.

YAZIN:  Our parties will not be as formal as yours—all that elegance, and T.V. cameramen.

SUFFIAN (*affectionately*):  Come on, it is time to go to your room.

ASMA (*looking at her wrist watch*):  You still have half an hour more to study.  Don't waste it.

YAZIN (*clinging to his father*):  I missed you, Dad.

ASMA:  And your books have missed you.  (*SUFFIAN hugs his son and leads him to a sofa.*)

SUFFIAN (*to his wife*):  Do you mind?  I missed him too.

ASMA:  You have no time and Yazin's time is precious.

SUFFIAN (*to YAZIN*):  Tell me, how are you getting on in mathematics?

ASMA:  He always takes the lead.

SUFFIAN (*to YAZIN*):  Do you have any difficulties in your literature courses?

ASMA:  Nothing is difficult for Yazin.

SUFFIAN (*looking at both, somewhat annoyed*):  And what about your tennis lessons?

ASMA:  They have to stop next week.

YAZIN:  Mother, tennis doesn't affect my studying.

ASMA (*to YAZIN with a slight warning*):  And the chess has to stop too.

YAZIN (*suppressing his anger*):  Mother!

SUFFIAN (*understanding the seriousness of the situation*):  I have forgotten to ask you about the play you are putting on at the end of the school year.

YAZIN (*joyfully*):  I have been chosen to play the leading role.

SUFFIAN:  It must be a great role.

YAZIN (*standing up as if ready to play the role*):  I have learned it by heart.

SUFFIAN:  I expect you to excel over all of your friends.

YAZIN:  I am the hero!

SUFFIAN:  What is the name of this hero?

YAZIN (*proudly*):  Oedipus.  (*SUFFIAN freezes in his place.  His lips quiver, but he soon regains his composure.*)

SUFFIAN:  Oedipus!  Why Oedipus?  Isn't that a mythical play?

YAZIN:  Our teacher likes it and I like it too.

SUFFIAN:  Aren't there any Arabic plays?

YAZIN:  But it is in Arabic.

SUFFIAN:  And you will play Oedipus?

YAZIN:  You will see me on the stage.  (*He stands up on the sofa and speaks theatrically.  His parents' eyes focus on him.*)  A plague spreads in the city. Its danger increases and threatens the people. King Oedipus sent someone to consult the Oracle. The Oracle said: "The plague will not leave the city until the king's murderer is punished." So, Oedipus declares that the king's murderer is the enemy of the people. No one should hide him or give him shelter. Then Oedipus discovers that he is the king's murderer.

SUFFIAN: Superstitions . . . superstitions.

YAZIN (*resuming with excitement*): And he marries his mother.

SUFFIAN: That is disgusting . . . disgusting.

YAZIN (*resuming*): And his sons are his brothers at the same time.

SUFFIAN (*getting up angrily*): Such a play is not suitable.

YAZIN (*resuming theatrically*): Oedipus punishes himself by putting out his eyes with his own hands, then lives in exile. (*Silence*) His mother strangles herself to death.

SUFFIAN: That is enough . . . that is enough! (*His wife looks at him with amazement and his son moves close to him.*)

YAZIN: You don't like the play.

SUFFIAN (*pulling himself together*): I like it, but I am worried that you will ruin yourself . . . I mean your time. Art is fine, but . . . (*He hides his confusion by kissing YAZIN's forehead.*) It is time to go to bed.

(*YAZIN looks a little sad, kisses his mother and goes to his room.*)

ASMA (*calling after YAZIN*): Don't forget to take your vitamins.

SUFFIAN (*preparing to leave*): May I say something?

ASMA: You are late for the party. (*She goes back to her book.*)

SUFFIAN (*with suppressed anger*):  Please put that book away for a
    moment.

ASMA (*putting the book aside*):  Go ahead, I'm listening.

SUFFIAN:  Don't treat our son too roughly.

ASMA:  I treat him roughly! (*Objecting strongly but lowering her
    voice*) I treat him roughly! I spend most of my time with
    him. I take care of him and make up for your absence at the
    university. And you claim that I treat him roughly? I won't
    allow you to say such a thing.

SUFFIAN:  Asma.

ASMA (*sadly and reproachfully*):  Is it time . . . has the time come,
    Suffian?

SUFFIAN:  What time, Asma . . . what time?

ASMA:  The time of grumbling and reproach. Do I treat my son
    roughly? Can't you see that I have devoted my entire life to
    him?

SUFFIAN:  I don't deny that. No one can deny that, but let him
    live his life. Who answered all the questions that I asked
    him . . . he or you? He can't answer a single question in
    your presence. Yazin is about to become a young man. He
    excels all his friends. I am proud of him . . . proud of my
    son.

ASMA (*slightly sarcastic*):  He is my son, too, and I am not ashamed
    of that.

SUFFIAN (*feeling that it is useless talking to her, tries to win her over
    with affection*):  Asma, dear Asma. (*He sits next to her.*) Let
    us calm down a little.

ASMA:  Do you see me tearing my clothes? Aren't I calm?

SUFFIAN (*helplessly*):  I don't think we can reach a solution.

ASMA:  What would be a solution in your opinion?

SUFFIAN (*hesitating, then speaking nervously*):  To stop humiliating those who love you and whom you love.

ASMA:  Come on, say it.  (*She stops talking as if she is trying to hide something.*)

SUFFIAN:  I will not say anything more, and I apologize.

ASMA:  Your apologies have increased lately.

SUFFIAN (*trying to be friendly and amiable with her*):  There must be something bothering you.  Come on, tell me.

ASMA (*harshly*):  Nothing is bothering me.

SUFFIAN:  Our life has never been like this . . . tension . . . tension . . . and the gap between us gets wider and wider.

ASMA:  Ask yourself.

SUFFIAN:  If I am the reason . . . (*suddenly*)  Does my job bother you?

ASMA:  It bothers me not seeing you advancing.

SUFFIAN:  Who has the ambition to become more than a professor at the university?

ASMA:  Why don't you try to become the dean or the president?

SUFFIAN:  Have I been offered those posts and refused them?  They only select the best, dear.

ASMA:  And the most active.

SUFFIAN: I try everything to be a successful professor.

ASMA (*harshly*): And you will remain in the back seat.

SUFFIAN (*trying to suppress his anger*): I am in the right place.

ASMA (*trying to annoy him*): I know you aren't ambitious.

SUFFIAN (*after a tense silence*): What does ambition mean to you? What does it mean?

ASMA: What it means to everybody: "advancement."

SUFFIAN (*sarcastically*): I advance in years.

ASMA: You have never been serious.

SUFFIAN (*seriously*): What happens if I advance according to your personal vision?

ASMA: When you advance, your family advances too.

SUFFIAN: Who denies that? But aren't we happy?

ASMA: Happy! Ours is the happiness of someone who is content to live in obscurity. All of your friends have better positions than yours.

SUFFIAN: Envy leads to evil.

ASMA (*with reserved resentment*): We are the only family among your friends that still lives in a crowded building. We are still using an old worn-out car. No doubt you like old cars!

SUFFIAN: I used to live in an old neighborhood and in an old house—a house in which more than one family lived together . . . and we still survived . . .

ASMA: You survived . . . and then you were poor and ignorant, but now!

SUFFIAN:  Now, we are in a much better situation.

ASMA:  Better!  Do you call these conditions better?  Are we able to send our son to Europe?  Forget about us, just think about him.  His knowledge might be enhanced if he could travel abroad.

SUFFIAN (*laughing painfully*):  Dear, there are many children and young men who never dream of moving out of their dirty quarters.

ASMA:  Can't you see how rooted you are in your own past?

SUFFIAN:  Who am I?  Am I a child of nothingness?  Of course I am the product of the past.

ASMA:  And the past enslaves you.

SUFFIAN:  I don't see it that way.  I learn from the past and there are things in the present situation that make me feel content.

ASMA (*shouting triumphantly*):  Content!  Ha . . . then contentment rules this house and it is doomed to remain backward.  Then let contentment make you the dean of the school of dreams or the president of the university of illusions.

SUFFIAN:  I would rather remain a professor of geography.  I hope my students, through me, will learn about the geography of their country and of the world.

ASMA:  How did Dr. Akram, your childhood friend, become a minister?  Does contentment make one a minister?  Is he better than you?  Smarter than you?  I know how stupid he is.  You know that too.  Won't you admit it?  But he knows how to eliminate contentment from his life.

SUFFIAN:  Everyone has a way to live.

ASMA:  And your way is to avoid the evils of high position!

SUFFIAN (*entreatingly*):  They can't create high positions for everyone, and my job is limited to teaching and scientific research.

ASMA:  Then we will remain in this little house; we will never have a villa.  Do you have comfortable houses?

SUFFIAN:  I feel very comfortable in our little house.

ASMA (*with unexpectedly gentle accusation*):  You know that I like to grow flowers.  In a villa I could grow and take care of roses.  I could fill all the rooms with roses.

SUFFIAN (*gently*):  You will have a garden when conditions get better.

ASMA:  You are the one who creates those conditions.

SUFFIAN:  I will do my best.

ASMA (*crying out, bitterly*):  To stay in the back seat?

SUFFIAN:  Please, don't speak so loudly.  I don't want Yazin to hear us.

ASMA:  You are ashamed of being seen as lazy by your son.

SUFFIAN (*ready to leave*):  I will not continue this discussion with you.  It is a useless dialogue.

ASMA:  Is this the first time that you have tried to avoid the truth?  Is it painful?

SUFFIAN (*stopping briefly*):  The truth painful?  I think we have accomplished wonderful things.  We have a cozy house and a son worthy of affection and respect, and . . .

ASMA (*interrupting*):  You should thank me for taking care of him.

SUFFIAN:  I don't deny you gratitude.  But isn't he your son too?

ASMA (*emotionally*):  This is not what you promised me.

SUFFIAN:  What did I promise?

ASMA:  Have you forgotten?

SUFFIAN:  I don't remember any promise that I haven't kept.

ASMA (*trying to remind him gently*):  The day we got married.

SUFFIAN:  What happened the day we got married?

ASMA:  You made several wonderful promises.

SUFFIAN:  Did I break any of them?

ASMA:  Have you forgotten?  You always forget.

SUFFIAN:  I haven't forgotten that I bought the car on installment and I haven't forgotten that I am still paying the mortgage on the house.

ASMA:  The car and the house no longer suit your scientific position.

SUFFIAN:  My scientific position qualifies me to ride on an ass.

ASMA (*angry*):  Do you mean I don't deserve more than an ass?

SUFFIAN:  I don't mean anything.  One day you complained about living in a densely populated quarter.  I made a promise to move you to a modern house and I kept my promise.

ASMA (*sarcastically*):  And the heating system in this oh-so-modern house!  The family of a university professor still lives in a house equipped with an ancient heating system!

SUFFIAN (*with light sarcasm*):  One day, the university will appreciate my efforts and your dreams will be fulfilled and we will have a new heating system.

ASMA:  That is where we differ.  You deserve more praise but you don't make any effort to get it.  You treat yourself unjustly and you do us wrong.

SUFFIAN:  Do you know what I am thinking about right now?

ASMA:  About what I am saying.

SUFFIAN:  No, I am thinking I am late for the party.

ASMA (*angry*):  No doubt I rank second or third in your priorities.

SUFFIAN (*annoyed*):  Do you want me to give up?  All right, I give up.  I am lazy and unambitious.  The curse of laziness fell upon me.  With all respect and humbleness, goodbye, madam.  (*He exits as ASMA is at the peak of her anger.*)

ASMA:  You have destroyed everything.  Even your respect for me is gone.  (*She paces the room like a wounded beast.  She tries to take up the book again, then changes her mind.  YAZIN cautiously appears.  She becomes aware of him.  She looks at him, then both remain silent.*)

ASMA (*with affected tenderness*):  You have not gone to bed yet?  (*He does not answer.*)  Is there anything you want to say?

YAZIN (*after some hesitation*):  I want to say: "Good night."

ASMA (*holding out her hands to him*):  Without a kiss!  (*YAZIN moves closer to kiss her.*)  I want you to be the greatest of men.

YAZIN (*as he leaves*):  That is what Dad wants me to be.  (*He goes into his room as ASMA remains gloomy.*)

THE CHORUS:    The worm weaves its cocoon.
               The cocoon is narrow.
               And sorrow is close, as close as breath.

**Darkness**

## Scene 3
## The Rapture of Life

*It is night, a little after SUFFIAN has left his house. We find him in
SULAF's house. The scene suggests relaxation. There is a large couch, a
carpet, and several cushions scattered on the floor. SUFFIAN is sitting
on the floor dressed in a strangely designed robe and smoking happily.
SULAF, dressed in a nightgown, comes from behind SUFFIAN to
embrace him. Drinking glasses and various dishes are on a low table.
SUFFIAN and SULAF kiss.*

THE CHORUS:    Love is close, as close as breath.
                The worm weaves the cocoon of happiness.
                The cocoon is narrow.
                And love is close to the abyss of sorrow.

SULAF:  And now the time for confession has come.

SUFFIAN:  I am at your disposal.

SULAF:  Why did you come late tonight?  What kept you?
     (*Tenderly*) I was worried.

SUFFIAN:  You know that I don't break appointments.

SULAF:  You frightened me when you came in.  The look on your
     face expressed the troubles of the whole world.

SUFFIAN:  A casual discussion disturbed my peace of mind.

SULAF:  I left you with Dr. Al-Bahi.

SUFFIAN:  It was not Al-Bahi.  (*He pauses a moment.*)  Nevertheless,
     our friend the scientist has caused me some misery that will
     be hard to forget.

SULAF:  I will punish him.  I will not work for somebody who
     makes my love unhappy.

SUFFIAN: Forget about it. It was only a joke. It evaporated like water from the ocean.

SULAF: I like your geographical images. (*She pours a glass.*)

SUFFIAN (*seriously*): Do you really love me?

SULAF (*gravely*): I don't know.

SUFFIAN (*with resignation*): I am content that I love you.

SULAF: I don't know if I have loved you since I met you or since I was born or before I was born. Do you yourself know? Tell me if you know.

SUFFIAN: I no longer understand anything.

SULAF: A month in love! Or is it a whole century? It seems like an entire history.

SUFFIAN: I don't know anything about time anymore.

SULAF: Time is mixed up with birth and my love has become boundless and eternal.

SUFFIAN: I was interested in you from the beginning. A serious girl, I thought. She knows when to speak and when to be silent.

SULAF: And I was then watching your seriousness and your balanced character. (*Joyfully*) Why are you so serious?

SUFFIAN: So that a girl like you will admire me.

SULAF: Did you imagine that you would love me?

SUFFIAN: I did not think that I could touch your hand.

SULAF: What a shy man you are, like an Oriental.

SUFFIAN:  Through you my shyness dies and with you I have
    become courageous and more aware of my humanity.

SULAF (*coquettishly*):  Do you think I seduced you?

SUFFIAN:  I admit that you fascinated me.  Here I am like clay in
    your hands.  Through you I breathe and through you I take
    form.

SULAF (*moving around like a butterfly, moving her hands as if she
    were making shapes*):  I made you my heart and out of your
    clay I made my face.  I molded you into an idol, in my arms
    you stay and you bear only my prayers.  I press you and
    embrace you and you become my skin so that no cold or
    fear can attack me.  (*Rapturously*)  I am happy with you and
    with myself.

(*SUFFIAN is absorbed in watching her postures.  As she stops to hug her
body with her arms, he motions her to come to him.*)

SUFFIAN:  Come here . . . come here.  I want a confirmation.

SULAF (*going to him eagerly*):  I am at your disposal, sir.

SUFFIAN:  Let us talk about the future.

SULAF (*with resignation*):  Let us talk about everything.

SUFFIAN:  What do you wish for me in the future?

SULAF:  To be mine.  I don't want anything except you.

SUFFIAN:  Do you expect a better future for me?  Do you want
    me to be a dean . . . or a university president?

SULAF:  I just want to see you and hide myself in your arms.

SUFFIAN:  Do you imagine your love becoming a minister?

SULAF:  I always imagine you in the forefront of the world.  Of all the people, you are the best.

SUFFIAN (*fondles her rapturously*):  You, a graduate of the electronic institute, have such emotional expressions at your command.

SULAF:  I am in command of what I feel and my feeling is about you.

SUFFIAN (*embracing her affectionately*):  I love your smell, I love the tone of your voice, and I love the roundness of your breast.

SULAF (*moving away coquettishly*):  Don't speak so loudly.

SUFFIAN:  Are you shy or do you expect an uninvited visitor?

SULAF:  I am not shy.  (*As if she remembers an unimportant thing*) But I may have an unexpected guest.

SUFFIAN:  Who may come?

SULAF:  My father.

SUFFIAN (*shocked*):  Your father!  Why didn't you tell me before?

SULAF:  I took care of everything.  Don't worry, love.  My father makes two or three visits every year.  The bird goes back to its nest when it gets tired.

SUFFIAN:  I don't know why I feel guilty.

SULAF:  Does my love for you make you feel guilty?

SUFFIAN:  It has nothing to do with your love.  It is something personal.

SULAF (*moving close to him*):  I am proud of you and proud of my love for you.  I wish I could display my pride and my love openly before everyone.

SUFFIAN (*he seems to be thinking of changing the direction of the conversation which is likely to cause some embarrassment*): What was I talking about a little while ago?

SULAF (*she seems to have understood his allusion*): You were speaking loudly and I think I asked you not to speak in such a loud voice.

SUFFIAN: I love your sharp mind. (*With a fleeting sadness*) How much I have missed your compassion and tenderness. (*Rapturously*) I love you. Oh, how intelligent you are. (*Cheering up*) I would like to drink a toast . . . to your intelligence, tenderness and compassion. I want to go back to the time of my youth. Men like me have forgotten the joy of being young and we have moved on . . . (*He moves vigorously*) And now I want us also to move on, beyond our misery and forget it. (*He takes a scarf and wraps it around one of his eyes, shouting rapturously*) Behold the pirate of the seven seas! (*As if looking from the top of a sailing ship*) Life is close, beautiful . . . life is very close. (*He squints and cheers*) I can see the people on the coast. I see savages. How cruel they are . . . they are roasting an old horse that fell in love with a young mare.

SULAF (*joining his mood*): No one eats horsemeat, nor mares either.

SUFFIAN: Hey, you beasts, keep that heart away from the fire. The horse's heart is full of the warmth of love. It is hotter than the fire. Release that beautiful mare. Let her go to the forest to meet her beloved stallion. (*He looks at the horizon*) I see birds in the sky. We are near land. The waves roll, the foam floats, then disappears. The waves die on the rock of love that knows no death. (*He becomes more cheerful*) I want to live. I want to love. I want to remain your love, Sulaf. You will be the master of my heart, mind and body. (*His voice gradually lowers*) I want to live. The pirate wants to live. I want to live, to love and be loved. (*He sways. SULAF rushes to embrace him. He hides his face in her arms.*)

SULAF (*rocking him like a child*):  Are you crying, my love? Cry, my little child. Wet my breast with your tears. Cry, cry, and don't fear that others will hear you. Cry, my little one, and sleep. Don't fear. Don't be afraid. I will be near you until death.

(*The scene continues in silence for a little while. Then SUFFIAN lifts his head slowly. They exchange compassionate looks. He suddenly rises and cheers up.*)

SUFFIAN:  Talk to me about Sulaf.

SULAF:  Talk to me about Suffian. Sulaf is nothing.

SUFFIAN:  You are infinite. You are the great thing that I needed and now have found.

SULAF:  You are everything to me. You were not mine, but you have become part of me.

(*SUFFIAN pauses suddenly and looks frightened. SULAF is worried.*)

SUFFIAN:  Do you ever think that some day we may part?

(*SULAF rushes frightened toward SUFFIAN and embraces him. They remain a while in each other's arms.*)

SULAF:  Please don't say things like that! (*After a quiet moment*)  I wish I were a bit stupid so that I could consult the computer about whether a single flesh could divide, whether the heart could be deprived of its blood or the eye deny its power to see.

SUFFIAN:  Don't remind me of that machine. It despises men.

SULAF (*laughing*):  You have never felt at ease with that machine. But I . . .

SUFFIAN:  I understand . . . it too feels comfortable with you.

SULAF:  I have truly gotten used to it and I feel that it obeys my orders in an extremely efficient way.

SUFFIAN:  Nevertheless, it is a liar and has an ability to tell disgusting stories.

SULAF (*laughing, then with amazement*):  Who has the ability to tell disgusting stories?

SUFFIAN:  Your friend, the computer.

SULAF:  It will be your friend too someday.  You will need it in your research.

SUFFIAN:  I have decided to depend only on my own mind and hands.  (*SULAF goes happily to the record player and turns it on.*)  Oh God, I always remember this piece of music!

SULAF:  I want to dance with you . . .  I want to dance for you.  (*She twirls around.*)  Oh God, how happy Sulaf is!  How happy I am!

SUFFIAN:  Happy, although you know that I have to leave in a little while.

SULAF:  And I know that I can't see you without an appointment and only on certain days, but still I am happy.  (*She pulls him to dance.  He slowly responds.*)

SUFFIAN:  What a capacity for contentment you have!

SULAF:  I am in love, but also content.

SUFFIAN:  But this hurts me, my little sweetheart, because I am not content.

SULAF:  Don't talk about achieving the impossible.  Otherwise we might lose what we have.

SUFFIAN:  I wish I could smile at you in the university or on the street.

SULAF:  I like this drama because I am the only one who knows that you love me and I love you.  Aren't you proud of our secret?

SUFFIAN:  I am frightened that one day I will no longer be able to keep our secret.

SULAF:  Then I will be proud of being exposed.

SUFFIAN:  And proud of seeing me exposed?

SULAF:  I would rather die than hear a bad word against you.

SUFFIAN:  How courageous you are!  How wonderful and noble! (*She clings to him like a child.*)

SULAF:  Tell me about yourself.

SUFFIAN:  You know everything about me.

SULAF:  I am always eager to know more about you.

SUFFIAN (*embracing her eagerly*):  I am glad that you want to talk about me.

SULAF (*pausing and reflecting*):  I want to know something about your infatuations.

SUFFIAN (*laughing*):  My scientific ambitions prevent me from having infatuations.

SULAF (*with childish stubbornness*):  I want to know something about Suffian's infatuations.

SUFFIAN:  Will you believe what I tell you?

SULAF (*interrupting him*):  You didn't know any women before
  me?

SUFFIAN (*after a hesitation*):  In fact, I am a shy person . . .  I am not
  shy in the traditional sense of the word . . . but I had an
  affair with a woman . . . it was a question of satisfying a
  young man's need.  The affair went on for a year.  The
  relationship was purely social.  I did not experience love . . .
  the woman was married . . . she was the wife of a neighbor.
  I was ashamed of everything that happened.

SULAF:  I don't want you to continue.

SUFFIAN:  You already know everything.

SULAF:  I just wanted to know if you have loved a woman before
  me . . . as you do me.

SUFFIAN:  As I do you, I don't think so . . .  I loved my wife in the
  beginning.

SULAF:  How lucky she was!

SUFFIAN:  But that love didn't last long.

SULAF:  How lucky I am!

SUFFIAN:  And you?

SULAF:  Do you want to know if I loved before you?

SUFFIAN:  Have you encountered any other man before me?

SULAF:  Two or three times.

SUFFIAN (*trying to suppress and hide his jealousy*):  Any real love?

SULAF:  Real love does not happen more than once.  I was a lonely little girl.  The first one I thought I loved was the son of our neighbor . . . we had two kisses and some tears . . . the second one was my classmate.  He wanted to marry me, but he was young, too emotional and jealous.  I tried to respond to his love but I could not . . . I felt only a sisterly affection . . . then everything came to an end.

SUFFIAN:  And the third time?

SULAF:  That was a passing infatuation with an Orientalist who came to visit our university.  I hated myself at that time. (*SUFFIAN can't hide his feelings of sadness and frustration.*)  Do you feel jealous?

SUFFIAN:  I will try to be honest and courageous.  I must say, yes.

SULAF:  An intelligent man like you shouldn't indulge in petty jealousy.

SUFFIAN:  Can jealousy be petty or big?

SULAF:  Here we are now, you and I.  Believe me, I will always be yours.

SUFFIAN:  But I am not only for you.

SULAF:  I understand that.  I never accepted a fate like this before, but despite everything I am happy and content.

SUFFIAN:  But how . . . ?  I don't understand you sometimes.

SULAF:  I understand myself.  My love for you is my understanding of myself.

SUFFIAN (*to himself*):  Will that last?  (*More cheerfully*)  Can our happiness last despite all these dangers?  Are you optimistic?

SULAF:  You are asking as if some dark bird were hovering over our heads.

SUFFIAN:  My concern for our happiness makes me pessimistic.

SULAF:  And my love for you makes me optimistic.

SUFFIAN:  What a happy woman you are!  Your age helps you to be optimistic.

SULAF:  Didn't that medical examination prove that you are still young?

SUFFIAN:  Had it not been for you I wouldn't have had that check-up.

SULAF:  It was a challenge.  Do you remember?  And I am happy about it.  I wish I could always challenge you so that you feel at ease. (*After a moment*)  And me too.

SUFFIAN (*preparing to leave*):  I fancy that I was born here.  Because of you I like this place.  Your scent pervades every corner. (*He sniffs her hair*.)  There is life in every atom of you.  Sulaf, you are wonderful!

SULAF (*smoking in a corner*):  I wish you knew what I am thinking about.

SUFFIAN:  I feel more attracted to you when I don't understand what you are thinking.

SULAF:  I bet you don't know what I am thinking.

SUFFIAN:  You are thinking of me.

SULAF:  Of course, of you.

SUFFIAN:  Of our meeting next week.

SULAF:  Of all our future days.

SUFFIAN:  Are you making any plans?

SULAF:  I'm dreaming of something small but wonderful.

SUFFIAN:  I promise to bring it about.

SULAF:  Don't make promises, love.

SUFFIAN:  I swear.

SULAF:  Don't swear by your love for me.

SUFFIAN (*looking worried about SULAF's seriousness*):  Come on, tell me about your dream.

SULAF:  I dream of becoming pregnant by you.

(*SUFFIAN looks frightened for a moment.  He then smiles to hide his fears.*)

SUFFIAN:  What did you say, Sulaf?

SULAF:  I said, I dream of becoming pregnant by you.

SUFFIAN:  Sulaf.

SULAF:  Didn't I say, don't swear.

SUFFIAN (*confused*):  I mean . . . this is embarrassing, you know.

SULAF:  What is embarrassing about it?

SUFFIAN:  Sulaf.

SULAF (*dreamily*):  I dream of a beautiful child like you, intelligent . . . wonderful. (*With overwhelming rapture*) How wonderful the children of love are!

SUFFIAN:  Don't you understand that it would be an illegitimate child?

SULAF:  What is legitimate and what is illegitimate?  The children of love are legitimate, dear love.

SUFFIAN (*still frightened*):  Sulaf.

SULAF:  Don't panic, love, it is merely a dream.  As you know, I have a few dreams.  My life doesn't allow me to dream, but with you things change and the dream makes me feel my existence.  Don't worry. (*She looks at her watch.*)  It is time to go, love.

SUFFIAN (*grieved*):  Your time is the time I love.  I don't like the time I spend with others.

SULAF (*returning to the music in an attempt to hide her feelings*):  I will be waiting for you. (*She weeps softly as he prepares to leave.*)

THE CHORUS:    Love is near the verge of sorrow,
The tears are salt,
And time is long, time is brief,
Sweet . . . bitter . . . painted with dreams.

**Darkness**

## PART TWO

### The end of the week

### Scene 4
### The Shredded Present

*The end of the week, an afternoon in SUFFIAN's house.  YAZIN is
playing chess alone.  After a moment, SUFFIAN comes in with a package
in his hand.  He looks at his son with admiration.*

THE CHORUS:      The lie comes near to the truth.
                 As one week approaches another,
                 And the truth comes near to the lie.
                 Has the programmed mind lied?
                 Has the programmed mind spoken the truth?

YAZIN: I've never lost a game yet, Dad.  Would you like to play
     with me?

SUFFIAN: I don't have enough courage, my dear.  Do you want to
     prove that you are smarter than me?

YAZIN: Smartness alone doesn't help you win.  You win when
     you have a will, persistence as well as intellect.

SUFFIAN: And that is exactly why I don't dare to play with you.

YAZIN: Try, please.

SUFFIAN (*going toward a couch, but watching YAZIN*): Do you
     know what I have in my hand?

YAZIN (*occupied by the game*): A present for my mother.

SUFFIAN: No, it is something for you.

YAZIN (*happily*): A new tennis racket!

SUFFIAN: Wrong! What did you dream about last week?

YAZIN (*confidently*): About spending summer vacation in the mountains.

SUFFIAN: This is something concrete, and you operate it with your fingers.

YAZIN (*brightening*): It must be a guitar. (*Hugs his father*) A guitar! I love you, Dad!

SUFFIAN (*as YAZIN is unwrapping the package*): Do you know . . . (*after a short silence*) that I love you?

(*YAZIN holds the guitar, passing his fingers over the strings, then he hugs his father.*)

SUFFIAN: You are my hope. I imagine you as a perfect man embodying all the potentials of this age: science, art, and the determination to excel. (*He looks like someone dreaming.*) I have dozens of plans in my head for your future. I want to prove that you can do what I could not.

YAZIN (*amazed*): But you have done everything!

SUFFIAN (*laughing a little sadly*): Shall I tell you a secret, son? It was not geography that I intended to study. In the beginning I dreamed only of becoming an elementary school teacher. My main intention was to help my family, but unexpected conditions cropped up and I got a scholarship . . . and so I found myself a geographer. (*He laughs.*) And I want to be a man for this age. (*Seriously*) While you should become a man for history.

YAZIN (*reproachfully*): But you are a great geographer!

SUFFIAN: That is how impossible things get accomplished.

YAZIN (*confidently*): How can a man fail to achieve what he wants?

SUFFIAN (*smiling affectionately*):  In our days—the old difficult
days—hope was like a bird in the sky.  One had nothing to
hold on to with except one's eyes, but your hope, my dear, is
a bird that lands on your shoulders or takes seeds from your
hand without fear.  Our hope was fearful of us, my son.

YAZIN:  Then our time is better than yours.

SUFFIAN:  Your generation is more fortunate than ours.

YAZIN:  It isn't a question of good fortune, Dad.

SUFFIAN (*giving up*):  Your generation is better than ours in
everything.

YAZIN:  Because we don't depend on or believe in luck.

SUFFIAN (*laughing as he recalls something*):  In the past we would
consult a palm reader to help us understand what the future
held for us. Now your generation makes fun of fortune
tellers and astrologers.  You are an anti-prophecy
generation.  (*Speaking simply*)  I wish I could become a record
and book dealer.

YAZIN (*amazed*):  A record and book dealer!

SUFFIAN:  Yes, so I could read all the books and journals and
listen to music continually.

YAZIN:  But you are a scientist of geography.

SUFFIAN (*correcting him*):  I am a professor of geography.

YAZIN:  But you are also a scientist, and an important one.

SUFFIAN:  Probably my good reputation and the students' respect
for me are the reasons that . . .

YAZIN (*interrupting him firmly*):  You are a great scientist and I love you.

SUFFIAN:  I want you to become a great scientist.  My entire life is devoted to that purpose.  (*He hugs YAZIN.*)  Where is your mother?

YAZIN:  She either went shopping or is visiting some people.  Do you want to play with me?

SUFFIAN:  Haven't I told you that I don't dare?  Come on, it's time to study.

YAZIN:  My break isn't over yet, and today is Thursday.

SUFFIAN:  You like Thursdays.

YAZIN:  It's the end of the week!  Do you like the end or the beginning of the week?

SUFFIAN:  I like both.

YAZIN:  But why?

SUFFIAN (*after a little thought*):  Because one is the beginning of work and the other of pleasure.

YAZIN (*toying with the chess pieces*):  Dad . . . do you believe in fate?

SUFFIAN (*looking a little apprehensive*):  Why do you ask such a question?

YAZIN:  It puzzles me that our teacher keeps saying that everything is predetermined but when we study the sciences we find the opposite.

SUFFIAN:  I would rather see you concentrating on the sciences now — leave those issues for later.  You will find out the truth for yourself.

YAZIN:  I have another question.

SUFFIAN (*giving up*):  Another question!

YAZIN:  Do you love my mother?

SUFFIAN (*silent for a moment, thinking*):  Why such a strange question?

YAZIN:  Because there is always friction between the two of you. You act like negative and positive charges, and everybody knows that when those two poles unite they produce electricity, namely life!

SUFFIAN:  You little scientist! (*Seriously*) Who said there was always friction between us?

YAZIN:  I always hear you in loud discussions.

SUFFIAN (*reproachfully*):  Yazin . . . Yazin . . . Where do you get these strange ideas: loud discussions . . . negative and positive!

(*The outside door opens. Both look toward the entrance. ASMA comes in heavily laden. YAZIN rushes to her. She exchanges a few indifferent looks with SUFFIAN.*)

YAZIN (*reproachfully*):  Mother . . . you're late! (*Happily*) Look what Dad bought me.

ASMA (*as she goes to a distant seat*):  I stopped to see the wife of the university president. I had a cup of coffee and a little chat with her.

SUFFIAN (*muttering*):  The witch!

ASMA (*after looking suspiciously at SUFFIAN*):  I got some news along with the coffee.

SUFFIAN: The weekend news.

ASMA (*to YAZIN*): What did Dad get you?

YAZIN: A guitar! (*He goes to bring it.*)

ASMA: A guitar in the middle of the academic year?

YAZIN (*deciding not to bring the guitar*): I want to learn to play it.

ASMA (*sarcastically as she glares at SUFFIAN*): You want to become a musician? A guitar for a scientist!

YAZIN: It won't hurt my studies. You know, mother, that it won't affect my studying.

ASMA: I know better than you do what you need. (*After a little thought*) Put this thing away until summer. (*She looks at her watch.*) You promised to help your cousin in math. You should go to her house now.

(*SUFFIAN does not make any comment. YAZIN looks at his father and mother alternatively, then goes out quickly.*)

YAZIN: So long.

ASMA: Don't stay there more than half an hour.

SUFFIAN: It must be a serious problem if you let Yazin leave the house during his study time.

ASMA: I don't want him to hear any more of your arguing.

SUFFIAN: You mean your arguing.

ASMA: You know how concerned I am about keeping him from being exposed to emotional disturbance.

SUFFIAN: And you know how concerned I am to disturb my son

emotionally.

ASMA:  I can't abide your sarcasm.

SUFFIAN:  And I can't abide your falsification of the facts.

ASMA (*shouting angrily*): Suffian! (*She tries to control herself.*)  At the university people were talking about something in whispers.

SUFFIAN:  I must be getting a new promotion soon.

ASMA (*bitterly*):  With you I no longer dream of such a thing.

SUFFIAN:  Probably my new lectures on geography and man . . . (*Enthusiastically*)  My last lectures were most interesting. They attracted students from other departments.  I talked about the desire of modern man to break down the barriers between peoples.

ASMA:  So many women admire you!

SUFFIAN:  You know that my students include both men and women.

ASMA:  And college employees.

SUFFIAN:  College employees have nothing to do with my lectures.

ASMA:  But rumors are going around that some employees have relationships with some professors.

SUFFIAN (*pulling himself together*):  I don't understand what you're hinting at.

ASMA (*coldly*):  Then who is this woman they are talking about?

SUFFIAN:  Who is talking about some woman?

ASMA:  They call her an admirer!  A friend!  They are talking about a relationship between a professor and a menial employee, one who specializes in stealing men from their wives!

SUFFIAN (*controlling himself*):  I don't understand anything of what you are saying.

ASMA:  The rumors have reached the houses of professors, scientists, even the university president!  Do you think, my dear doctor, that a community of this kind can keep a secret?

SUFFIAN:  I am sorry to tell you that I can't make heads or tails of what you are saying.

ASMA:  It is something related to you.  You know that very well.

SUFFIAN (*angrily*):  I'm sorry, but I have nothing to do with rumors.

ASMA (*screaming*):  I will find out who she is . . . and I know how to deal with this too!

SUFFIAN (*controlling himself, aware that his wife is ignorant of the truth*):  My dear Asma . . .

ASMA:  I am not your dear.

SUFFIAN (*trying to mollify her*):  Dear Asma, this week began with pain and continued in deadly silence.  I don't want it to end with more pain.

ASMA (*sadly*):  Is it only one week, Suffian?  Is it only one week . . . or long years?  (*Suddenly*)  Do you really love me, Suffian?

SUFFIAN:  I love my family, and you are the principle element in it.

ASMA:  Do you love me as a wife or as a woman?

SUFFIAN (*with affected joy*):  Who am I married to if not a woman?

ASMA (*angrily*):  This is no time to show joy.  Our joy has died.

SUFFIAN:  Can joy die, Asma?  We were very happy.

ASMA (*firmly*):  This is no time to lie to each other.

SUFFIAN:  Who is lying?

ASMA:  Come on, admit that you are not happy.  Be courageous
    and admit it.

SUFFIAN (*hastily*):  Admit it yourself.

ASMA (*looking as if she might collapse*):  I am miserable . . .
    miserable!  (*She covers her face with her hands.  SUFFIAN
    approaches her tenderly and affectionately.*)

SUFFIAN:  Are you crying?  (*To himself*)  Has the ice melted?

ASMA (*controlling herself*):  I am not crying.  Miserable people
    don't cry.

SUFFIAN:  Asma.

ASMA:  I don't cry and I never will.

SUFFIAN (*as if speaking to himself*):  The end of the week has turned
    into an island of sorrow and misery — an island devoid of
    any kind of hope.

ASMA:  Who is it that has killed hope, then?

SUFFIAN:  And here comes the salty water to flood the island's
    coast.

ASMA:  Which of us is that salty water, you or I?

SUFFIAN (*shouting*):  I am tired . . . I am tired.

ASMA (*cruelly*):  You are a master of nothing but evasion.  This is how our life has passed, in evading any challenge.  You could not once face up to reality!

SUFFIAN (*standing defiantly before her*):  Here I am, facing it!

ASMA:  Look at me carefully.

SUFFIAN:  I am looking.

ASMA:  You don't love me any more.

SUFFIAN (*about to say something, he changes his mind, and continues, but avoiding looking at ASMA*):  Let's calm down a little.  You're confusing me.  First you ask me if I still love you.  Then you try to extract the truth, then force me to admit that I don't love you.  Have mercy on me, woman.

ASMA (*in a distant corner*):  Everything is torn apart . . . it has all torn apart.

SUFFIAN (*trying to create a new atmosphere*):  Can't we calm down?  Aren't these just the difficulties of life?

ASMA:  It would have been easy to calm down before I heard this new story.

SUFFIAN:  Don't we have enough misery?  Do we have to crown it with scandal?

ASMA (*crying out triumphantly*):  So you admit you are miserable!

SUFFIAN (*confused*):  I mean . . . the misery we have been through lately.

ASMA:  Admit that our whole life has been miserable!

SUFFIAN:  I don't want to admit anything and I don't want to talk about anything. (*Muttering*)  I feel that the present is disintegrating, the past is in shreds.  What does the future hold for us?

ASMA:  What are you muttering?  What are you saying?

SUFFIAN:  I am not saying anything and I'm not going to say anything later either. (*He goes out angrily.*)

THE CHORUS:    What is said is said.
And that which will happen will happen,
When will it happen
And what does the future hold . . . ?

**Darkness**

## Scene 5
## Catastrophe

*The same day, a little after sunset. It is evening. In SULAF's house, SUFFIAN is seen pacing anxiously. He looks at his wrist watch more than once and smokes nervously.*

THE CHORUS:    It is not the clock that keeps the time,
Which slips out of our hands.
And the coming sorrow is self-evident.
What if the future comes early, today?

SUFFIAN (*talking to himself*):  I hope she won't be late.  She won't be late.  It's been a horrible week.  Sulaf offers me love and Asma deprives me of security.  And a computer with a perverse imagination.  We consume our days in a search for happiness.  (*He looks at his watch.*)  She hasn't come yet.  (*He looks at Sulaf's picture on the table.*)  My wonderful little one, I have no one but you.  Sulaf, you are the source of mercy, my refuge.  (*He pours himself a drink.*)  I can do nothing but wait. (*With a nervous motion*)  I have not felt good throughout this week.  It has passed as slowly as a cloud of atomic dust.  (*He looks at his watch.*)  It is the tide's ebb and flow!  That is life, feelings and sentiments.  Can't we dream of happiness and then attain it?  (*He looks toward the entrance, sensing some kind of movement.*)  She has come; Sulaf must have come.  The mild winds of dawn have come.  (*SULAF comes in worried. SUFFIAN rushes to embrace her.*)  You are late, but I knew you would come.

SULAF:  How could I not come?  Your voice on the phone was trembling.  (*She looks at SUFFIAN.*)  But you are safe, you are all right, that is my happiness.

SUFFIAN:  My beloved little one, don't worry about me.

(*She takes his hand and leads him like an obedient child.  They sit next to each other.*)

SULAF:  Don't speak.  Let me look at you.  You seem all right; nothing is threatening you.  I was overcome with worry!

SUFFIAN:  Your worry was justified.  I am miserable.

SULAF:  My beautiful dear one, you are with me.  You frightened me, but I am happy now.  Did you find the door key where I told you?

SUFFIAN:  It was in its place.  (*Hopelessly*)  I had no other refuge.

SULAF:  I am glad you came a little early.  We'll have a beautiful time.  (*Laughing*)  I apologized to Dr. Al-Bahi for leaving early by making up a little lie.  Sulaf is lying!  For your sake, love, I lied!  (*She hugs him.*)  Imagine, he was annoyed and said he would stop working today because I wasn't there!

SUFFIAN:  He really respects you and needs you.

SULAF:  By the way, he asked after you and said you didn't stop by as usual.

SUFFIAN:  I hate that lying machine.

SULAF (*laughs*):  He is engaged in using the computer to explore the depths of humanity and I believe he will succeed.

SUFFIAN (*cautiously*):  Did he talk to you about the results of his research?

SULAF:  It's confidential.

SUFFIAN:  Confidential!

SULAF:  He hides the results of his research in special files, and he is right.  (*After a moment*)  Maybe he doesn't trust me any more.

SUFFIAN:  Who doesn't trust you?

SULAF (*kissing him*): Come on, tell me about your problem. (*Coquettishly*) Are you going to stay with me until midnight?

SUFFIAN: I want to stay with you until the end of my life.

SULAF (*sighing painfully*): Is it possible that such a dream will come true? (*Seriously*) I want a detailed account of my love's problems.

SUFFIAN: Worries can't be articulated.

SULAF (*placing her ear close to him*): Share your worries with me. I am ready to bear your sufferings and sorrows. Aren't we one?

SUFFIAN (*kissing her ear*): My beloved little one, it is my wife.

SULAF (*honestly concerned*): Is she sick?

SUFFIAN: It doesn't look like she will recover.

SULAF: Poor woman! (*As if making a decision*) She should be taken to a specialist. At the university there are doctors for all kinds of diseases.

SUFFIAN: Except for her disease. Her illness lies in the university.

SULAF: I don't understand . . .

SUFFIAN: My lovely little one. You won't understand. Neither do I. After living so many years with her, I no longer understand her.

SULAF: She is a riddle.

SUFFIAN: My wife has heard some rumors at the university.

SULAF: Rumors? About what?

SUFFIAN:  She must have heard something about our love.  But she does not know anything about you.

SULAF:  It is impossible.  Nobody knows anything.  I swear . . .

SUFFIAN:  I understand that.  Maybe she is fantasizing . . . she has always been like that, and she will never change her suspicious nature.

SULAF:  Nobody is as cautious in love as I am.

SUFFIAN:  And so am I.  It is confusing.  (*He thinks.*)  Do you think she is playing a role in order to find out something she doesn't know?

SULAF:  She has reason to do that.  A husband like you can't be easy to give up.  You are the kind of husband women fight over.

SUFFIAN (*sarcastically*):  So she has the right to use all kinds of tricks to upset my life.  I am unhappy.  This woman has made me very unhappy, Sulaf.

SULAF (*reproaching him*):  Suffian.

SUFFIAN:  Her unbearable cruelty may drive me to the brink of madness.

SULAF (*embracing him compassionately*):  I hope she will always be cruel so that I can see you more.  Come on, lie down.  I will give you a massage.  I want to offer you more happiness and pleasure.

SUFFIAN (*laying his head in her lap*):  I want to sum up life in this single rendezvous.

SULAF:  I want all of life to be here.  I don't want anything else.

SUFFIAN:  My real life is the one I live here with you, the rest is nothing. Had it not been for you and for Yazin, my son, I could have thought of other things . . . I could have thought seriously of death.

SULAF (*frightened*): Death! You will not die. Men like you don't die. I can't imagine you dying. You are life, love and the source of life . . . I love you. I love you. And I wish (*standing up*) that I could dance the dance of joy with you.

SUFFIAN: Sulaf . . . Sulaf.

(*She turns the record player on and sways rapturously.*)

SULAF: Do I satisfy you . . . do I make you happy? I want to dance. Can I express my love and happiness to you? I love you . . . I loved you a thousand years ago . . . I loved you from the beginning of creation . . . since you and I were one being . . . one body. (*She suddenly stops and thinks.*) Isn't it strange what happens, Suffian?

SUFFIAN: What is strange?

SULAF: At the university, I deal in figures and concrete facts, but here with you I think in mythical categories. Isn't that strange? Maybe I have two personalities within me. At the university, I am a woman bound up by the restrictions of existing realities. With you, I am a being with two imaginary wings, one connecting me to the past, the other pulling me into the future. (*Rapturously*) With you I am free . . . at the university, I am in chains.

SUFFIAN: Sulaf . . . Sulaf.

SULAF: I was ambitious in my studies. They accused me of having a scientific mind which could only deal with actual facts. Here I am. I believe in fate . . . (*She looks at him affectionately.*) You are my fate . . . You are my destiny!

SUFFIAN: Let us not talk about fate. I hate that word.

SULAF (*amazed*):  You hate being my fate?

SUFFIAN (*nervously*):  This is something I don't understand.  I
     don't know why I hate that ugly thing . . . with its elegantly
     lighted façade.

SULAF:  Suffian . . . Suffian.

SUFFIAN:  I wish I understood my attitude towards that machine.
     (*Pulling himself together*)  I love you, that is one thing I know
     despite all the things that surround my life.  I love you and I
     wish I could create the words that could match my love for
     you.  I want to express my love for you in a real way.
     (*Suddenly*)  Will you really stay with me?  Are you going to
     stay with me until the last moment?  Do you promise . . . ?  I
     only want you to promise me a lasting love.

SULAF:  I've already promised, and I promise to keep my vow till
     the moment of death.  (*Like someone struck by a crisis of nerves*)
     For you, I refuse to die.  Promise me that you also refuse
     death.  I hate it and I hate . . . (*She suddenly stops.*)  Why are
     we talking about misery when it never enters this house?  I
     defy misery to knock at our door.  (*She pours two drinks.*)  Let
     us drink to these happy moments.  These are immortal
     moments.  I have read novels and poetry.  (*As if she were
     reading*)  My feelings for you began from the moment you
     lent me a novel.  (*With determination*)  As if I were not the
     child of this complicated and ordered age.  (*She contemplates
     SUFFIAN as if seeing him for the first time.*)  Your love, my . . .
     (*After some hesitation*)  Your love, my poor little one, is
     something I can't describe in words invented by writers and
     poets.  (*Looking at herself in a mirror*)  How strange!  (*She
     motions SUFFIAN toward her.*)  Isn't that strange?  I look like
     you!  Look at this strange likeness.  Are we twins?  Look at
     me, love.  Am I not like you?!

SUFFIAN (*looking in the mirror which SULAF brings close to him*):
     Our eyes look alike . . . and our noses a little . . . (*He feels
     her hand.*)  There is a big difference between the softness of

your hands and the roughness of mine. (*He caresses her . . . she gives up and sits on his lap.*) My little one . . . my little one.

SULAF (*like a little girl*): Spoil me . . . spoil me. (*She hides her face in his chest.*)

SUFFIAN: My little one . . . my butterfly . . . talk to me about your childhood, love.

SULAF (*with childish joy*): Haven't I shown you my childhood photos? (*She rushes to bring an album. She points to the first page proudly.*) This is me.

SUFFIAN: I wish I were able to follow your growth moment by moment.

SULAF (*pointing to a picture joyfully*): And this is Sulaf, the infant.

SUFFIAN: It looks like my son Yazin when he was a baby.

SULAF (*turning a page*): This is when I was one year old. I used to like cold milk; that is what my father once said.

SUFFIAN (*laughing*): Drinking cold milk indicates fine taste.

SULAF (*as she turns a page*): When I was ten years old.

SUFFIAN (*annoyed*): And where are the pictures of the nine years between?

SULAF (*sadly*): My father did not have enough time to take pictures of me. He was busy with commerce. It is like a dead period in my life.

SUFFIAN: And your mother?

SULAF (*sadly and regretfully*): My mother! I never knew her.

SUFFIAN: Oh, poor one . . . I wish I were your mother and . . .

SULAF:  She deserted us.

(*There is a knock at the outside door.*)

SUFFIAN (*frightened*):  Who is at the door?

SULAF (*calmly*):  Neighbors, I don't care.

(*SUFFIAN goes inside with his drink.*)

SUFFIAN:  We should be careful.

SULAF:  Don't worry.  I don't give a damn about the whole world.

(*She goes to the outside door.  SUFFIAN disappears.  SULAF's voice is heard saying "Dad."  After a few moments her father comes in.  He looks tired.  Although he has drunk a lot, he is still able to pull himself together and try to be pleasant.*)

MUDER (*reproachfully*):  I hear nothing except the word "Dad." You didn't expect to see your father coming to his own house?  (*Affectionately*)  You don't give a kiss to the old bird which has returned to its nest?

SULAF (*kissing his forehead*):  I didn't expect you at the end of the week.

MUDER:  Don't I have the right to come at the end of the week?

SULAF:  You used to come in the middle.

MUDER:  Fatigue, my dear, breaks rules.  (*He looks around the room.*)  Do you expect guests or do you already have some?

SULAF (*hesitating, then admitting it*):  I have a friend.

MUDER (*looking around*):  I don't see him.  Is he playing hide and seek?

SULAF (*speaking loudly so that SUFFIAN can hear*):  My friend will be here in a little while.

MUDER:  Do you have a drink?

SULAF (*tiredly*):  I think you have drunk enough.

MUDER (*sitting*):  I have drunk enough but I am also tired enough. (*Threateningly*)  I want to stay with you, Sulaf.  Come close to me.  I want to feel that I have a daughter and a friend. Come closer to me, my poor one.  I have neglected you terribly.

(*SUFFIAN comes in in a way so that her father does not see him.*)

SULAF (*trying to stop her father from talking*):  Dad!

MUDER (*resuming*):  I have lost everything, even that lousy job which took me around the country . . . I lost it.  I'm finished, Sulaf.  The businessman is reduced to a cheap salesman and then to nothing.

(*He buries his face in his hands.  SULAF stands near him, confused. SUFFIAN searches around for something to do, but he does not find anything except the album, which he looks at again.*)

SULAF:  Shall I get you something to eat?

MUDER (*in a subdued voice*):  I no longer sell that much of their merchandise.  I got old and tired and I want to sleep.  I want to sleep for years and dream too.  (*To SULAF*)  I have neglected you, my little one.  I hope I can make it up to you. I know I am worth nothing, but let me try.

SULAF:  Father, I would like to introduce you to my friend, Dr. Suffian.

SUFFIAN (*paying no attention to her introduction*):  Who is this woman, Sulaf?  (*He points to a picture in the album to the astonishment of the father and the bewilderment of SULAF.*)

SULAF (*resuming her introduction, pointing to MUDER*):  My father.

(*SUFFIAN and MUDER stand face to face, silent, as if recalling a forgotten past.  MUDER speaks first.*)

MUDER:  It seems I know your friend.  (*He stretches out his hand to SUFFIAN.*)

SUFFIAN (*shaking hands with MUDER*):  I'm trying to remember you, sir.  I'm sorry, but my memory is getting weak.

MUDER (*cheering up as he remembers*):  You are Suffian.  I remember, you are Suffian.  (*He laughs as SUFFIAN remains silent and SULAF looks amazed.*)  Suffian, the platonic lover, that was your nickname among your friends.

SUFFIAN (*remembering*):  Suffian, the platonic lover.  (*He brightens.*) You are Muder.  I remember you now.  (*To SULAF*)  Did you say he is your father?

MUDER:  Aren't I worthy to be the father of a beautiful girl like Sulaf?

SUFFIAN (*shocked*):  You are Muder, Sulaf's father.  (*To SULAF, as he points to a picture in the album*)  And who is this lady, Sulaf?

SULAF (*annoyed*):  My mother.  (*To MUDER*)  Isn't she my mother? (*MUDER nods as SUFFIAN throws the album aside.*)

SUFFIAN (*his strength giving out*):  This is impossible . . . impossible.

SULAF:  What is impossible?  I don't understand.  I don't understand anything.

MUDER (*in a friendly way*):  Is it twenty years or more?  You were shy and polite, and you are still.  (*To SULAF*)  You said Dr. Suffian.  He must be a great physician.

SULAF:  He is a professor of geography at the university.

SUFFIAN:  This is impossible . . . impossible.

MUDER:  You have chosen the right path, my friend, but I have lost everything, even myself.

SUFFIAN (*standing up wildly and addressing MUDER*):  What happened to your wife?

SULAF:  Do you know my mother?

SUFFIAN (*repeats*):  What happened to your wife?

MUDER:  She deserted her home and daughter.

SUFFIAN:  What a miserable man I am!  I have discovered everything!

SULAF:  I don't understand anything.

SUFFIAN (*shouting again*):  But I understand everything.  (*He seizes MUDER's clothing.*)  Don't you understand, you poor fool?  Don't you understand?

(*SULAF is bewildered and unable to do anything.*)

MUDER (*trying to shake off SUFFIAN's wild hold*):  Don't be cruel to me.  I am as light as a feather.  I fall down when the slightest wind blows.

SUFFIAN (*shaking him*):  You must know the truth.  You must know why your wife deserted you.  You were weak and you were sick.  You were useless and that shy young man replaced you.  Do you understand that?

SULAF (*sitting hopelessly*):  I don't understand . . . I don't understand anything.

SUFFIAN:  We are doomed to understand every truth at the wrong time . . . understand to bring us to misery . . . understand to bring us to death itself.

SULAF (*looking to MUDER, who sits humiliated and distant*):  I don't understand anything.

SUFFIAN:  You poor thing, of course you cannot understand any of this.

SULAF:  Will no one have mercy on me and tell me what is going on here?

SUFFIAN:  Your mother deserted this man (*pointing to MUDER*) because he was not a man, and I was doomed, I who stand before you now . . . I was doomed to be the man who . . . (*screaming wildly*) Sulaf . . . what a disaster! It seems that I am the man who brought you into this world!

SULAF:  What do you mean?

SUFFIAN:  I mean, I am your father, Sulaf. (*A short, horrified moment of silence.*)

SULAF (*screaming in intense pain*):  Oh, God . . . Oh, God of misery! I can't believe it!  I am pregnant . . . I am pregnant by my . . . (*She stops, unable to speak the word. A deadly silence interrupted only by SULAF's weeping. SUFFIAN looks at her and cries out.*)

SUFFIAN:  I want to die.  May God's curse fall on the computer.

(*He goes out as SULAF collapses on the floor. MUDER pours a drink.*)

THE CHORUS:     The incident took place and the moon shattered.
The incident took place and the moon shattered.

**Darkness**

## Scene 6
## Killing

*In SUFFIAN's house, soon after SUFFIAN has left SULAF's house. It is night and the stage is dim. SUFFIAN smokes in a frantic way. He paces the floor like a wild animal. After a little while, ASMA comes in.*

THE CHORUS:    You make your daughter pregnant.
With your own hands you kill the one
You love the most.

ASMA: Listen to me. This is going to be the last time that I will ask you about your strange behavior. (*SUFFIAN doesn't respond.*) If you don't tell me what has happened, I will leave the house. Will you tell me what happened to you? I know you won't say and I know that I don't mean anything to you. That is clear. (*SUFFIAN doesn't respond.*) I will leave everything for you and I won't return unless you get your sanity back. I've tolerated a lot. I put up with your surrender to existing conditions. I put up with your lack of ambition. But I can't take your silence. It shows your resentment of me. You have been drinking and smoking for hours. You've made no effort to answer my questions. (*Less severely*) I am not a merchant who mourns over the money he has lost. I am not a candidate who gets angry when he loses an election. (*Angrily*) I don't understand what has happened to you. (*After thinking*) Is there a woman in your life? There must be another woman. (*Angrily*) Listen, if I leave now I will never come back. I am tired of you. Answer me! Say something, or you will never see me again! (*She leaves, but SUFFIAN is unaffected. After a moment, she comes back.*) Yazin is asleep. I don't want to disturb him today. I will be here tomorrow to take him. You don't deserve him. (*She goes out. SUFFIAN doesn't move. After a little while, he moans.*)

SUFFIAN: Has the computer's prediction come true? May heaven's curse fall on that infernal machine. May Dr. Al-Bahi be cursed. May damnation take all science and technology. Sulaf, my love, is my daughter! Is this coincidence? What a horrible end I have come to! It is all over for me. (*He recalls the computer's words.*) "You will get your daughter pregnant." She is already pregnant by me. Oh God, what a bitter choice I made! I want to trample on everything: the laws of geography, history, and the sciences. (*After a moment*) I despise myself . . . I want to die. (*Determined*) Death is inevitable. (*He recalls the computer's prophecy.*) "You will wish to die, but you cannot." I am going to disappoint you, you ingenious machine! I will prove to you that I can expose your lies and discredit your cheap prophecies. (*Humbly*) But they were not cheap. (*Shouting*) I want to die! Death is inevitable, challenge is inevitable. I defy you. (*He goes to a nearby closet to take out a bottle. He pours out pills into his palm.*) Two . . . ten. (*He puts the pills in a glass and pours in water, then stirs it with his pen.*) They have begun to dissolve and death approaches. Soon your lies will be exposed . . . you foolish machine. (*To himself*) Is it truly foolish? (*He puts the glass aside and takes up a scrap of paper.*) I will write a letter to Yazin. "Dear Yazin, please forgive me. I failed to stay with you till the end of the road." (*He writes, then thinks, then paces.*) "Dear Yazin . . . (*He erases the phrase.*) My dear son, Yazin, I know you will forgive what I have done. I have left you midway in your path, but my confidence in you makes me feel secure. Dear Yazin, you have the mind of a scientist and the vision of an artist. You are an example of the new man that I have always dreamed of for us. In the past, different conditions, such as poverty and backwardness, have conspired against me, but I survived them all. Today, new conditions conspire against me, and I can no longer resist. I have to give up. I wish I could . . . (*He stops writing and addresses himself.*) A machine has defeated you. Poetry moves you, and music draws you into a world of fantasy. A woman's tenderness enchants you. (*He contemplates the room and its details as if he is losing everything.*) I will lose everything, my memories and my friends. Will my friends and others miss me? A man commits suicide because he has failed, but I did not fail. I only lost my way. I am atoning for a desire that once moved my hungry youth. (*He ponders.*) Who would imagine that the girl I fell deeply in love with would turn out to be my daughter, the child of a woman I met long ago, whose name I don't even remember and whom I have totally forgotten? What a miserable creature you are, professor of geography! (*He pulls himself together as if he remembered something serious.*) What will happen to her? I left her so that I could find a solution for my own sorrows. What about her sorrows? Should I worry about the daughter or about the sweetheart? Can I see her again . . . should I look at her with the eyes of a father or with the eyes of a lover? Does she think of death as I do? I don't think that Asma does. It is clear that she thinks seriously of death—a death that can end a misery she is not responsible for. (*Frightened*) Does she really think of dying? (*He thinks intensely, then rushes out like a man on a rescue mission. After a little while, YAZIN comes out of his room. He seems to have just woken up.*)

YAZIN (*He calls his mother in a subdued voice. He waits for a moment, then calls again*): Dad, Mommy. (*He does not hear any answer, so he goes toward the water bottle and finds a glass full of water. He picks it up and calls.*) Dad! (*Then he drinks the water at one gulp.*) Mommy . . . (*To himself*) Maybe they went to a party. I hope they are having a good time. May peace return to this house. (*He feels pain in his stomach. He grabs his stomach in pain, then falls to the floor. After a moment SUFFIAN comes in as if he has backed down from the decision to go back to SULAF.*)

SUFFIAN (*to himself*): It is useless . . . what should I say to her . . . how should I address her? I am ashamed before her. I don't think seeing her is any solution. The world has collapsed and the boundaries between happiness and misery have disappeared. The night has blended with the day . . . the earth has brought forth its burdens . . . the future is coming out of the womb of the unknown. Before the eyes of the defeated knight the words of failure and frustration dance. (*A long silence.*) I declare your death, Suffian! (*He suddenly looks in the corner and finds YAZIN. He approaches him with fear and finds the empty glass. He kneels down, then screams wildly and bends over YAZIN's body.*)

THE CHORUS:     You will get your daughter pregnant.
                You will kill with your own hands
                The one you love most.
                You will wish to die,
                But your wish does not come true.
                You will wish to die,
                But your wish does not come true.


**Darkness**

## Scene 7
## Revenge

*In the computer center of the university. It is morning, several days after the previous scene. Dr. SUFFIAN is in the depths of despair. He has let his beard grow. The tears in his eyes have dried. He is as silent as a sphinx. Dr. AL-BAHI moves slowly as though he was plagued by the same problem. Sorrow permeates the place.*

THE CHORUS:    Hopelessness is akin to sorrow.
You wish to die,
But your wish does not come true.
You wish, you did not wish.
Then, keep silent, death, keep silent.

AL-BAHI:  You know that I have no talent for the language of consolation, but (*hesitant*) . . . you are killing yourself with sadness. You have been silent for three days. Come now, say something. Sorrow doesn't bring back a dear one we have lost. (*The phone rings and he answers it.*) Yes . . . the work has stopped. I can't do everything myself. My secretary has quit. Yes, she quit and I can't work miracles. Tell the university president I am on leave. (*He hangs up.*) Nobody thought that Sulaf would quit. There was no reason for her to quit without giving me notice. Didn't I treat her as though she were my colleague?

SUFFIAN (*speaking very slowly*):  Did Sulaf leave?

AL-BAHI:  Imagine, that wonderful girl suddenly dropped out of my life!

SUFFIAN (*in a subdued voice*):  You loved her too.

AL-BAHI (*resuming*):  I have quite lost my balance.

SUFFIAN:  It's about time we lost our balance. It's all up with me now.

AL-BAHI:  A man like you can't be ruined by an unexpected disaster.

SUFFIAN:  An unexpected disaster?  Yazin, my beautiful son, dies suddenly before my eyes.  All my dreams fade away. That was a deadly tale your computer told.  (*After a moment*) Your machine gave some information and then withdrew into silence.  What more does it have to say?

AL-BAHI:  I don't think you really care what the computer has to say.

SUFFIAN (*with deadly sarcasm*):  Then who does care?  It was your machine that tied my life to a slender thread.  As I fell, all my hope and love collapsed.

AL-BAHI:  What does the sudden death of your son have to do with the computer?

SUFFIAN:  What does it have to do with it?  Nothing, except in the relationship between life and catastrophe.  (*Painfully*) "You will get your daughter pregnant."  My daughter is now pregnant by me!

AL-BAHI (*innocently*):  I didn't know that you had a daughter.

SUFFIAN (*resuming*):  And "You will kill with your own hands the one you love most."  Thus, I killed my son with the poison I prepared for myself.

AL-BAHI (*in wonder*):  Did you really intend to kill yourself?

SUFFIAN:  I was challenging your damned machine in an attempt to prove that I could put an end to my life, which your machine denied.  Thus I made myself ready to die, but death became the lot of the one I loved most.  Did you know Yazin?  I don't think you did.  All the hopes of the future were latent in him.  He was such a smart and intelligent boy, ahead of his time.  Yazin used to bring balance into our disturbed life.  Yazin died and his mother abandoned me.

What evil luck I have!  Your computer  has mastered the art of prophecy.

AL-BAHI (*consoling him*):  My friend, I don't think you believe that the computer can predict.  It only helps us to discover some inner truths.

SUFFIAN:  But that's just what happened.  Your machine has discovered those deadly truths.  The poisonous claws of your machine reached out and burst the tumors.  Once those tumors burst, misery and frustration poured out.  (*In a deep voice*)  I want to die.

AL-BAHI:  Pull yourself together, man.  You are the child of a scientific civilization.  You are not a weak being to give up so easily.

SUFFIAN:  Who wants to give up?  We are forced to.

AL-BAHI:  Sorrow is inevitable, but it is not a lasting fact.

SUFFIAN (*addressing himself in a loud voice*):  Is it true that sorrow is inevitable?  If so, then let sorrow, like cancer, tear bodies and souls to pieces.  (*He addresses AL-BAHI like a madman.*)  I will bow in great respect to your computerized mind.  You are the priest of science.  In you hands lie the keys of sorrow.  (*He  sinks into a chair and cries.*)  My daughter became pregnant by me and I killed my son with my own hands.  (*He shouts entreatingly*)  I want to die.  Is your new electronic God able to help me die?  I entreat you, crushed. I beg of you, Lord of science and technologY, to help this weak insect to die swiftly.

AL-BAHI (*bewildered*):  There has to be a solution for this misery. I'm going to call a doctor.  (*AL-BAHI moves toward the exit, but SUFFIAN stops him.*)

SUFFIAN:  Do you really like me, my friend?  Does the time of our study and our struggle for science together mean anything to you?  Then help me, please!

AL-BAHI:  I swear, I am ready to offer you any possible help.

SUFFIAN:  Swear by what you truly believe.

AL-BAHI:  I swear by my firm faith in man's power to control the mysteries of man and nature.

SUFFIAN:  Then help me challenge the prophecy of your electronic God.

AL-BAHI:  But how can I help you?  I don't understand anything. Your sorrow has infected me.  I can't think anymore.

SUFFIAN:  Ask your God to make me die quickly.  I am unable to kill myself.  (*He shouts.*)  I wish to die, but I cannot find death.  And I don't want this machine to defeat me a third time.  It has achieved enough victories already.

AL-BAHI:  You are crazy.

SUFFIAN:  But you swore.  Are you repudiating your scientific honor?

AL-BAHI:  I will never renounce that as long as I live.

SUFFIAN:  Then do what I want.

AL-BAHI:  I don't understand how a sophisticated machine of the kind that serves humanity can . . .

SUFFIAN (*interrupting sarcastically*):  Serves humanity!  I am humanity and I am moving step by step toward an inevitable destruction, according to laws and equations beyond man's understanding.  Come on, ask your machine to help me, because I am not strong enough to find an easy death.  (*Entreatingly*)  I am ready to kiss the ground upon which your God stands.  Just help me, my friend.

AL-BAHI:  You are becoming more and more confused.  Like you, I have gone through crises, but I pulled myself together.

SUFFIAN:  Shouldn't I implore your God to save my soul from cowardice and helplessness?

AL-BAHI:  I was raised an orphan.  I lost my father when I was still a child.  I experienced orphanhood and poverty.  I knew sorrow very early, but I continued my struggle.

SUFFIAN:  Long live your courage.  You can spit in my face, but help me, please.  I am a rotten body, weighed down with sin and transgression.  (*Shouting*)  For the sake of your God, save me.

AL-BAHI (*hopelessly confused*):  But the computer can't think without help.

SUFFIAN:  Then help it find death for me.  You have all the data you need: my name, my condition, my misery and my frustration.

AL-BAHI:  I can't do anything.

SUFFIAN:  And you conspire against your friend!

AL-BAHI:  I conspire against you!  You are out of your mind!

SUFFIAN:  What is the use of the mind when the soul has lost its bearings?  I have lost my soul; help me to get rid of its body, my friend, before it decays and spreads a stinking odor through your clean, calm, disinfected temple.  (*He bows to the computer.*)  If I am predestined to be one of the miserable, please, my modern God, free me from my misery and guide me to death.  If I am set down to face a death that does not come, then erase that third curse from your tape.  Your prophecies have come true.  Your hatred for a weak man—one who sought only love, happiness, and dreams—has been satisfied.  (*To himself*)  What a greedy man you are, Suffian!

AL-BAHI:  That is enough, my friend.  That is enough.

SUFFIAN (*on his knees*):  I admit your infinite greatness, but are your powerless worshipers not worthy of a sign that can come from your depths and wipe out their fears?

AL-BAHI:  That is enough.  Are you insane?

SUFFIAN:  Nobody says he is insane.  They say, it is all over for him now.  (*Becoming angry*)  Watch out, I can't tolerate incorrect expressions.  (*Very angry*)  Our scientific honor no longer means anything to me.  (*In a sudden outburst*)  I hate you, oh false God.  I don't believe in you and I don't believe in myself.  (*To AL-BAHI*)  I don't believe in you either.  (*As if searching for something, he finds a piece of glass.  He holds it up.*)  Is this enough to smash your power?  (*He throws the piece of glass.  It falls.*)  I wish I could smash this solemn edifice of meanness and hatred.

AL-BAHI (*holding SUFFIAN back*):  You are addressing an inanimate body made by man.  We use it for our own purposes.  It helps us solve many problems.  It does not do us any harm.  Wake up, man!  Your son is dead and it is impossible to bring him back.  You should try to get your sanity back.

SUFFIAN (*sadly*):  My son has died, Sulaf has gone, and Asma's hatred for me has solidified into fact.

AL-BAHI (*amazed*):  Sulaf!  What does Sulaf have to do with the things that have happened to you?

SUFFIAN:  Sulaf . . . Sulaf, my friend, was the beloved woman who promised me a paradise.  Then she turned out to be my daughter.  All the happiness we dreamed of turned into an endless hell.

AL-BAHI (*shocked by SUFFIAN's words*):  I can't understand this.  It sounds like an ancient tale.  How can I believe this when I refuse to believe in fables!

SUFFIAN:  We denied several facts . . . and crushed our dreams with our heavy feet. (*In a strangely calm voice*)  Shall I admit something to you, dear friend . . . shall I?

AL-BAHI:  Do you still have something to admit?

SUFFIAN:  I admit that happiness is an illusion and I am unable to avenge myself.

AL-BAHI (*consolingly*):  But you made your students happy and you will continue to do so because that is in your nature.

SUFFIAN (*sadly sarcastic*):  It is true that I shall go on, simply because I cannot experiment with something as horrible as death. (*He goes out.*)

AL-BAHI (*calling after him*):  Suffian . . . Suffian!  Don't leave!  (*No one answers, so he goes back into his office.*)  Poor Suffian. (*He addresses the computer.*)  Please, stop your prophecies.  Let us stick to actual facts . . . there are so many things in life and we need a lifetime to explore some of them. (*To himself*)  Poor Suffian. (*Thinking*)  Has he turned himself into Oedipus, or was Oedipus latent in him without his knowledge? (*He begins to work on some papers.*)

THE CHORUS:  We run, we dream, we get tired, we suffer.
These are man's good deeds.
We crawl, we hate, we become content.
We give up, we refuse, we transcend, we neglect.
All good deeds are done by man.
They are done by the great memory,
They are the product of days charged with hope.

**Darkness**


**END**

# NOTES ON PLAYWRIGHTS

## Ali Ahmad Bakathir (1915-1959)

Born in Indonesia of Arabic parents, Bakathir settled in Egypt in 1934 where he became fascinated by English literature and especially by Shakespeare, whose *Romeo and Juliet* he translated.  He wrote a number of novels, over thirty plays, and an epic dramatization in nineteen volumes of early Islamic history and conquests. He was awarded many medals, including the State Prize of Egypt for his play *Harot and Marot*.  His passionate commitment to Islam and to Arab nationalism resounds throughout his work.

## Tawfiq Al-Hakim (1898-1987)

Born in Alexandria and educated in law in Cairo and Paris before turning to writing.  Although he wrote novels, poems and essays, he is best known as a dramatist, generally regarded as the founder of the modern literary drama in Egypt and the most important dramatist Egypt has yet produced.  His *People of the Cave* was the first production by the Egyptian National Theatre Troupe in 1935.

## Walid Ikhlasi (b. 1935)

A novelist, playwright, and short story writer, Walid Ikhlasi, one of Syria's most distinguished authors, was born in Alexandretta and holds a degree in agricultural science.  His collected plays were published, in ten volumes, in 1999.  He has also produced a collection of short plays (1997), a work on the nature of Arabic culture (1995) and, most recently, a book on culture and modernism (2002).

**Ali Salim (b. 1936)**

One of the leading satirists and comic dramatists of contemporary Egypt. Originally an actor, Salim turned to writing serious and comic studies of contemporary society, among them *The Wheat Well* (1968) and *Our Children in London* (1975).

# NOTES ON TRANSLATORS

## Dalia Basiouny

Dalia Basiouny is an Egyptian artist, academic and translator. As a theatre director she has 11 plays to her credit performed in Egypt, Morocco, England and the USA. She has a B.A. in English Literature, Cairo University, Diploma in Translation, AUC, Egypt and M.A. in Drama, Bristol University, UK. She has received a Fulbright Arts Grant and British Council Chevening Scholarship. Currently she is writing her Ph.D. thesis on "Arab American Women Theatre" at the Graduate Center of the City University of New York.

## Pierre Cachia

Professor Cachia recently retired after a distinguished career as scholar and professor in Arabic literature. He served as editor of the *Journal of Arabic Literature* and is the author of many articles in the field, some collected in *An Overview of Modern Arabic Literature* (1990). His *Popular Narrative Ballads of Modern Egypt,* a major study of this genre, appeared in 1989.

## Marvin Carlson

Marvin Carlson is Sidney E. Cohn Professor of Theatre and Comparative Literature at the Graduate Center of the City University of New York. He has previously translated plays from French, German, Italian, and Arabic and is the author of many books and articles on theatre and performance history and theory. He edited the Martin E. Segal publication *Contemporary Drama in Egypt* in 2000.

## Admer Gouryh

Admer Gouryh is Assistant Professor of English at the Borough of Manhattan Community College. His previous publications include *The Prague Semiotics of Theatre*, published by the Syrian Ministry of Culture Press in 1997, and *Touma Al-Khoury: A Stranger at the Door* (2003). His translation of Walid Ikhlasi's play *Pleasure Club 21* appeared in *Short Arabic Plays,* ed. S. K. Jayyusi (2003).

## William Maynard Hutchins

Professor Hutchins teaches at Appalachian State University of North Carolina. He is a leading translator of modern Arabic literature. His two-volume *Plays, Preface and Postscripts of Tawfiq Al-Hakim* appeared in 1984. He was the principal translator of *The Cairo Triolgy* by Naguib Mahfouz, and his translation of *Anubis* by the Libyan Tuareg author Ibrahim Al-Koni appeared in 2005.

## Desmond O'Grady

Born in Limerick, Ireland, took a Harvard M.A. in Celtic Studies, and as a lecturer in English at the University of Cairo became interested in Arabic literature, especially classic poetry. Among his many publications are several collections of poetry and some verse translations, including the famous ode of the pre-Islamic poet, Imru al-Qays.

OTHER MARTIN E. SEGAL THEATRE CENTER PUBLICATIONS

*Contemporary Theatre in Egypt*, edited by Marvin Carlson, contains the proceedings of a Symposium on this subject held at the CUNY Graduate Center in 1999 along with the first English translations of three short plays by leading Egyptian playwrights who spoke at the Symposium, Alfred Farag, Gamal Maqsoud, and Lenin El-Ramley. It concludes with a bibliography of English translations and secondary articles on the theatre in Egypt since 1955.

*Pixérécourt: Four Melodramas*, translated and edited by Daniel Gerould and Marvin Carlson, contains four of Pixérécourt's most important melodramas: *The Ruins of Babylon, The Dog of Montargis, Christopher Columbus*, and *Alice* as well as Charles Nodier's "Introduction" to the 1843 edition of the author's plays and two theoretical essays by the playwright.

*The Heirs of Molière*, translated and edited by Marvin Carlson, contains four representative French comedies of the period from the death of Molière to the French Revolution: Regnard's *The Absent-Minded Lover,* Destouches's *The Conceited Count,* La Chaussée's *The Fashionable Prejudice,* and Laya's *The Friend of the Laws.*

*Witkiewicz: Seven Plays*, translated and edited by Daniel Gerould, contains seven of Witkiewicz's most important plays: *The Pragmatists, Tumor Brainiowicz, Gyubal Wahazar, The Anonymous Work, The Cuttlefish, Dainty Shapes and Hairy Apes,* and *The Beelzebub Sonata,* as well as two of his theoretical essays: "Theoretical Introduction" and "A Few Words about the Role of the Actor in the Theatre of Pure Form."

*Four Works for the Theatre by Hugo Claus* contains translations of four plays by the foremost contemporary writer of Dutch language theatre, poetry, and prose. Flemish by birth and upbringing, Claus is the author of some ninety plays, novels, and collections of poetry. The plays collected here, edited and with an introduction by David Willinger, include *The Temptation, Friday, Serenade,* and *The Hair of the Dog.*

***Zeami and the Nô Theatre in the World***, edited by Benito Ortolani and Samuel Leiter, contains the proceedings of the "Zeami and the Nô Theatre in the World Symposium" held in New York City in October 1997 in conjunction with the "Japanese Theatre in the World" exhibit at the Japan Society. The book contains an introduction and fifteen essays, organized into sections on "Zeami's Theories and Aesthetics," "Zeami and Drama," "Zeami and Acting," and "Zeami and the World."

***Theatre Research Resources in New York City*** is the most comprehensive catalogue of New York City research facilities available to theatre scholars, including public and private libraries, museums, historical societies, university and college collections, ethnic and language associations, theatre companies, acting schools, and film archives. Each entry features an outline of the facility's holdings as well as contact information, hours, services, and access procedures.

For further information on the
Martin E. Segal Theatre Center visit:
http://web.gc.cuny.edu/mestc